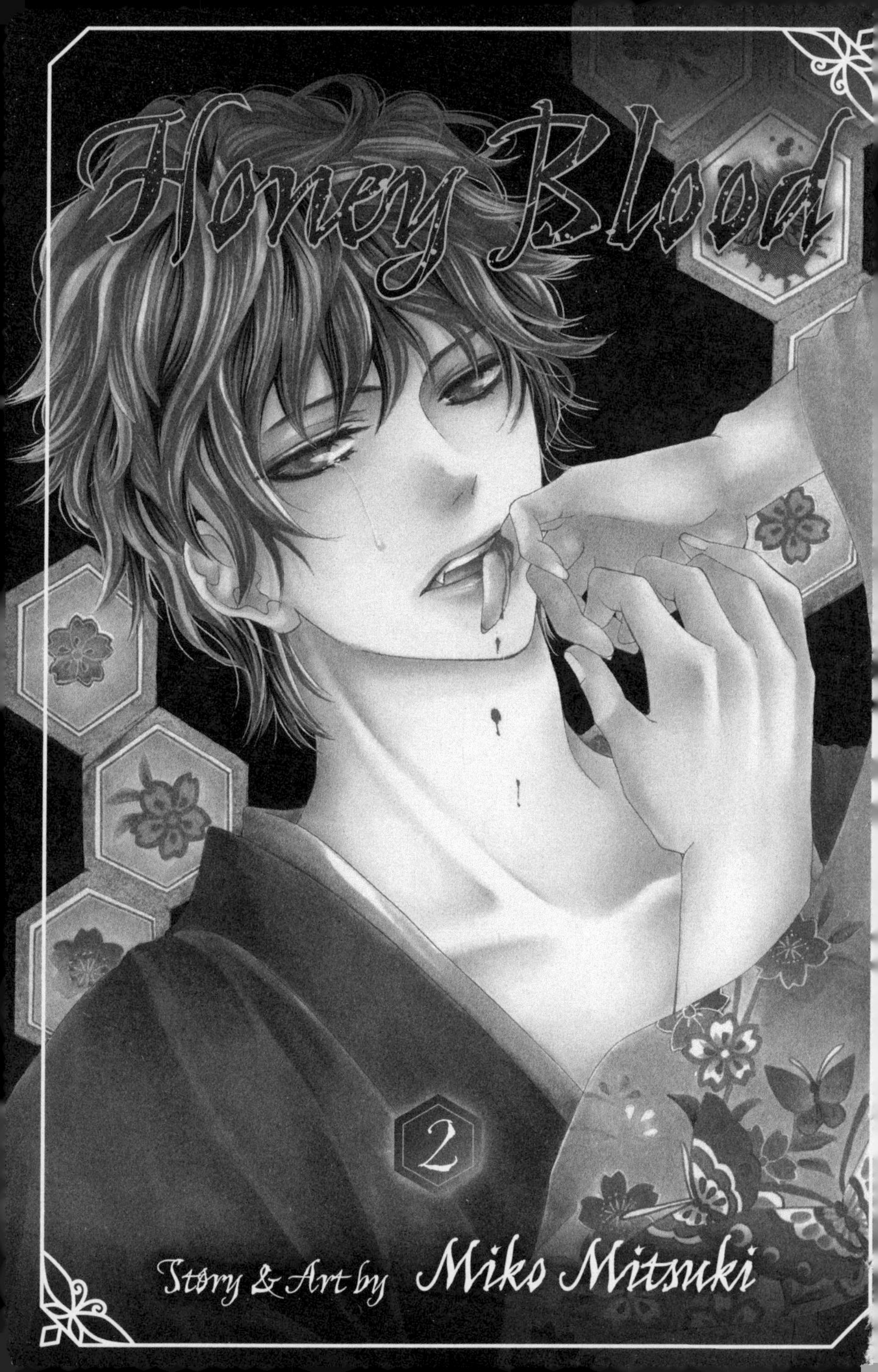
Honey Blood
2
Story & Art by Miko Mitsuki

Honey Blood

2

Contents

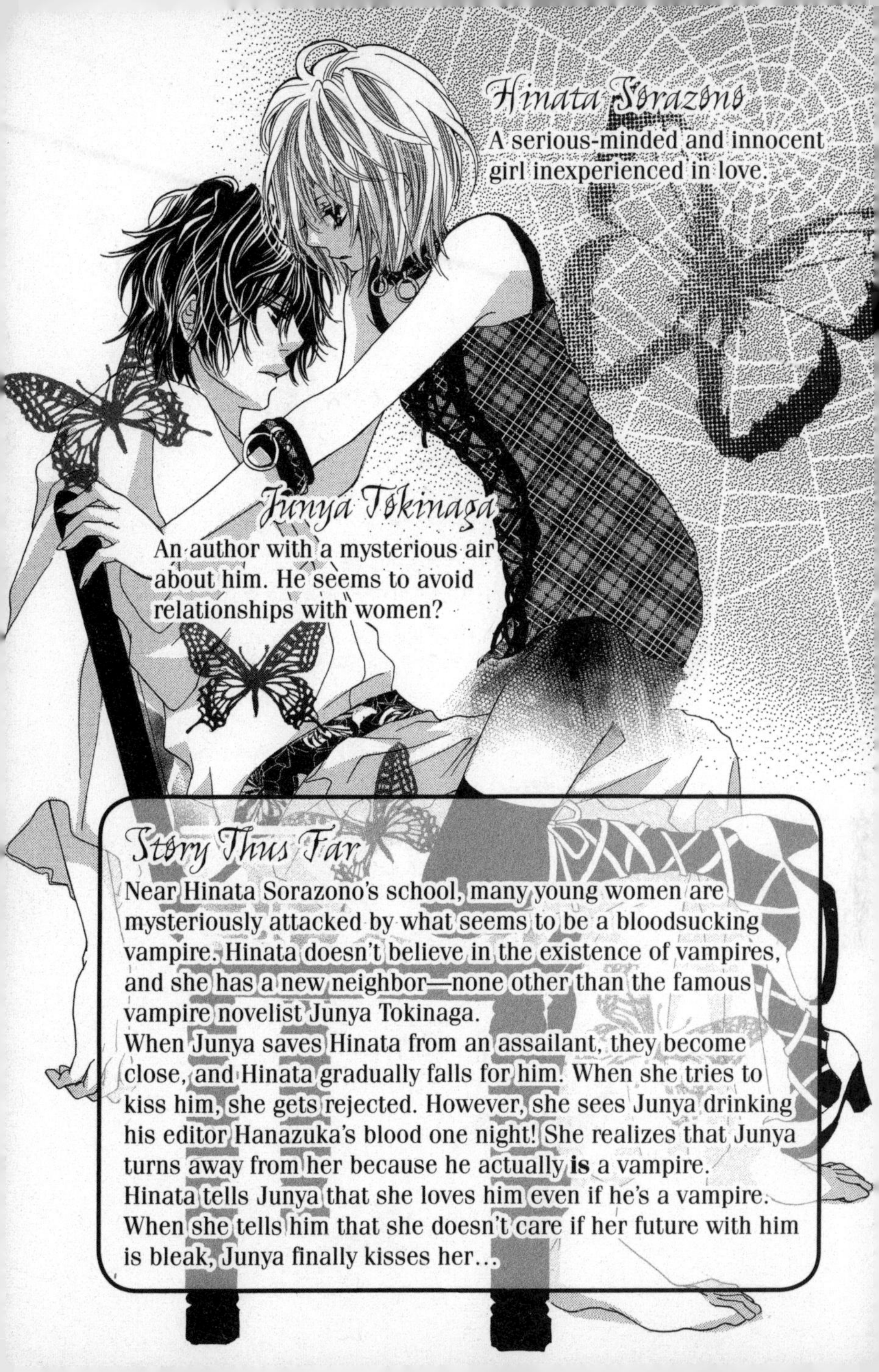

Hinata Sorazono

A serious-minded and innocent girl inexperienced in love.

Junya Tokinaga

An author with a mysterious air about him. He seems to avoid relationships with women?

Story Thus Far

Near Hinata Sorazono's school, many young women are mysteriously attacked by what seems to be a bloodsucking vampire. Hinata doesn't believe in the existence of vampires, and she has a new neighbor—none other than the famous vampire novelist Junya Tokinaga.

When Junya saves Hinata from an assailant, they become close, and Hinata gradually falls for him. When she tries to kiss him, she gets rejected. However, she sees Junya drinking his editor Hanazuka's blood one night! She realizes that Junya turns away from her because he actually **is** a vampire.

Hinata tells Junya that she loves him even if he's a vampire. When she tells him that she doesn't care if her future with him is bleak, Junya finally kisses her...

❀ Greetings! ❀

Thank you so much for picking up this book!
Honey Blood volume 2 is my ✧tenth✧ manga volume!!

I'm so happy to have reached this milestone
with Honey Blood. ♥ It's all thanks to you readers!

I hope you enjoy this final volume. ♥ ৩

Chapter 6

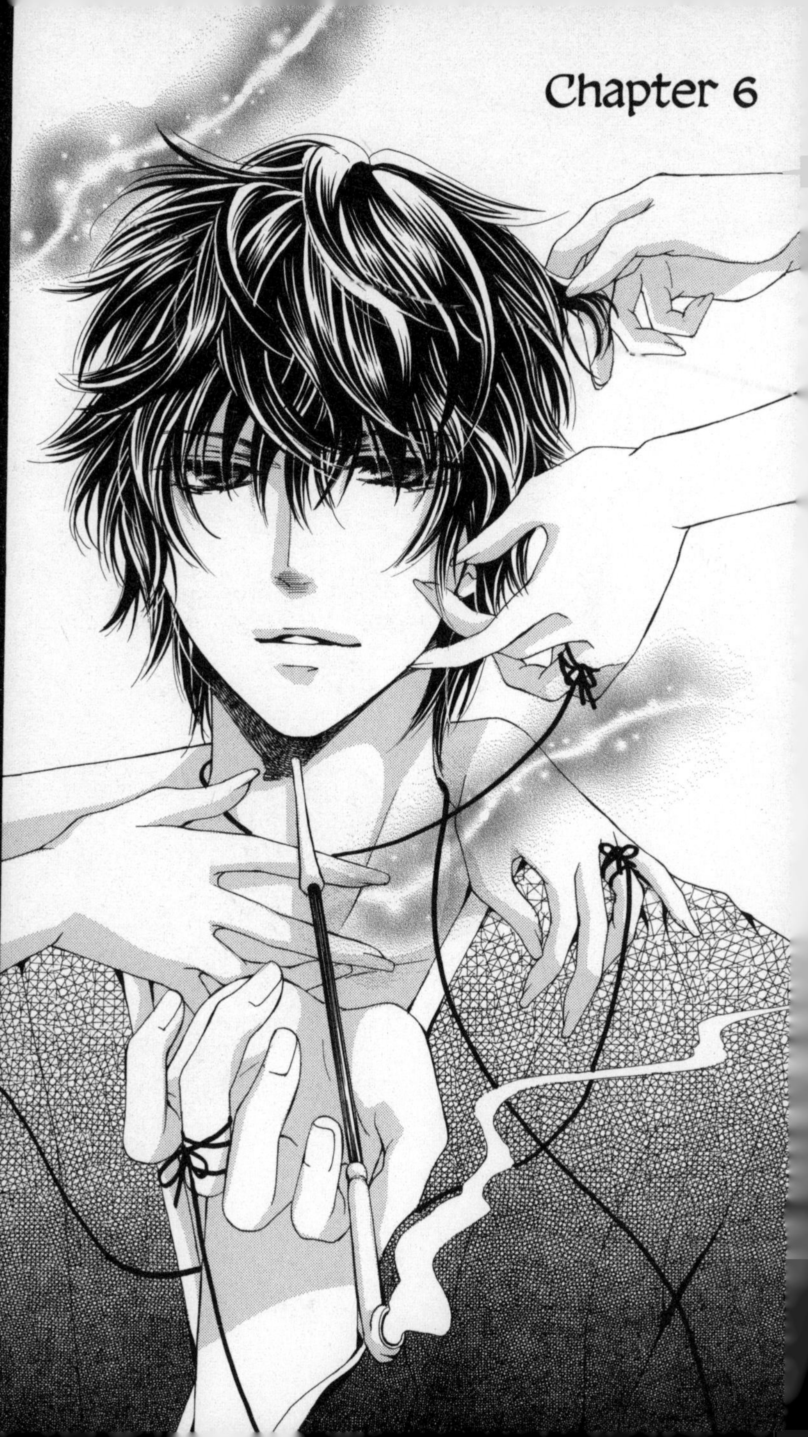

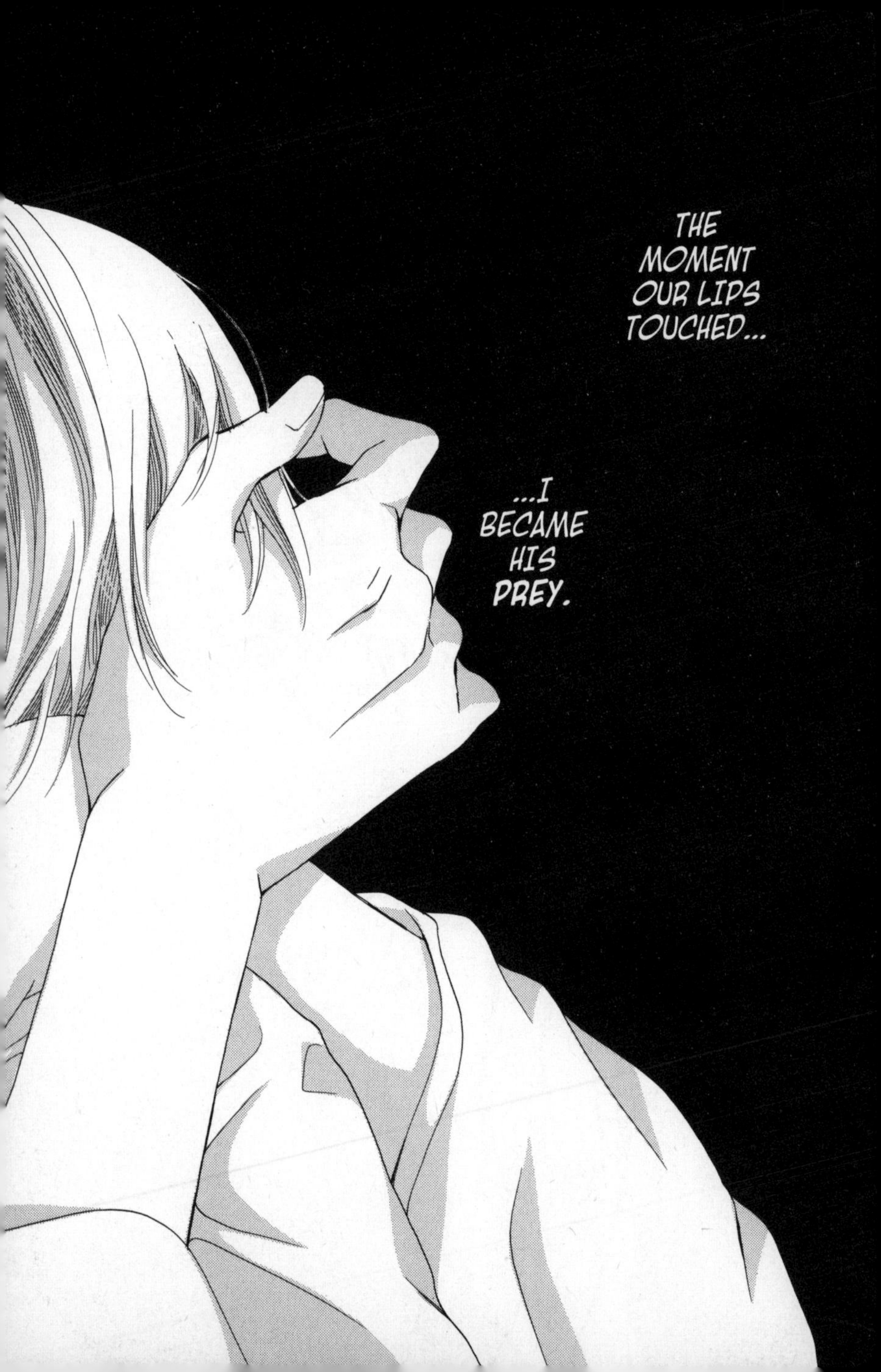
THE MOMENT OUR LIPS TOUCHED...
...I BECAME HIS PREY.

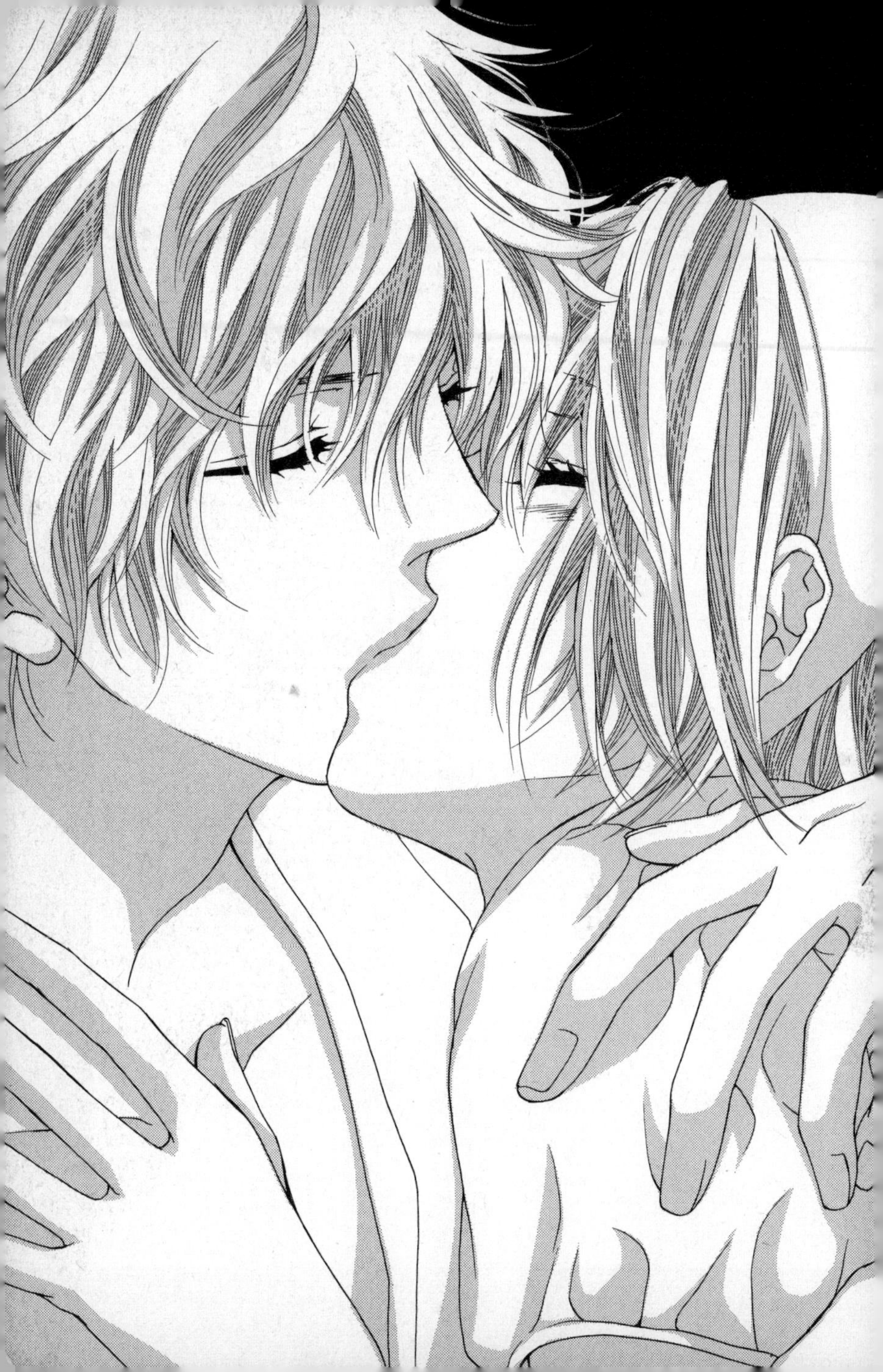

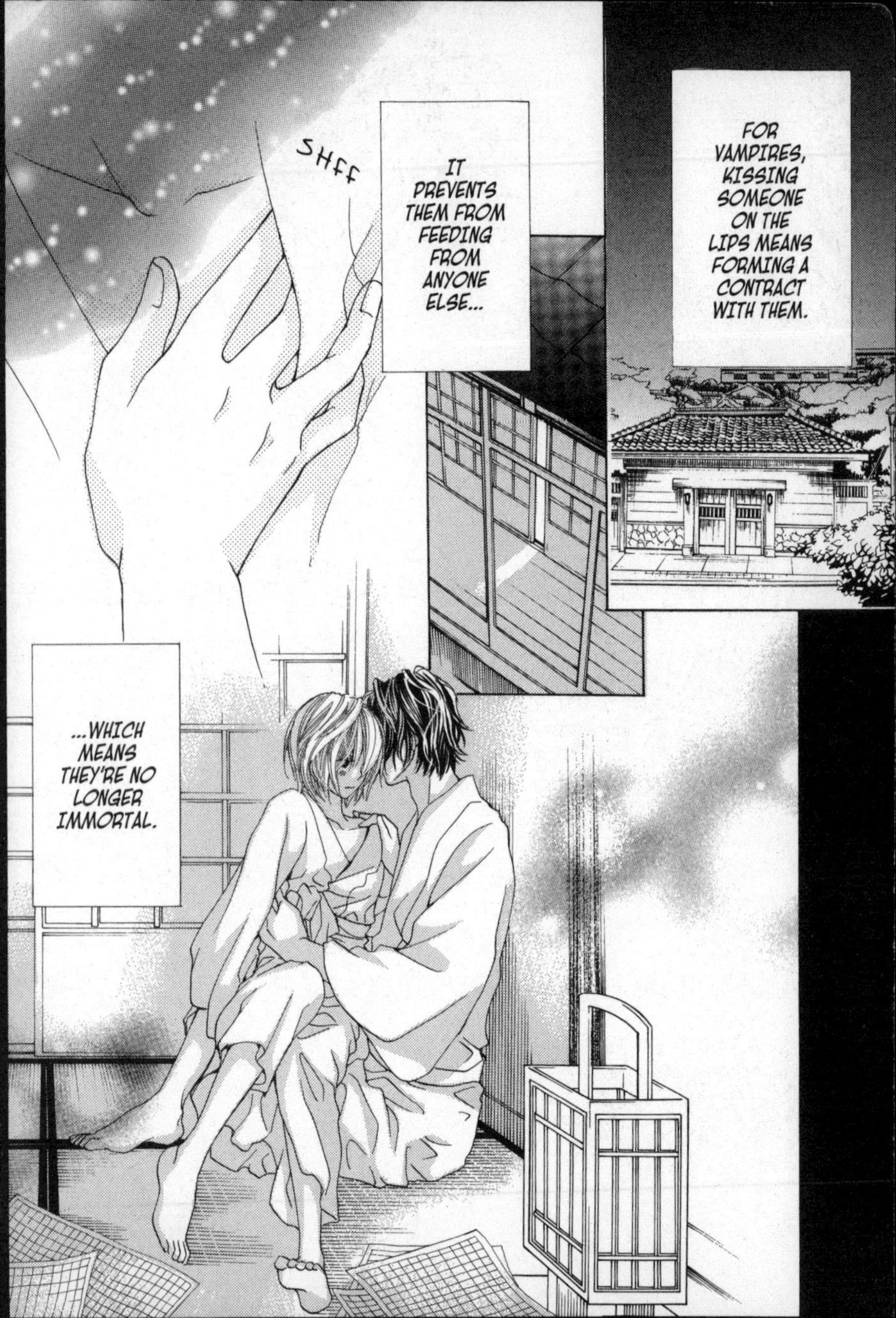

FOR VAMPIRES, KISSING SOMEONE ON THE LIPS MEANS FORMING A CONTRACT WITH THEM.
IT PREVENTS THEM FROM FEEDING FROM ANYONE ELSE...
SHFF
...WHICH MEANS THEY'RE NO LONGER IMMORTAL.

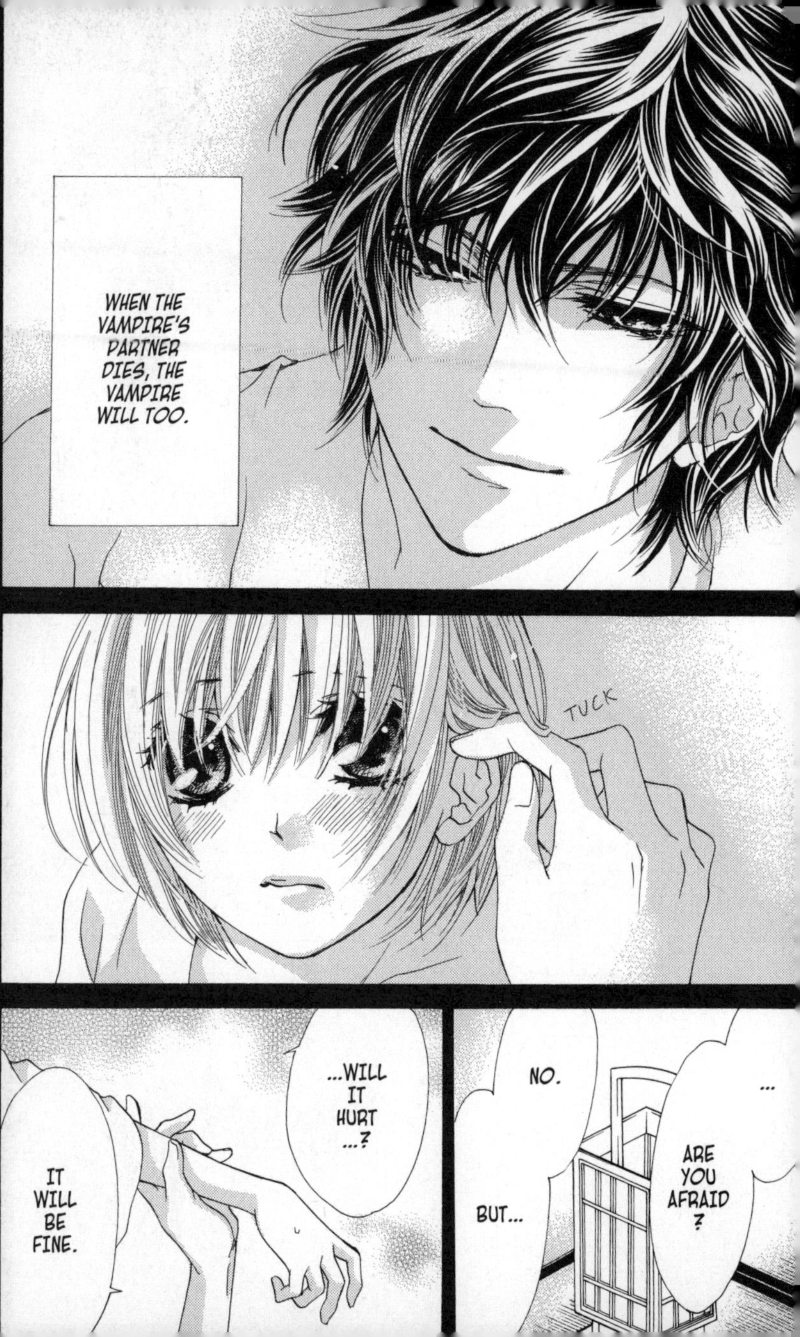
WHEN THE VAMPIRE'S PARTNER DIES, THE VAMPIRE WILL TOO.
TUCK
...
ARE YOU AFRAID?
NO.
BUT...
...WILL IT HURT...?
IT WILL BE FINE.

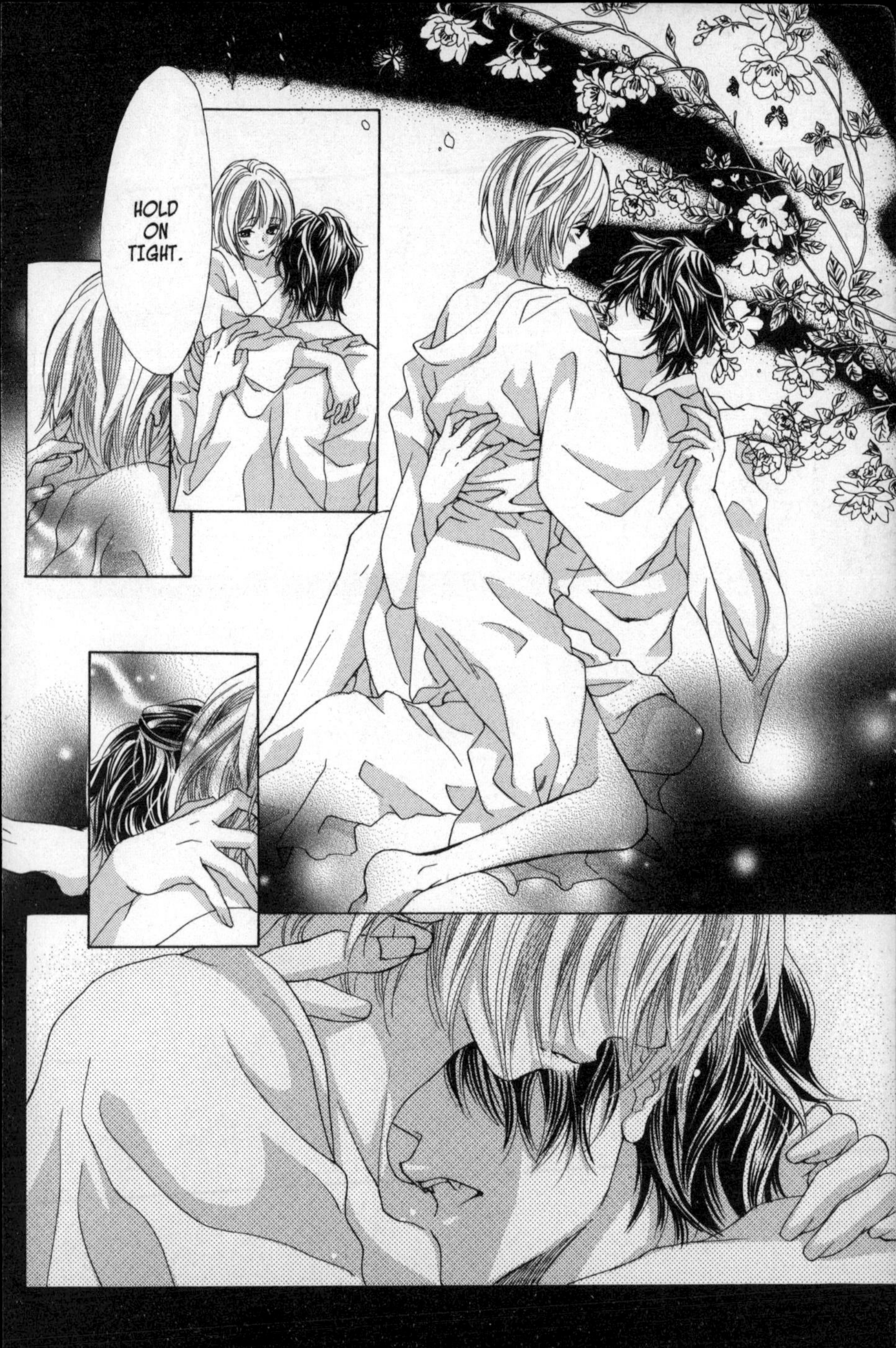
HOLD ON TIGHT.

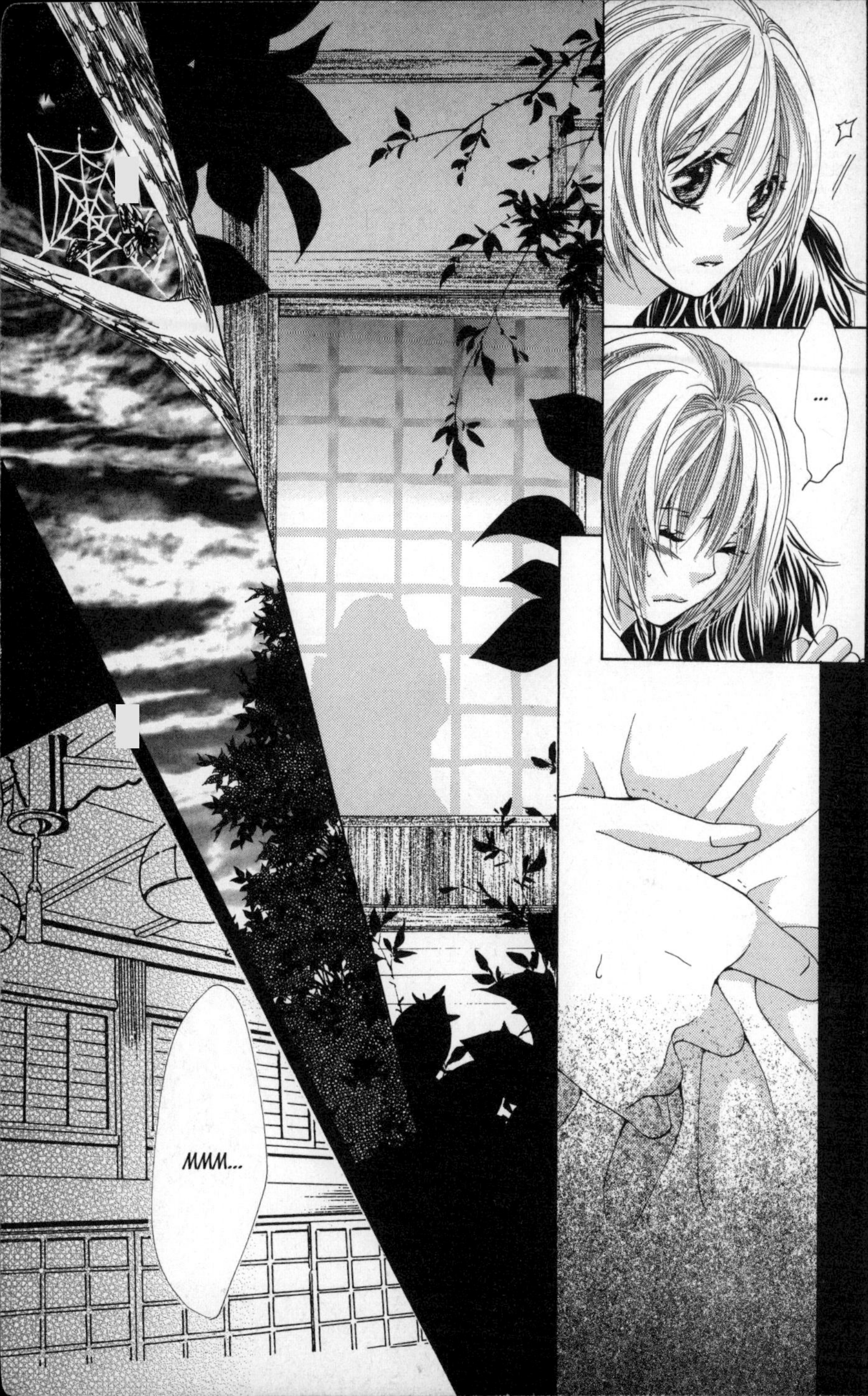
...
MMM...

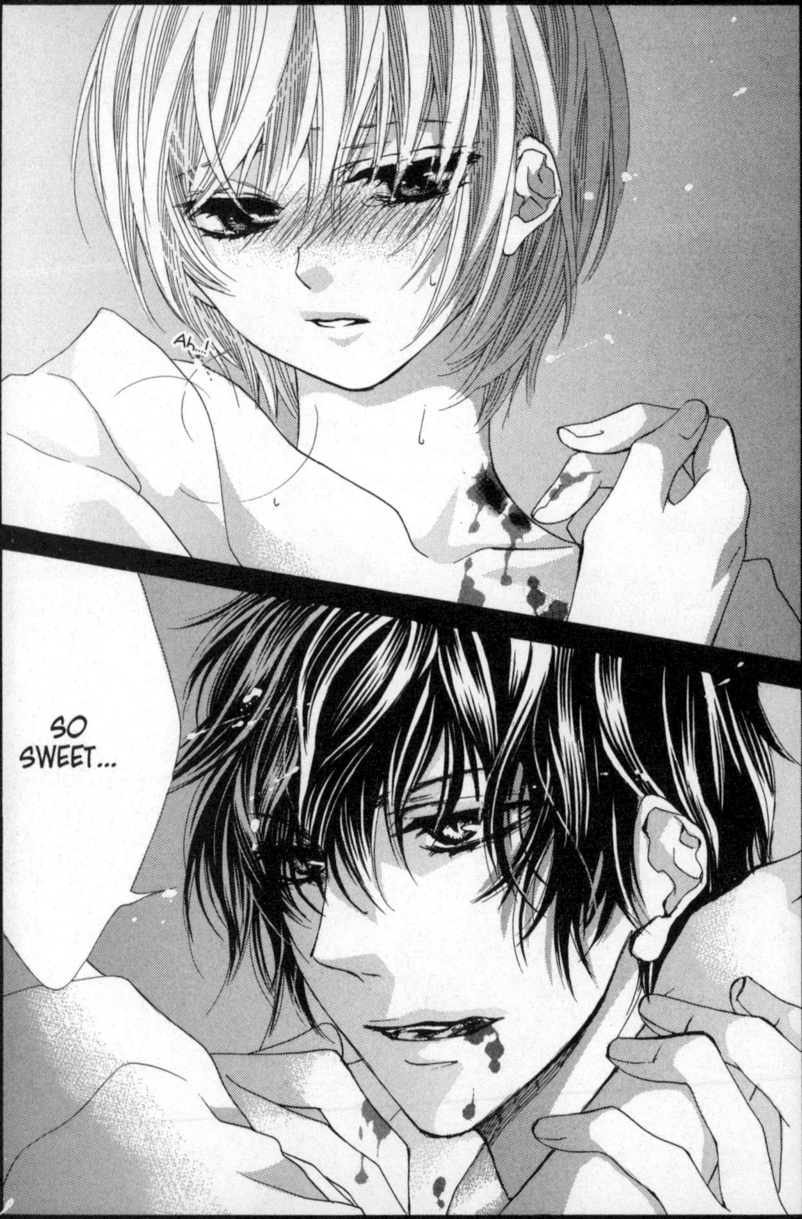
Ah...!
SO SWEET...

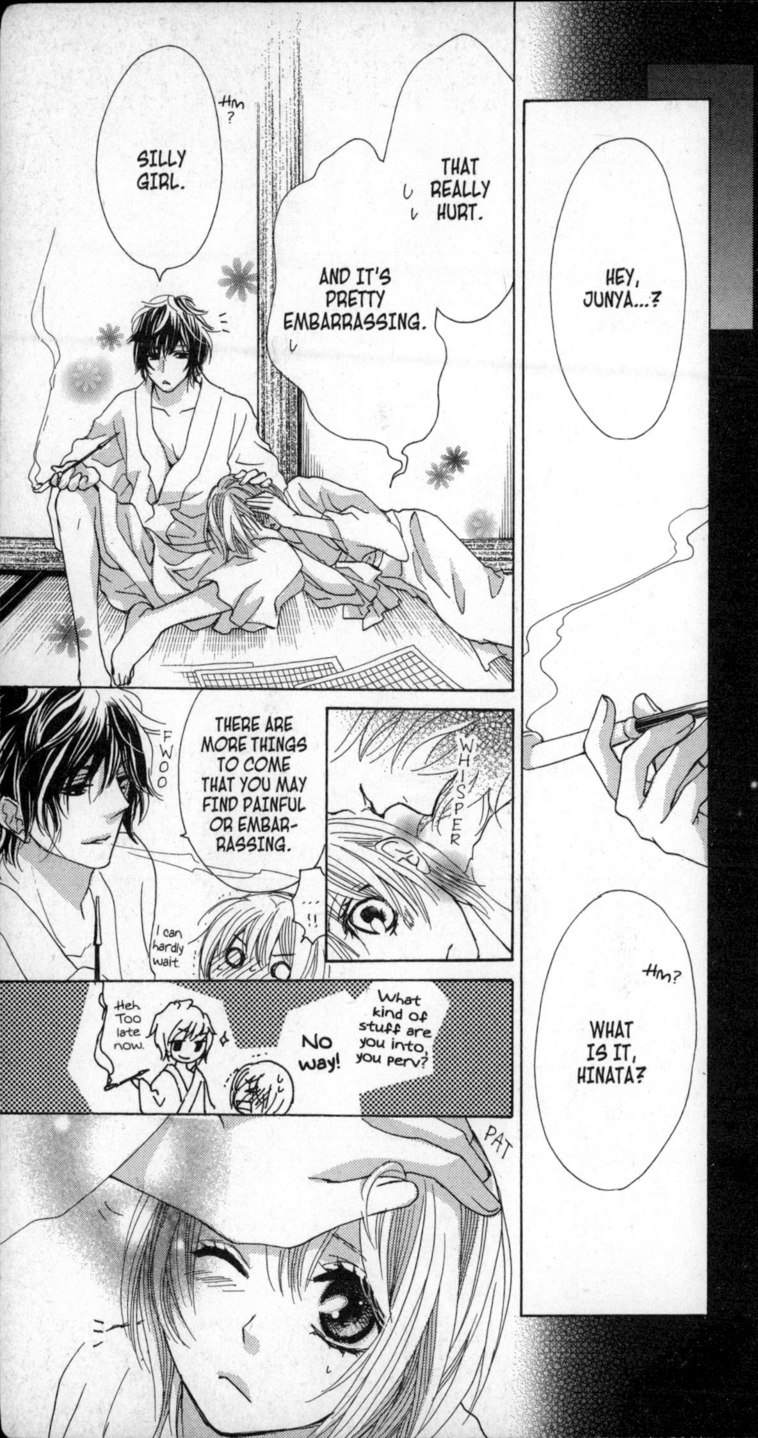
HEY, JUNYA...?
Hm?
WHAT IS IT, HINATA?
THAT REALLY HURT.
AND IT'S PRETTY EMBARRASSING.
Hm?
SILLY GIRL.
WHISPER
FWOO
THERE ARE MORE THINGS TO COME THAT YOU MAY FIND PAINFUL OR EMBARRASSING.
...!!
I can hardly wait.
What kind of stuff are you into, you perv?
No way!
Heh Too late now.
PAT

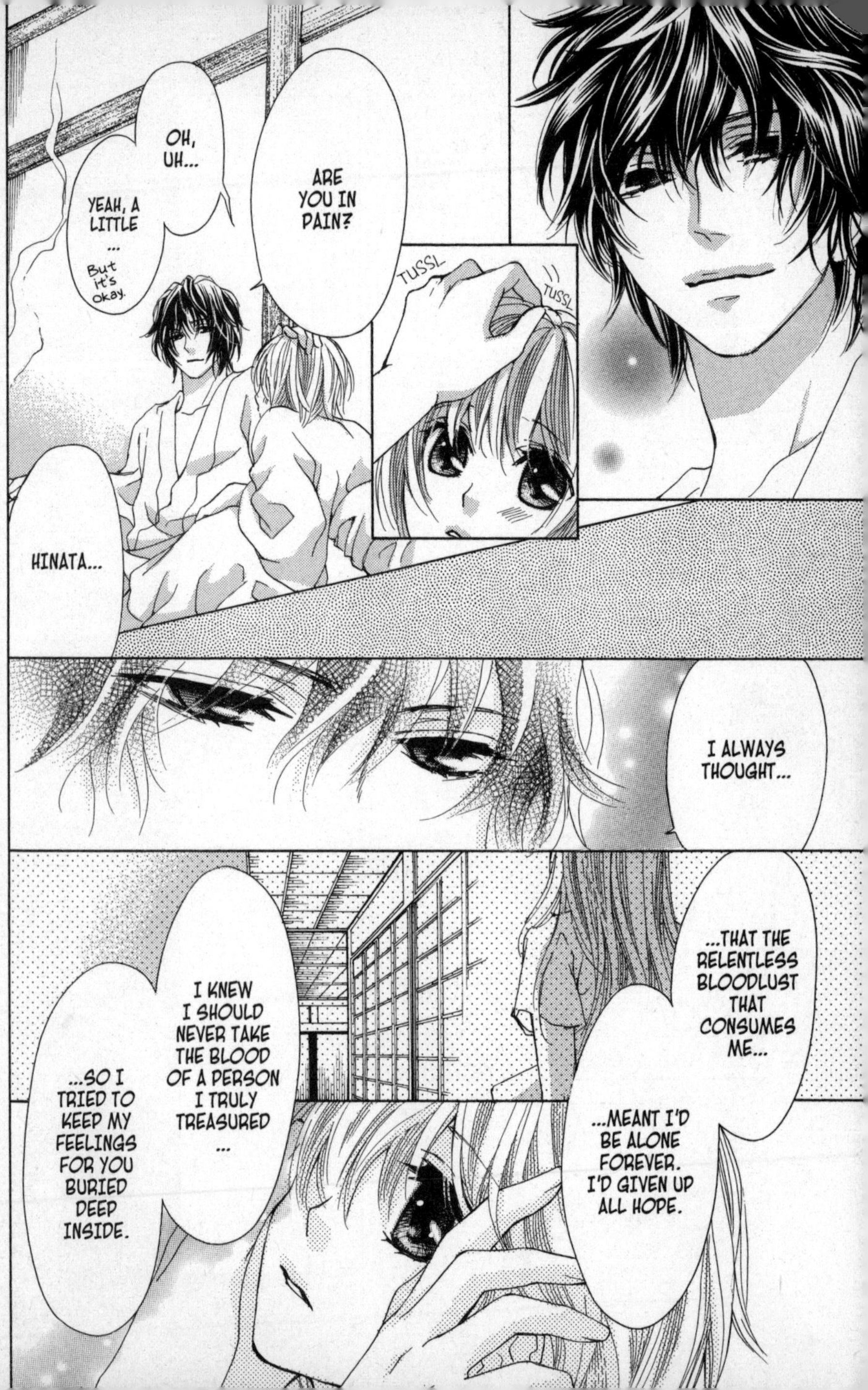
TUSSL
TUSSL
ARE YOU IN PAIN?
OH, UH...
YEAH, A LITTLE ...
But it's okay.
HINATA...
I ALWAYS THOUGHT...
...THAT THE RELENTLESS BLOODLUST THAT CONSUMES ME...
...MEANT I'D BE ALONE FOREVER. I'D GIVEN UP ALL HOPE.
I KNEW I SHOULD NEVER TAKE THE BLOOD OF A PERSON I TRULY TREASURED ...
...SO I TRIED TO KEEP MY FEELINGS FOR YOU BURIED DEEP INSIDE.

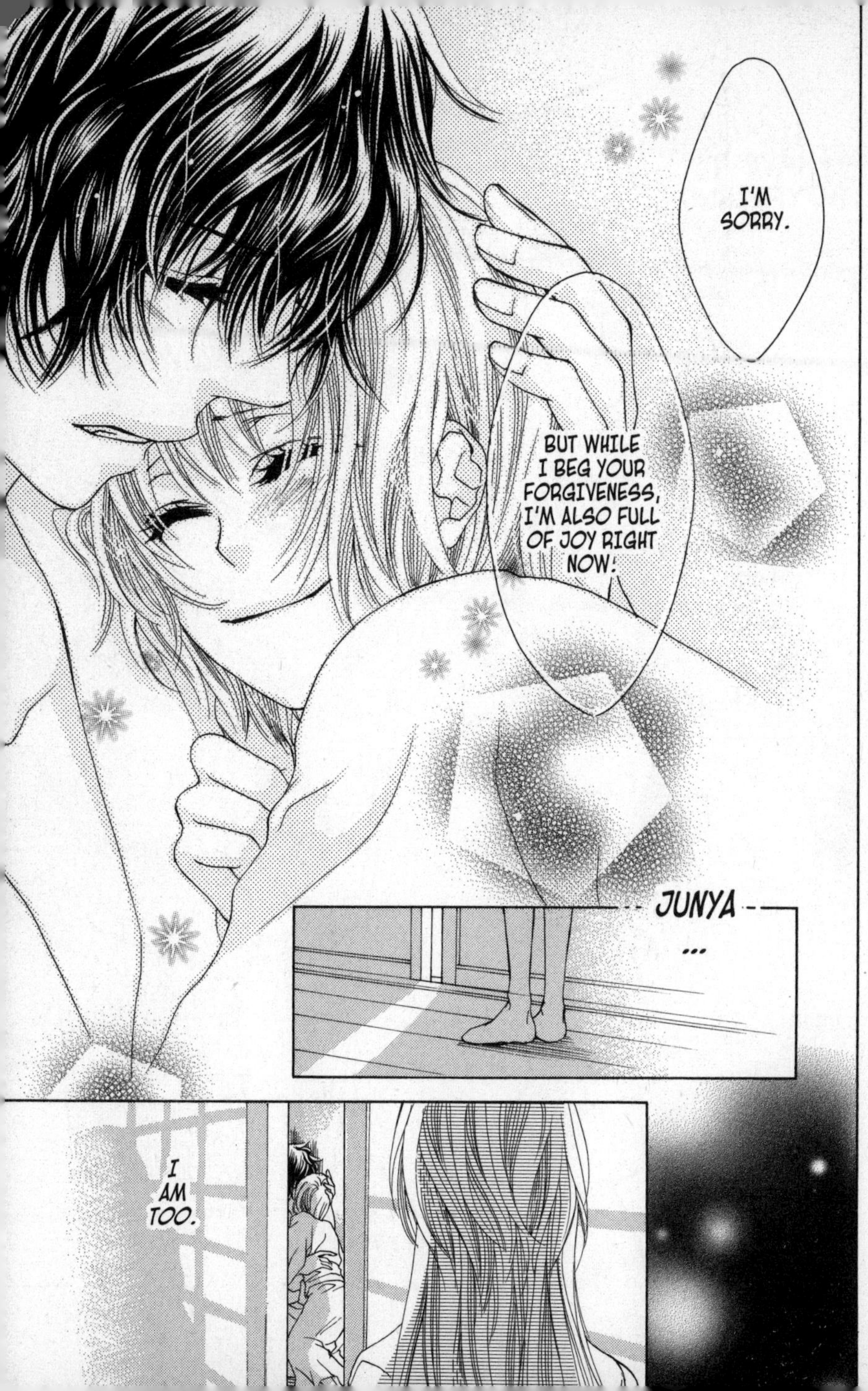
I'M SORRY.
BUT WHILE I BEG YOUR FORGIVENESS, I'M ALSO FULL OF JOY RIGHT NOW.
JUNYA ...
I AM TOO.

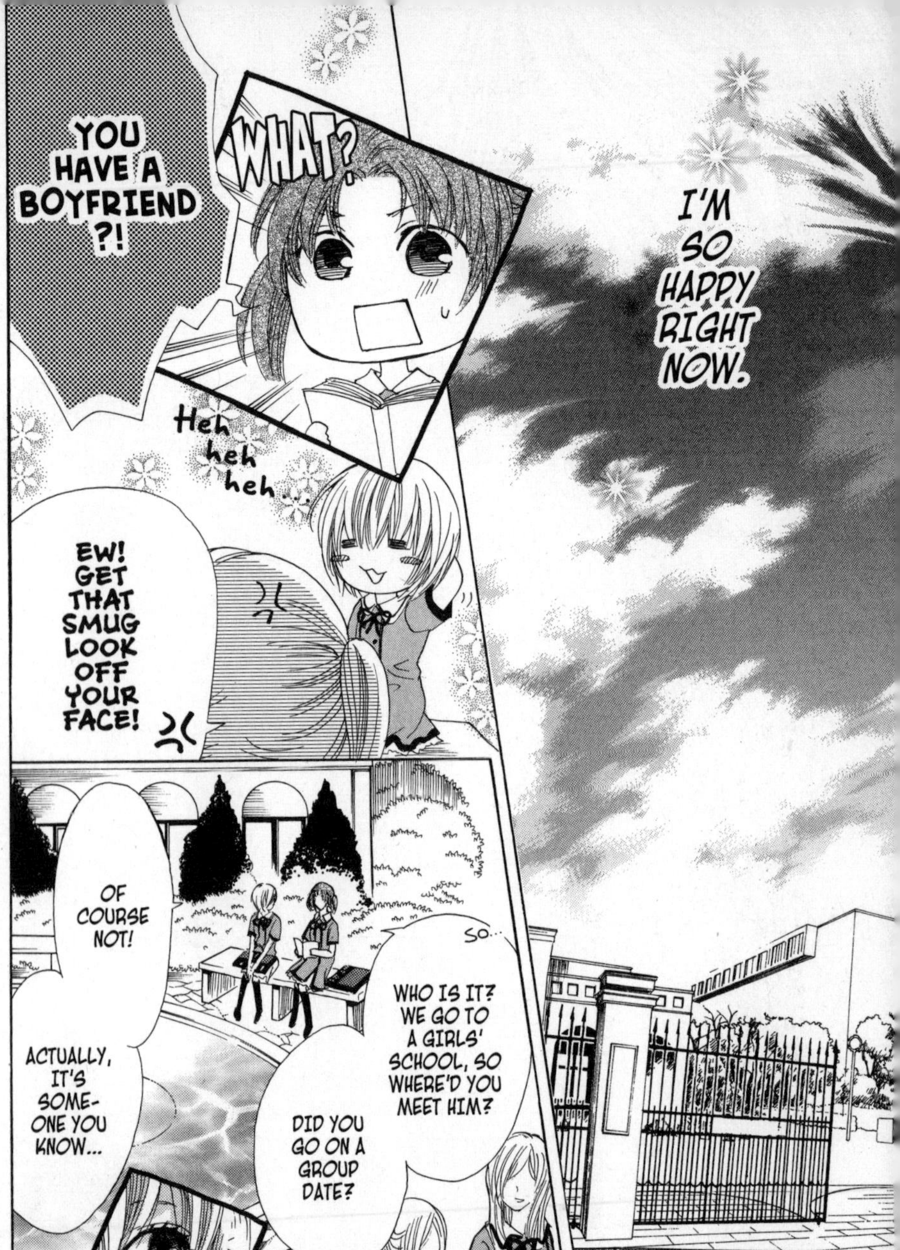
I'M SO HAPPY RIGHT NOW.
WHAT?
YOU HAVE A BOYFRIEND?!
Heh heh heh...
EW! GET THAT SMUG LOOK OFF YOUR FACE!
SO...
WHO IS IT? WE GO TO A GIRLS' SCHOOL, SO WHERE'D YOU MEET HIM?
DID YOU GO ON A GROUP DATE?
OF COURSE NOT!
ACTUALLY, IT'S SOME-ONE YOU KNOW...

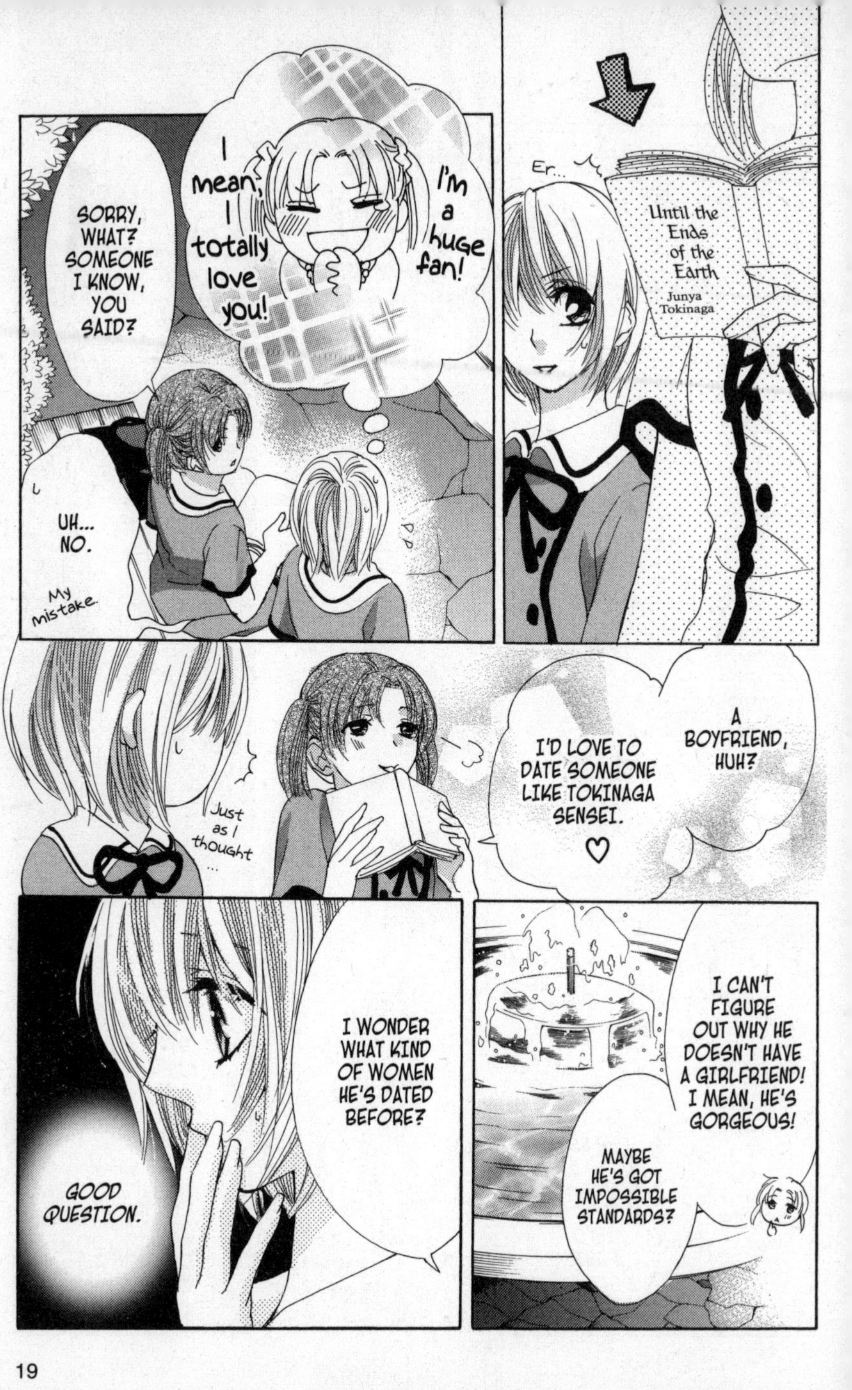
Er...
Until the Ends of the Earth
Junya Tokinaga
I mean, I totally love you!
I'm a huge fan!
SORRY, WHAT? SOMEONE I KNOW, YOU SAID?
UH... NO.
My mistake.
A BOYFRIEND, HUH?
I'D LOVE TO DATE SOMEONE LIKE TOKINAGA SENSEI. ♥
Just as I thought...
I CAN'T FIGURE OUT WHY HE DOESN'T HAVE A GIRLFRIEND! I MEAN, HE'S GORGEOUS!
MAYBE HE'S GOT IMPOSSIBLE STANDARDS?
I WONDER WHAT KIND OF WOMEN HE'S DATED BEFORE?
GOOD QUESTION.

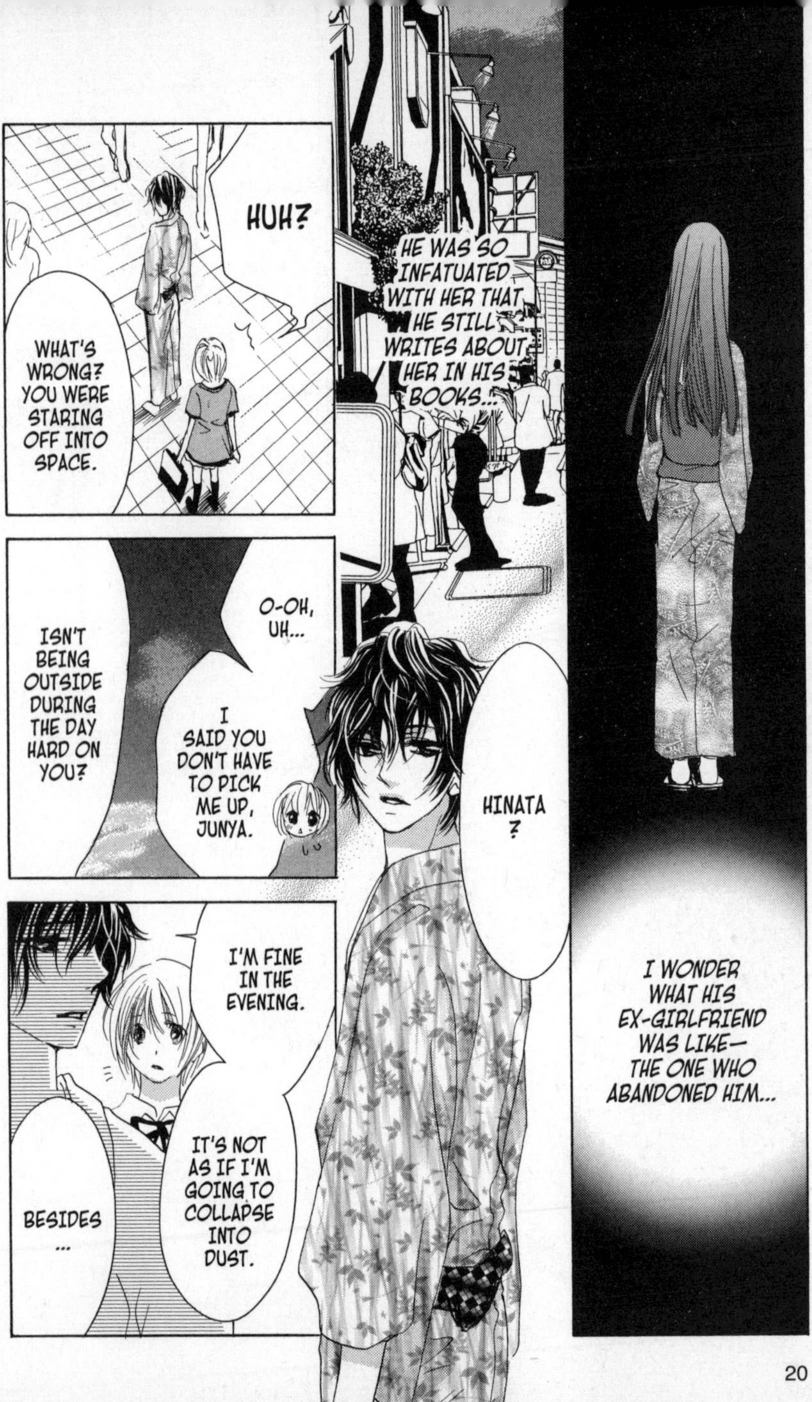
I WONDER WHAT HIS EX-GIRLFRIEND WAS LIKE— THE ONE WHO ABANDONED HIM...
HE WAS SO INFATUATED WITH HER THAT HE STILL WRITES ABOUT HER IN HIS BOOKS...
HINATA?
HUH?
WHAT'S WRONG? YOU WERE STARING OFF INTO SPACE.
O-OH, UH...
I SAID YOU DON'T HAVE TO PICK ME UP, JUNYA.
ISN'T BEING OUTSIDE DURING THE DAY HARD ON YOU?
I'M FINE IN THE EVENING.
IT'S NOT AS IF I'M GOING TO COLLAPSE INTO DUST.
BESIDES ...

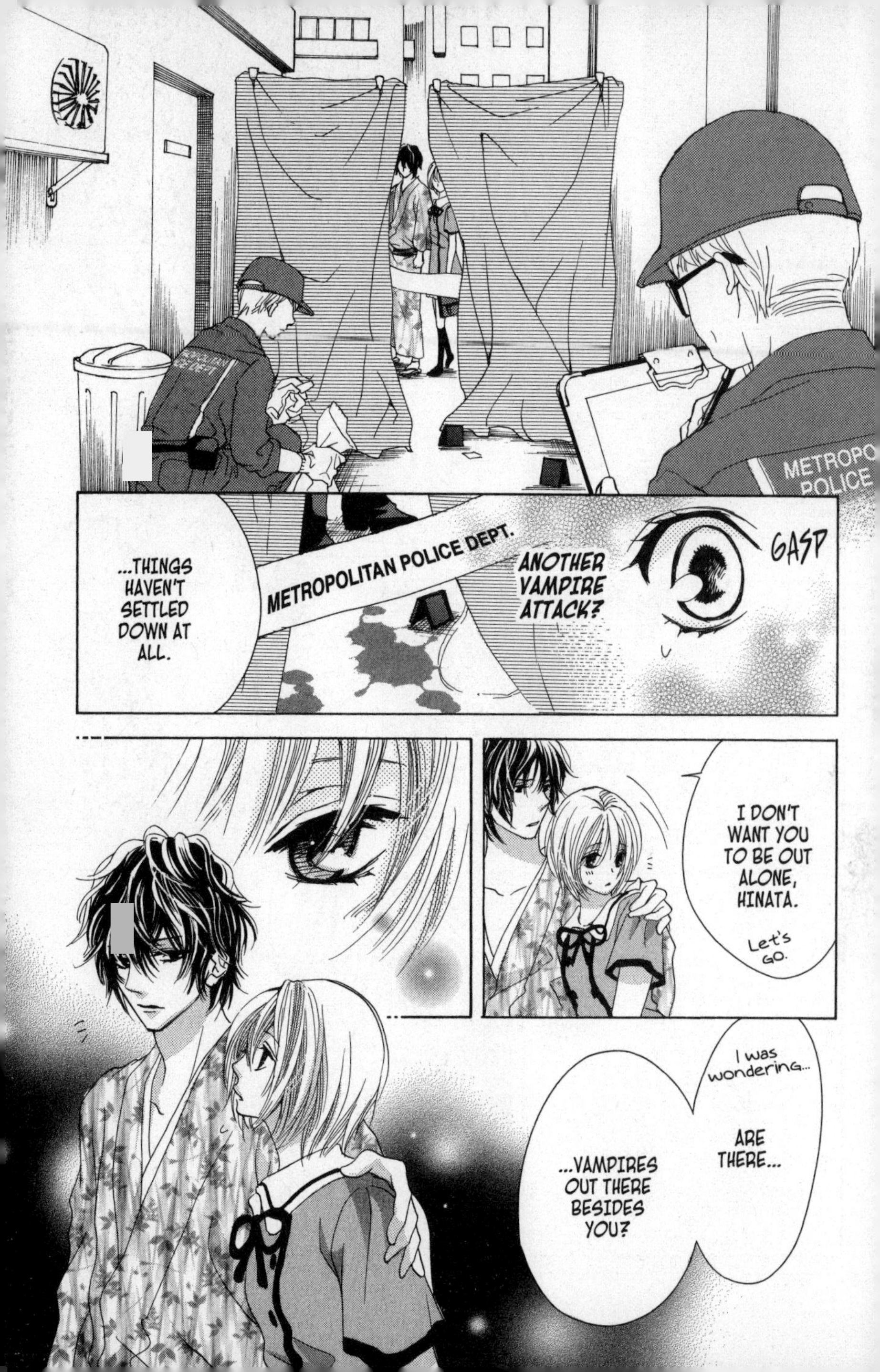
METROPOLITAN POLICE
GASP
ANOTHER VAMPIRE ATTACK?
METROPOLITAN POLICE DEPT.
...THINGS HAVEN'T SETTLED DOWN AT ALL.
I DON'T WANT YOU TO BE OUT ALONE, HINATA.
Let's go.
I was wondering...
ARE THERE...
...VAMPIRES OUT THERE BESIDES YOU?

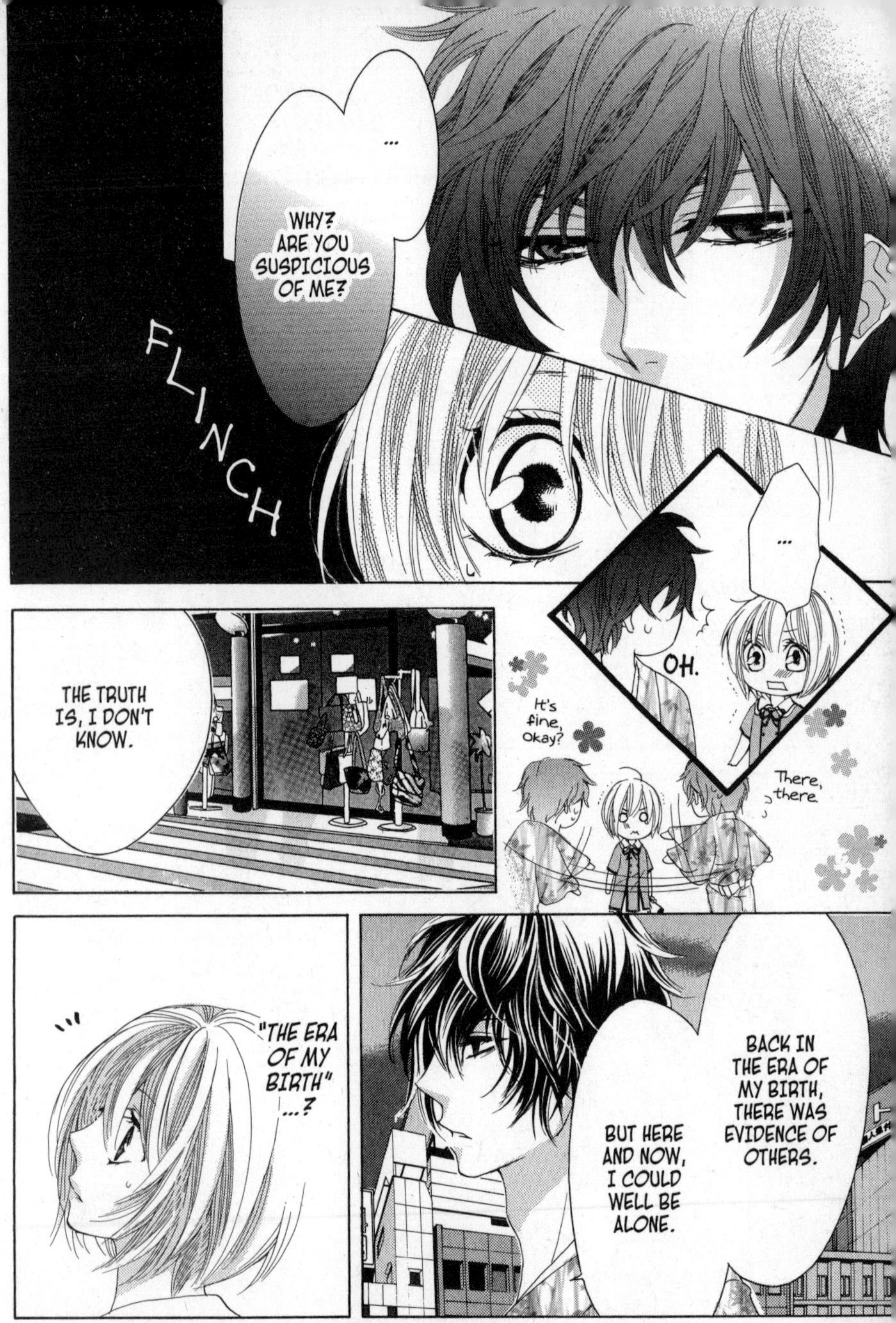
...
WHY? ARE YOU SUSPICIOUS OF ME?
FLINCH
...
OH.
It's fine, Okay?
There, there.
THE TRUTH IS, I DON'T KNOW.
BACK IN THE ERA OF MY BIRTH, THERE WAS EVIDENCE OF OTHERS.
BUT HERE AND NOW, I COULD WELL BE ALONE.
"THE ERA OF MY BIRTH" ...?

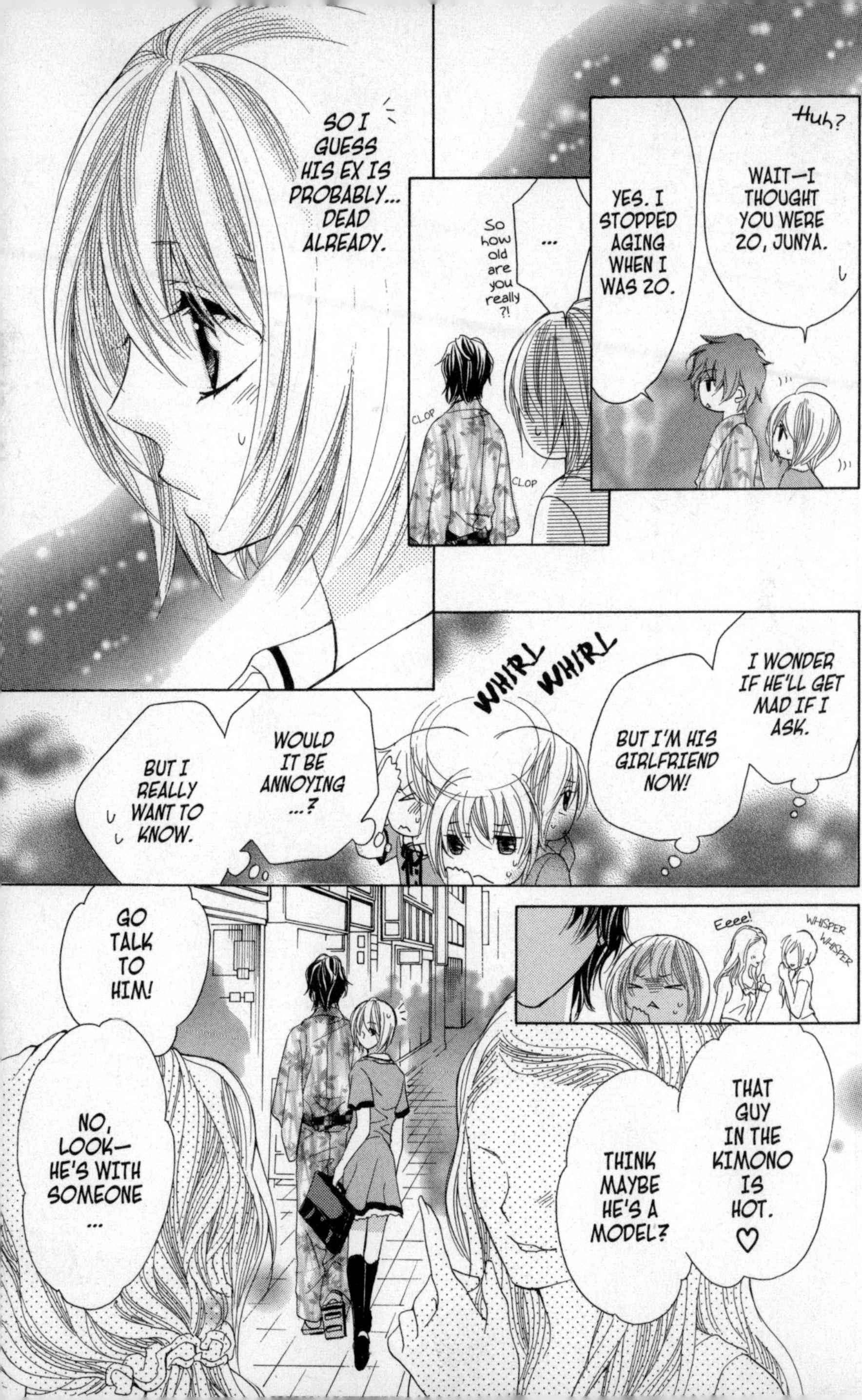
Huh?
WAIT—I THOUGHT YOU WERE 20, JUNYA.
YES. I STOPPED AGING WHEN I WAS 20.
...
So how old are you really?!
CLOP
CLOP
SO I GUESS HIS EX IS PROBABLY... DEAD ALREADY.
I WONDER IF HE'LL GET MAD IF I ASK.
BUT I'M HIS GIRLFRIEND NOW!
WHIRL WHIRL
WOULD IT BE ANNOYING...?
BUT I REALLY WANT TO KNOW.
WHISPER WHISPER
Eeee!
THAT GUY IN THE KIMONO IS HOT. ♥
THINK MAYBE HE'S A MODEL?
GO TALK TO HIM!
NO, LOOK—HE'S WITH SOMEONE...

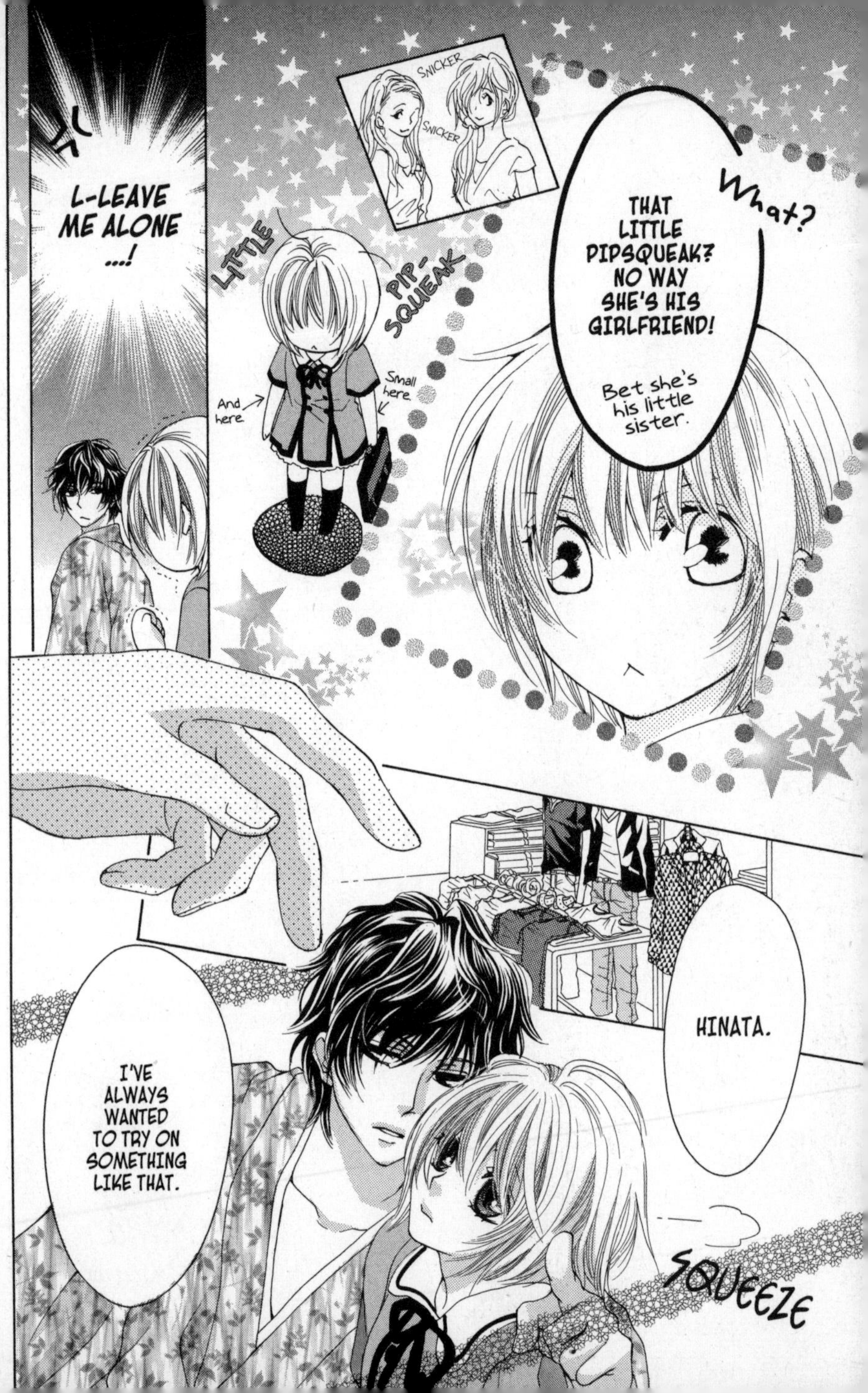
What?
THAT LITTLE PIPSQUEAK? NO WAY SHE'S HIS GIRLFRIEND!
Bet she's his little sister.
SNICKER
SNICKER
LITTLE
PIP-SQUEAK
Small here.
And here
L-LEAVE ME ALONE ...!
HINATA.
SQUEEZE
I'VE ALWAYS WANTED TO TRY ON SOMETHING LIKE THAT.

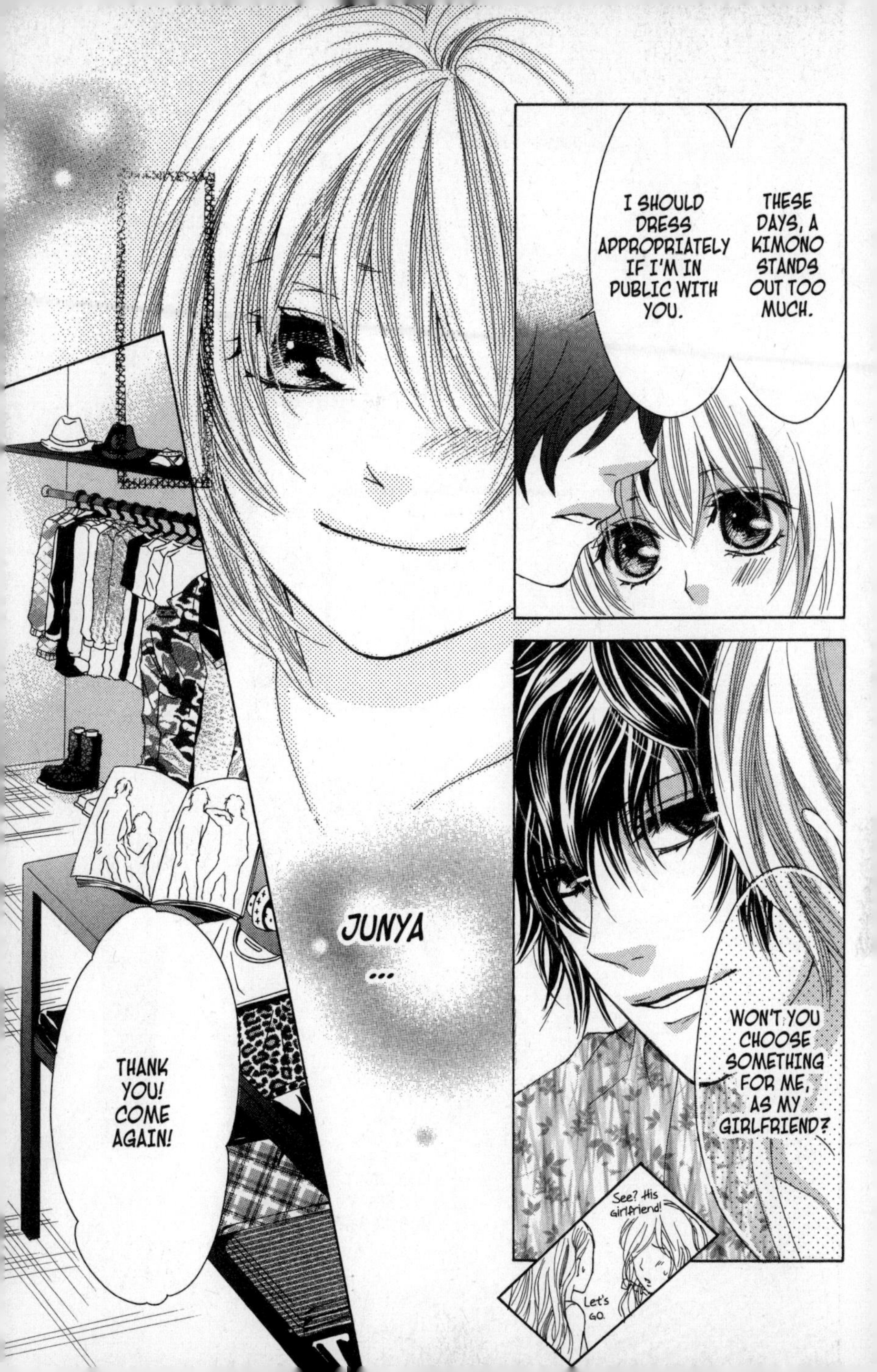
THESE DAYS, A KIMONO STANDS OUT TOO MUCH.
I SHOULD DRESS APPROPRIATELY IF I'M IN PUBLIC WITH YOU.
WON'T YOU CHOOSE SOMETHING FOR ME, AS MY GIRLFRIEND?
See? His girlfriend!
Let's go.
JUNYA...
THANK YOU! COME AGAIN!

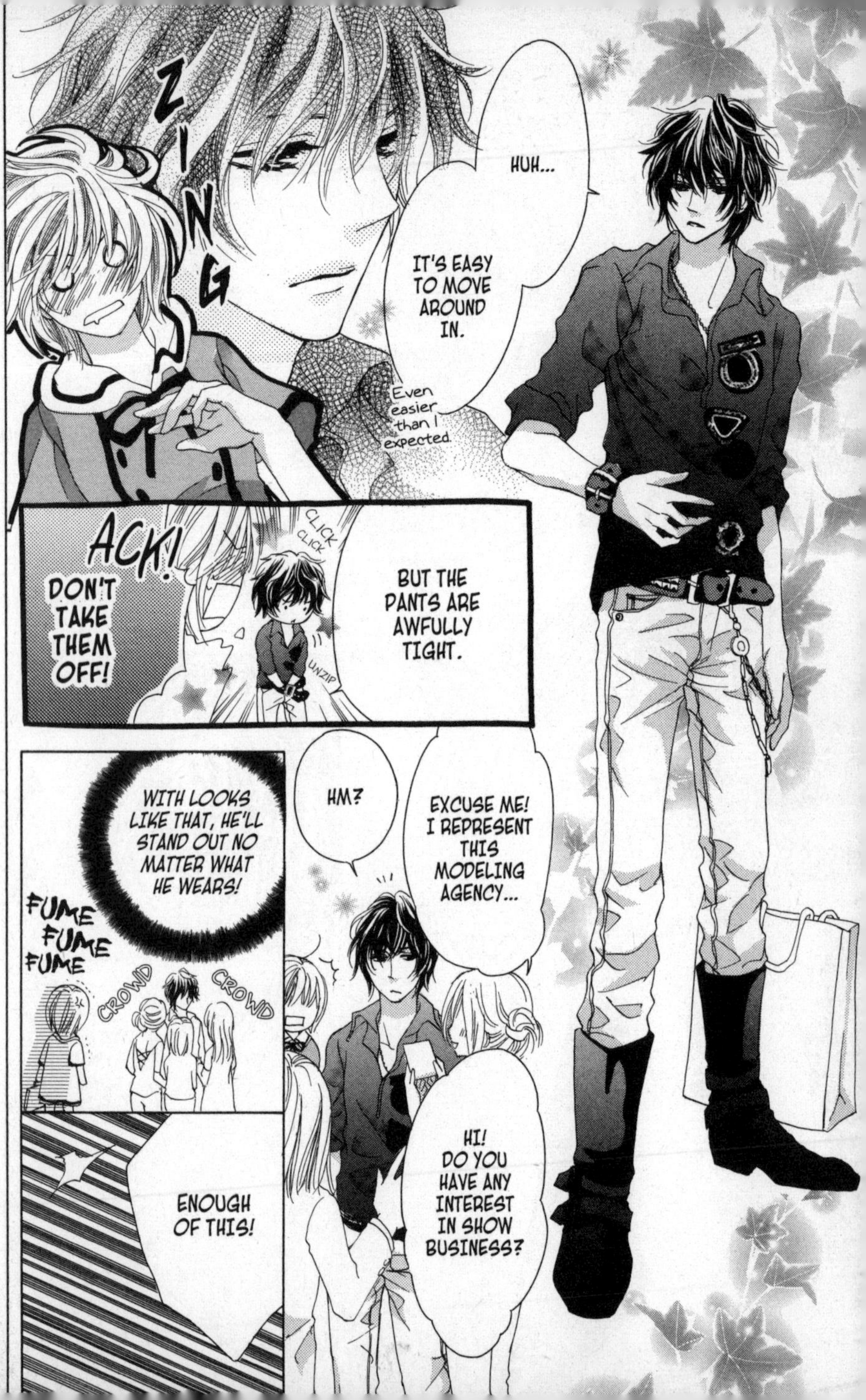
HUH...
IT'S EASY TO MOVE AROUND IN.
Even easier than I expected.
ZING
BUT THE PANTS ARE AWFULLY TIGHT.
CLICK CLICK
UNZIP
ACK!
DON'T TAKE THEM OFF!
EXCUSE ME! I REPRESENT THIS MODELING AGENCY...
HM?
HI! DO YOU HAVE ANY INTEREST IN SHOW BUSINESS?
WITH LOOKS LIKE THAT, HE'LL STAND OUT NO MATTER WHAT HE WEARS!
FUME FUME FUME
CROWD CROWD
ENOUGH OF THIS!

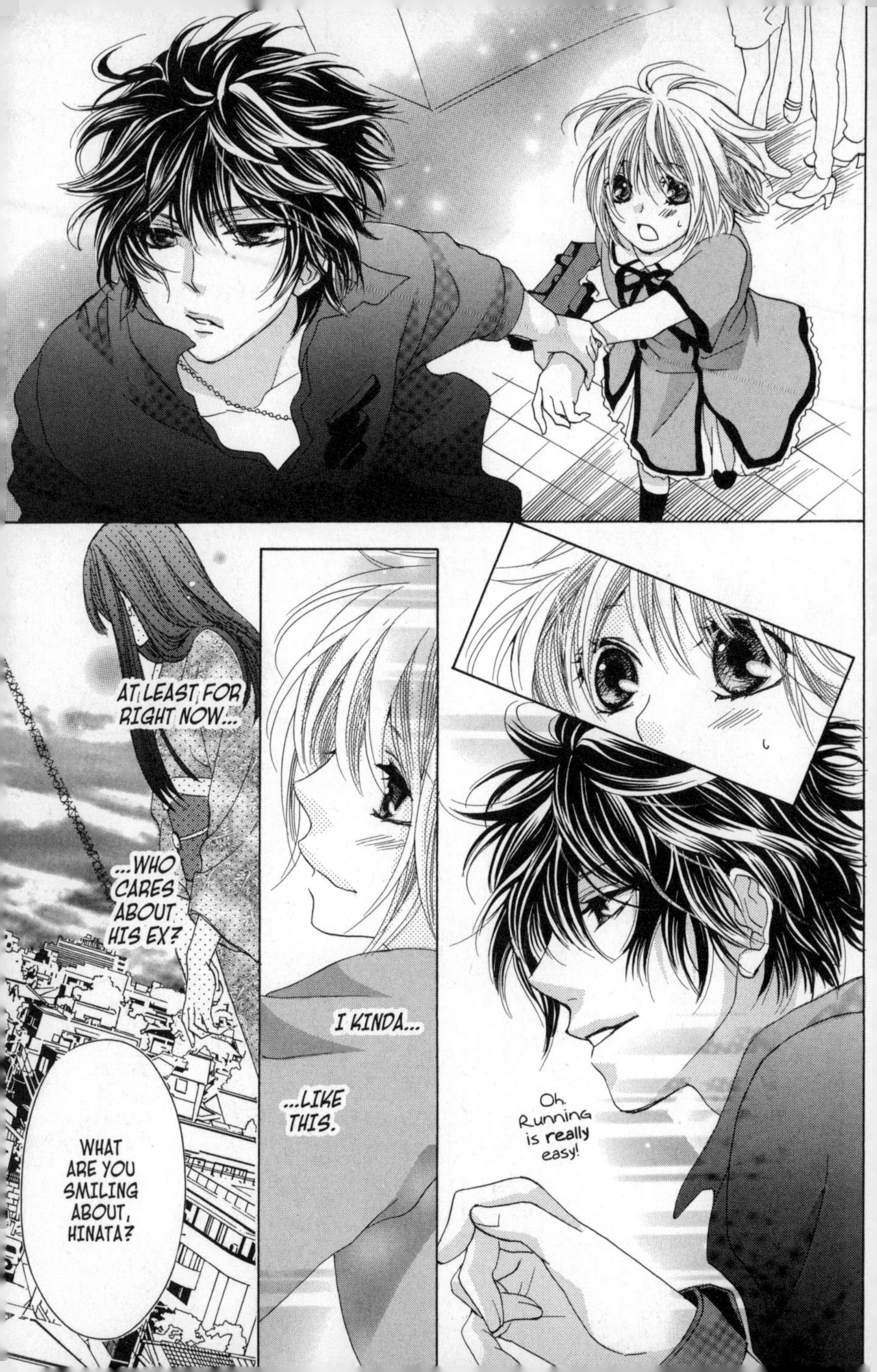
Oh. Running is really easy!
I KINDA...
...LIKE THIS.
AT LEAST FOR RIGHT NOW...
...WHO CARES ABOUT HIS EX?
WHAT ARE YOU SMILING ABOUT, HINATA?

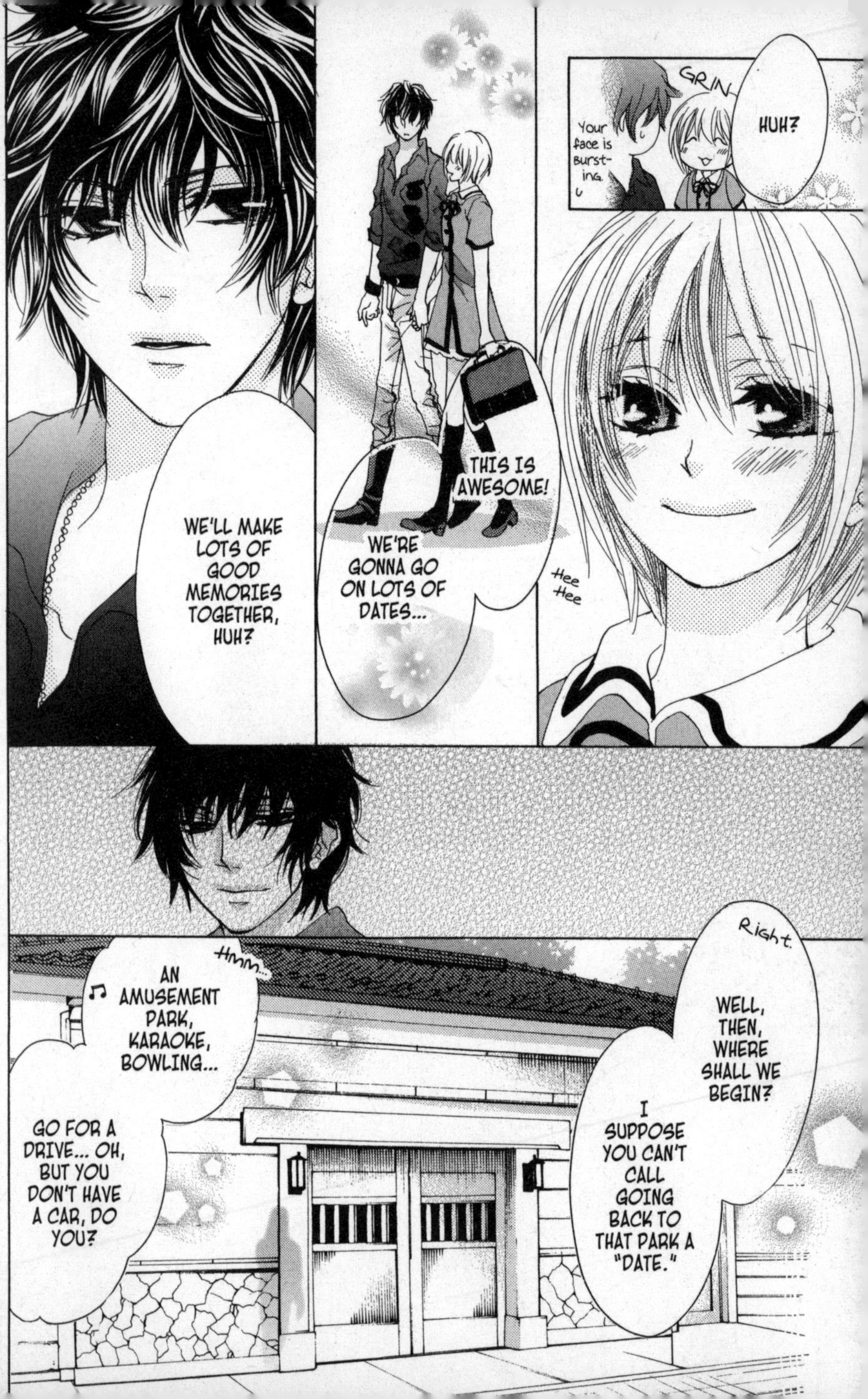
HUH?
GRIN
Your face is Burst-ing.
Hee Hee
THIS IS AWESOME!
WE'RE GONNA GO ON LOTS OF DATES...
WE'LL MAKE LOTS OF GOOD MEMORIES TOGETHER, HUH?
Right.
WELL, THEN, WHERE SHALL WE BEGIN?
I SUPPOSE YOU CAN'T CALL GOING BACK TO THAT PARK A "DATE."
Hmm...
AN AMUSEMENT PARK, KARAOKE, BOWLING...
GO FOR A DRIVE... OH, BUT YOU DON'T HAVE A CAR, DO YOU?

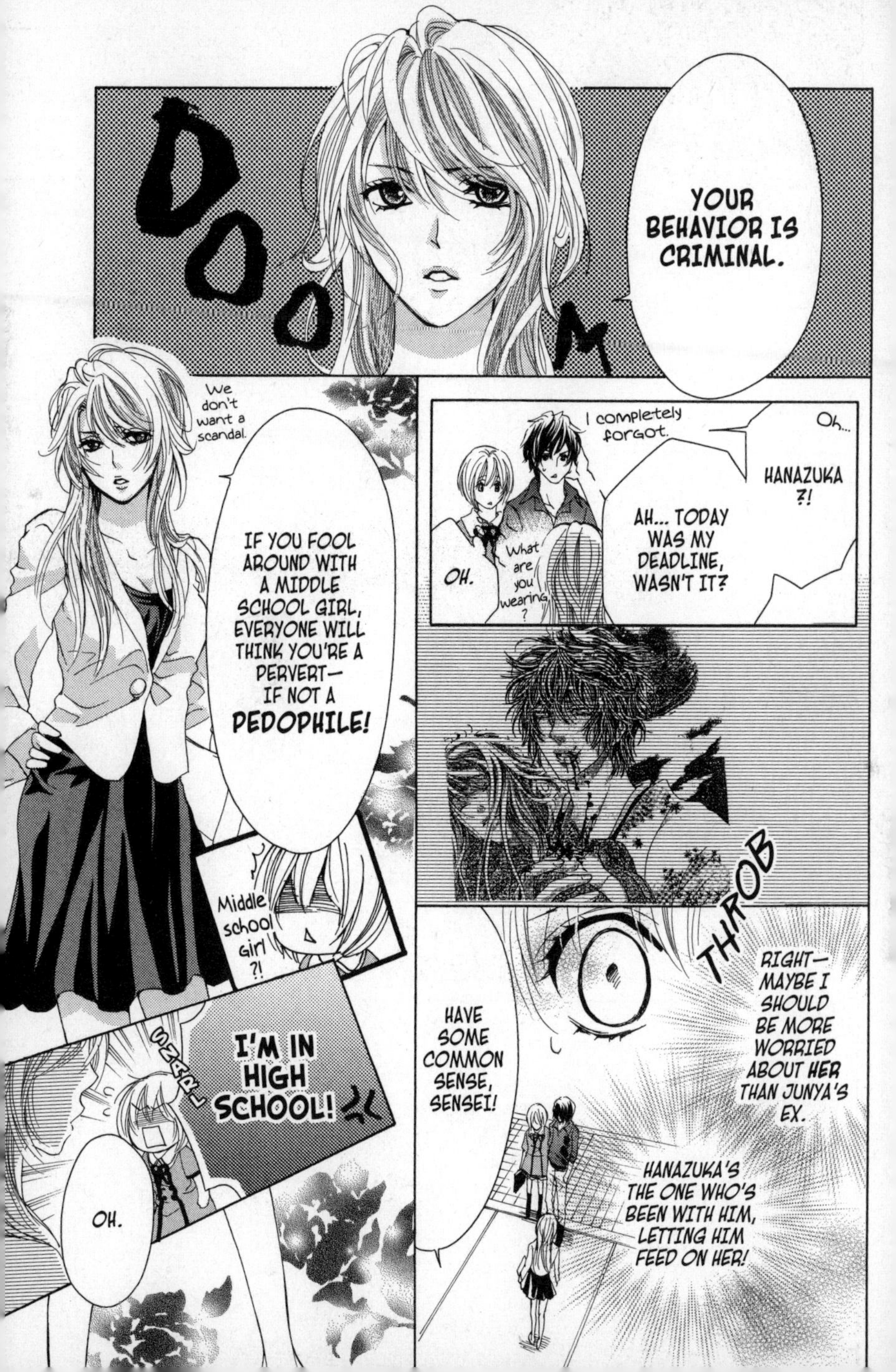
DOOOM
YOUR BEHAVIOR IS CRIMINAL.
Oh...
HANAZUKA?!
I completely forgot.
AH... TODAY WAS MY DEADLINE, WASN'T IT?
What are you wearing?
OH.
THROB
RIGHT—MAYBE I SHOULD BE MORE WORRIED ABOUT HER THAN JUNYA'S EX.
HAVE SOME COMMON SENSE, SENSEI!
HANAZUKA'S THE ONE WHO'S BEEN WITH HIM, LETTING HIM FEED ON HER!
We don't want a scandal.
IF YOU FOOL AROUND WITH A MIDDLE SCHOOL GIRL, EVERYONE WILL THINK YOU'RE A PERVERT— IF NOT A PEDOPHILE!
Middle school girl?!
SNARL
I'M IN HIGH SCHOOL!
OH.

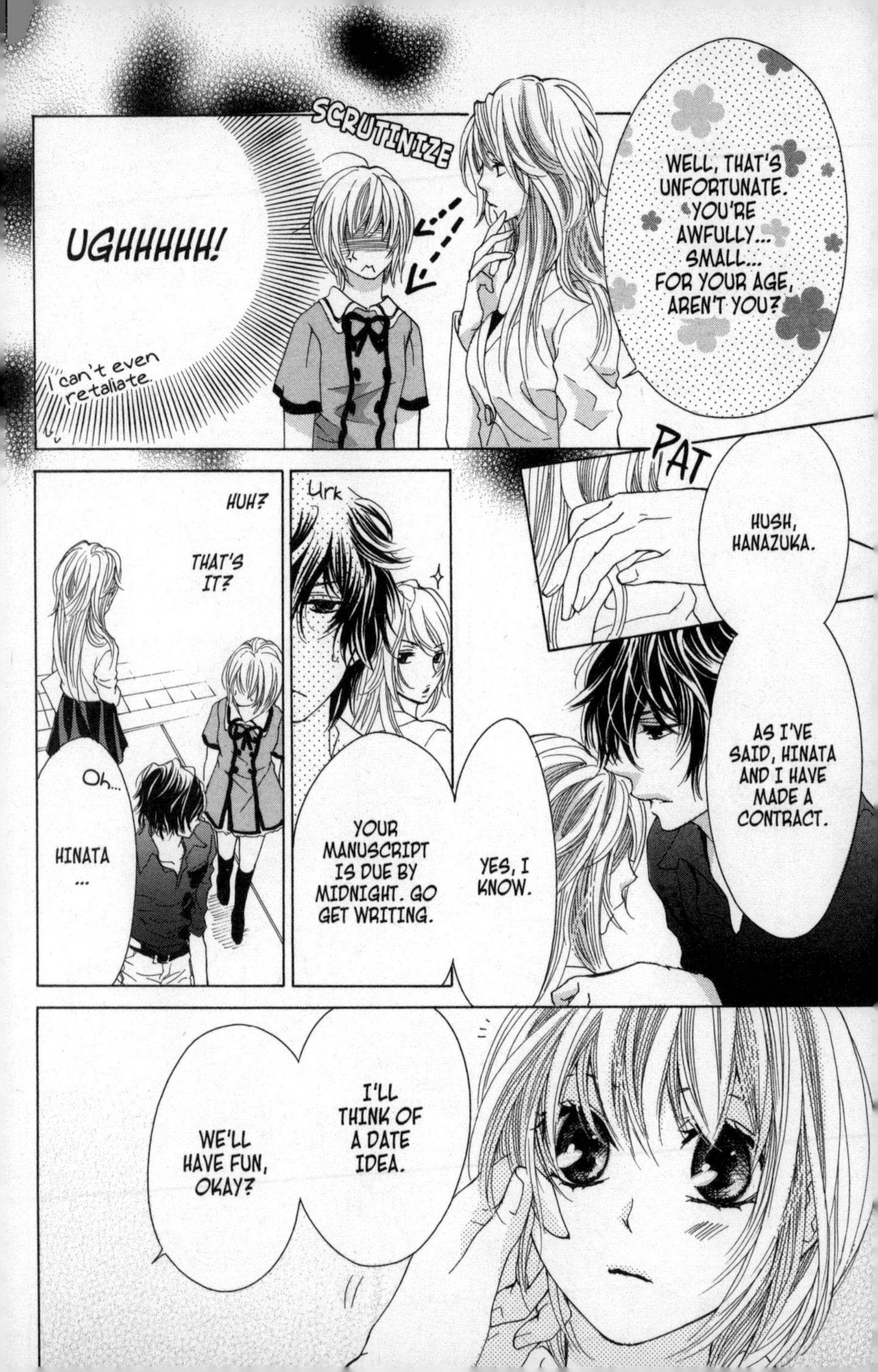
WELL, THAT'S UNFORTUNATE. YOU'RE AWFULLY... SMALL... FOR YOUR AGE, AREN'T YOU?
SCRUTINIZE
UGHHHHH!
I can't even retaliate.
PAT
HUSH, HANAZUKA.
AS I'VE SAID, HINATA AND I HAVE MADE A CONTRACT.
Urk
YES, I KNOW.
YOUR MANUSCRIPT IS DUE BY MIDNIGHT. GO GET WRITING.
HUH?
THAT'S IT?
Oh...
HINATA ...
I'LL THINK OF A DATE IDEA.
WE'LL HAVE FUN, OKAY?

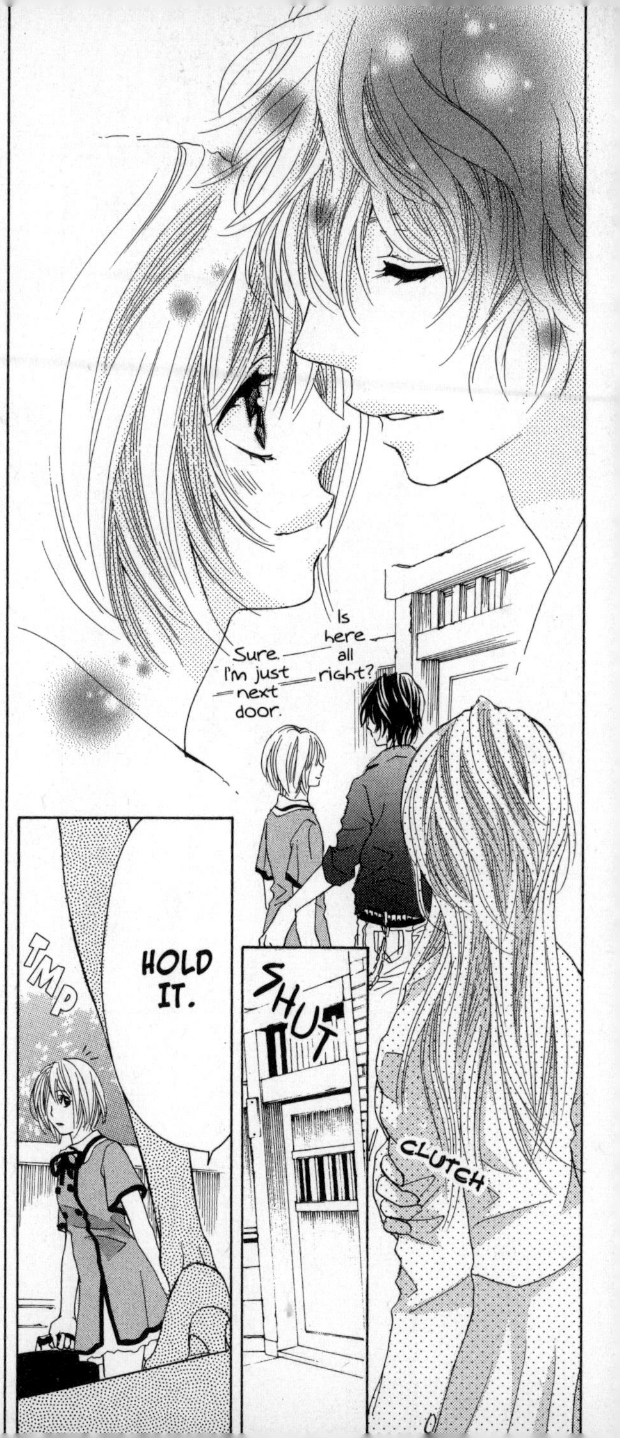
Is here all right?
Sure. I'm just next door.
SHUT
CLUTCH
TMP
HOLD IT.

Small Talk

①

Hello again!
Mitsuki here.

After I said that I was worried about what sorts of things to write about in this space before, a lot of you readers sent me suggestions.

I was surprised by how many of you expressed interest in my personal life! Then I started thinking about what to say about my life, but I kind of got depressed when I realized how little I have going on. But I've come up with a few things that I'll try to write about.

I'm sorry if you don't find them all that interesting, but please read them if you have the time!

← To be continued...

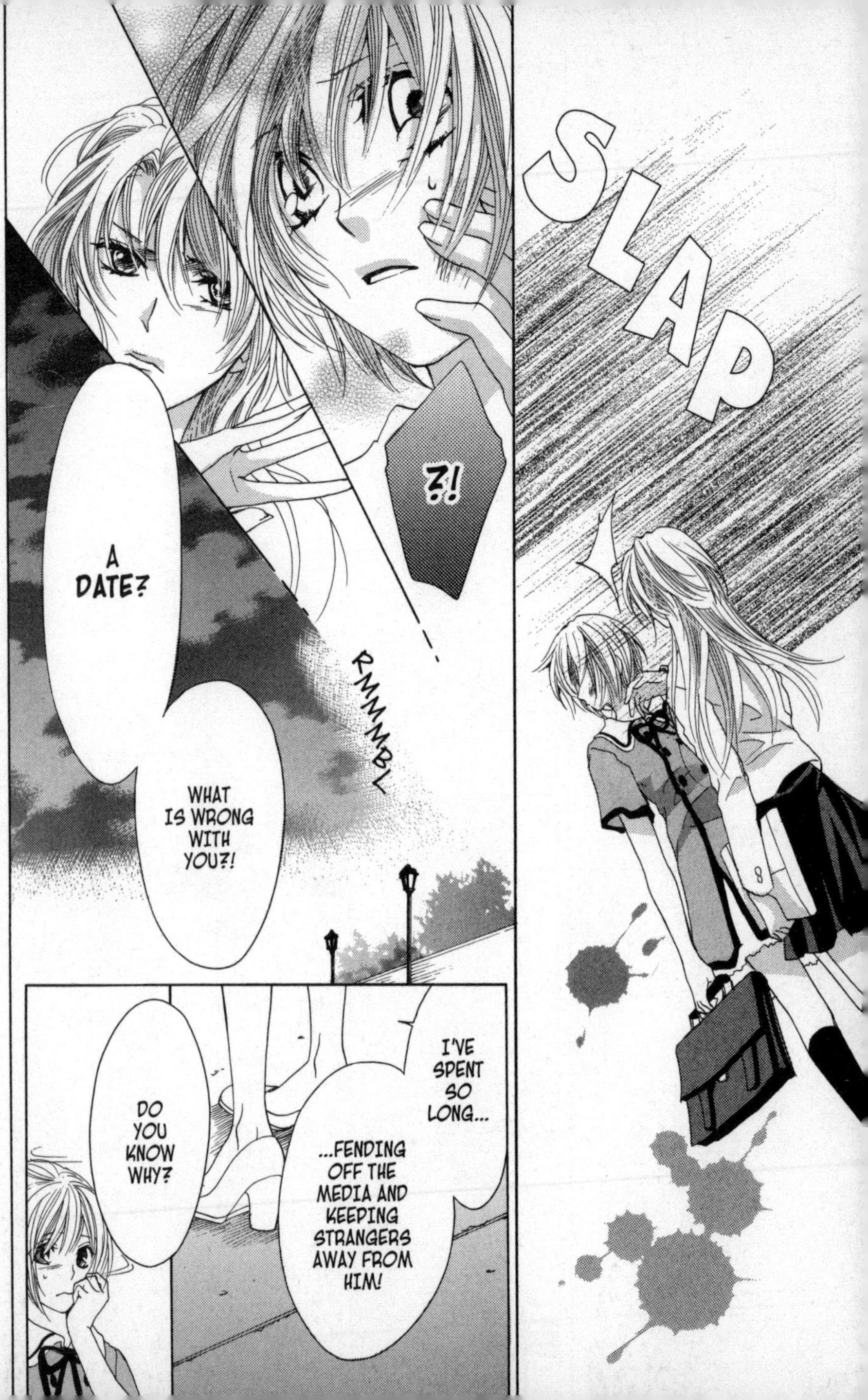
SLAP
?!
A DATE?
WHAT IS WRONG WITH YOU?!
RMMMBL
I'VE SPENT SO LONG...
...FENDING OFF THE MEDIA AND KEEPING STRANGERS AWAY FROM HIM!
DO YOU KNOW WHY?

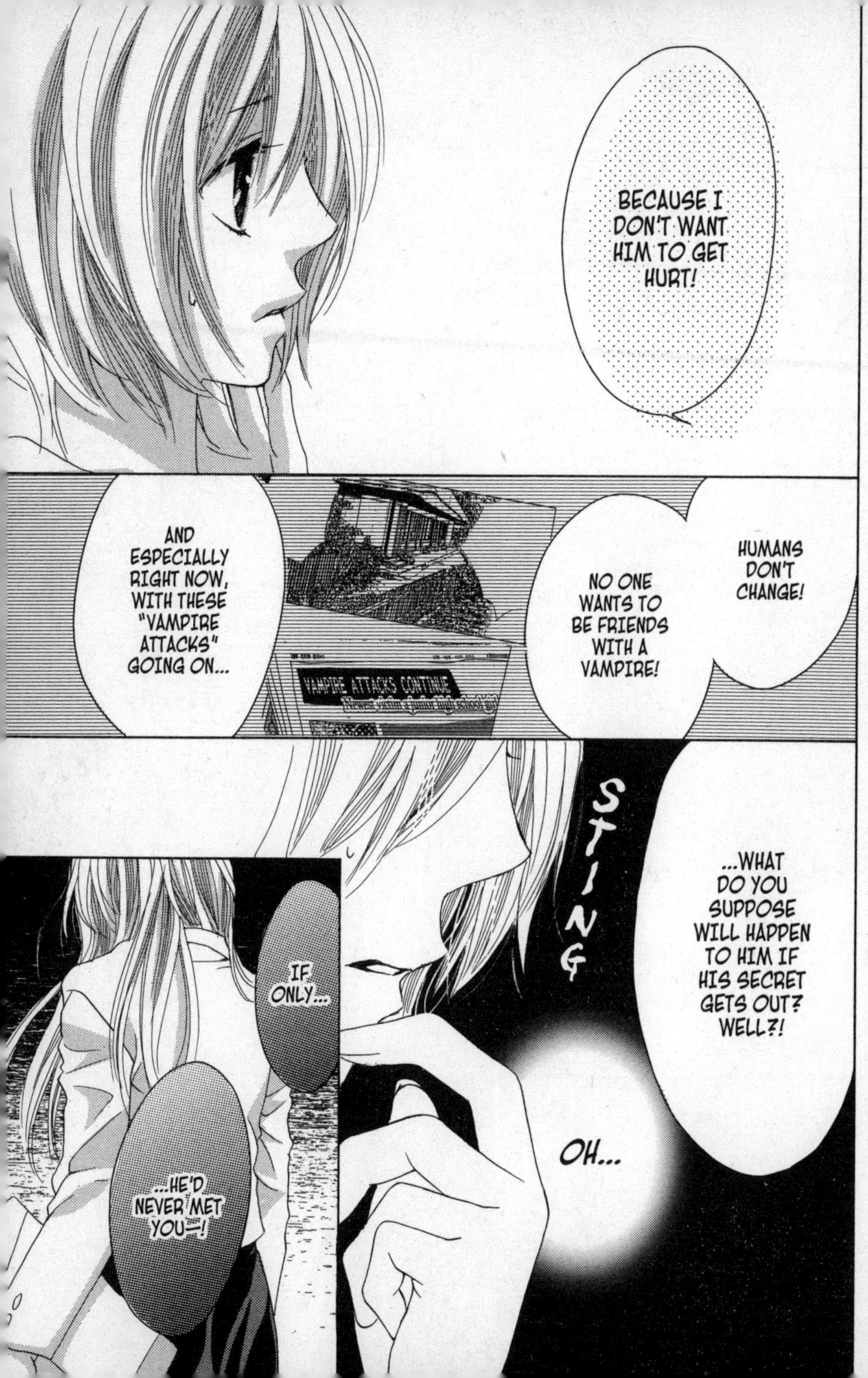
BECAUSE I DON'T WANT HIM TO GET HURT!
HUMANS DON'T CHANGE!
NO ONE WANTS TO BE FRIENDS WITH A VAMPIRE!
VAMPIRE ATTACKS CONTINUE
Newest victim a junior high school gi
AND ESPECIALLY RIGHT NOW, WITH THESE "VAMPIRE ATTACKS" GOING ON...
...WHAT DO YOU SUPPOSE WILL HAPPEN TO HIM IF HIS SECRET GETS OUT? WELL?!
STING
OH...
IF ONLY...
...HE'D NEVER MET YOU—!

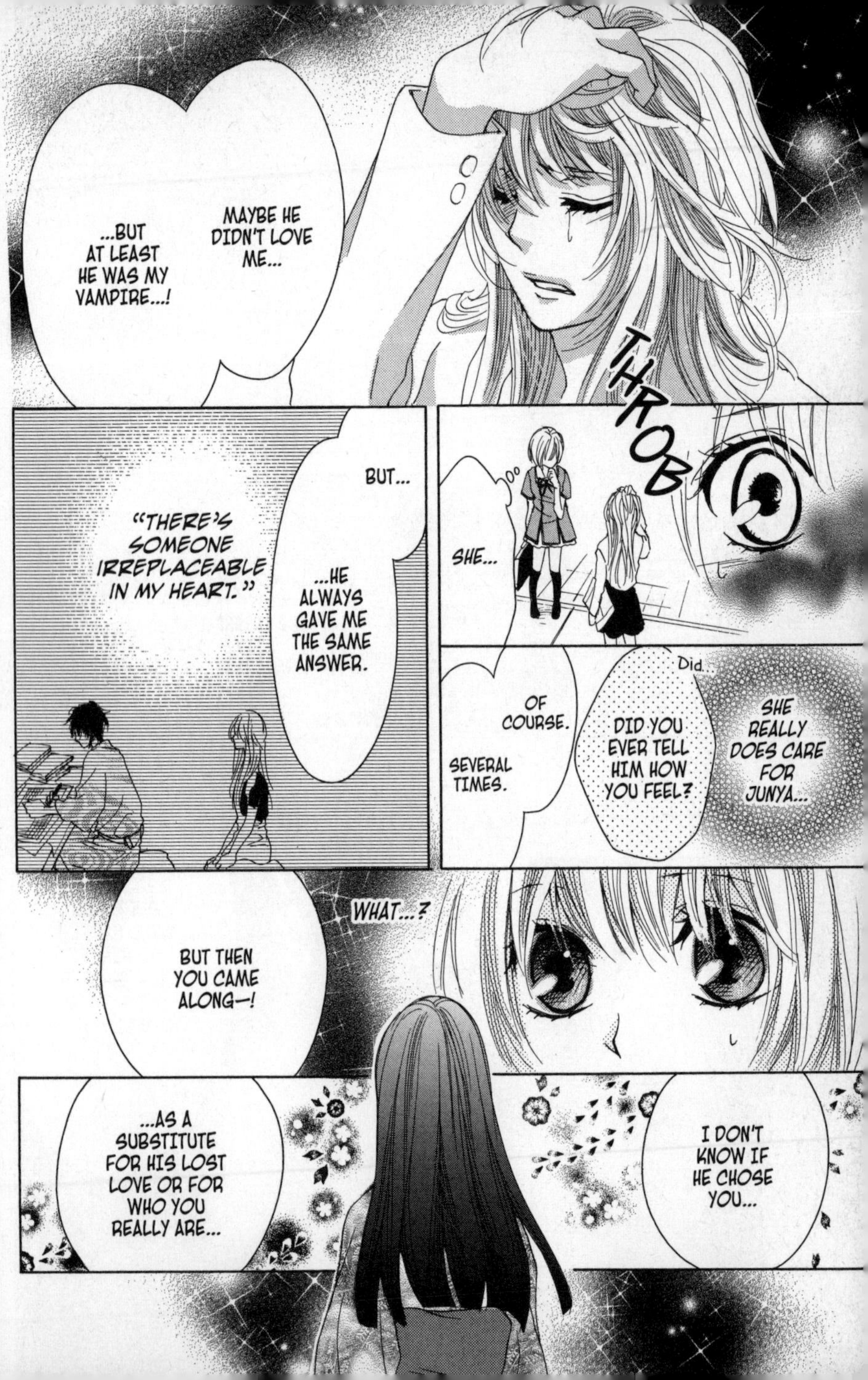
MAYBE HE DIDN'T LOVE ME...
...BUT AT LEAST HE WAS MY VAMPIRE...!
THROB
SHE...
Did...
SHE REALLY DOES CARE FOR JUNYA...
DID YOU EVER TELL HIM HOW YOU FEEL?
OF COURSE.
SEVERAL TIMES.
BUT...
...HE ALWAYS GAVE ME THE SAME ANSWER.
“THERE'S SOMEONE IRREPLACEABLE IN MY HEART.”
WHAT...?
BUT THEN YOU CAME ALONG—!
I DON'T KNOW IF HE CHOSE YOU...
...AS A SUBSTITUTE FOR HIS LOST LOVE OR FOR WHO YOU REALLY ARE...

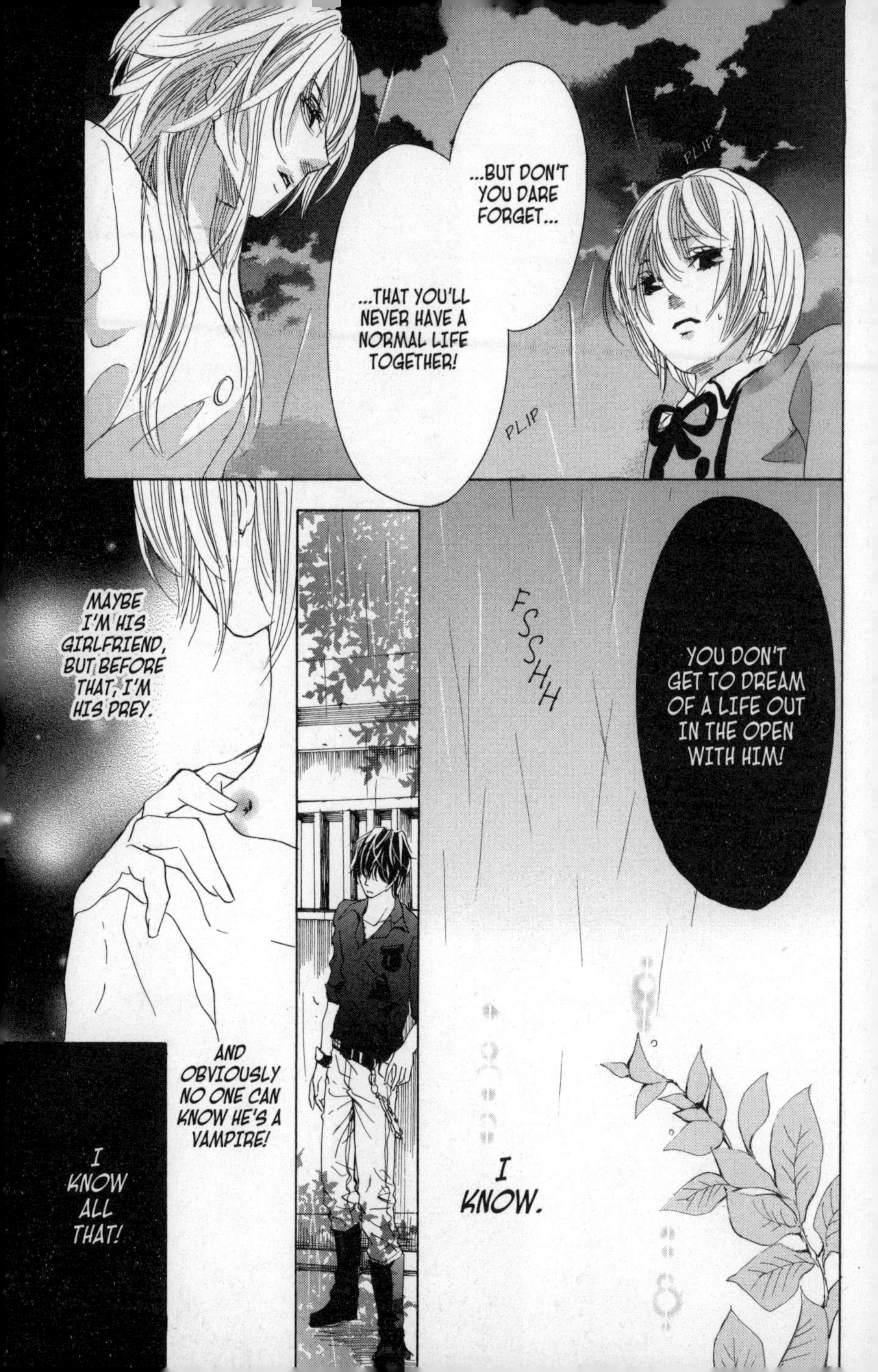
PLIP
...BUT DON'T YOU DARE FORGET...
...THAT YOU'LL NEVER HAVE A NORMAL LIFE TOGETHER!
PLIP
FSSHH
YOU DON'T GET TO DREAM OF A LIFE OUT IN THE OPEN WITH HIM!
I KNOW.
AND OBVIOUSLY NO ONE CAN KNOW HE'S A VAMPIRE!
MAYBE I'M HIS GIRLFRIEND, BUT BEFORE THAT, I'M HIS PREY.
I KNOW ALL THAT!

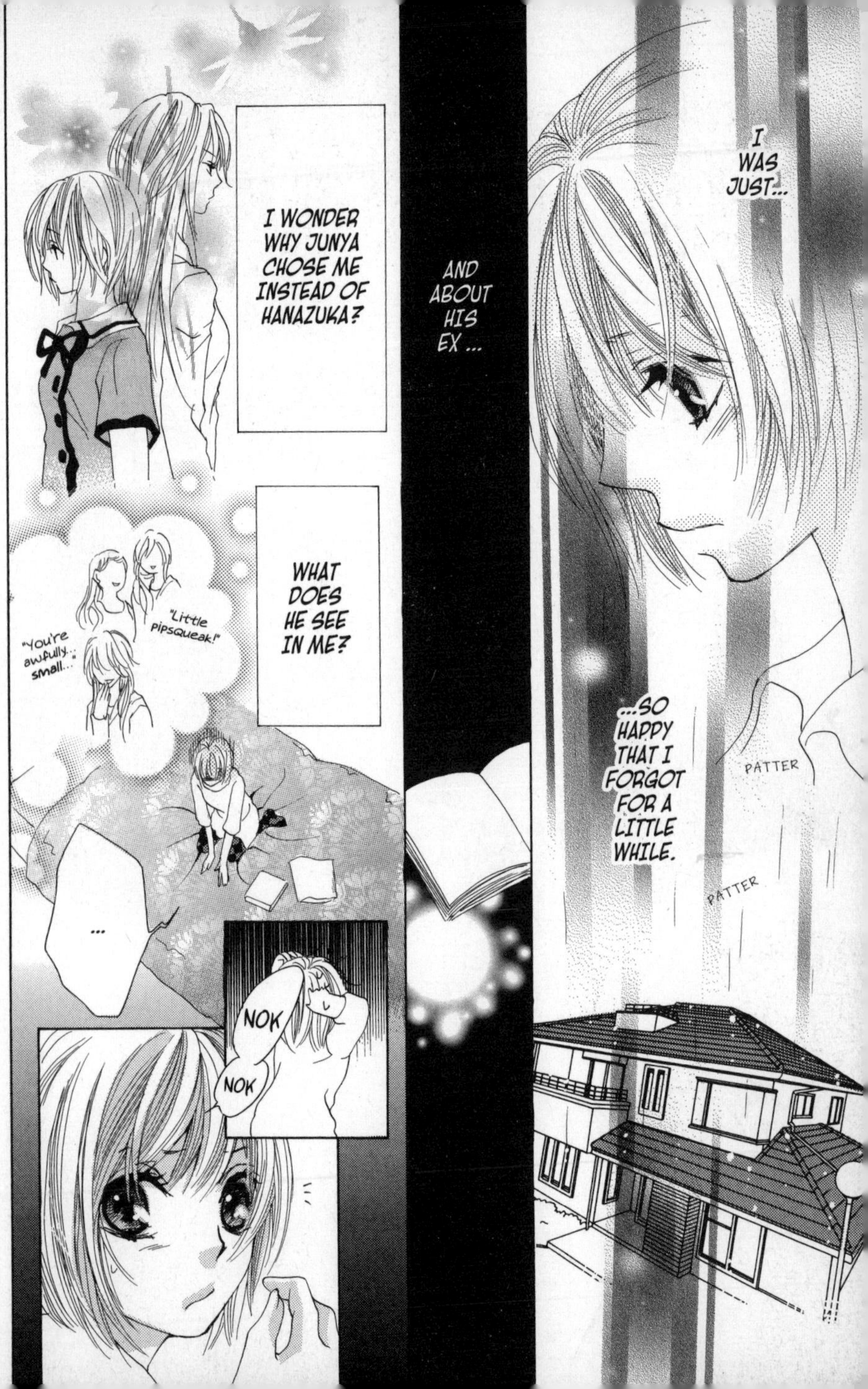
I WAS JUST...
...SO HAPPY THAT I FORGOT FOR A LITTLE WHILE.
PATTER
PATTER
AND ABOUT HIS EX ...
I WONDER WHY JUNYA CHOSE ME INSTEAD OF HANAZUKA?
WHAT DOES HE SEE IN ME?
"Little pipsqueak!"
"You're awfully... small..."
...
NOK
NOK

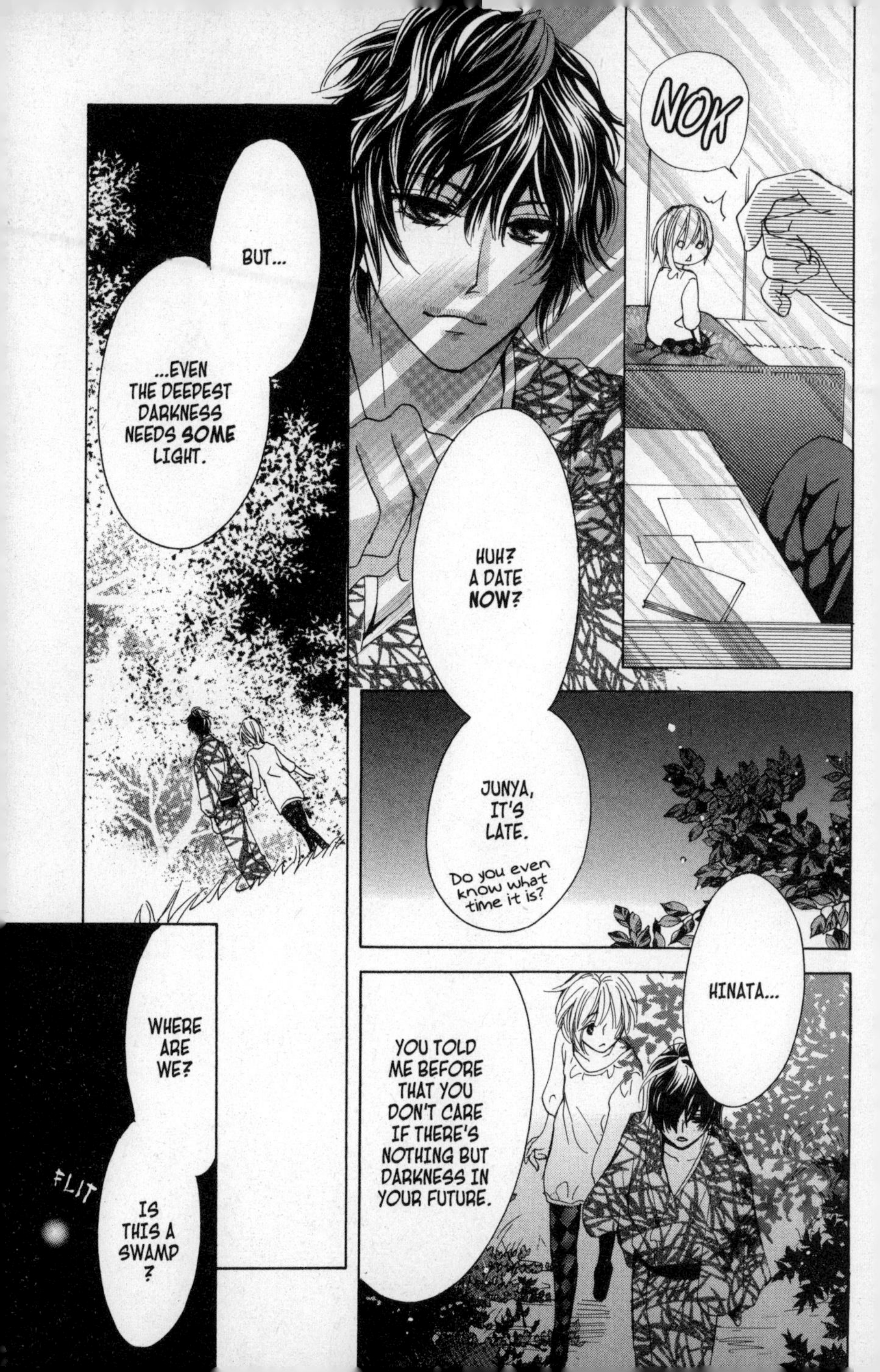
NOK
HUH? A DATE NOW?
JUNYA, IT'S LATE.
Do you even know what time it is?
HINATA...
YOU TOLD ME BEFORE THAT YOU DON'T CARE IF THERE'S NOTHING BUT DARKNESS IN YOUR FUTURE.
BUT...
...EVEN THE DEEPEST DARKNESS NEEDS SOME LIGHT.
WHERE ARE WE?
IS THIS A SWAMP?
FLIT

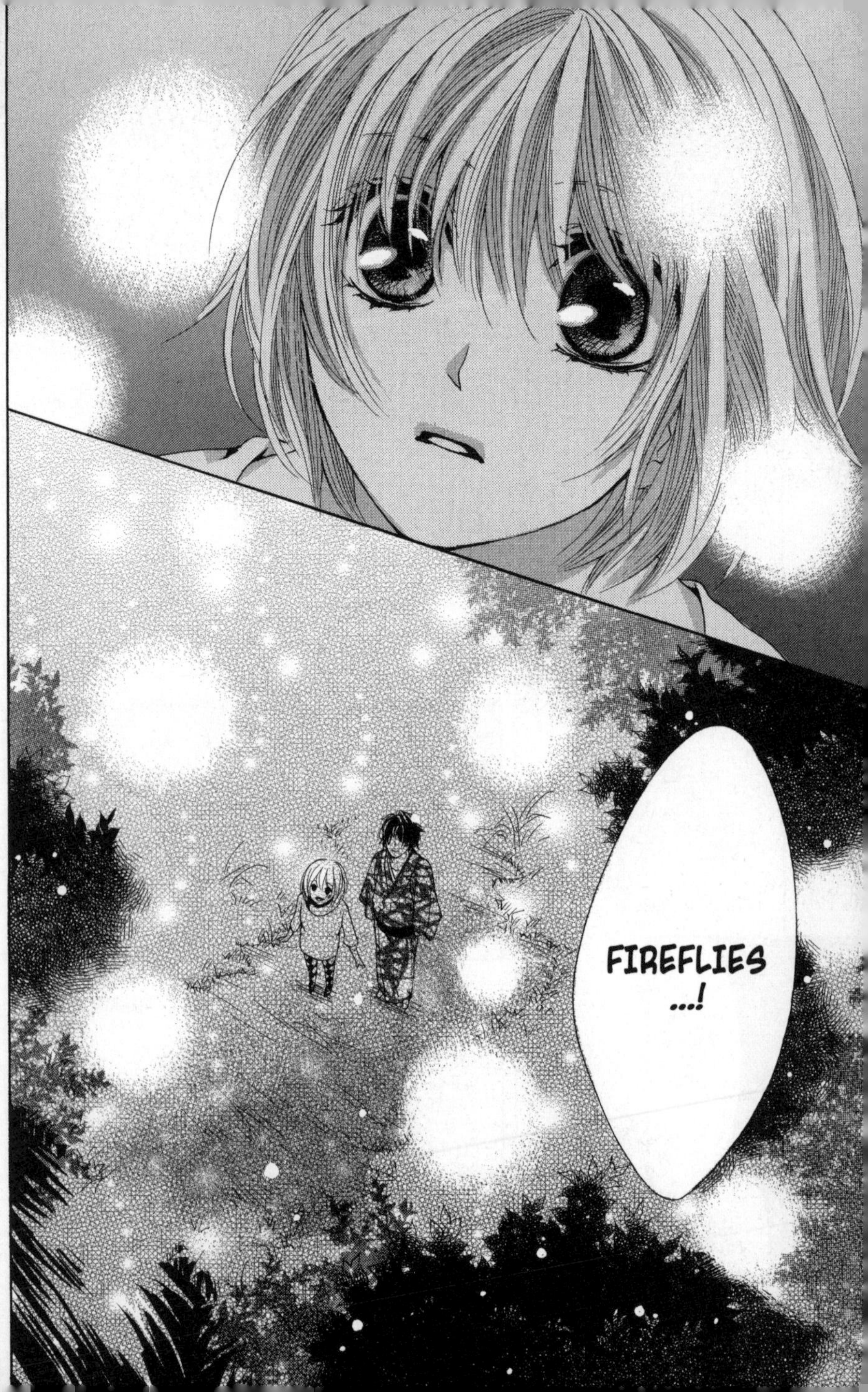
FIREFLIES ...!

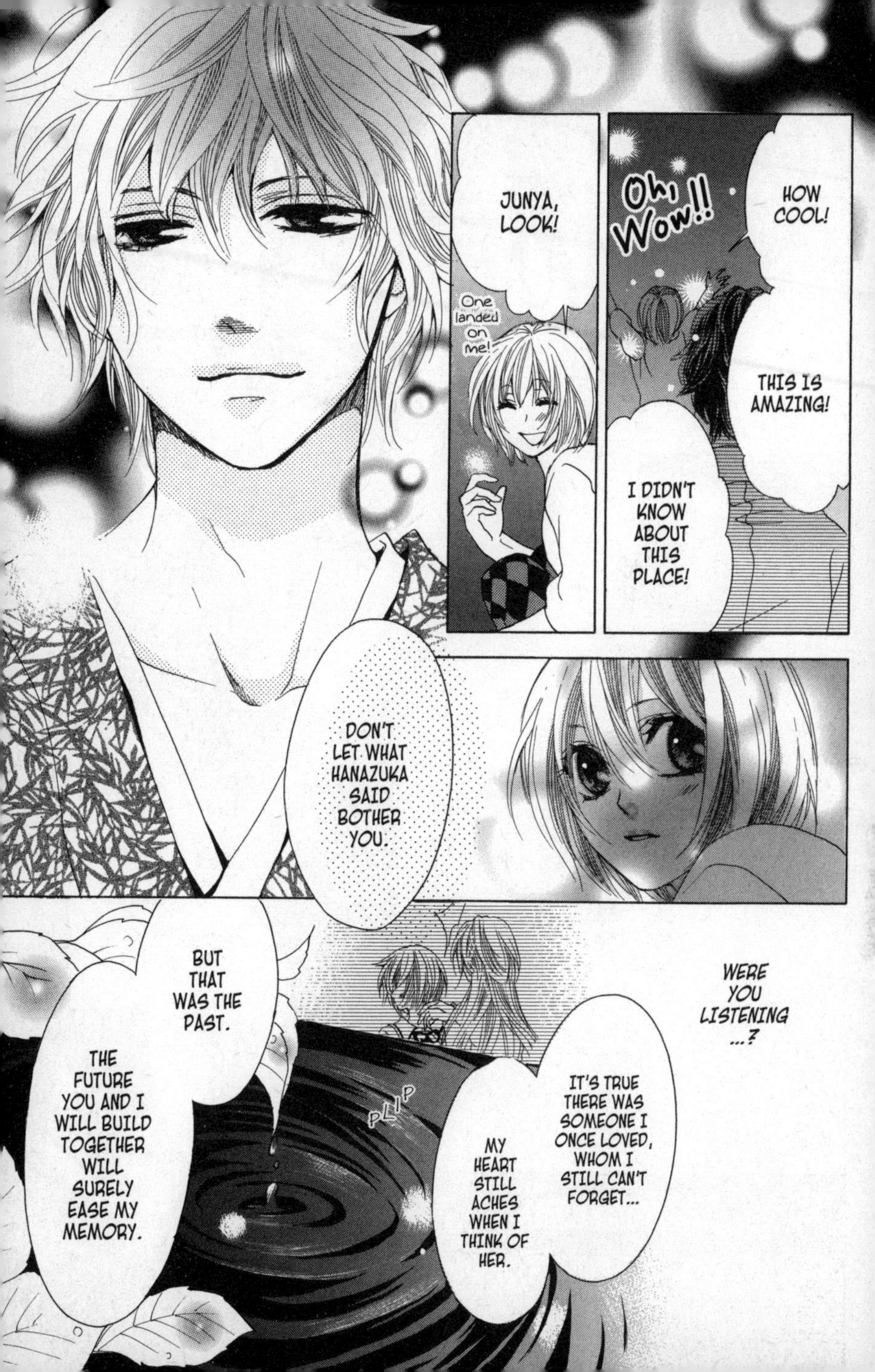
Oh, Wow!!
HOW COOL!
THIS IS AMAZING!
I DIDN'T KNOW ABOUT THIS PLACE!
JUNYA, LOOK!
One landed on me!
DON'T LET WHAT HANAZUKA SAID BOTHER YOU.
WERE YOU LISTENING ...?
IT'S TRUE THERE WAS SOMEONE I ONCE LOVED, WHOM I STILL CAN'T FORGET...
MY HEART STILL ACHES WHEN I THINK OF HER.
PLIP
BUT THAT WAS THE PAST.
THE FUTURE YOU AND I WILL BUILD TOGETHER WILL SURELY EASE MY MEMORY.

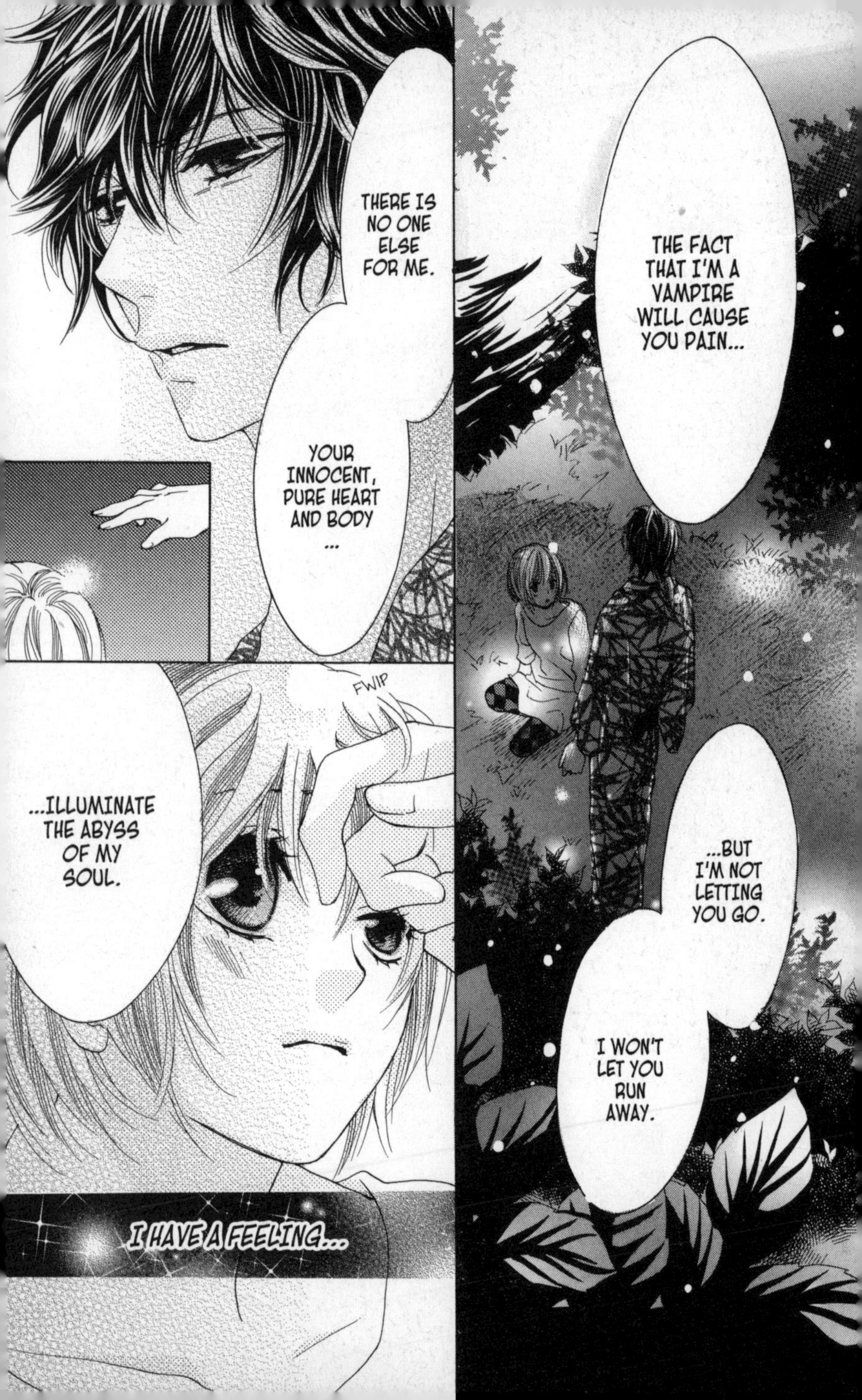
THE FACT THAT I'M A VAMPIRE WILL CAUSE YOU PAIN...
...BUT I'M NOT LETTING YOU GO.
I WON'T LET YOU RUN AWAY.
THERE IS NO ONE ELSE FOR ME.
YOUR INNOCENT, PURE HEART AND BODY ...
FWIP
...ILLUMINATE THE ABYSS OF MY SOUL.
I HAVE A FEELING...

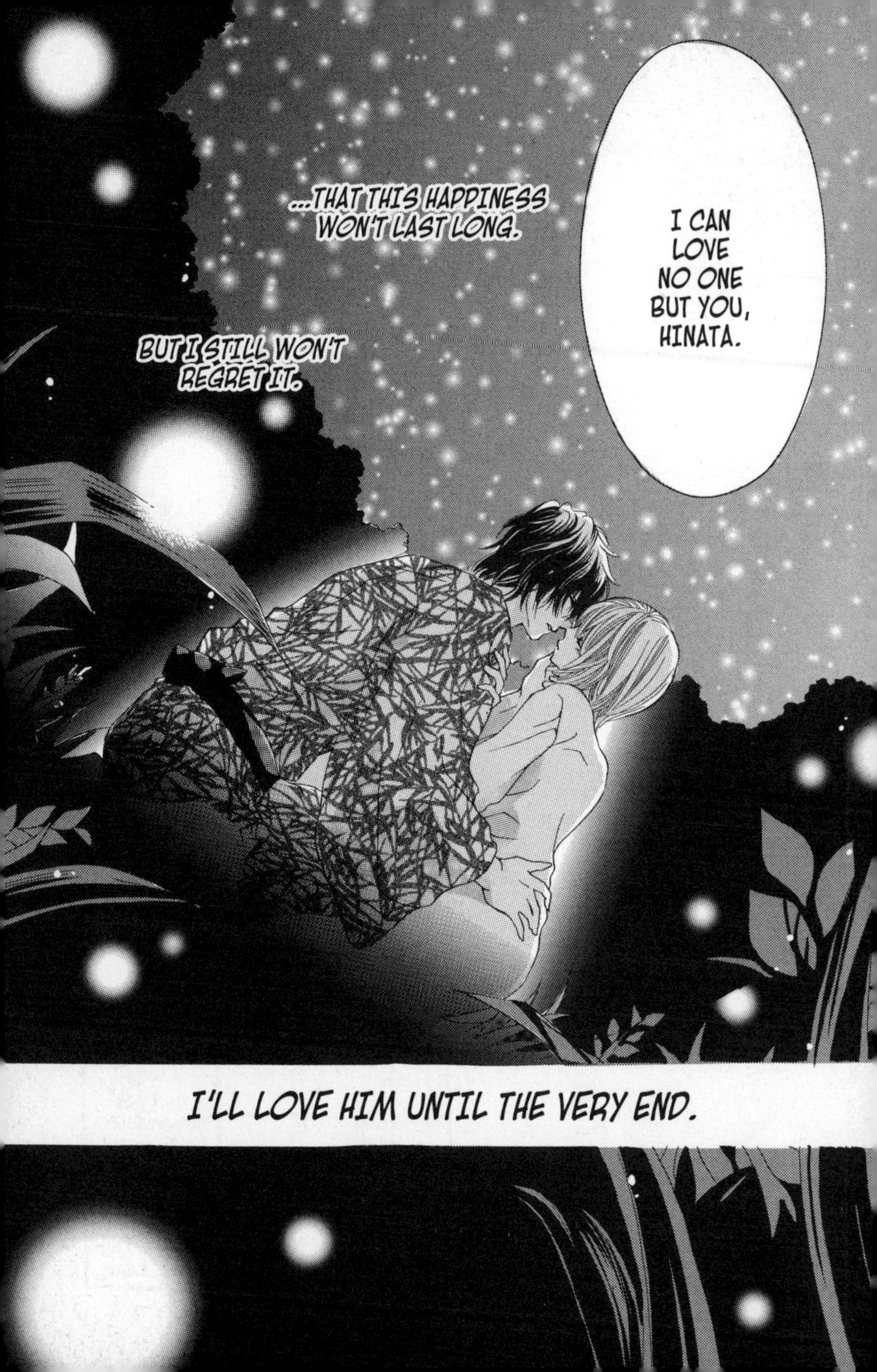
I CAN LOVE NO ONE BUT YOU, HINATA.
...THAT THIS HAPPINESS WON'T LAST LONG.
BUT I STILL WON'T REGRET IT.
I'LL LOVE HIM UNTIL THE VERY END.

I Went!

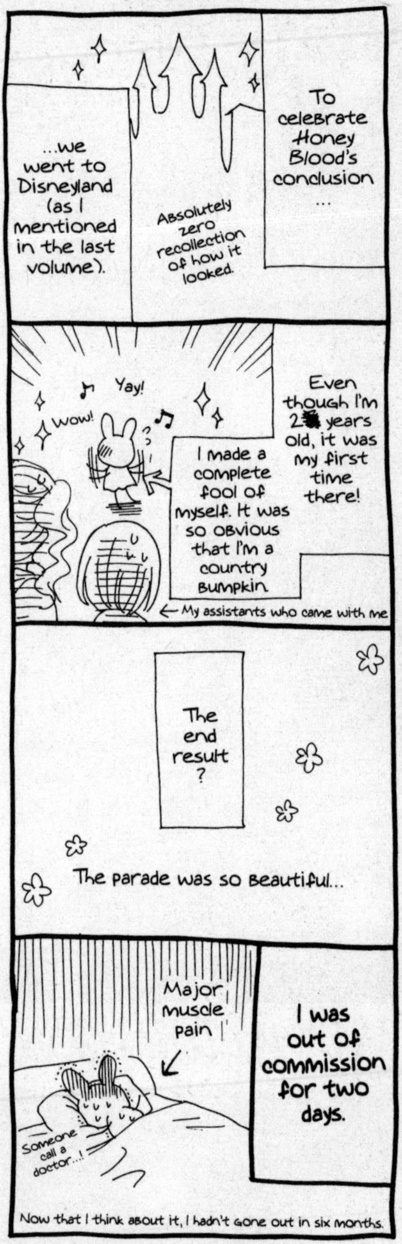
To celebrate Honey Blood's conclusion...
Absolutely zero recollection of how it looked.
...we went to Disneyland (as I mentioned in the last volume).
Even though I'm 2[redacted] years old, it was my first time there!
I made a complete fool of myself. It was so obvious that I'm a country bumpkin.
Yay!
Wow!
← My assistants who came with me
The end result?
The parade was so beautiful...
I was out of commission for two days.
Major muscle pain
Someone call a doctor...!
Now that I think about it, I hadn't gone out in six months.

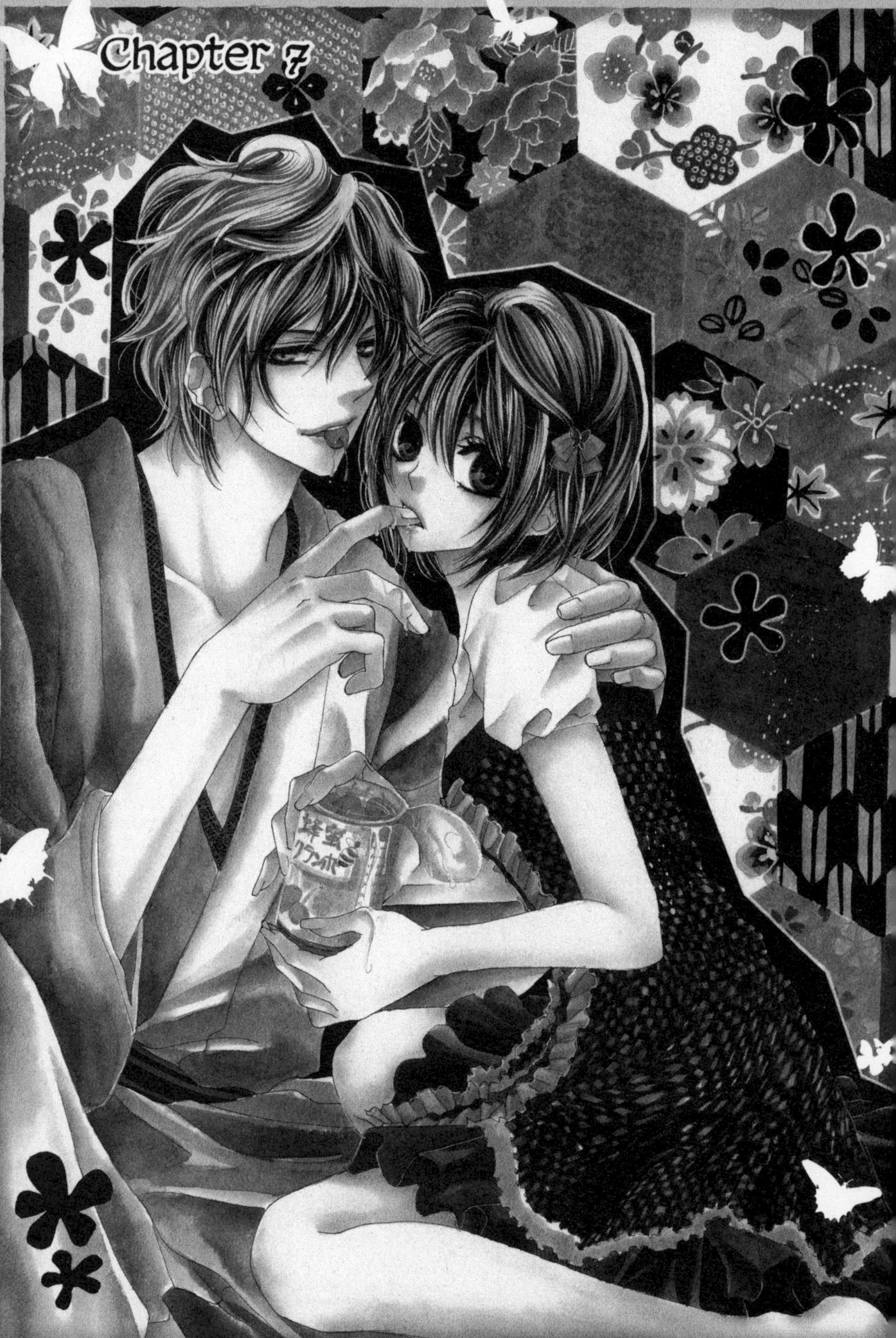
Chapter 7

Wait Time

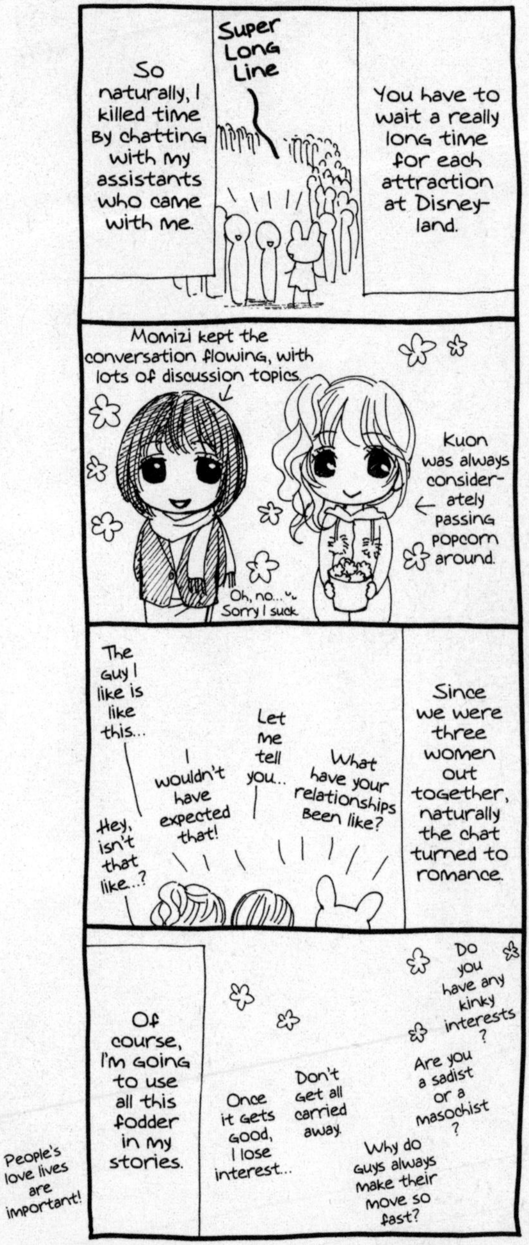
You have to wait a really long time for each attraction at Disney-land.
Super Long Line
So naturally, I killed time by chatting with my assistants who came with me.
Momizi kept the conversation flowing, with lots of discussion topics.
Kuon was always consider-ately passing popcorn around.
Oh, no... Sorry I suck
Since we were three women out together, naturally the chat turned to romance.
What have your relationships been like?
Let me tell you...
I wouldn't have expected that!
The guy I like is like this...
Hey, isn't that like...?
Do you have any kinky interests?
Are you a sadist or a masochist?
Don't get all carried away.
Why do guys always make their move so fast?
Once it gets good, I lose interest...
Of course, I'm going to use all this fodder in my stories.
People's love lives are important!

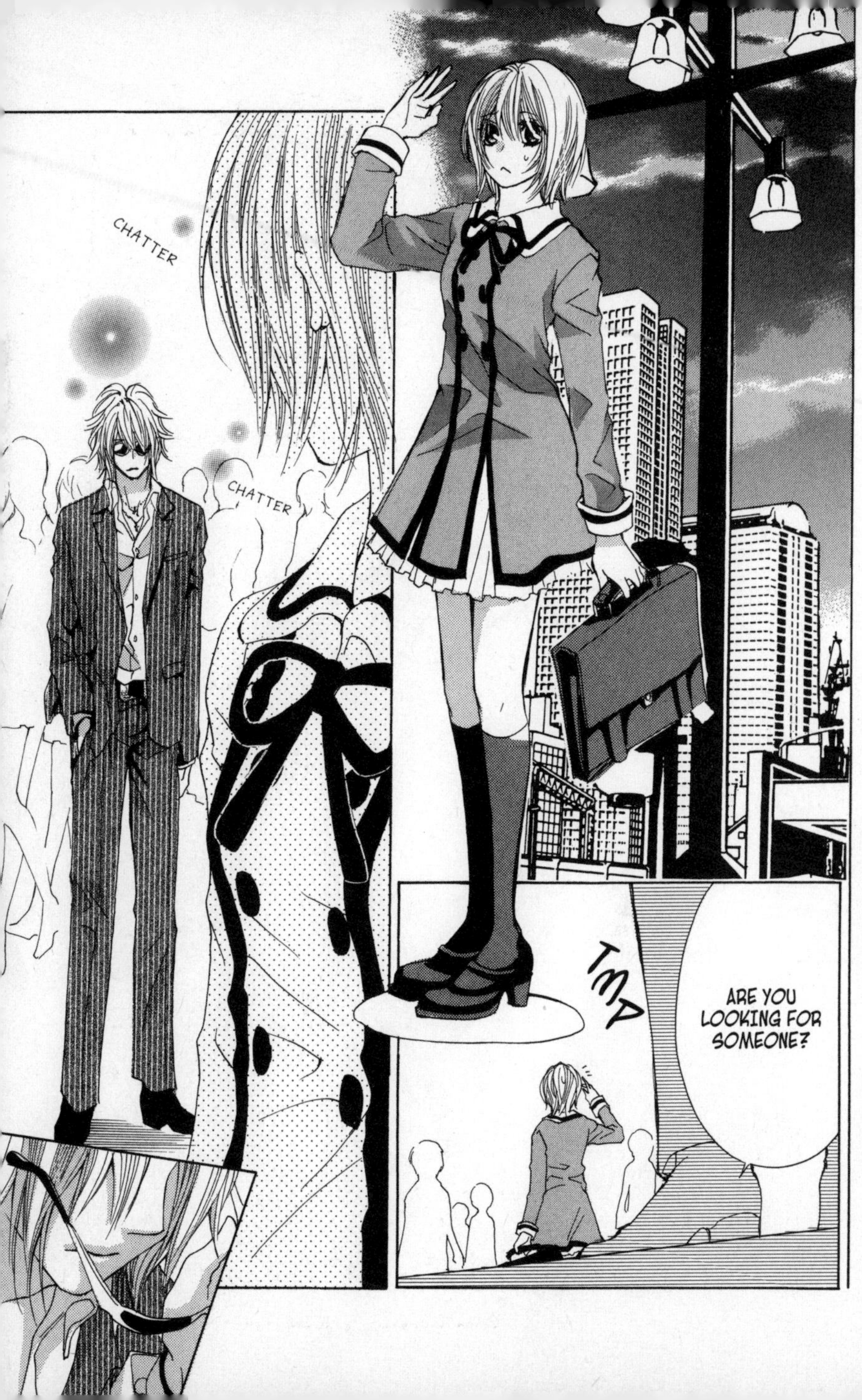
TMP
ARE YOU LOOKING FOR SOMEONE?
CHATTER
CHATTER

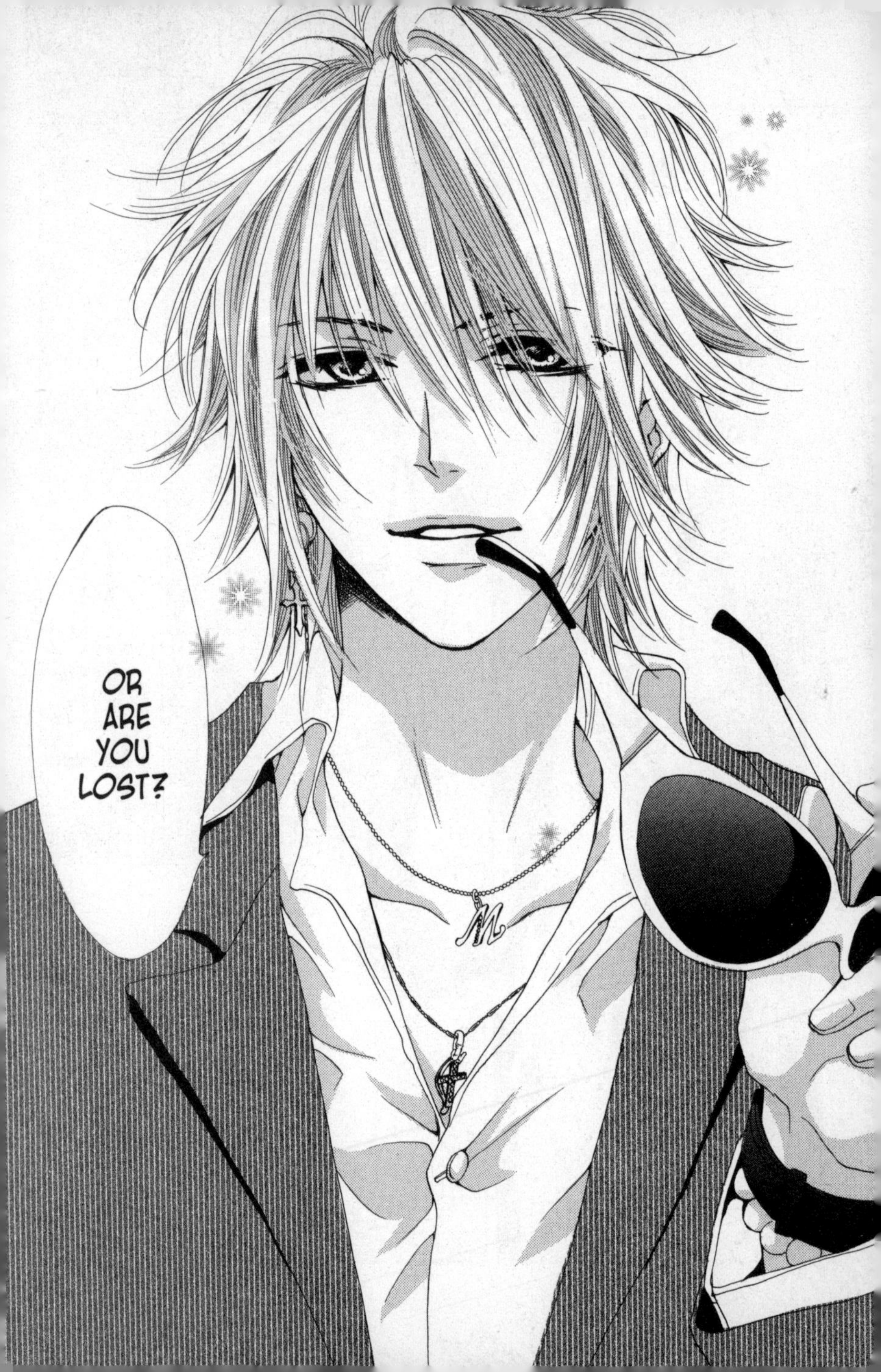
OR ARE YOU LOST?

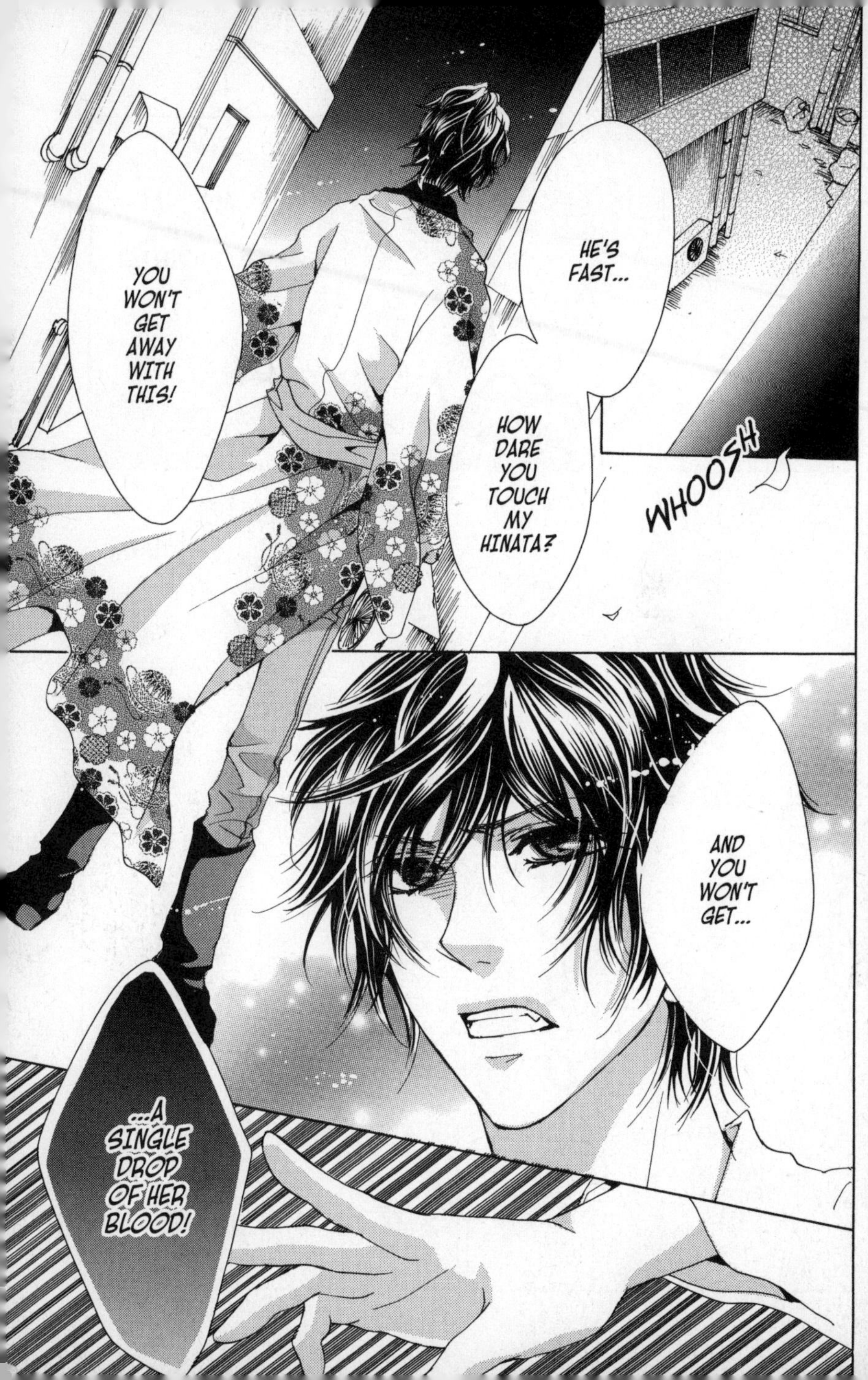
HE'S FAST...
HOW DARE YOU TOUCH MY HINATA?
WHOOSH
YOU WON'T GET AWAY WITH THIS!
AND YOU WON'T GET...
...A SINGLE DROP OF HER BLOOD!

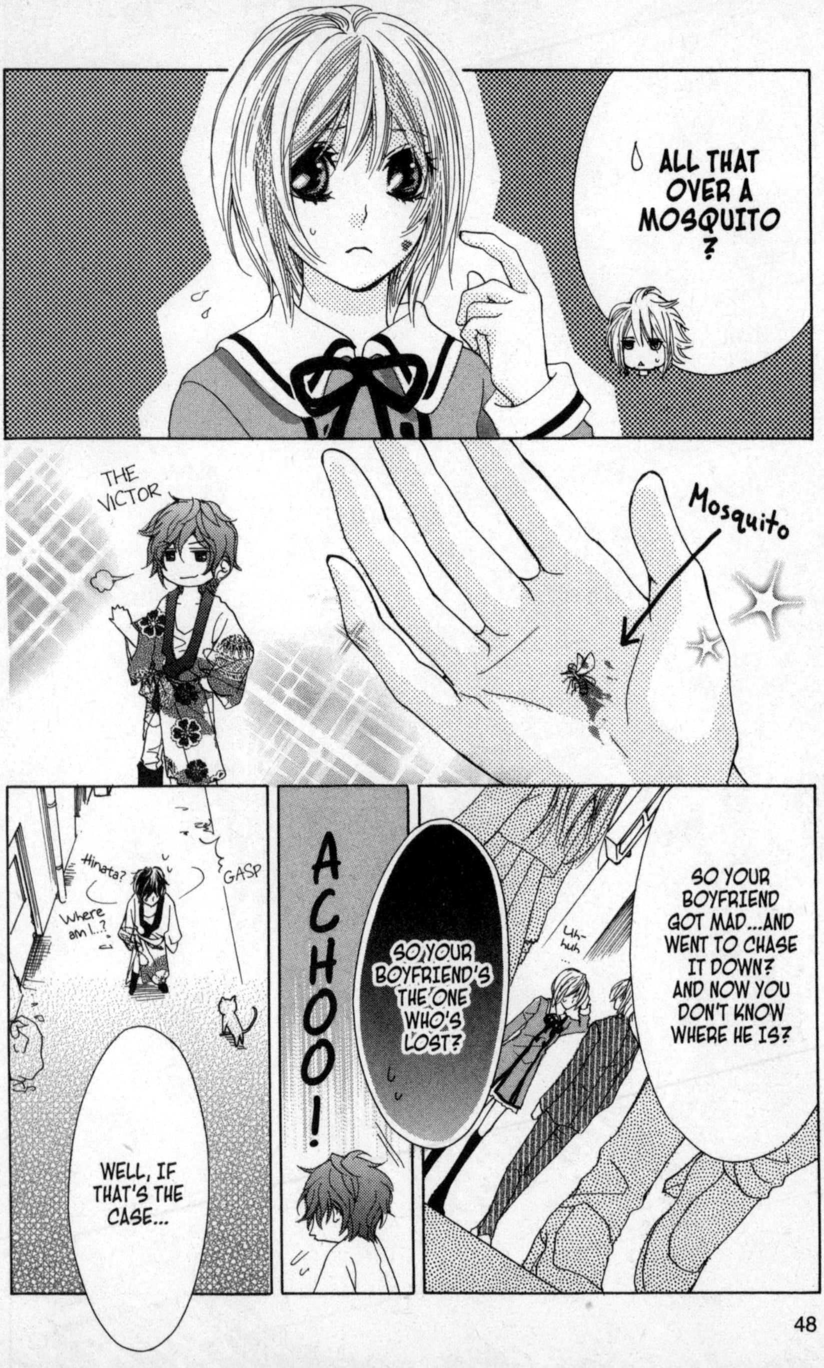
ALL THAT OVER A MOSQUITO?
Mosquito
THE VICTOR
SO YOUR BOYFRIEND GOT MAD...AND WENT TO CHASE IT DOWN? AND NOW YOU DON'T KNOW WHERE HE IS?
Uh-huh...
ACHOO!
SO YOUR BOYFRIEND'S THE ONE WHO'S LOST?
GASP
Hinata?
Where am I...?
WELL, IF THAT'S THE CASE...

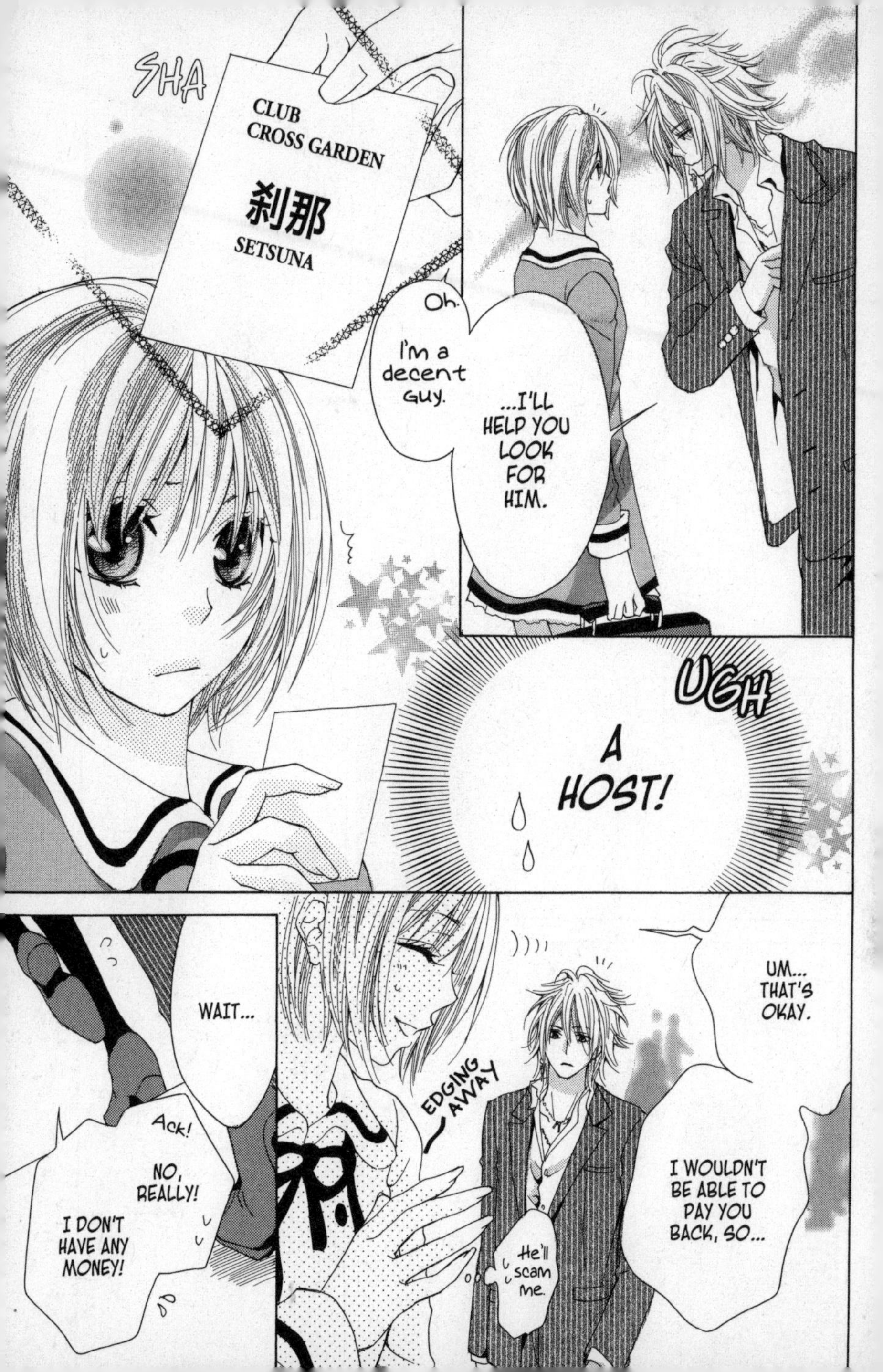
...I'LL HELP YOU LOOK FOR HIM.
Oh.
I'm a decent guy.
UGH
A HOST!
SHA
CLUB CROSS GARDEN
刹那
SETSUNA
UM... THAT'S OKAY.
I WOULDN'T BE ABLE TO PAY YOU BACK, SO...
He'll scam me.
EDGING AWAY
WAIT...
Ack!
NO, REALLY!
I DON'T HAVE ANY MONEY!

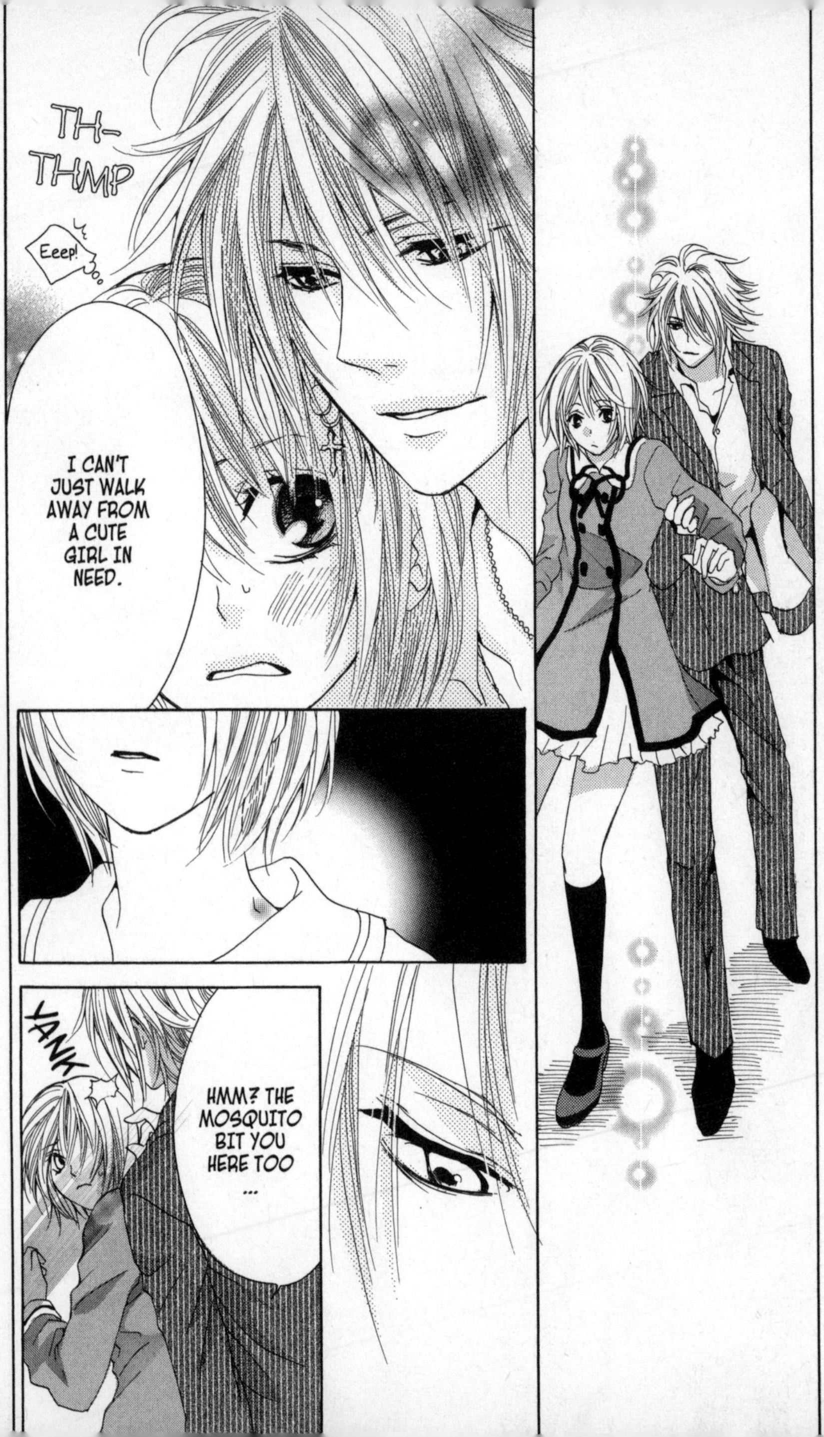
TH-THMP
Eeep!
I CAN'T JUST WALK AWAY FROM A CUTE GIRL IN NEED.
HMM? THE MOSQUITO BIT YOU HERE TOO ...
YANK

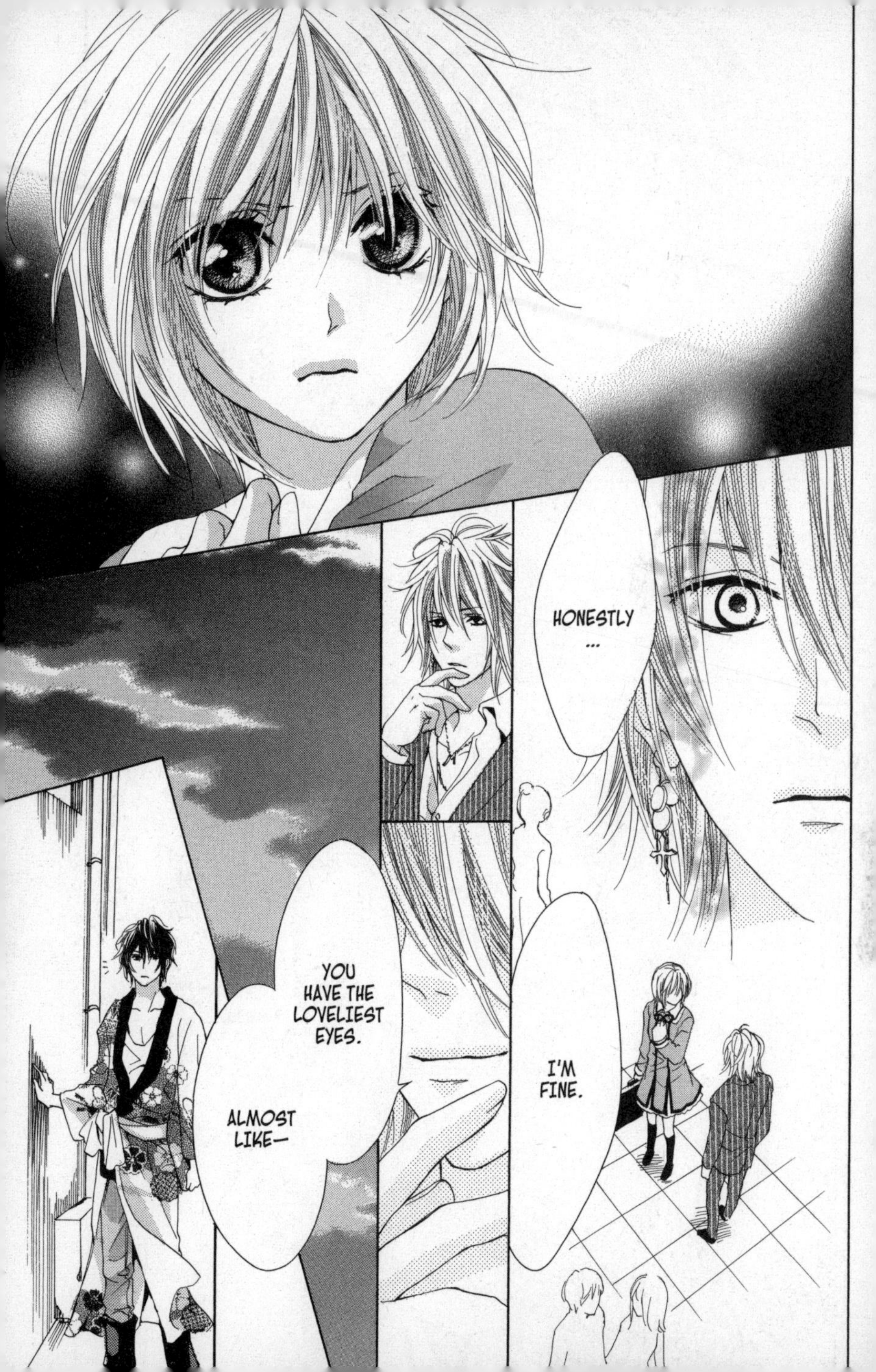
HONESTLY ...
I'M FINE.
YOU HAVE THE LOVELIEST EYES.
ALMOST LIKE—

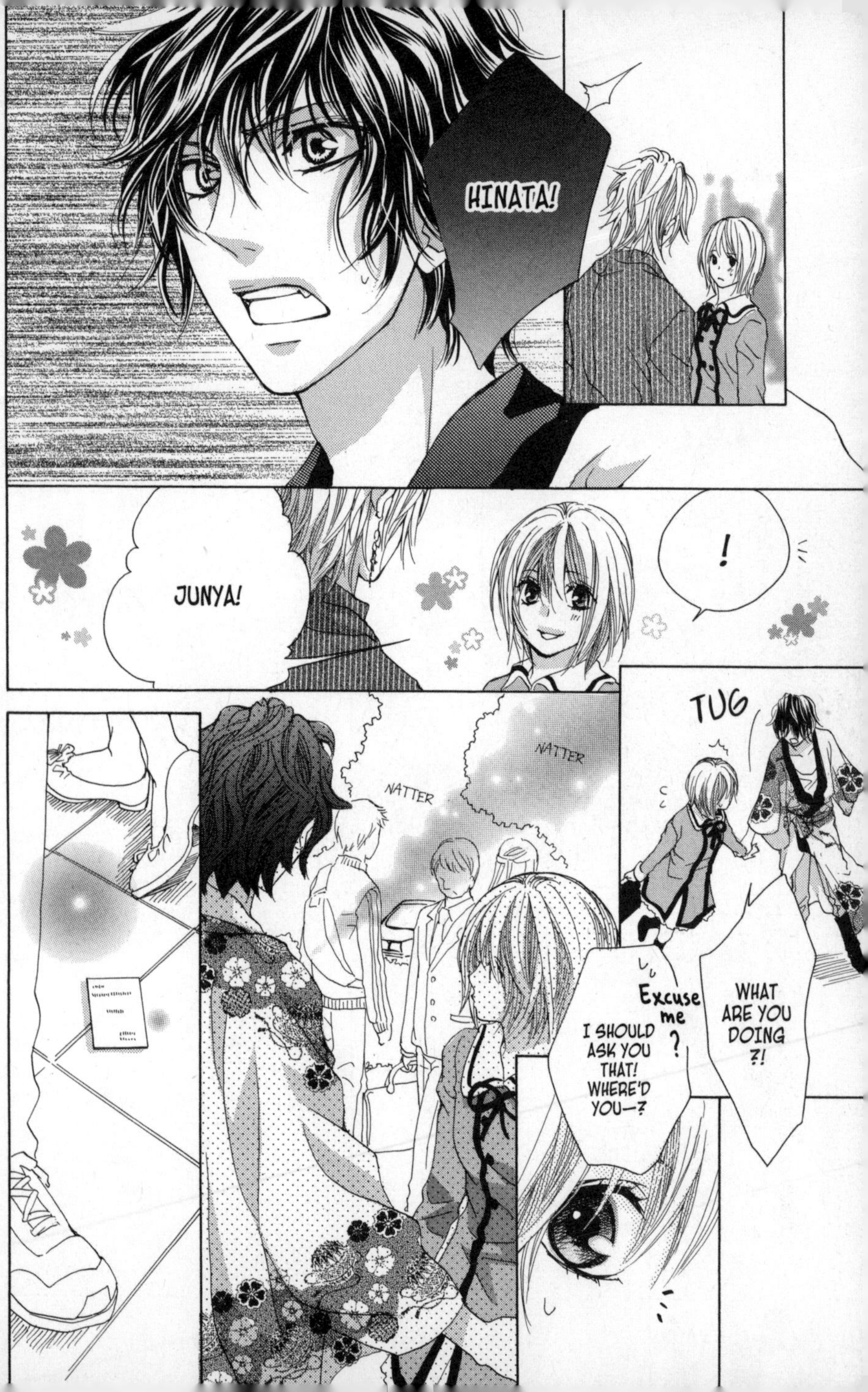
HINATA!
!
JUNYA!
TUG
WHAT ARE YOU DOING ?!
Excuse me ?
I SHOULD ASK YOU THAT! WHERE'D YOU—?
NATTER
NATTER

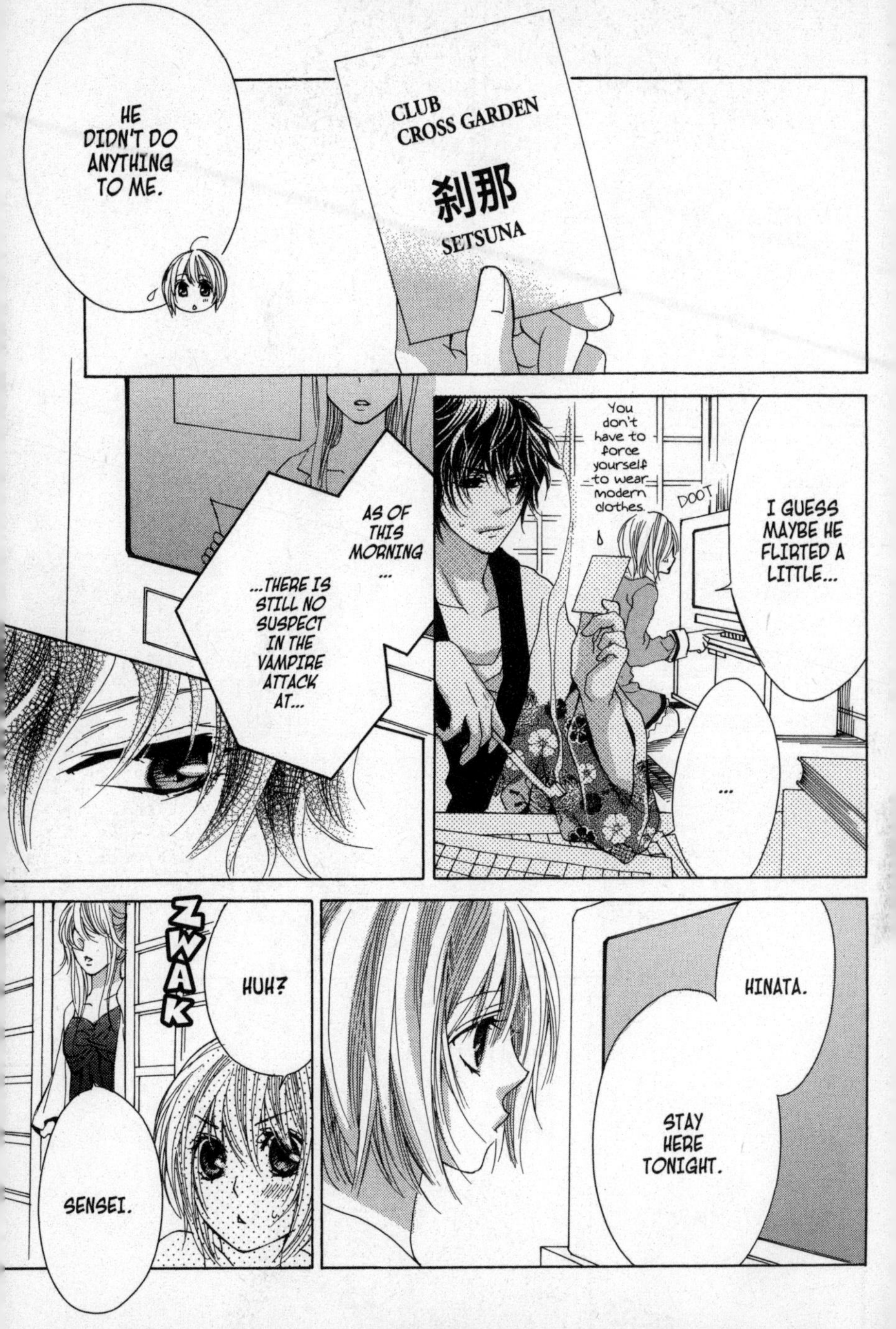
CLUB CROSS GARDEN
刹那
SETSUNA
HE DIDN'T DO ANYTHING TO ME.
I GUESS MAYBE HE FLIRTED A LITTLE...
You don't have to force yourself to wear modern clothes.
DOOT
...
AS OF THIS MORNING ...
...THERE IS STILL NO SUSPECT IN THE VAMPIRE ATTACK AT...
HINATA.
STAY HERE TONIGHT.
ZWAK
HUH?
SENSEI.

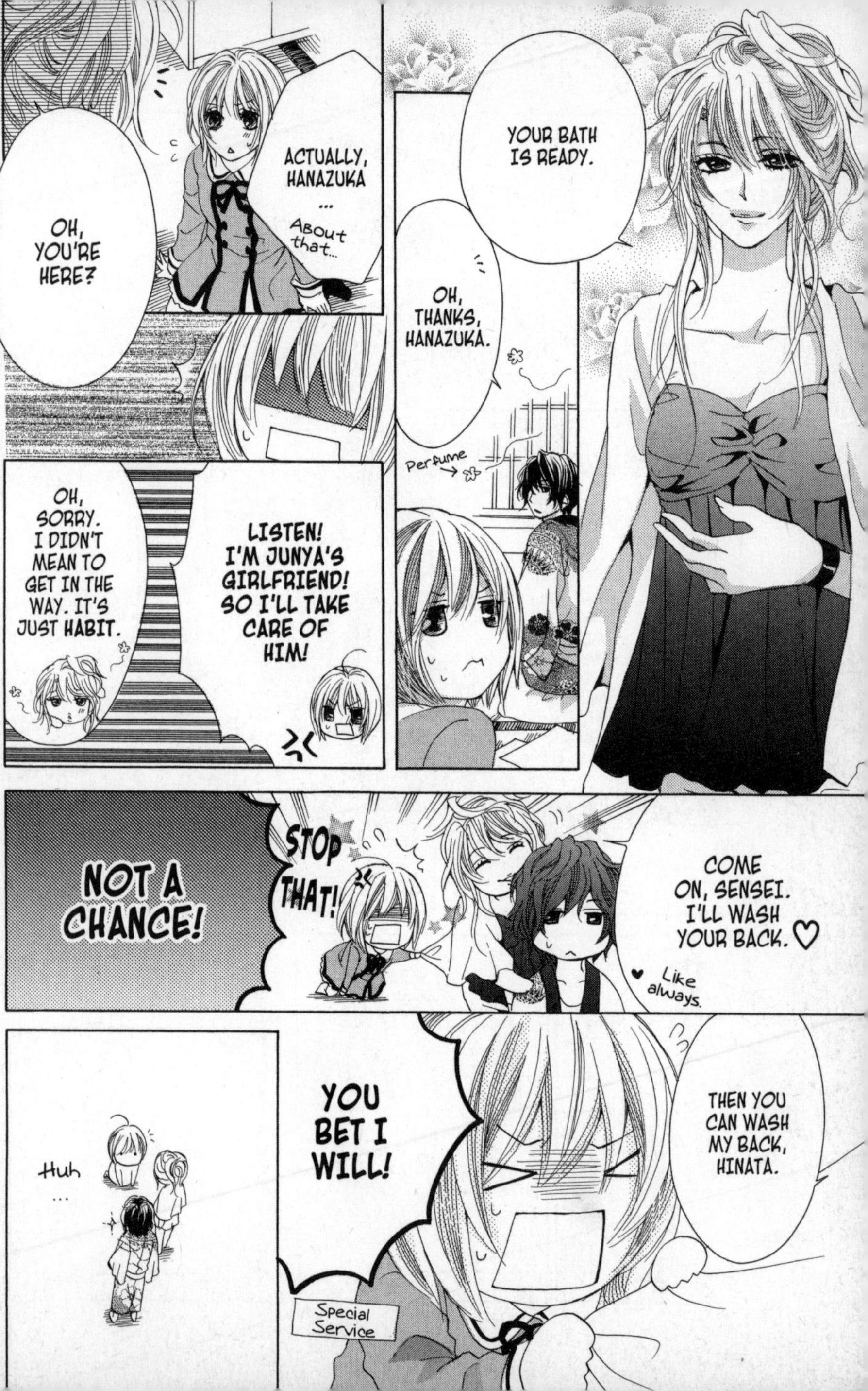

YOUR BATH IS READY.
OH, THANKS, HANAZUKA.
Perfume
ACTUALLY, HANAZUKA ...
About that...
OH, YOU'RE HERE?
LISTEN! I'M JUNYA'S GIRLFRIEND! SO I'LL TAKE CARE OF HIM!
OH, SORRY. I DIDN'T MEAN TO GET IN THE WAY. IT'S JUST HABIT.
COME ON, SENSEI. I'LL WASH YOUR BACK. ♡
Like always.
STOP THAT!
NOT A CHANCE!
THEN YOU CAN WASH MY BACK, HINATA.
YOU BET I WILL!
Special Service
Huh ...

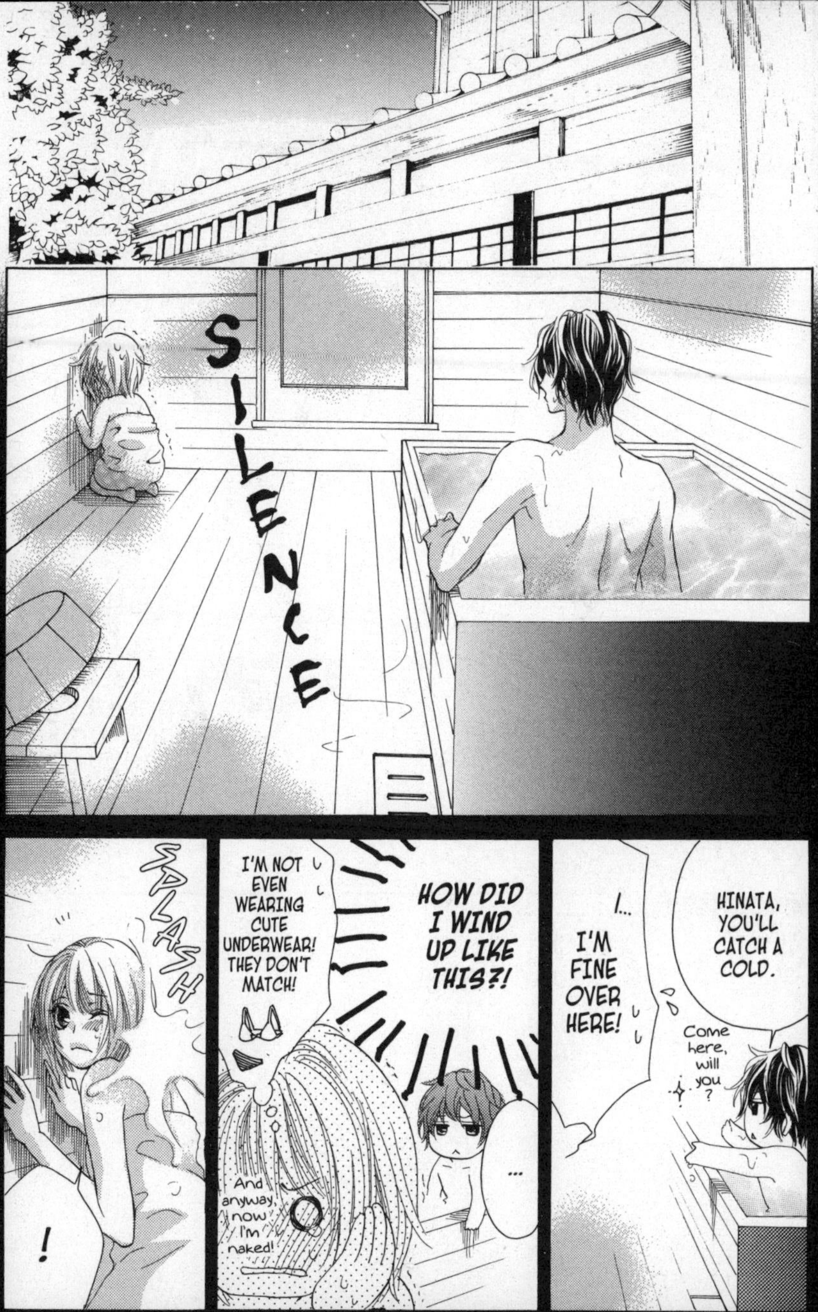
SILENCE
HINATA, YOU'LL CATCH A COLD.
Come here, will you?
I... I'M FINE OVER HERE!
HOW DID I WIND UP LIKE THIS?!
I'M NOT EVEN WEARING CUTE UNDERWEAR! THEY DON'T MATCH!
...
And anyway, now I'm naked!
SPLASH
!

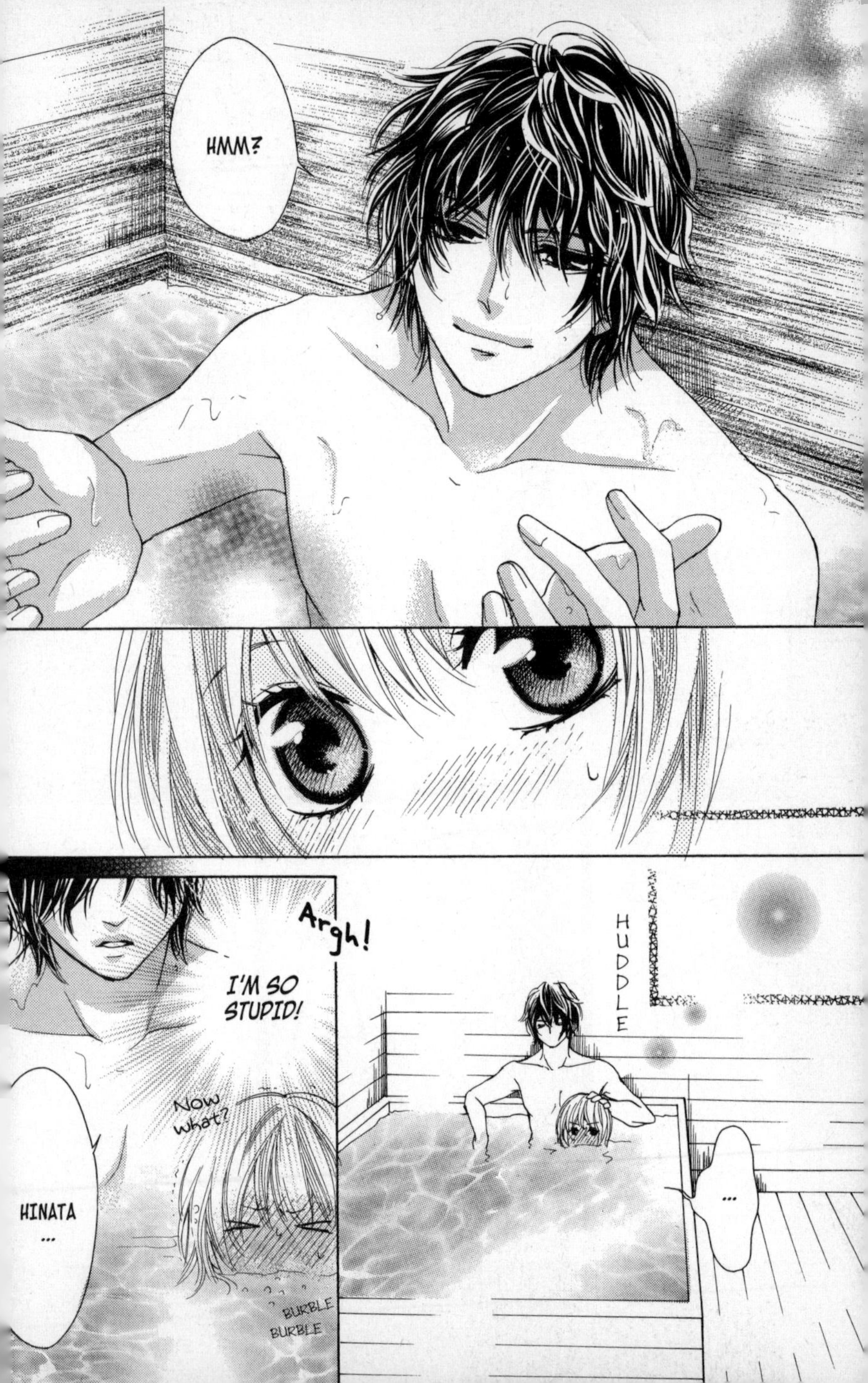
HMM?
HUDDLE
...
Argh!
I'M SO STUPID!
Now what?
HINATA ...
BURBLE
BURBLE

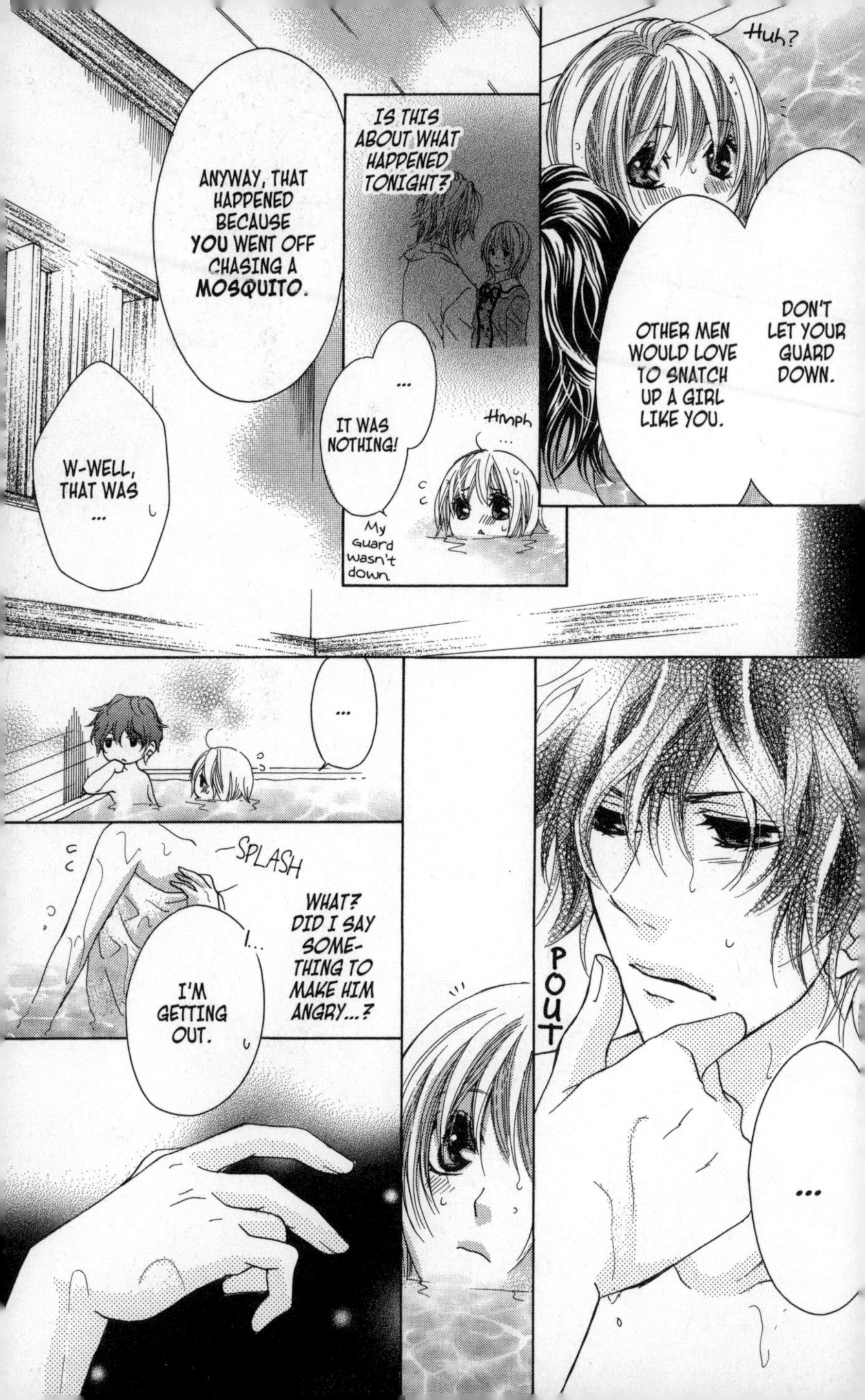
Huh?
DON'T LET YOUR GUARD DOWN.
OTHER MEN WOULD LOVE TO SNATCH UP A GIRL LIKE YOU.
IS THIS ABOUT WHAT HAPPENED TONIGHT?
... IT WAS NOTHING!
Hmph ...
My Guard wasn't down
ANYWAY, THAT HAPPENED BECAUSE YOU WENT OFF CHASING A MOSQUITO.
W-WELL, THAT WAS ...
POUT
...
...
SPLASH
I... I'M GETTING OUT.
WHAT? DID I SAY SOMETHING TO MAKE HIM ANGRY...?

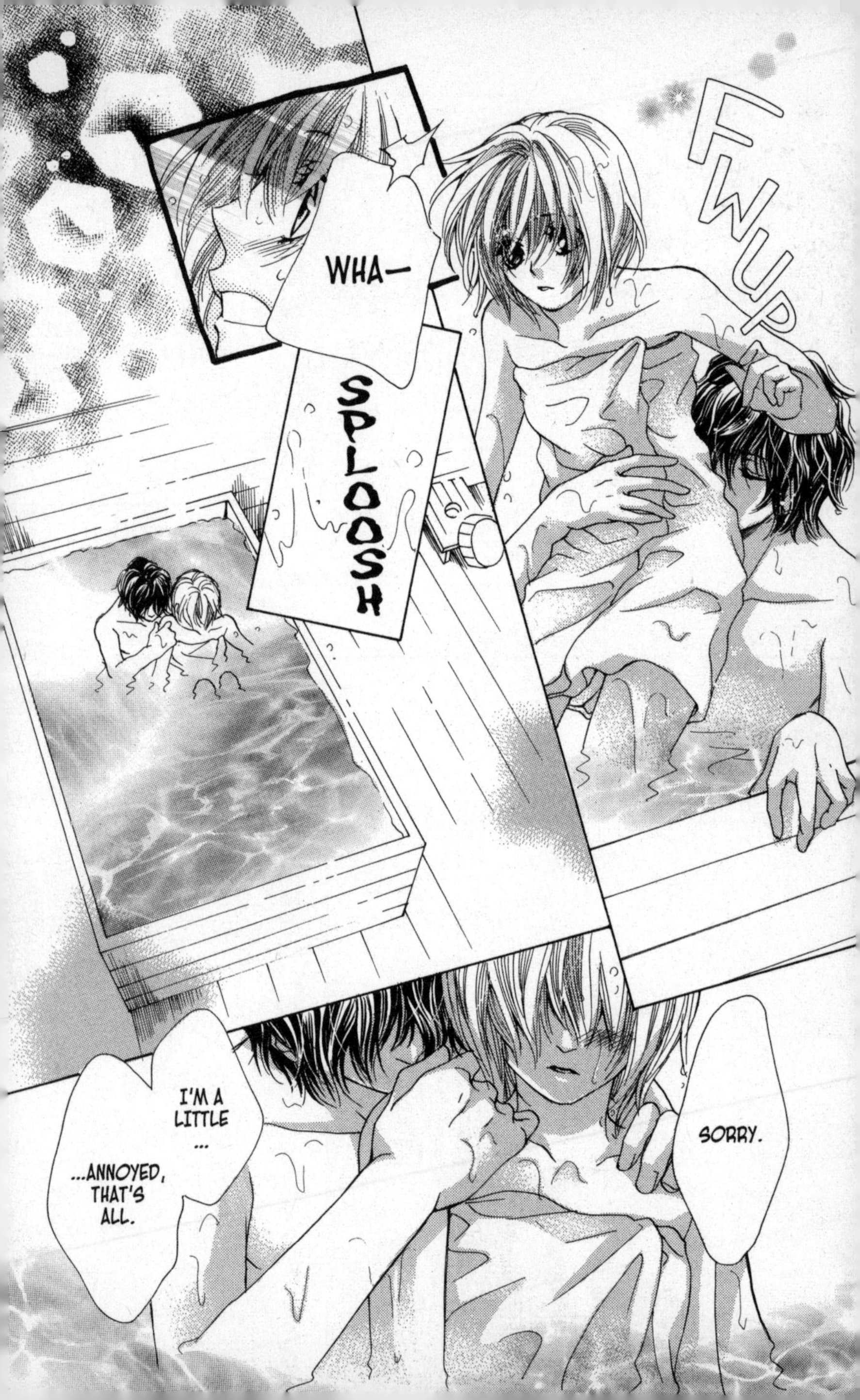
FWUP
WHA—
SPLOOOSH
SORRY.
I'M A LITTLE ...
...ANNOYED, THAT'S ALL.

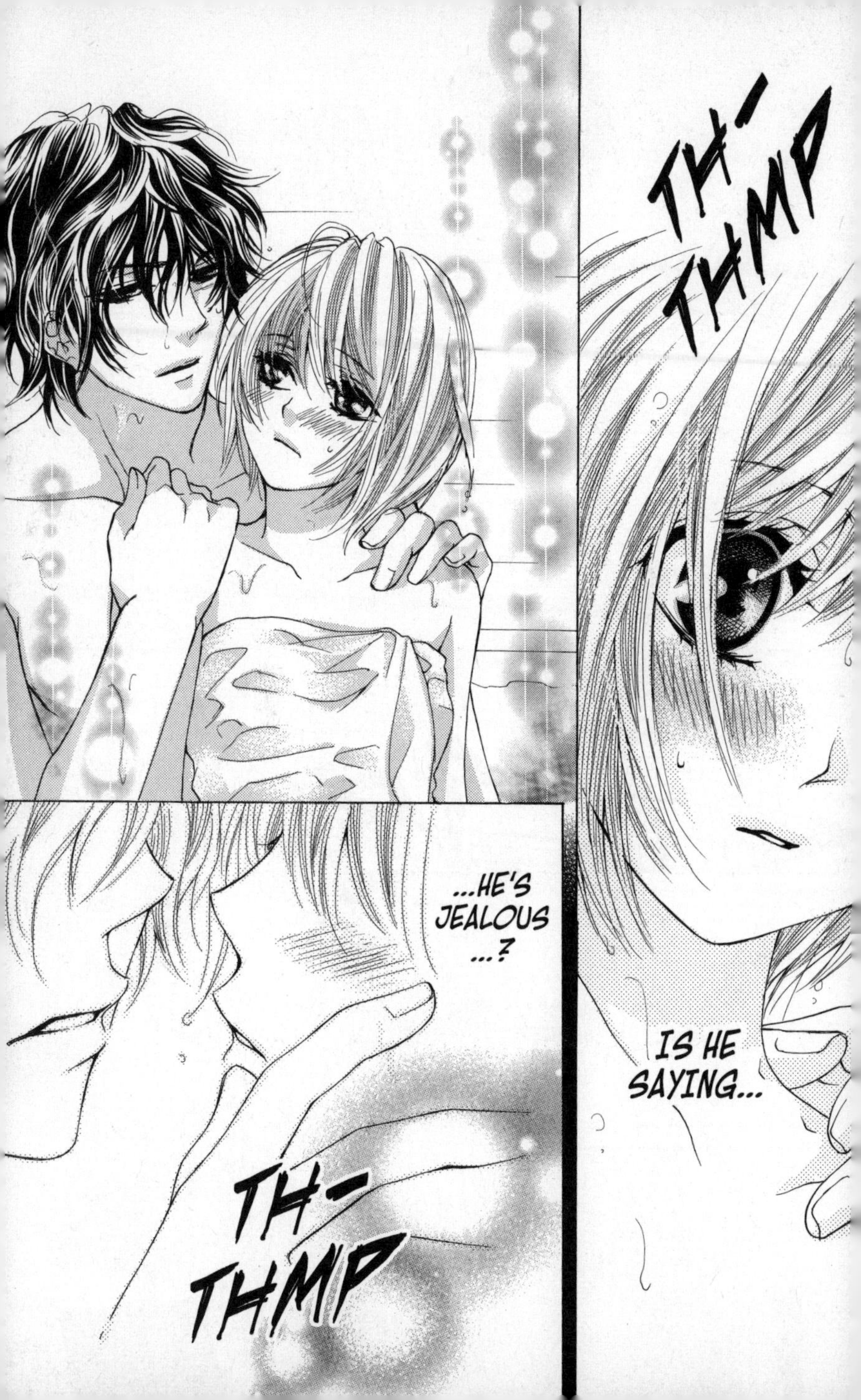
TH-THMP
IS HE SAYING...
...HE'S JEALOUS ...?
TH-THMP

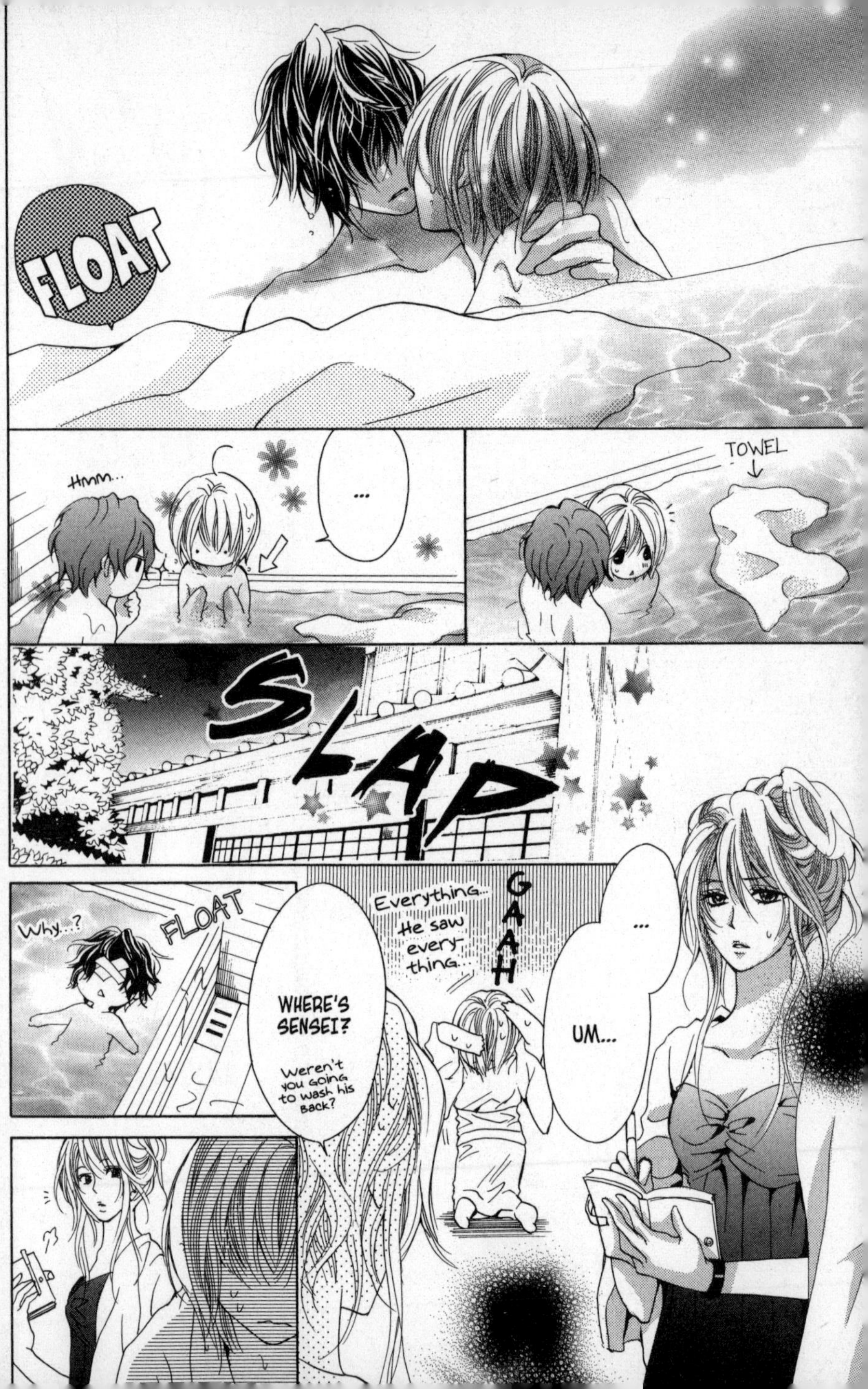
FLOAT
TOWEL
...
Hmm...
SLAP
...
UM...
GAAH
Everything... He saw every-thing...
WHERE'S SENSEI?
Weren't you going to wash his back?
FLOAT
Why...?

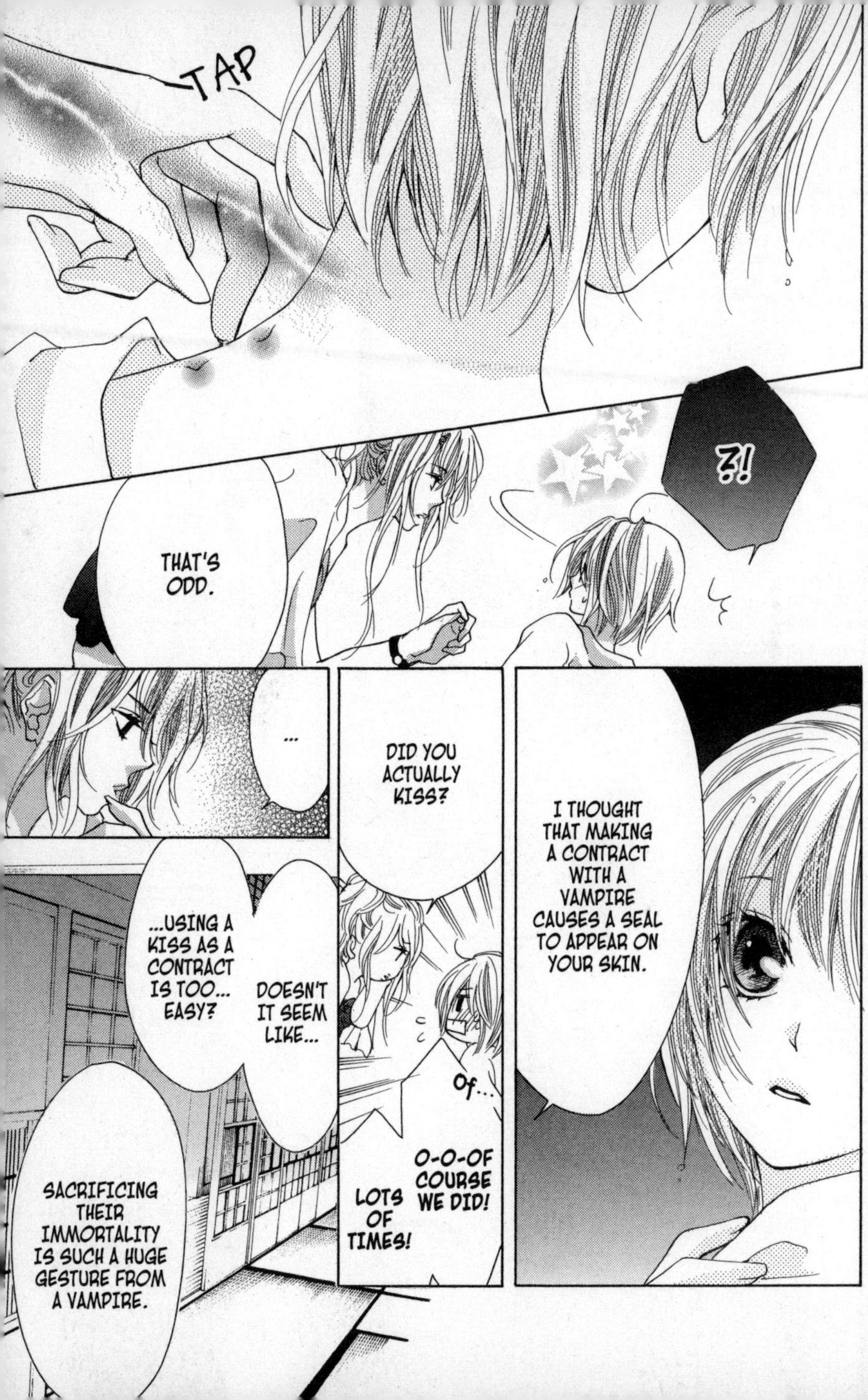
TAP
?!
THAT'S ODD.
I THOUGHT THAT MAKING A CONTRACT WITH A VAMPIRE CAUSES A SEAL TO APPEAR ON YOUR SKIN.
DID YOU ACTUALLY KISS?
Of...
O-O-OF COURSE WE DID!
LOTS OF TIMES!
...
DOESN'T IT SEEM LIKE...
...USING A KISS AS A CONTRACT IS TOO... EASY?
SACRIFICING THEIR IMMORTALITY IS SUCH A HUGE GESTURE FROM A VAMPIRE.

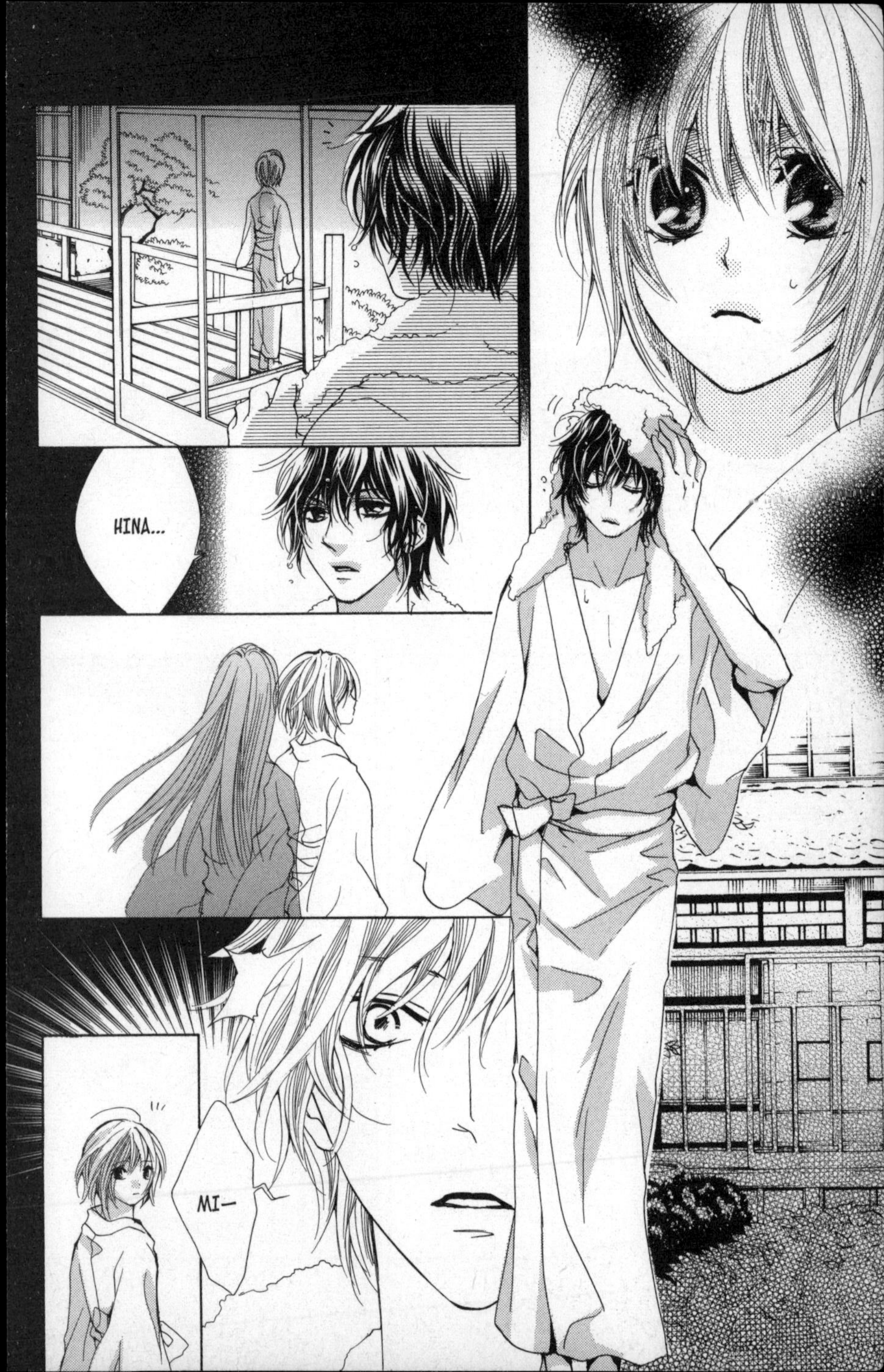
HINA...
MI—

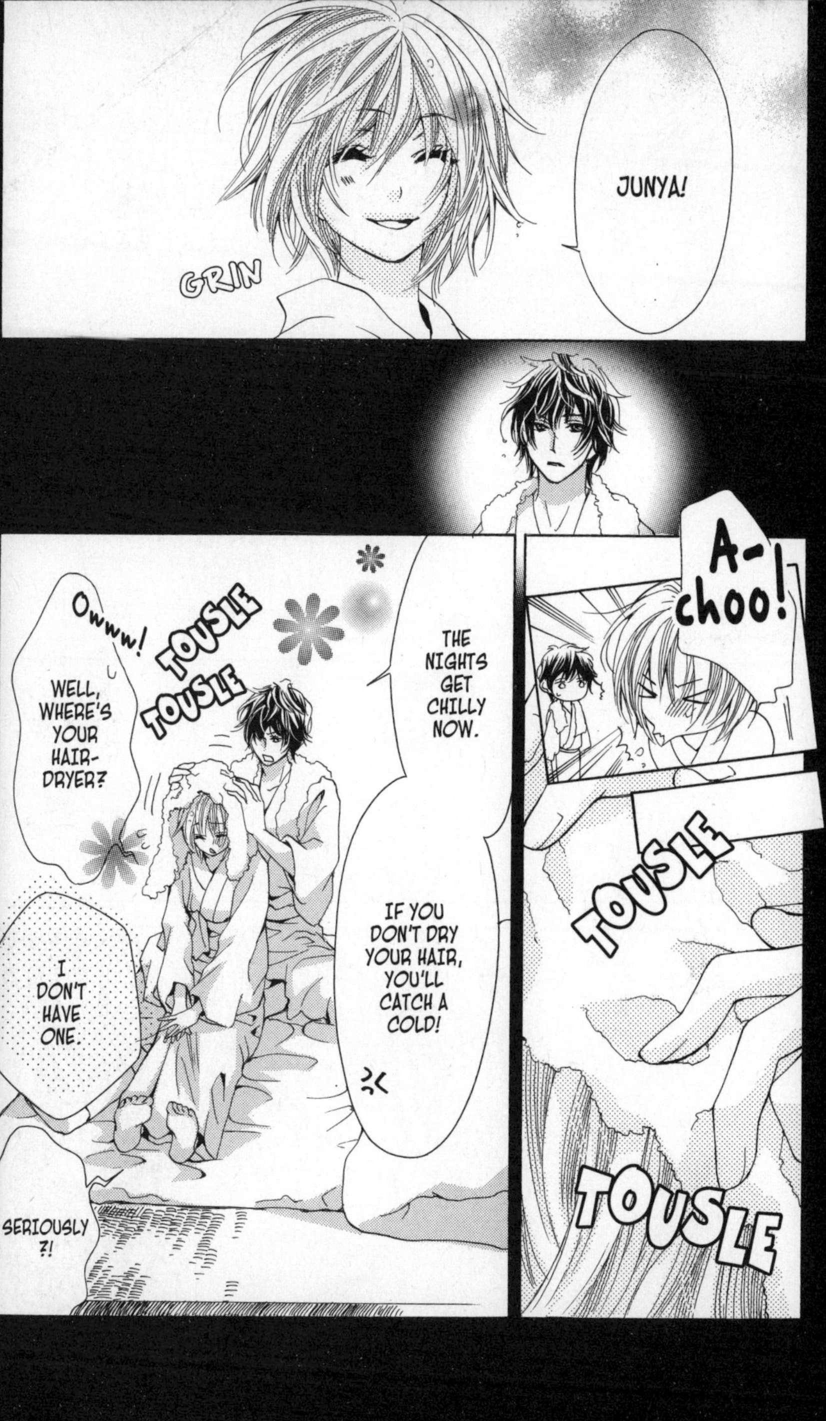
JUNYA!
GRIN
A-choo!
TOUSLE
TOUSLE
THE NIGHTS GET CHILLY NOW.
IF YOU DON'T DRY YOUR HAIR, YOU'LL CATCH A COLD!
TOUSLE TOUSLE
Owww!
WELL, WHERE'S YOUR HAIR-DRYER?
I DON'T HAVE ONE.
SERIOUSLY?!

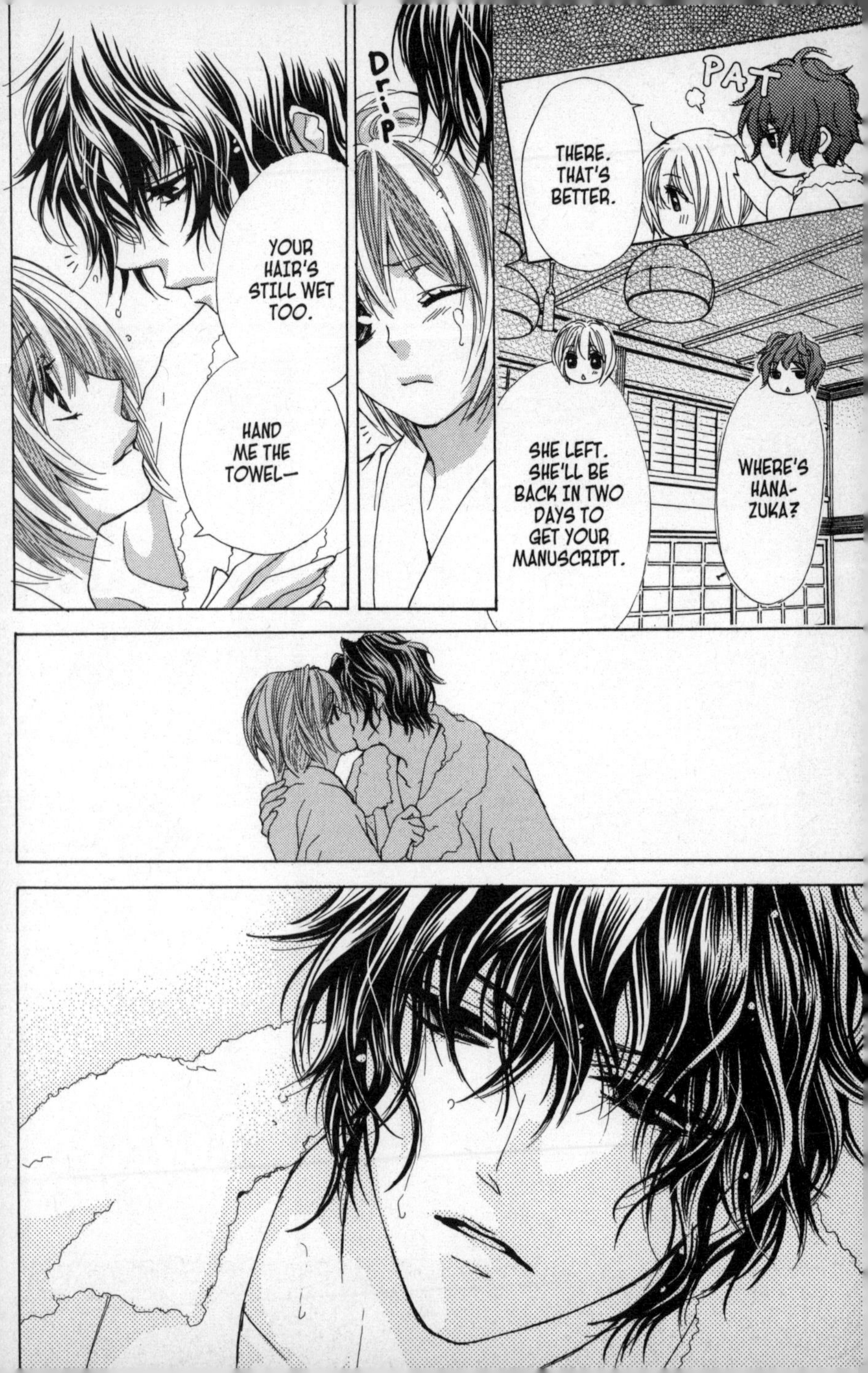
PAT
THERE. THAT'S BETTER.
WHERE'S HANA-ZUKA?
SHE LEFT. SHE'LL BE BACK IN TWO DAYS TO GET YOUR MANUSCRIPT.
DRIP
YOUR HAIR'S STILL WET TOO.
HAND ME THE TOWEL—

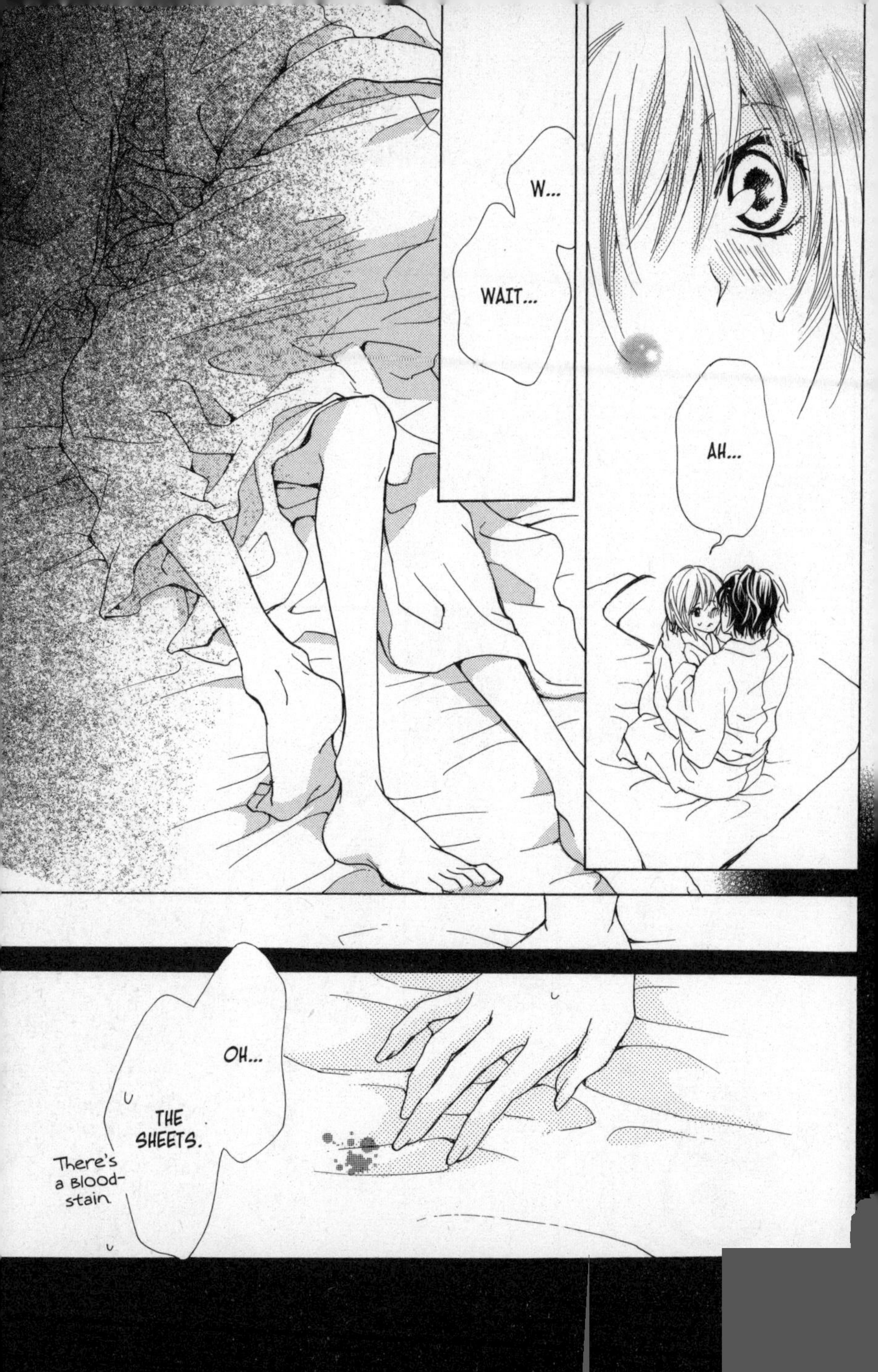
AH...
W...
WAIT...
OH...
THE SHEETS.
There's a blood-stain

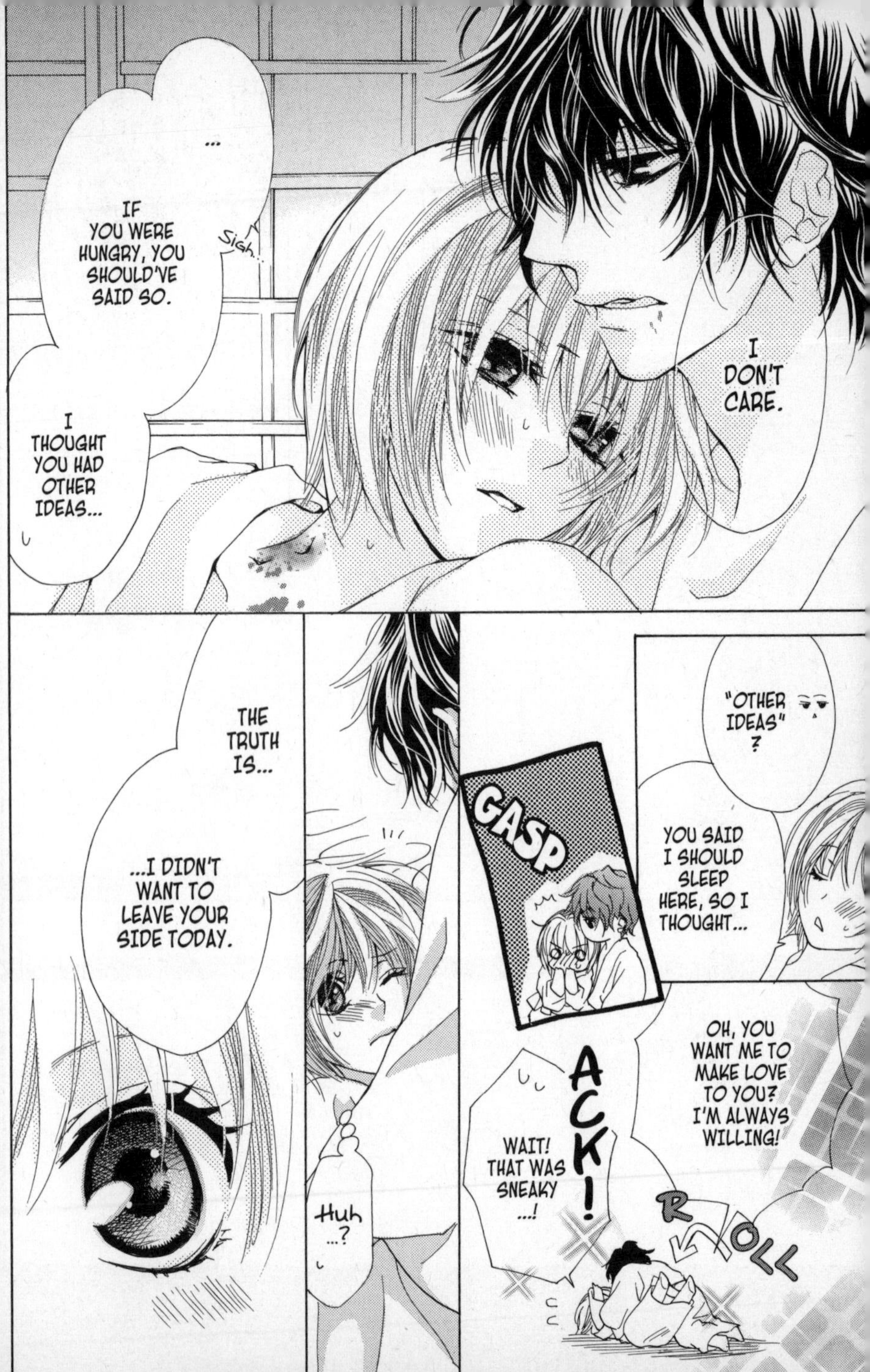
I DON'T CARE.
...
IF YOU WERE HUNGRY, YOU SHOULD'VE SAID SO.
Sigh..
I THOUGHT YOU HAD OTHER IDEAS...
"OTHER IDEAS"?
YOU SAID I SHOULD SLEEP HERE, SO I THOUGHT...
GASP
OH, YOU WANT ME TO MAKE LOVE TO YOU? I'M ALWAYS WILLING!
ACK!
WAIT! THAT WAS SNEAKY ...!
ROLL
Huh ...?
THE TRUTH IS...
...I DIDN'T WANT TO LEAVE YOUR SIDE TODAY.

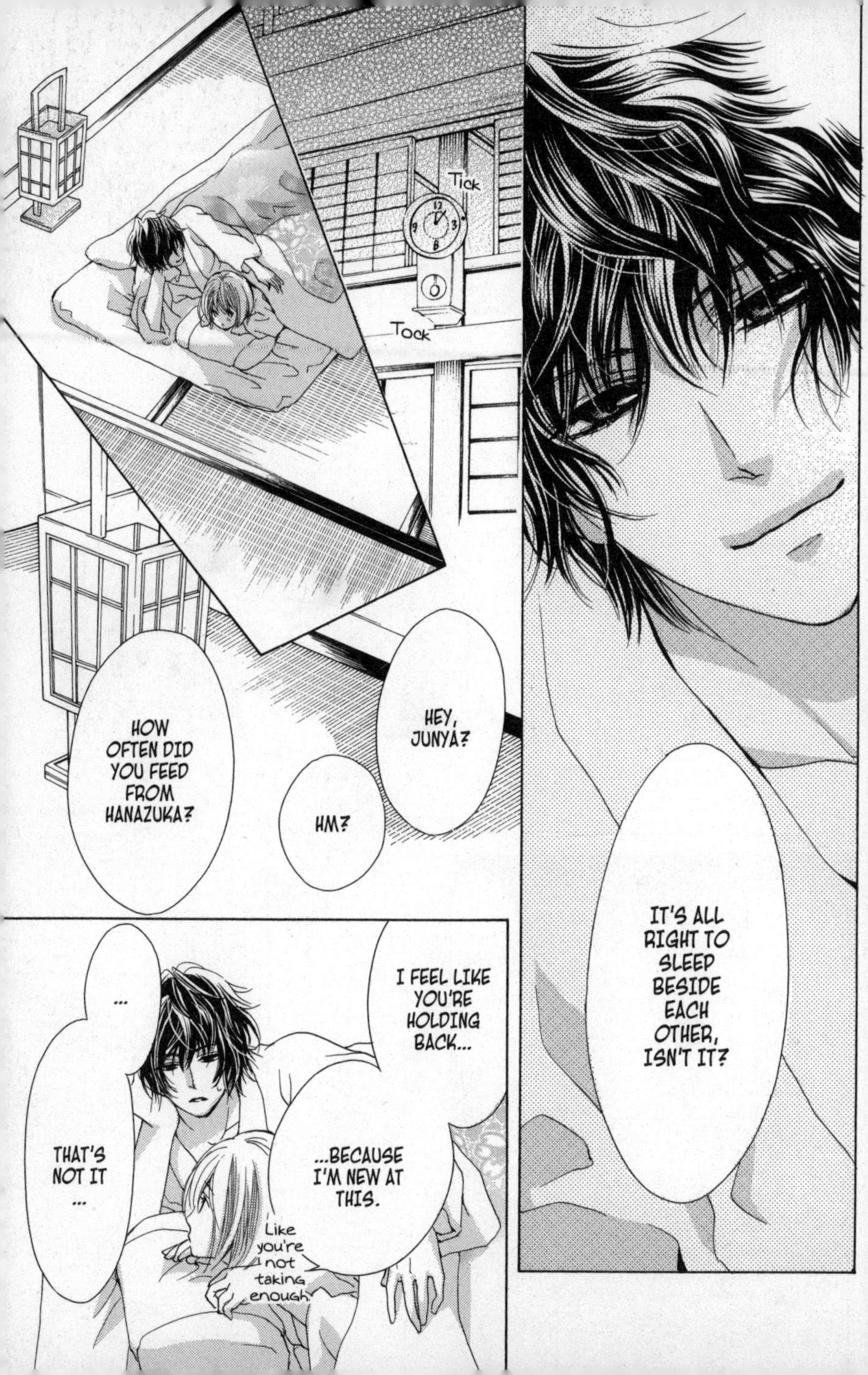
IT'S ALL RIGHT TO SLEEP BESIDE EACH OTHER, ISN'T IT?
Tick
Tock
HEY, JUNYA?
HM?
HOW OFTEN DID YOU FEED FROM HANAZUKA?
I FEEL LIKE YOU'RE HOLDING BACK...
...
...BECAUSE I'M NEW AT THIS.
Like you're not taking enough.
THAT'S NOT IT ...

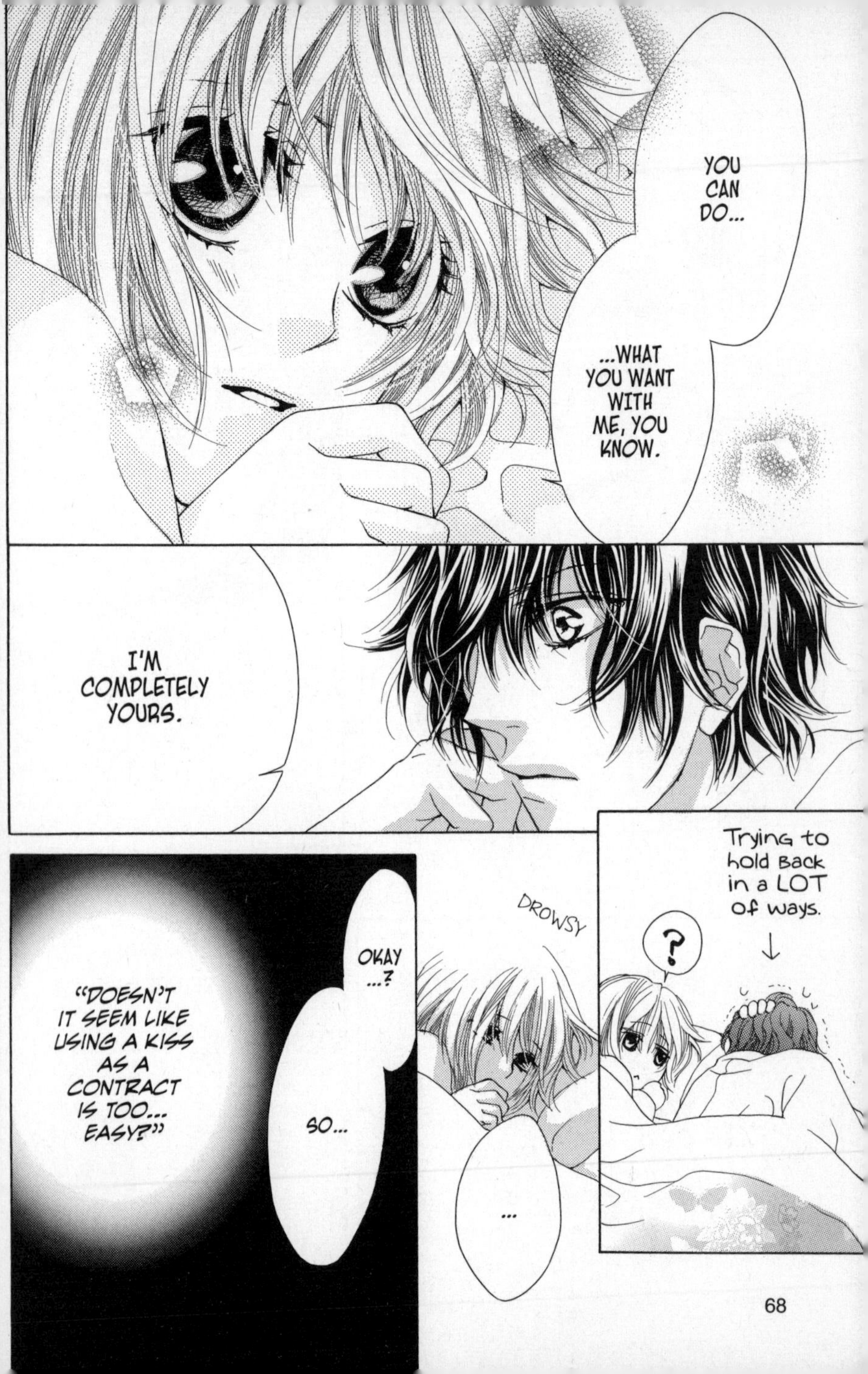
YOU CAN DO...
...WHAT YOU WANT WITH ME, YOU KNOW.
I'M COMPLETELY YOURS.
Trying to hold back in a LOT of ways.
?
DROWSY
OKAY ...?
SO...
...
"DOESN'T IT SEEM LIKE USING A KISS AS A CONTRACT IS TOO... EASY?"

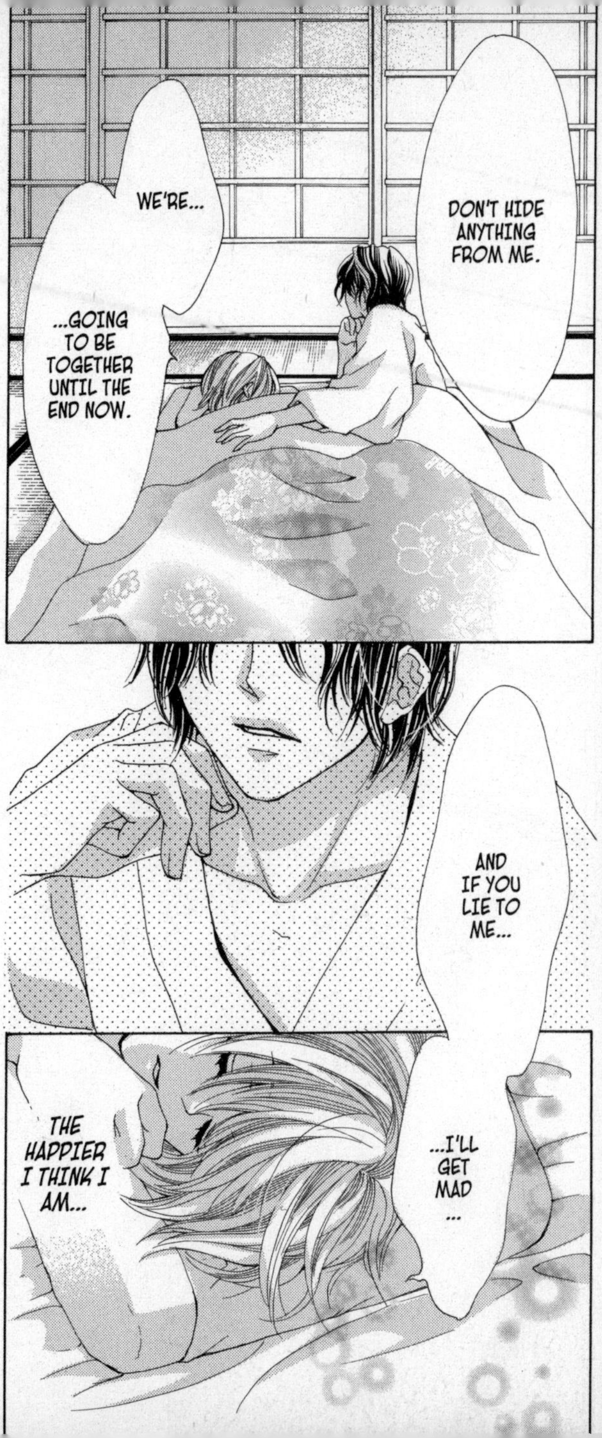
DON'T HIDE ANYTHING FROM ME.
WE'RE...
...GOING TO BE TOGETHER UNTIL THE END NOW.
AND IF YOU LIE TO ME...
...I'LL GET MAD ...
THE HAPPIER I THINK I AM...

Small Talk

②

✿ Things I've Bought Recently ✿

Copic (Color Markers)

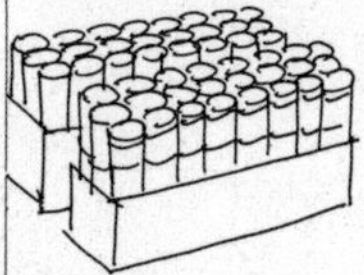

When I do my color pages, I usually try to use color ink. But it's such a hassle ← (Hey!) to moisten the paper and then wait for it to dry that I bought a whole bunch of Copic markers. They're much easier to use, but they're also pretty expensive, so I considered it for a long time before I decided to get them.

I'm going to practice with them a lot before I use them for real!

By the way, whether I'm using color ink or Copic markers, my color pages still suck. Sorry about that!

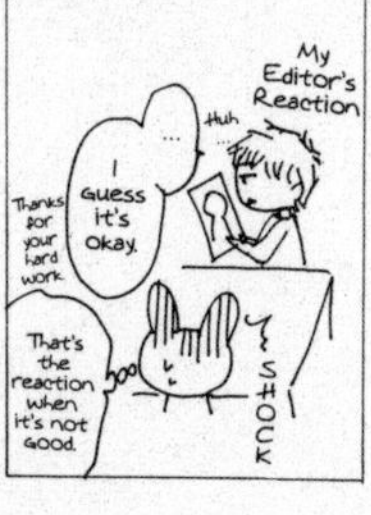
My Editor's Reaction
...
Huh
I guess it's okay.
Thanks for your hard work
That's the reaction when it's not good.
SHOCK

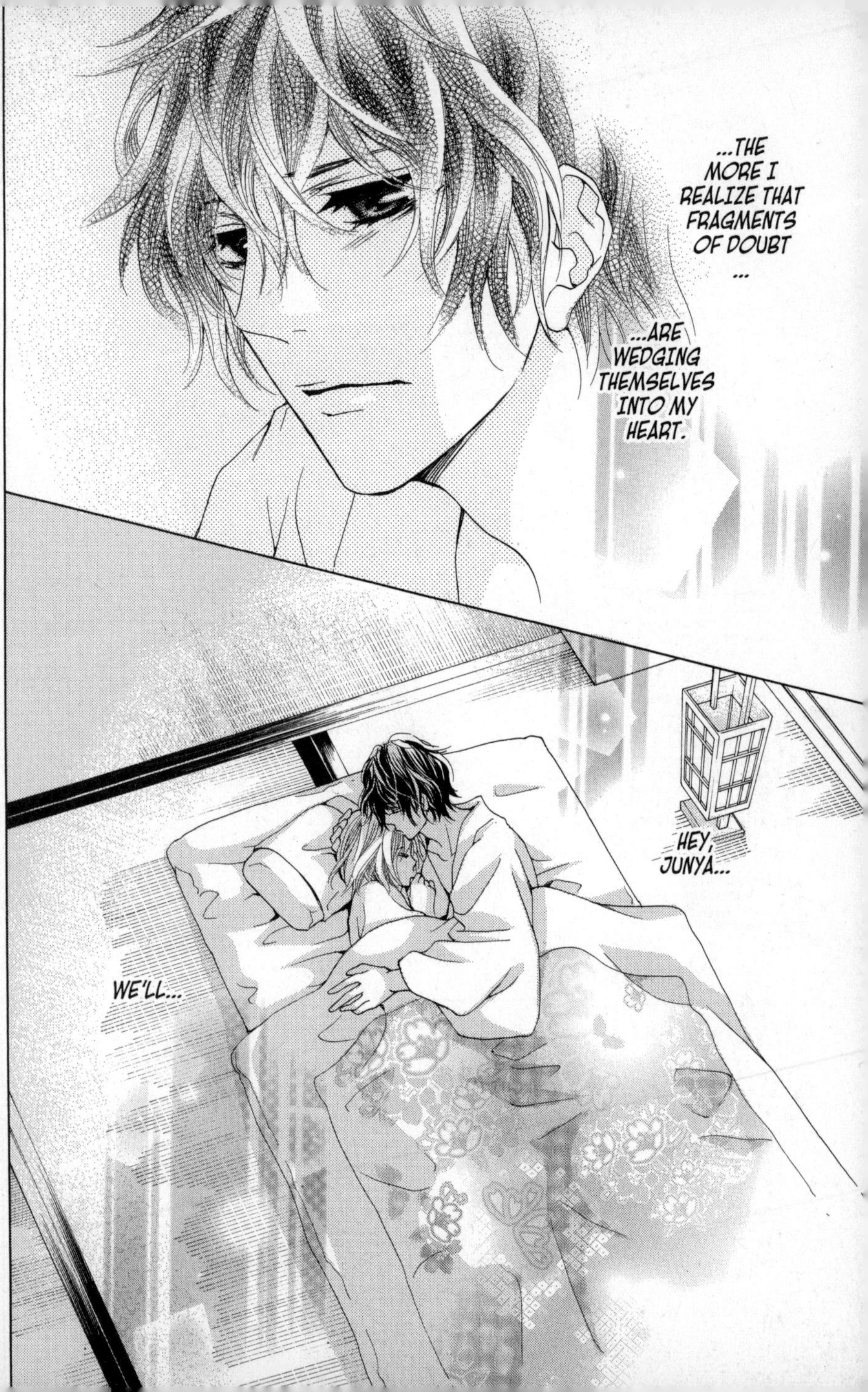
...THE MORE I REALIZE THAT FRAGMENTS OF DOUBT ...
...ARE WEDGING THEMSELVES INTO MY HEART.
HEY, JUNYA...
WE'LL...

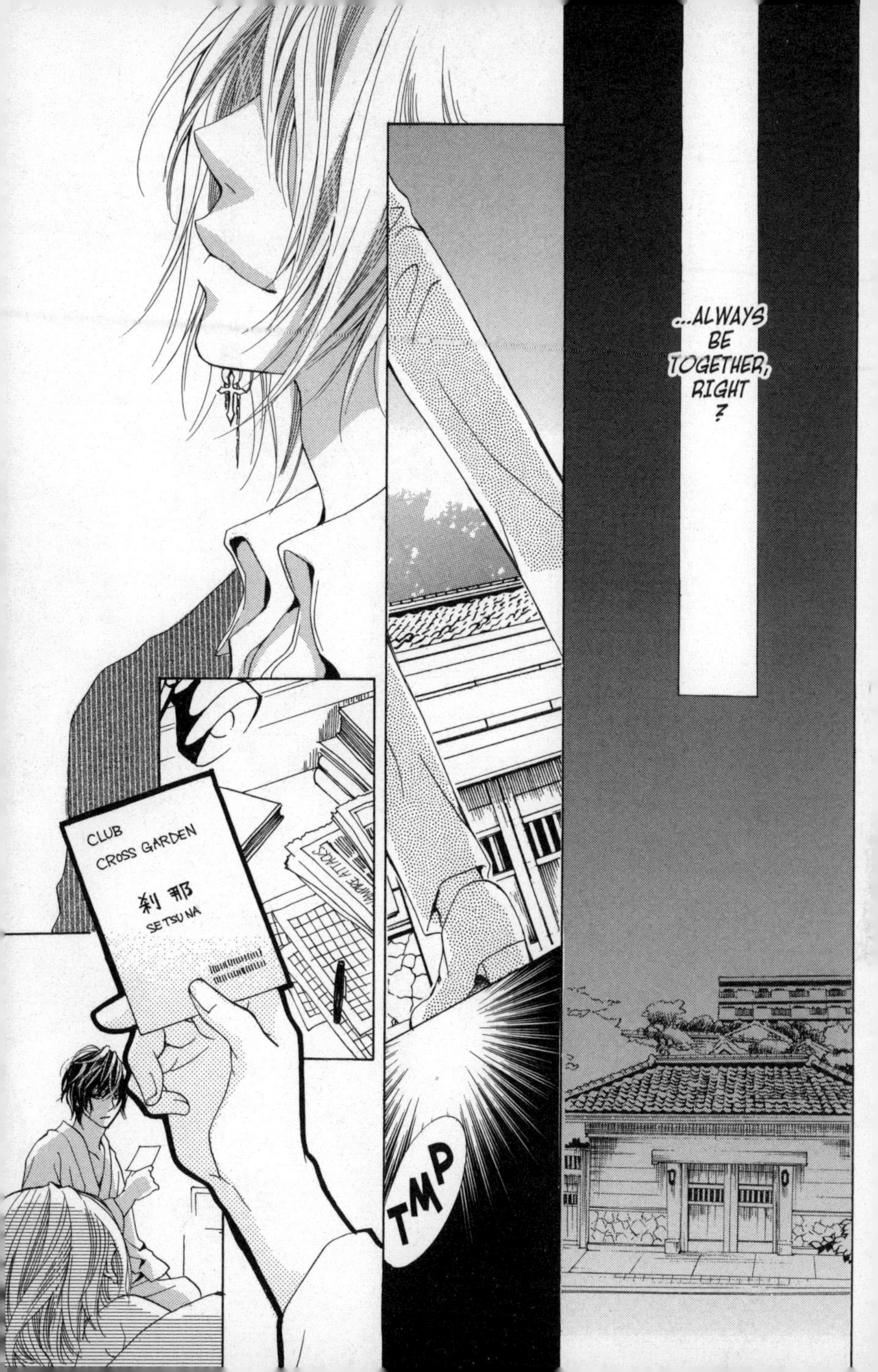
...ALWAYS BE TOGETHER, RIGHT?
TMP
CLUB
CROSS GARDEN
刹那
SETSUNA

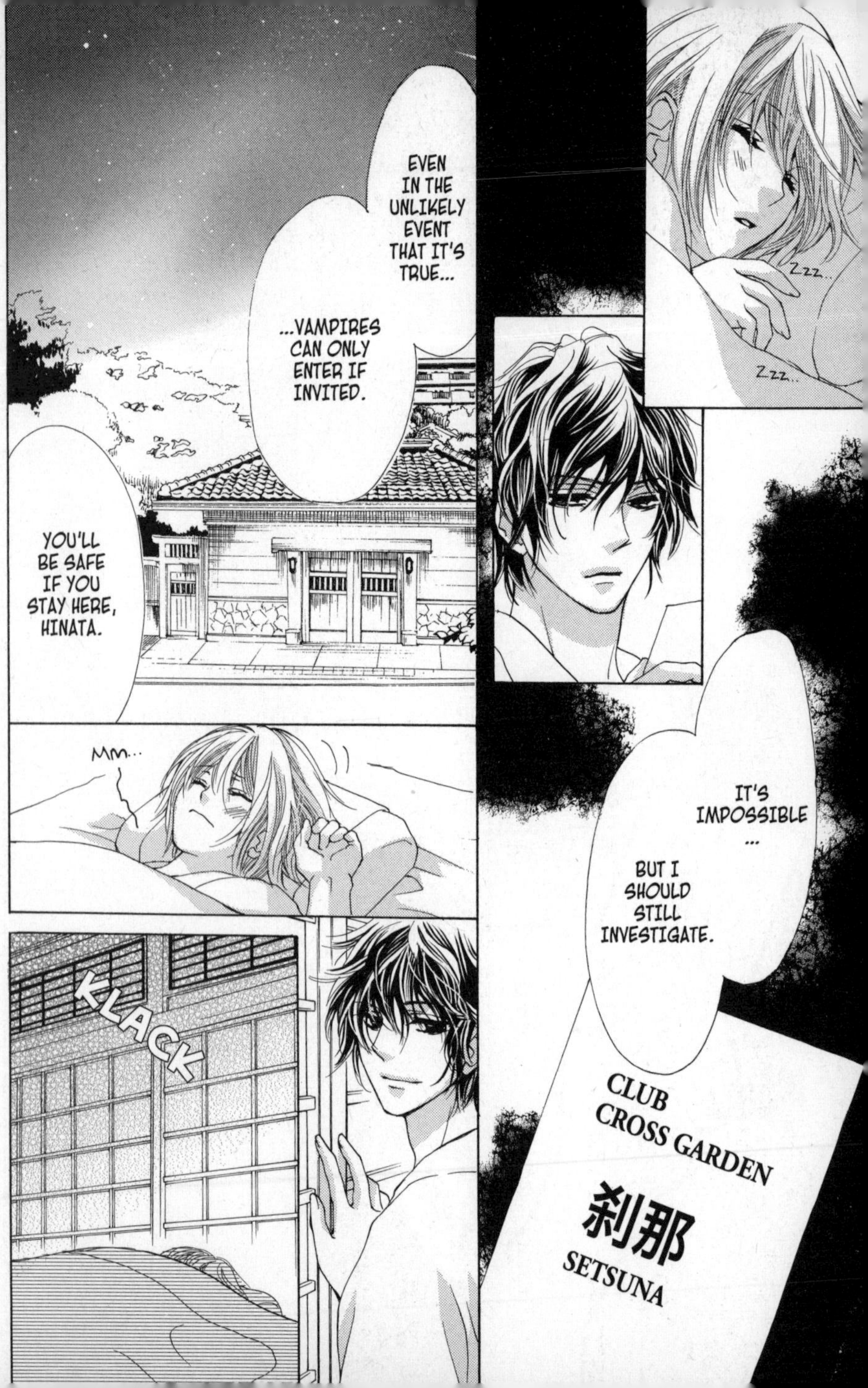
Zzz...
Zzz...
IT'S IMPOSSIBLE ...
BUT I SHOULD STILL INVESTIGATE.
CLUB CROSS GARDEN
刹那
SETSUNA
EVEN IN THE UNLIKELY EVENT THAT IT'S TRUE...
...VAMPIRES CAN ONLY ENTER IF INVITED.
YOU'LL BE SAFE IF YOU STAY HERE, HINATA.
MM...
KLACK

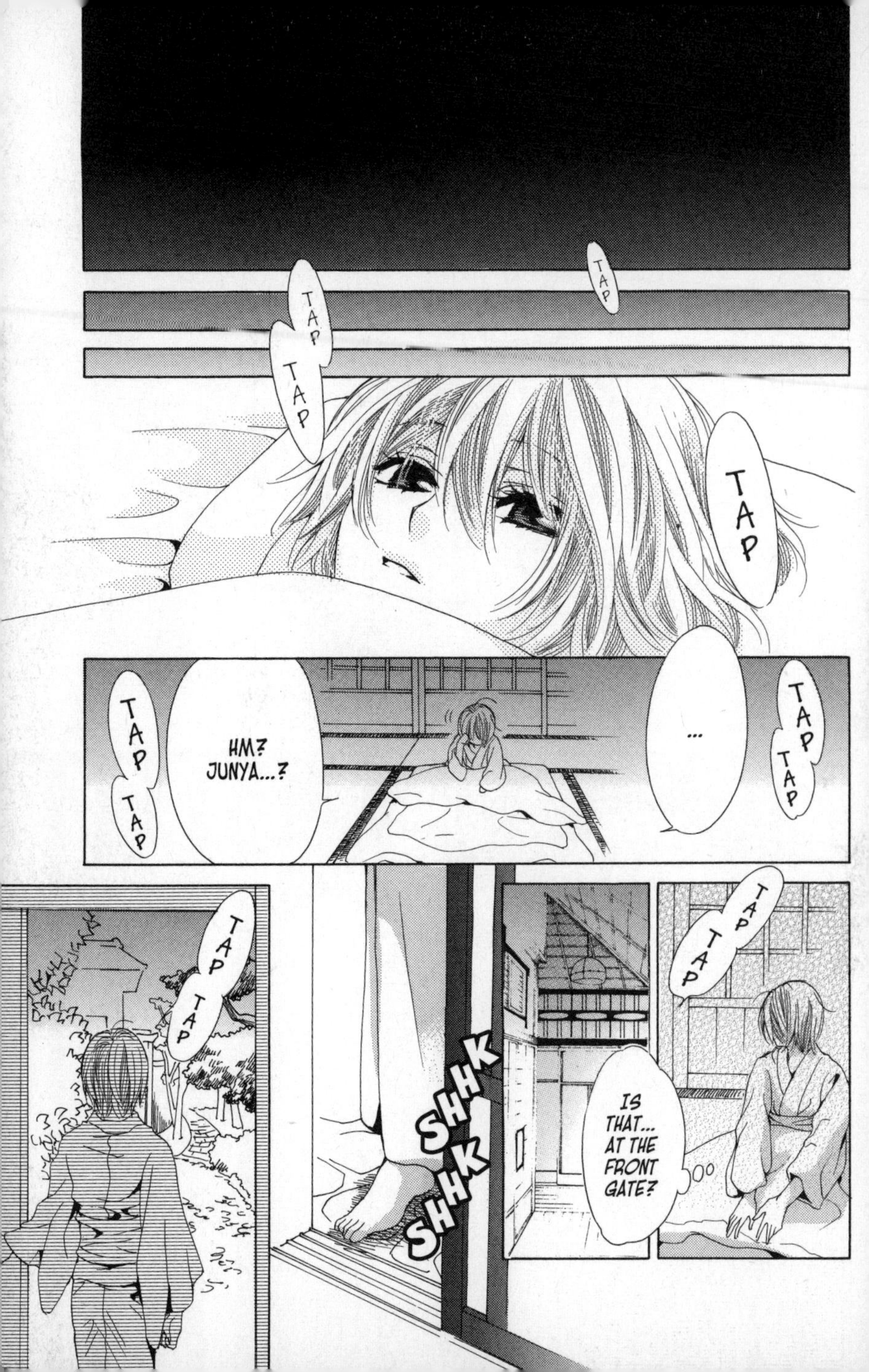
TAP
TAP TAP
TAP
TAP TAP
...
HM? JUNYA...?
TAP TAP
TAP TAP
IS THAT... AT THE FRONT GATE?
SHHK SHHK
TAP TAP

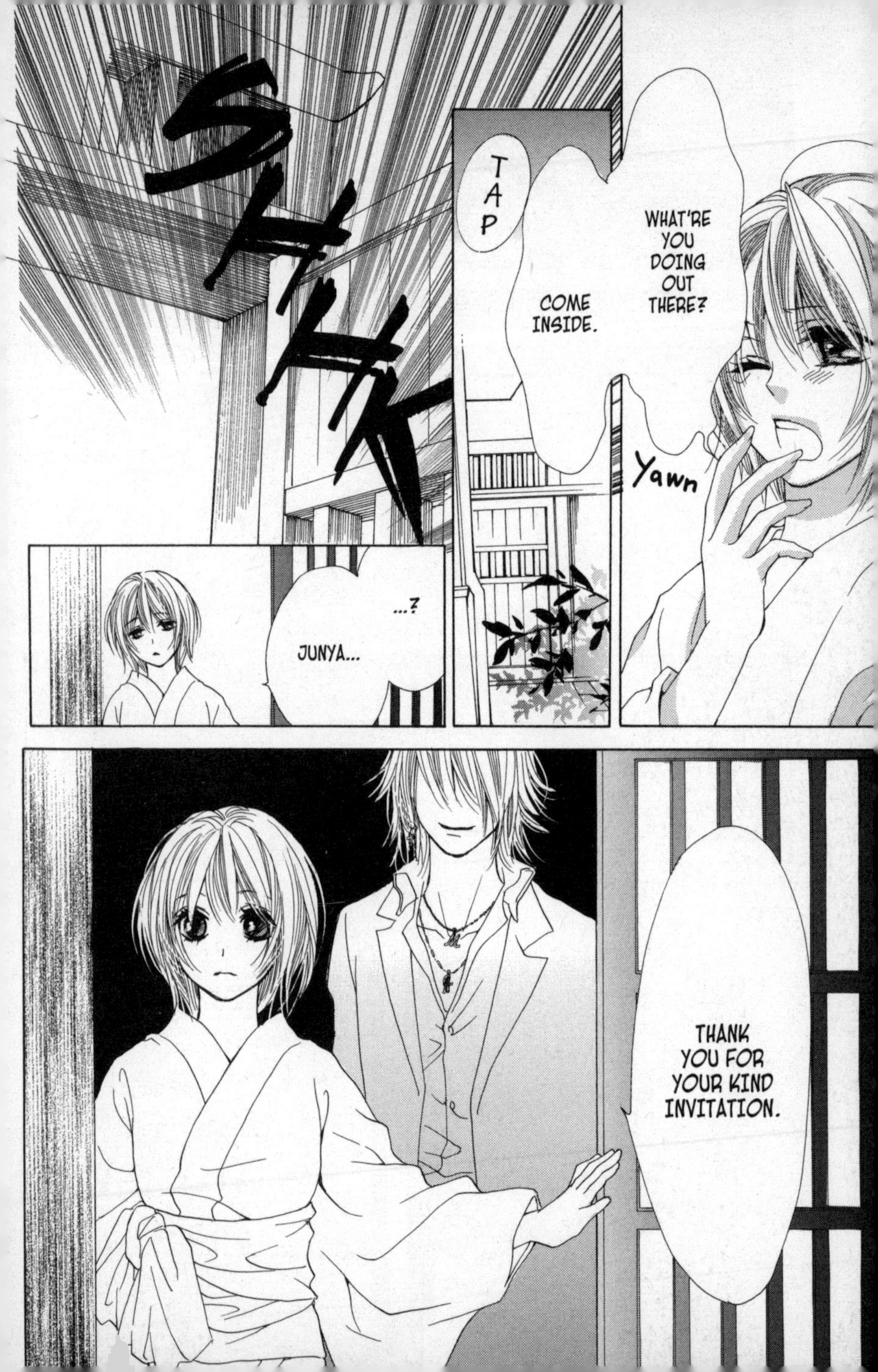
WHAT'RE YOU DOING OUT THERE?
COME INSIDE.
Yawn
TAP
SHHK
...?
JUNYA...
THANK YOU FOR YOUR KIND INVITATION.

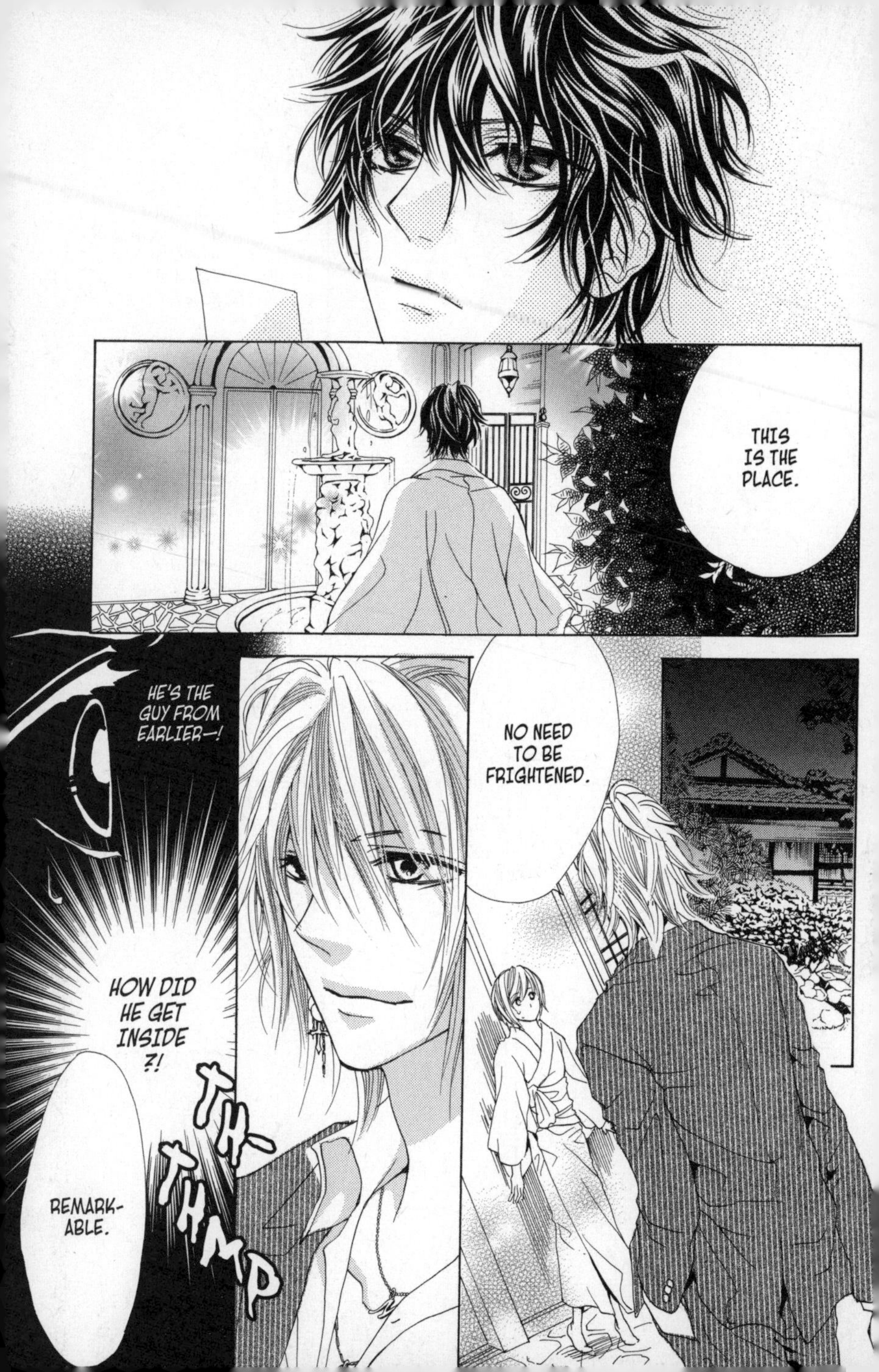
THIS IS THE PLACE.
NO NEED TO BE FRIGHTENED.
HE'S THE GUY FROM EARLIER—!
HOW DID HE GET INSIDE?!
TH-THMP
REMARK-ABLE.

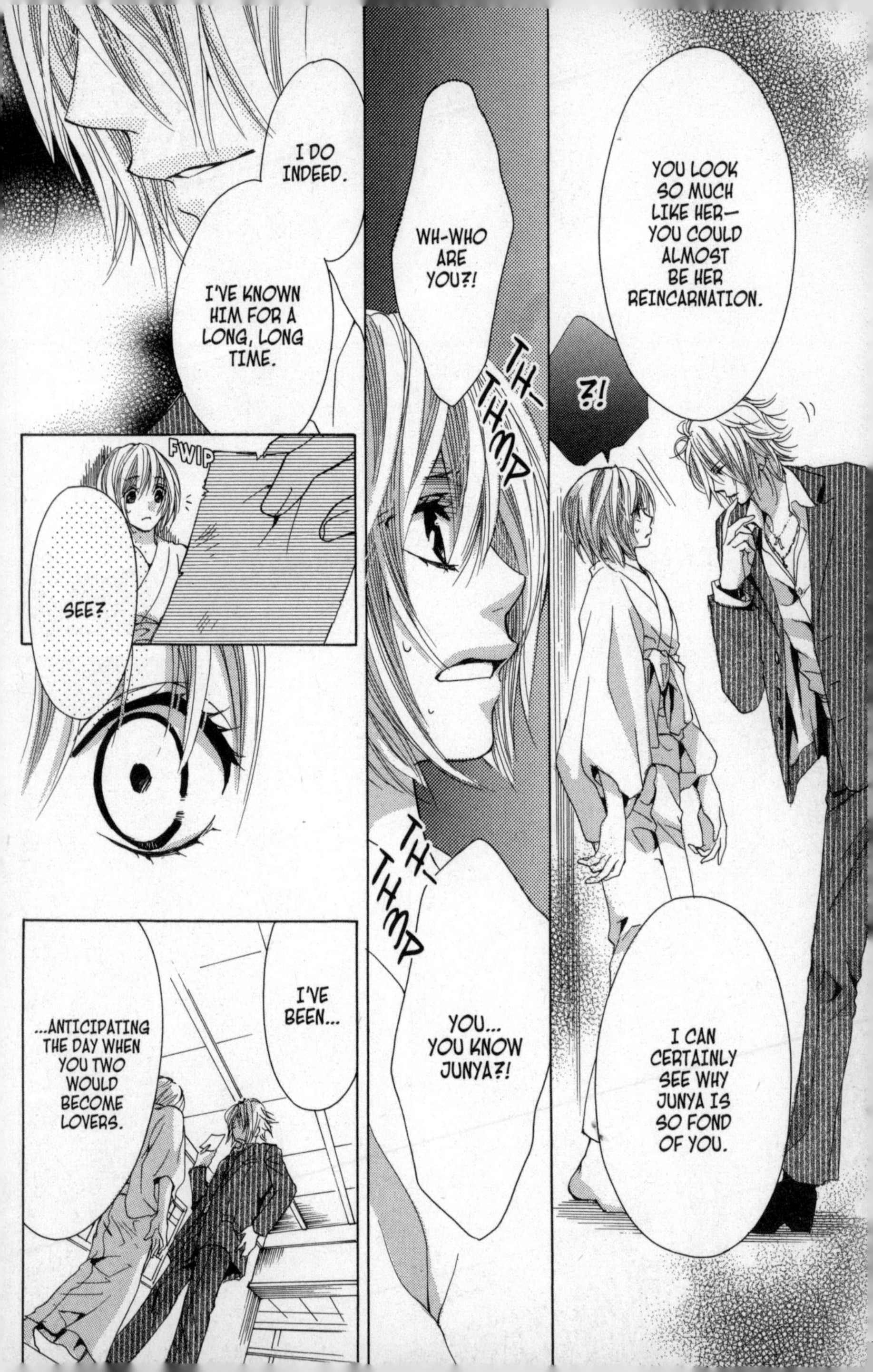
YOU LOOK SO MUCH LIKE HER— YOU COULD ALMOST BE HER REINCARNATION.
?!
I CAN CERTAINLY SEE WHY JUNYA IS SO FOND OF YOU.
WH-WHO ARE YOU?!
TH-THMP
TH-THMP
YOU... YOU KNOW JUNYA?!
I DO INDEED.
I'VE KNOWN HIM FOR A LONG, LONG TIME.
FWIP
SEE?
I'VE BEEN...
...ANTICIPATING THE DAY WHEN YOU TWO WOULD BECOME LOVERS.

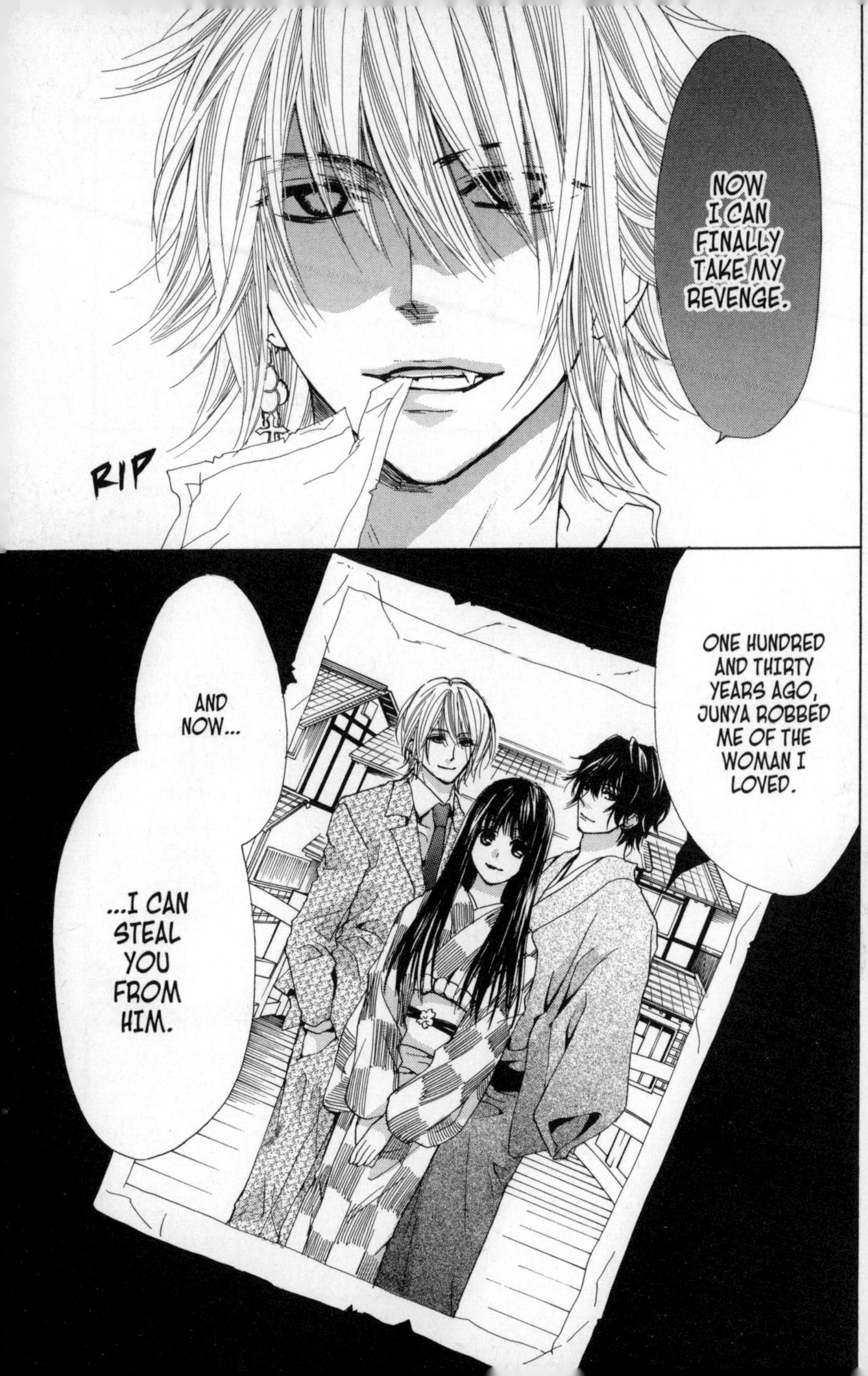
NOW I CAN FINALLY TAKE MY REVENGE.
RIP
ONE HUNDRED AND THIRTY YEARS AGO, JUNYA ROBBED ME OF THE WOMAN I LOVED.
AND NOW...
...I CAN STEAL YOU FROM HIM.

About My Editor

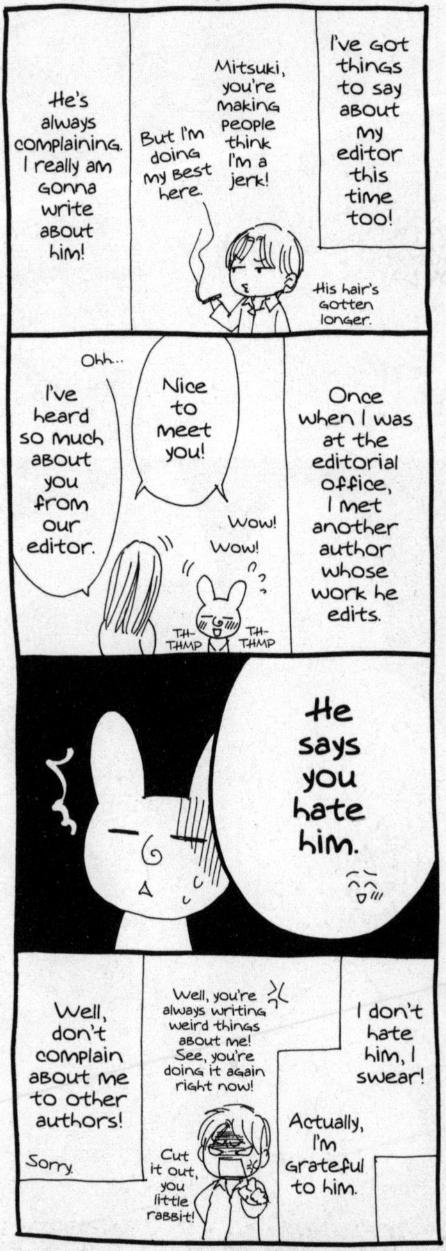
I've got things to say about my editor this time too!
His hair's gotten longer.
Mitsuki, you're making people think I'm a jerk!
But I'm doing my best here.
He's always complaining. I really am gonna write about him!
Once when I was at the editorial office, I met another author whose work he edits.
Nice to meet you!
Wow! Wow!
TH-THMP TH-THMP
Ohh...
I've heard so much about you from our editor.
He says you hate him.
I don't hate him, I swear!
Actually, I'm grateful to him.
Well, you're always writing weird things about me! See, you're doing it again right now!
Cut it out, you little rabbit!
Well, don't complain about me to other authors!
Sorry.

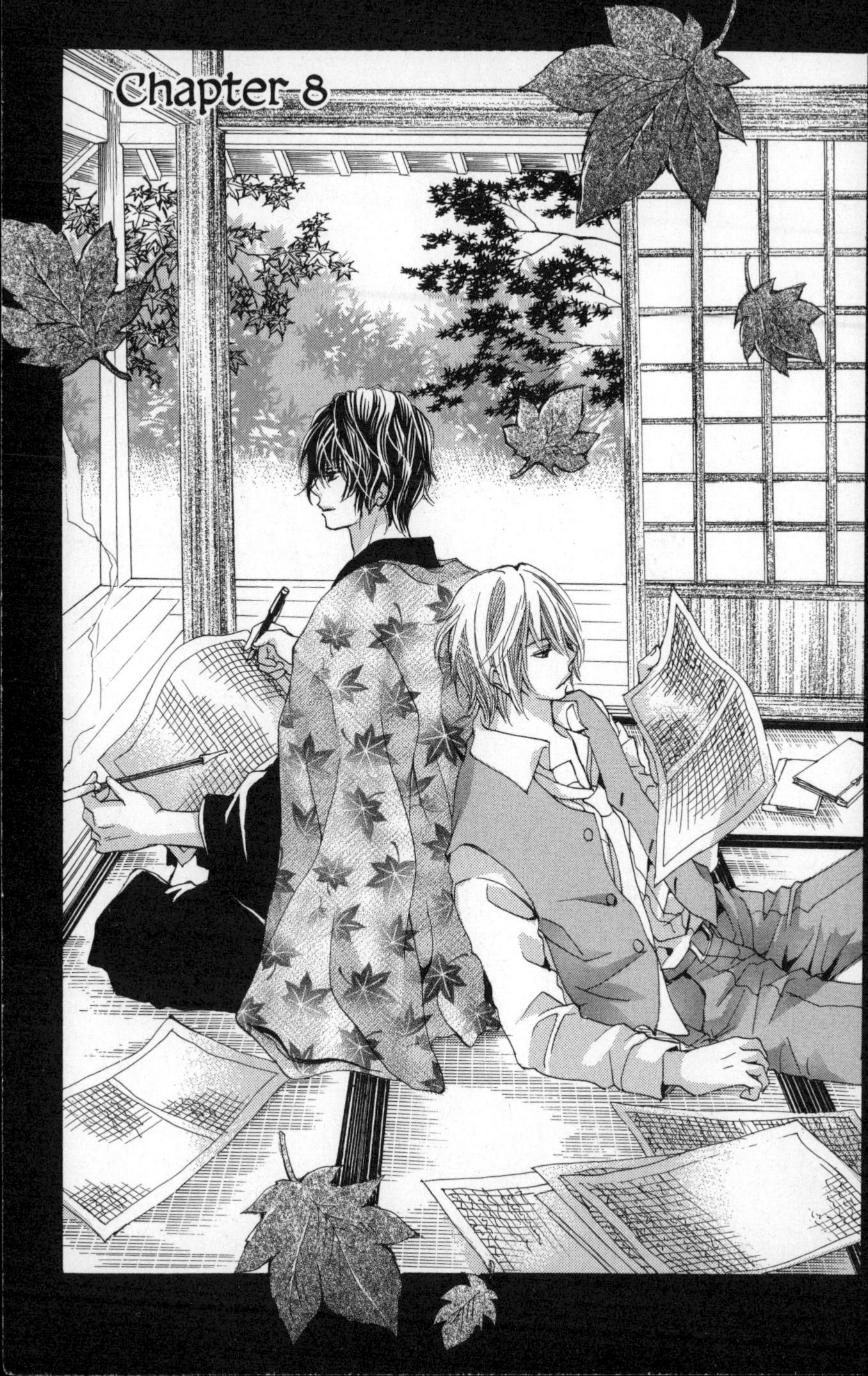
Chapter 8

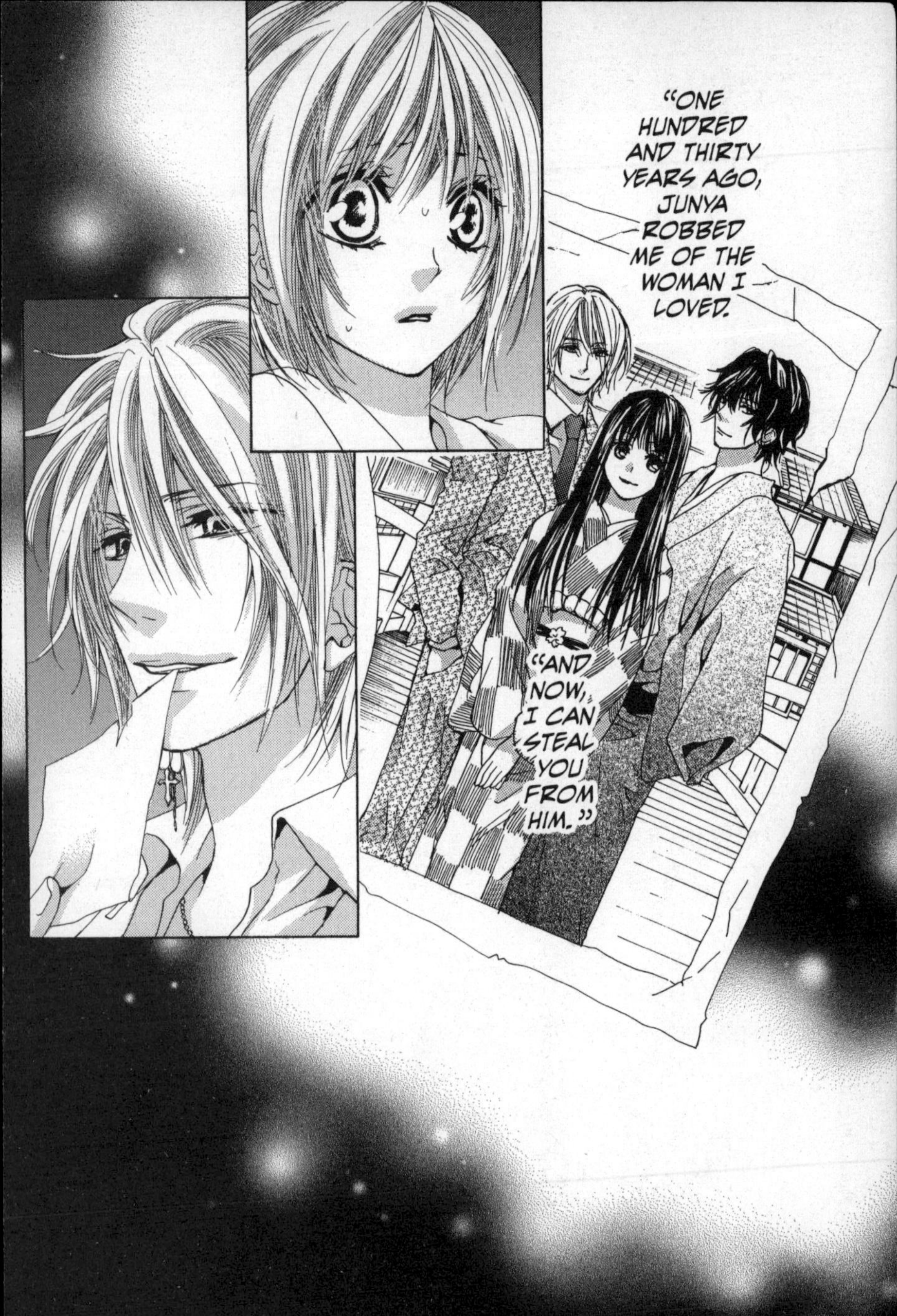
"ONE HUNDRED AND THIRTY YEARS AGO, JUNYA ROBBED ME OF THE WOMAN I LOVED.
"AND NOW, I CAN STEAL YOU FROM HIM."

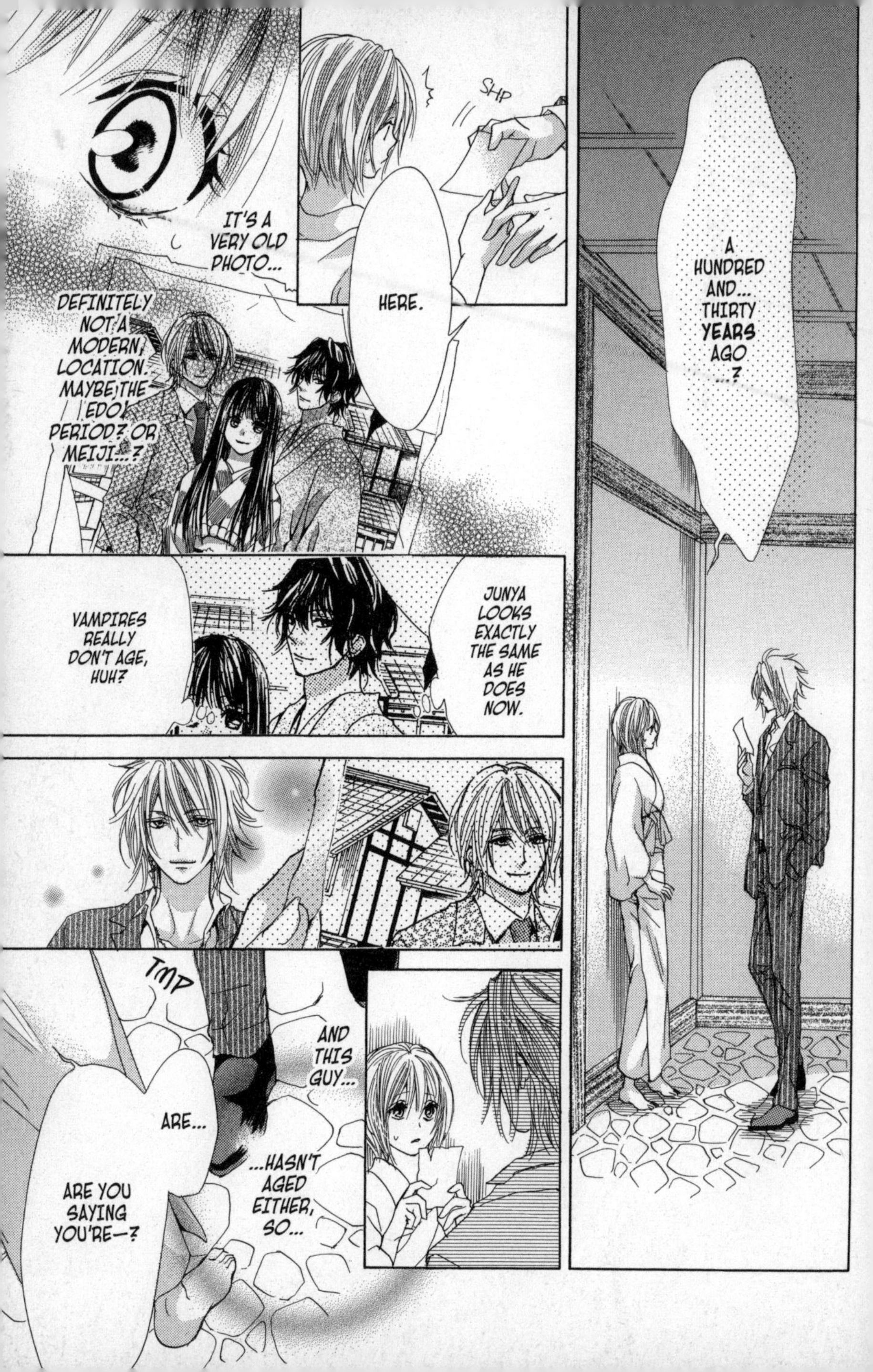
A HUNDRED AND... THIRTY YEARS AGO ...?
SHP
HERE.
IT'S A VERY OLD PHOTO...
DEFINITELY NOT A MODERN LOCATION. MAYBE THE EDO PERIOD? OR MEIJI...?
JUNYA LOOKS EXACTLY THE SAME AS HE DOES NOW.
VAMPIRES REALLY DON'T AGE, HUH?
AND THIS GUY...
...HASN'T AGED EITHER, SO...
TMP
ARE...
ARE YOU SAYING YOU'RE—?

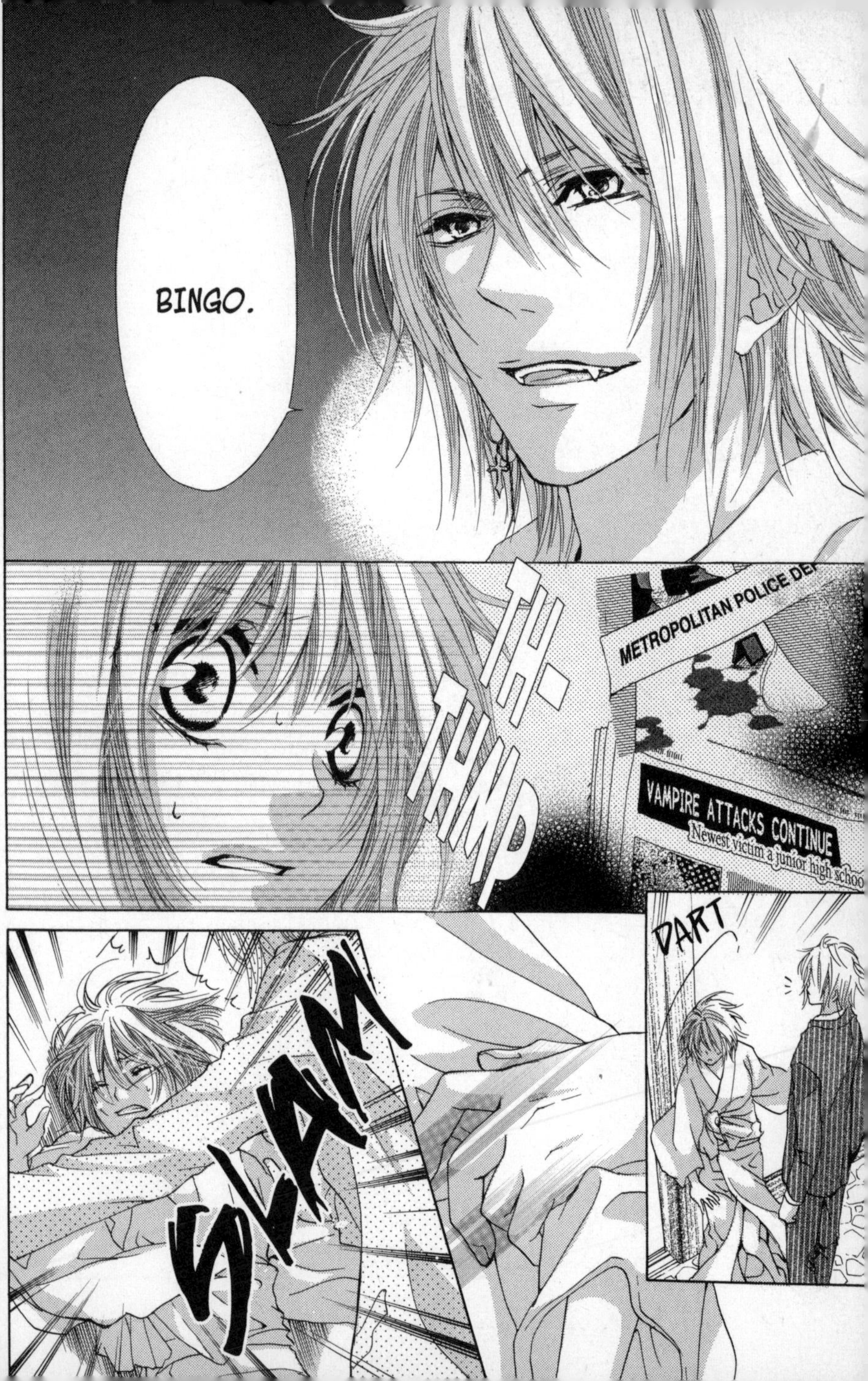
BINGO.
METROPOLITAN POLICE DE
VAMPIRE ATTACKS CONTINUE
Newest victim a junior high schoo
TH-THMP
DART
SLAM

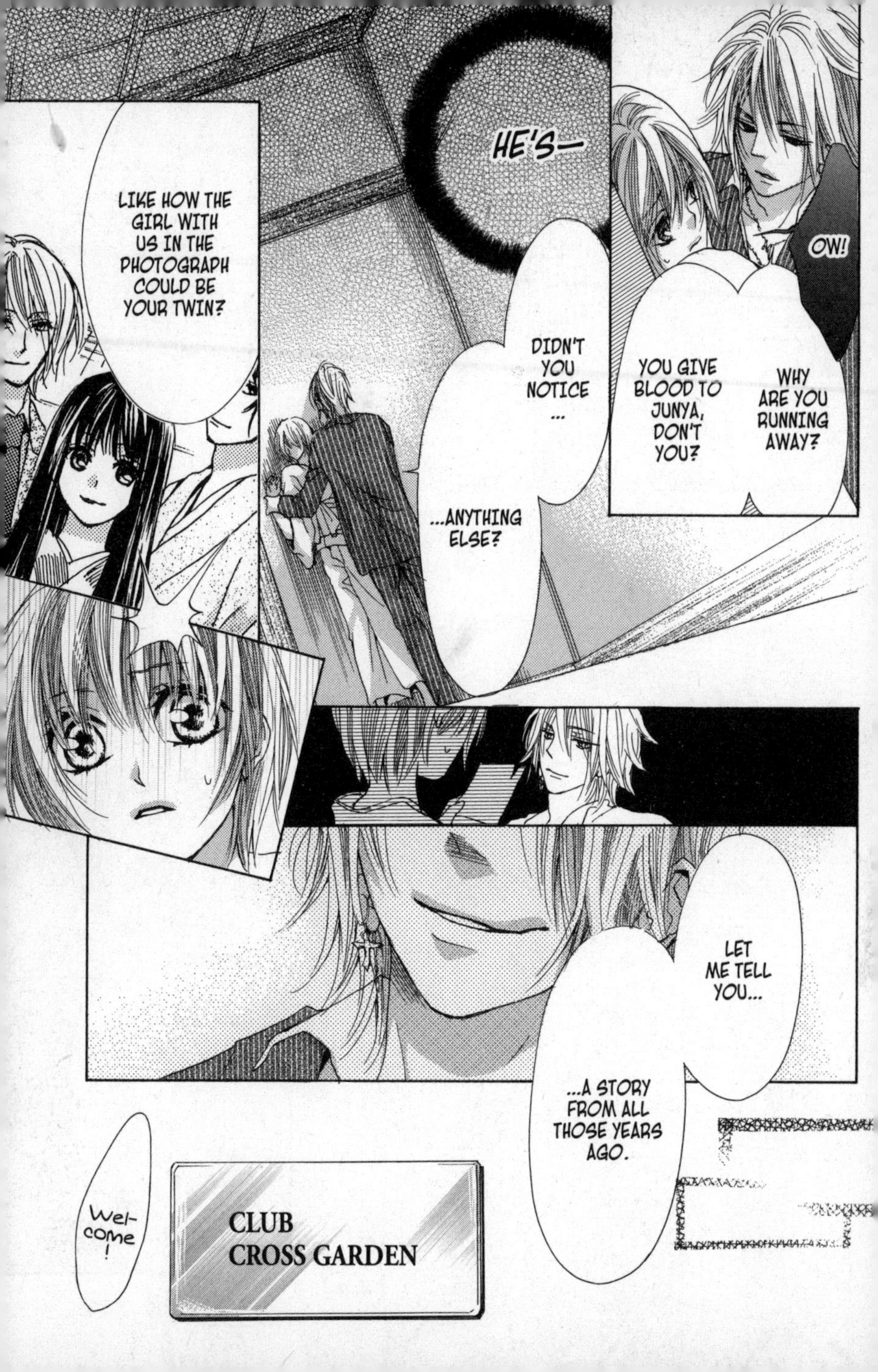
OW!
WHY ARE YOU RUNNING AWAY?
YOU GIVE BLOOD TO JUNYA, DON'T YOU?
HE'S—
DIDN'T YOU NOTICE ...
...ANYTHING ELSE?
LIKE HOW THE GIRL WITH US IN THE PHOTOGRAPH COULD BE YOUR TWIN?
LET ME TELL YOU...
...A STORY FROM ALL THOSE YEARS AGO.
CLUB CROSS GARDEN
Wel-come!

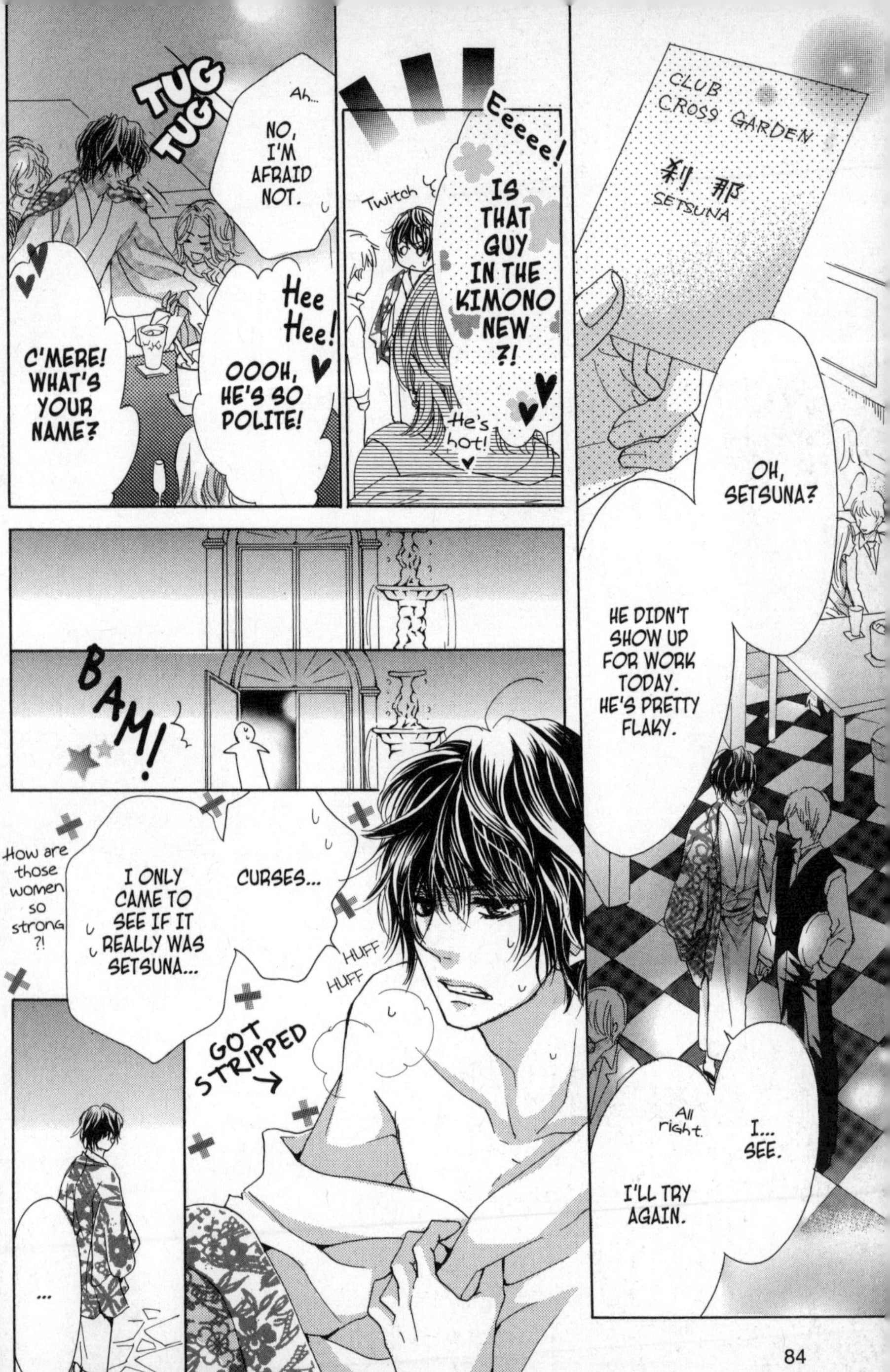
CLUB CROSS GARDEN
刹那
SETSUNA
OH, SETSUNA?
HE DIDN'T SHOW UP FOR WORK TODAY. HE'S PRETTY FLAKY.
I... SEE.
All right.
I'LL TRY AGAIN.
Eeeee!
IS THAT GUY IN THE KIMONO NEW?!
Twitch
He's hot!
TUG TUG
Ah...
NO, I'M AFRAID NOT.
Hee Hee!
OOOH, HE'S SO POLITE!
C'MERE! WHAT'S YOUR NAME?
BAM!
CURSES...
I ONLY CAME TO SEE IF IT REALLY WAS SETSUNA...
How are those women so strong?!
HUFF HUFF
GOT STRIPPED
...

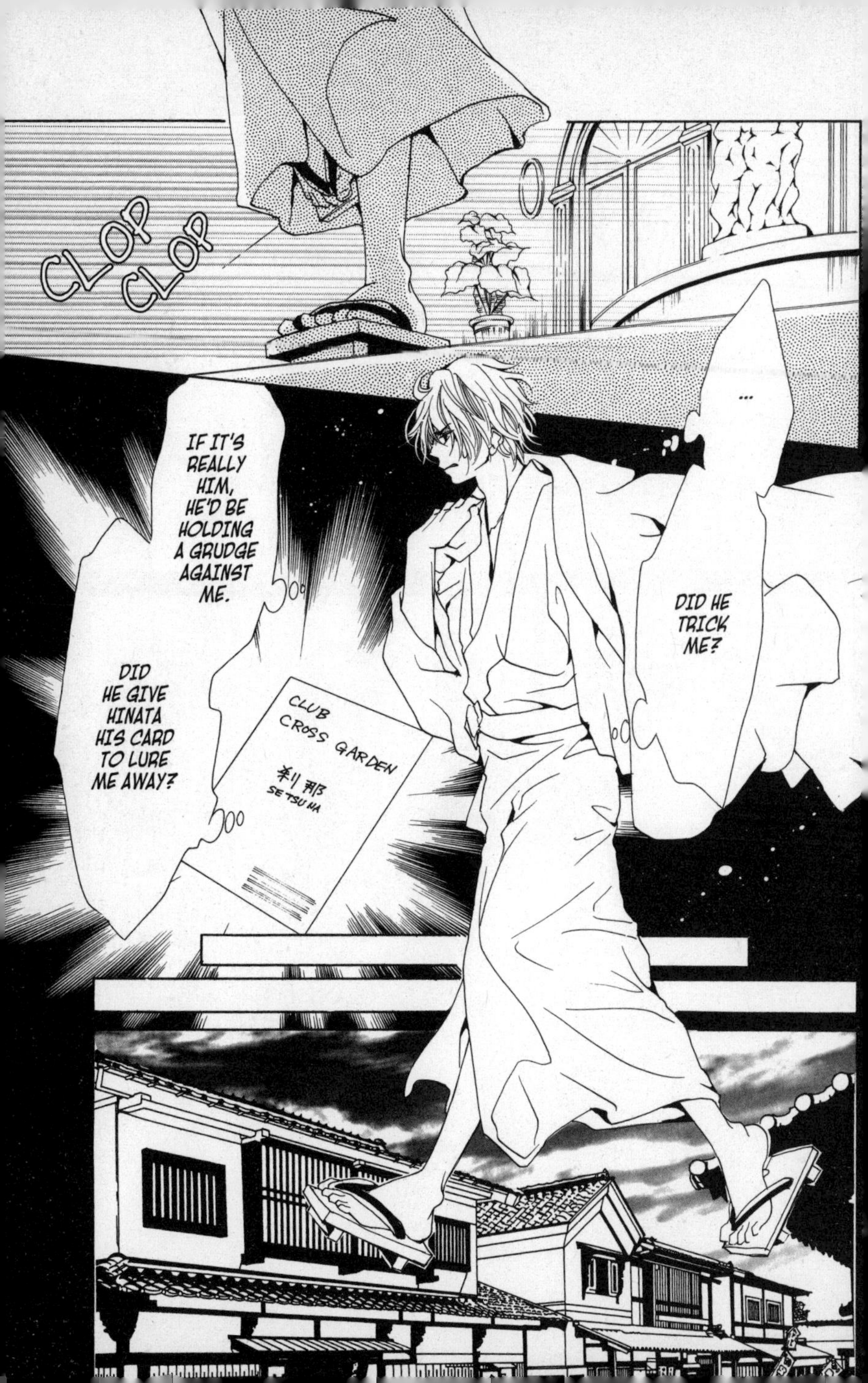
CLOP CLOP
...
DID HE TRICK ME?
IF IT'S REALLY HIM, HE'D BE HOLDING A GRUDGE AGAINST ME.
CLUB CROSS GARDEN
刹那
SETSUNA
DID HE GIVE HINATA HIS CARD TO LURE ME AWAY?

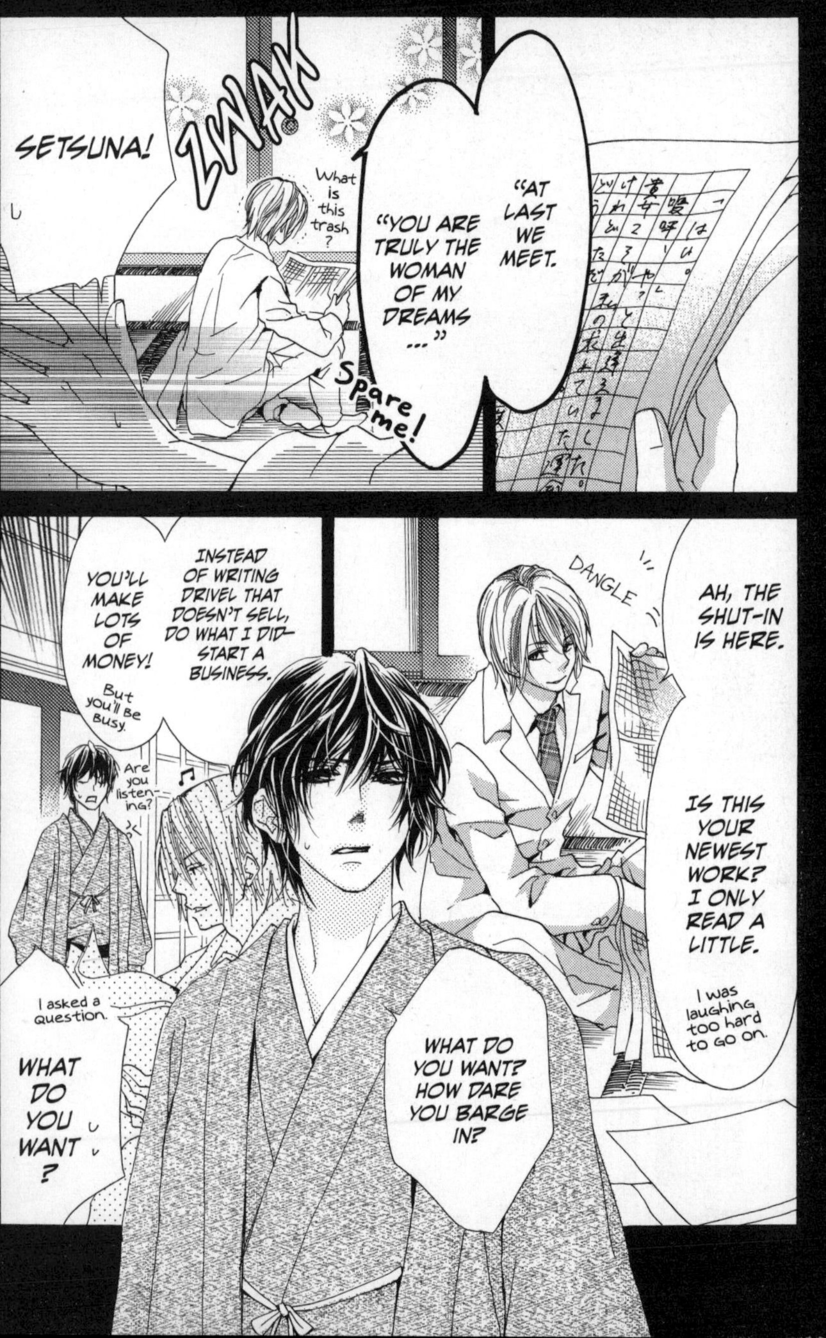
"AT LAST WE MEET.
"YOU ARE TRULY THE WOMAN OF MY DREAMS..."
What is this trash?
Spare me!
ZWAK
SETSUNA!
AH, THE SHUT-IN IS HERE.
DANGLE
IS THIS YOUR NEWEST WORK? I ONLY READ A LITTLE.
I was laughing too hard to go on.
INSTEAD OF WRITING DRIVEL THAT DOESN'T SELL, DO WHAT I DID-START A BUSINESS.
YOU'LL MAKE LOTS OF MONEY!
But you'll Be Busy.
Are you listening?
WHAT DO YOU WANT? HOW DARE YOU BARGE IN?
I asked a question.
WHAT DO YOU WANT?

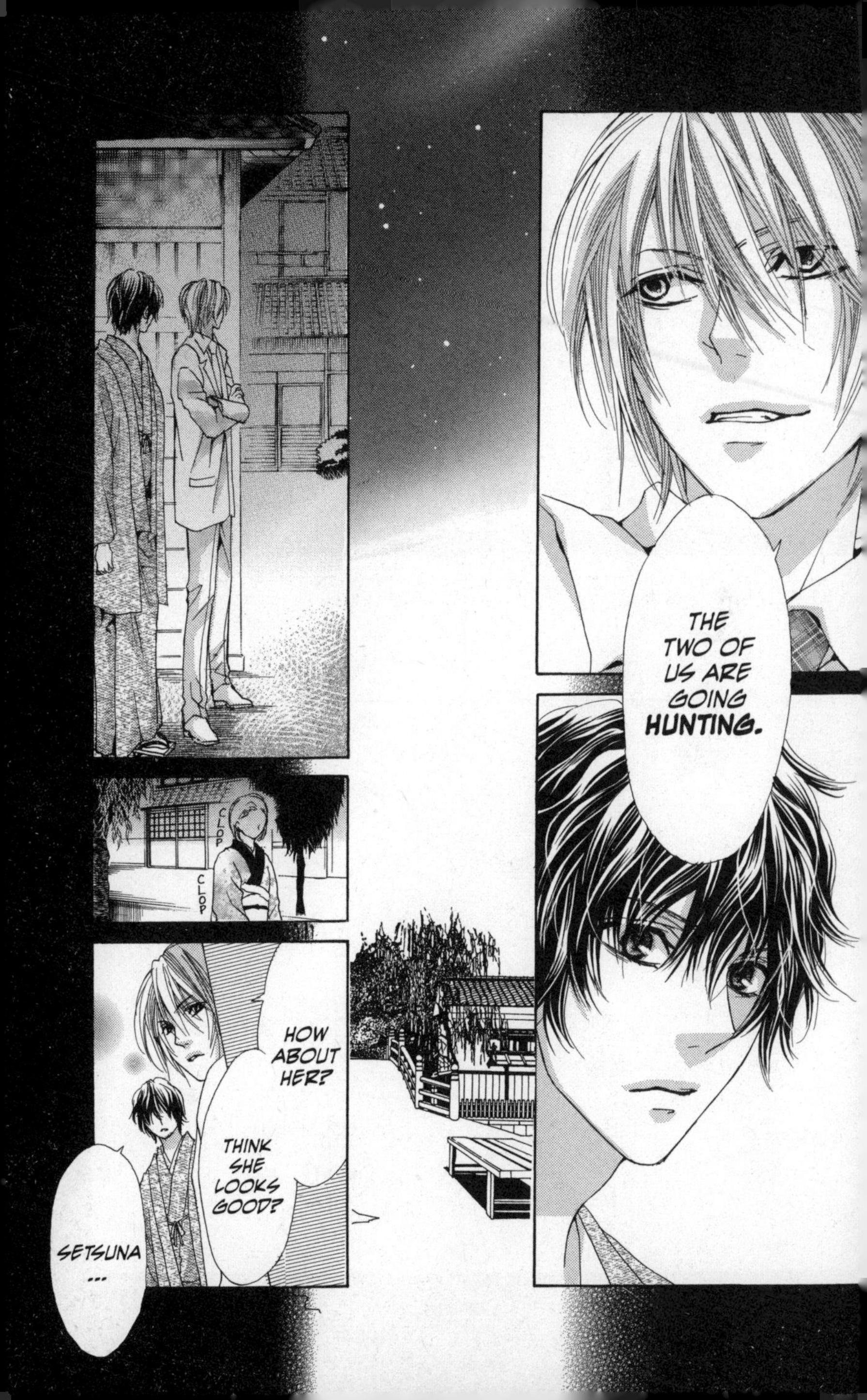
THE TWO OF US ARE GOING HUNTING.
CLOP
CLOP
HOW ABOUT HER?
THINK SHE LOOKS GOOD?
SETSUNA...

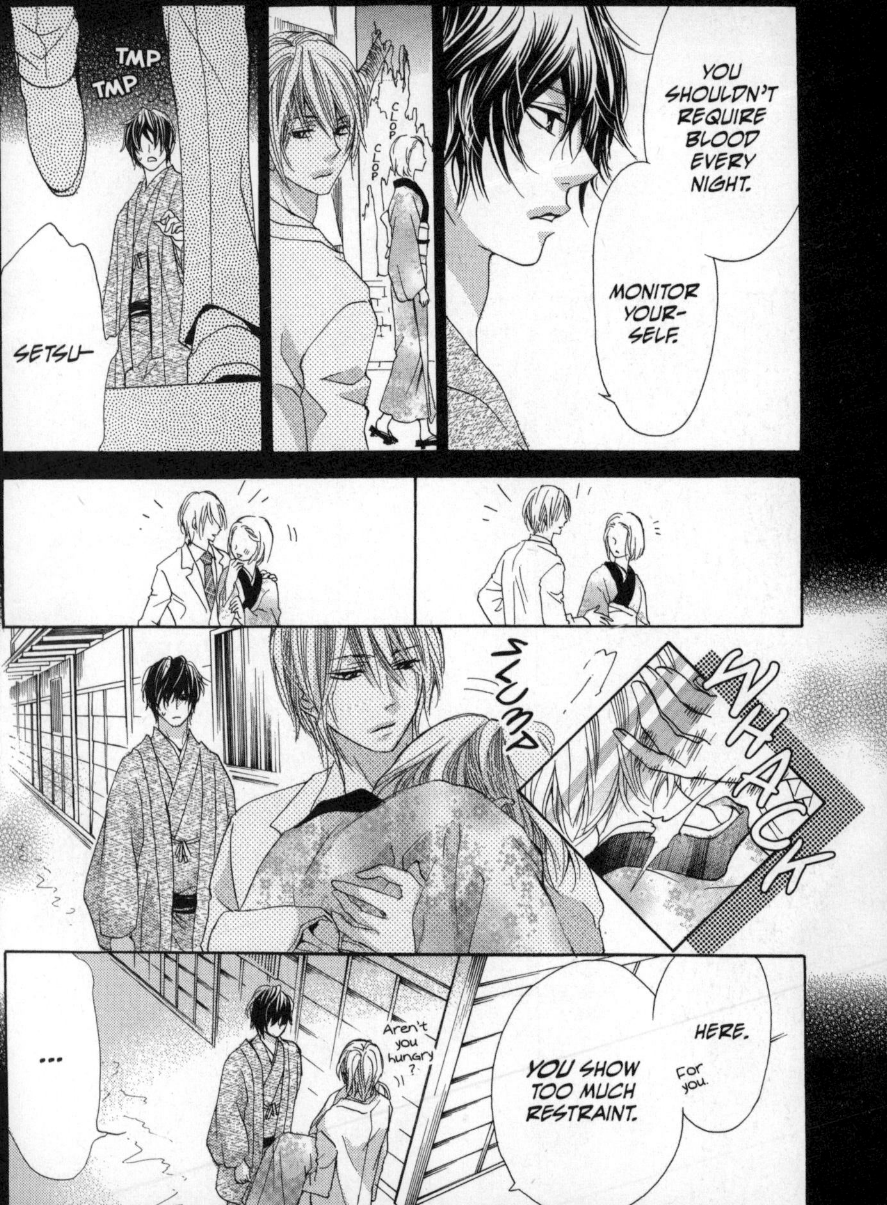
YOU SHOULDN'T REQUIRE BLOOD EVERY NIGHT.
MONITOR YOUR-SELF.
CLOP
CLOP
TMP
TMP
SETSU—
WHACK
SLUMP
HERE.
For you.
YOU SHOW TOO MUCH RESTRAINT.
Aren't you hungry?
...

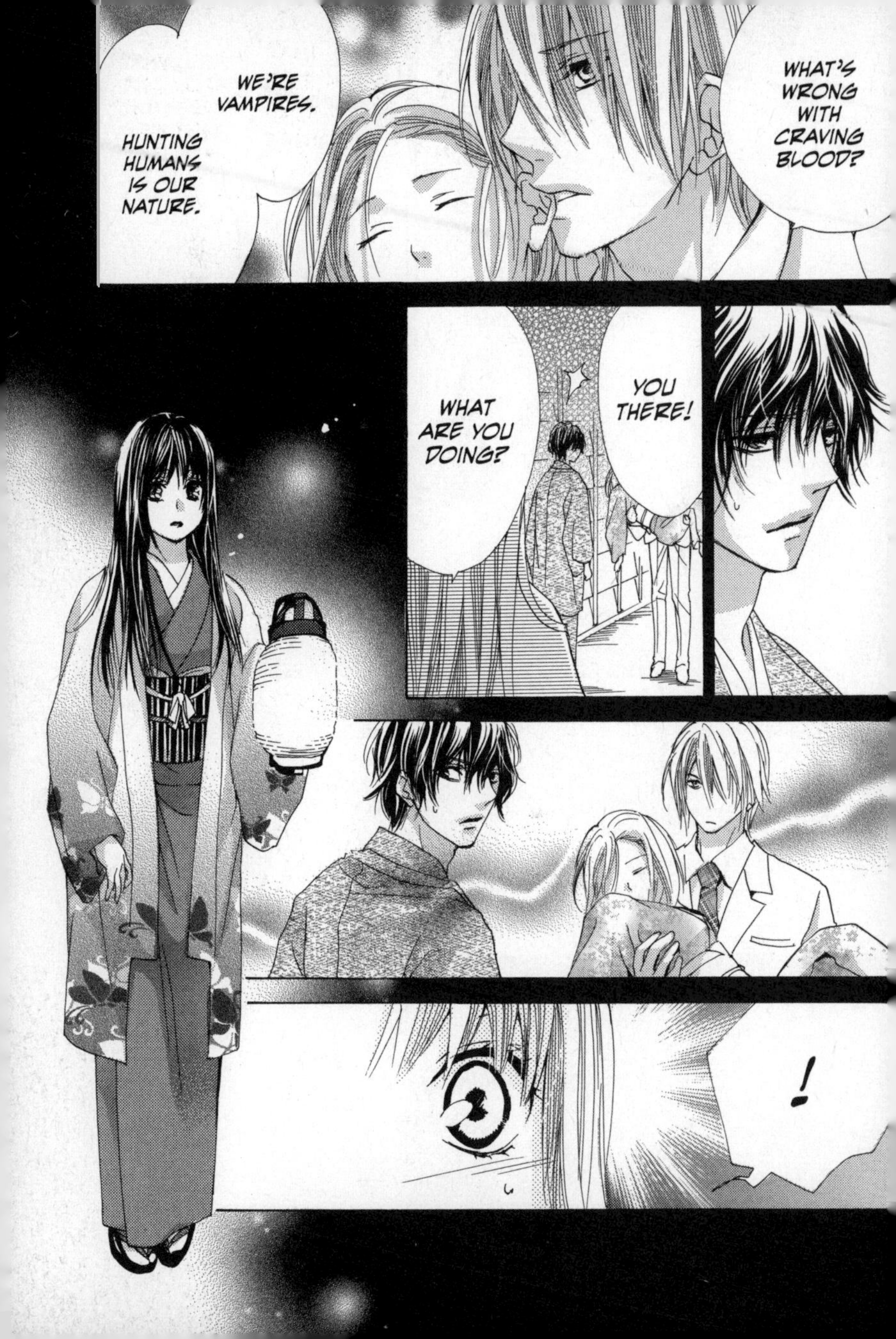
WHAT'S WRONG WITH CRAVING BLOOD?
WE'RE VAMPIRES.
HUNTING HUMANS IS OUR NATURE.
YOU THERE!
WHAT ARE YOU DOING?
!

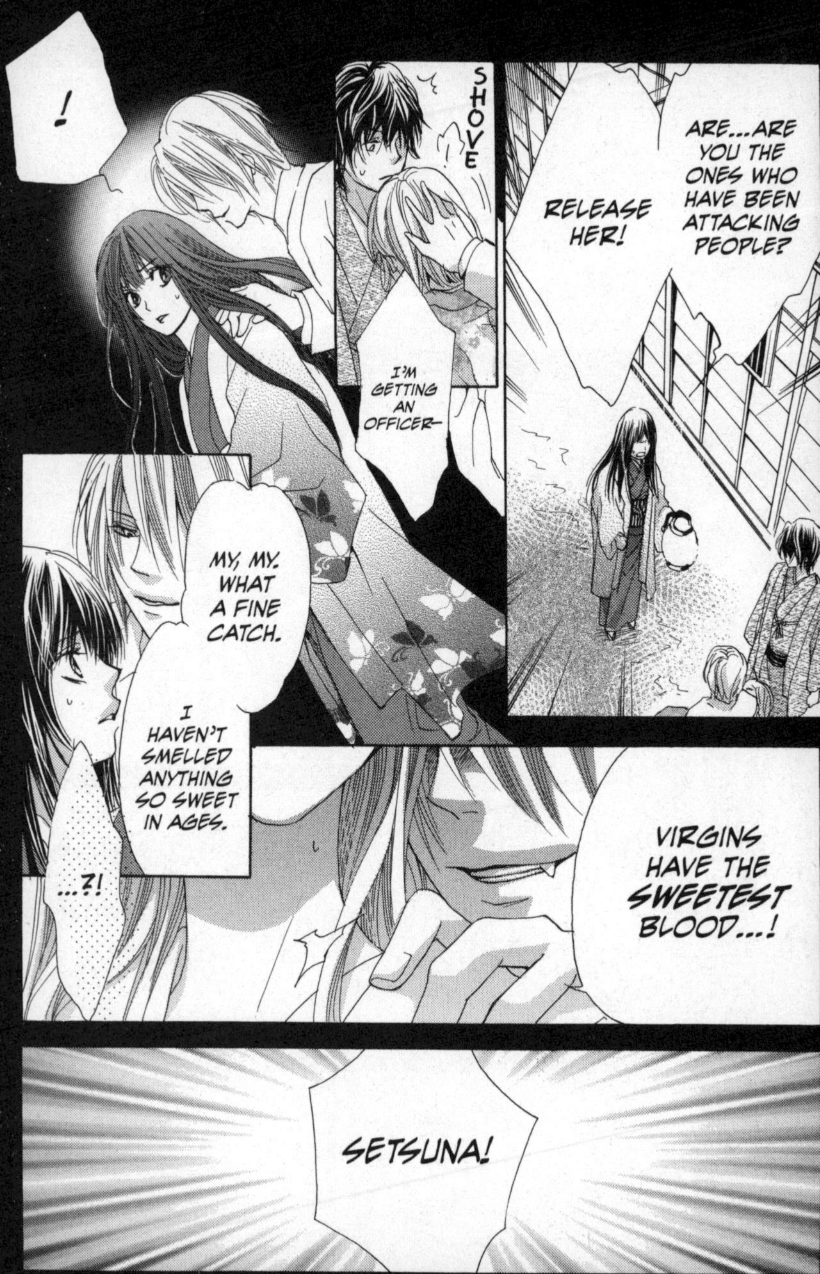
ARE...ARE YOU THE ONES WHO HAVE BEEN ATTACKING PEOPLE?
RELEASE HER!
SHOVE
I'M GETTING AN OFFICER—
!
MY, MY. WHAT A FINE CATCH.
I HAVEN'T SMELLED ANYTHING SO SWEET IN AGES.
...?!
VIRGINS HAVE THE SWEETEST BLOOD...!
SETSUNA!

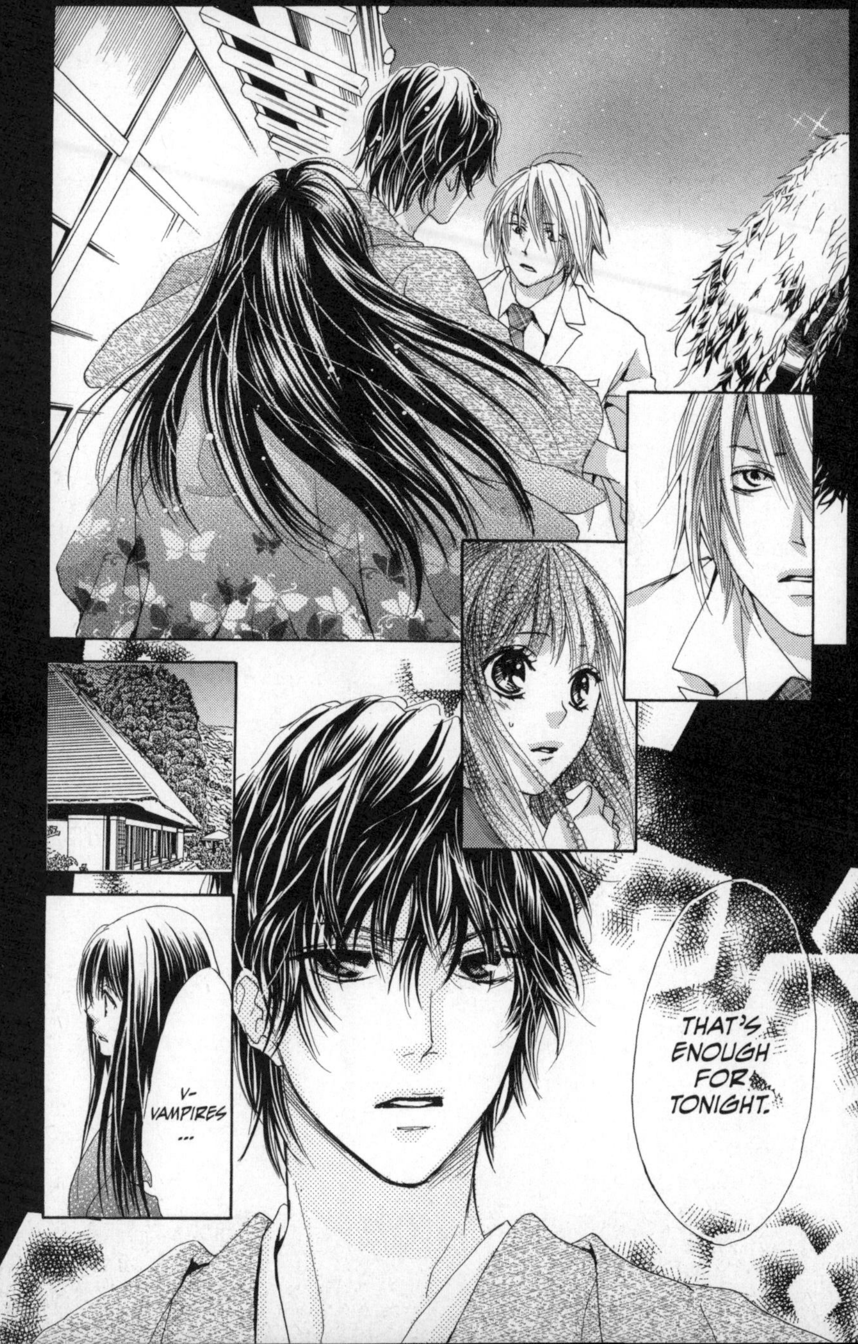
THAT'S ENOUGH FOR TONIGHT.
V-VAMPIRES...

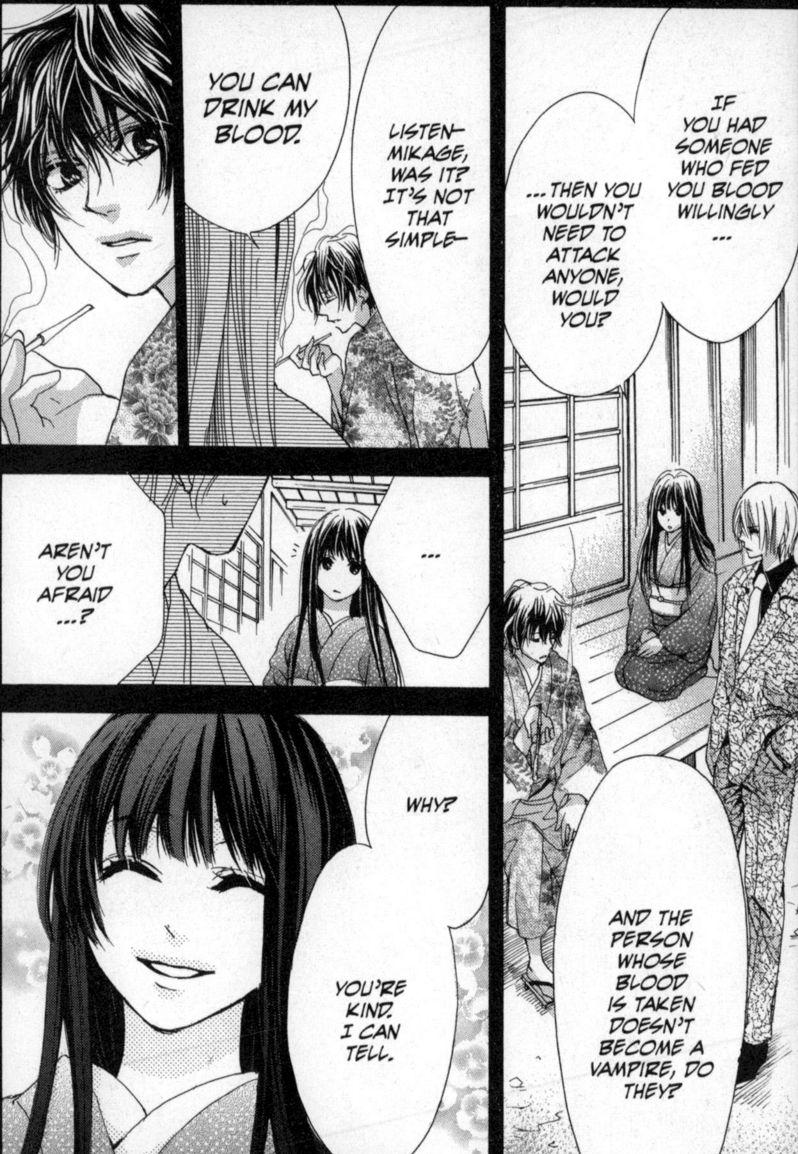
IF YOU HAD SOMEONE WHO FED YOU BLOOD WILLINGLY ...
...THEN YOU WOULDN'T NEED TO ATTACK ANYONE, WOULD YOU?
AND THE PERSON WHOSE BLOOD IS TAKEN DOESN'T BECOME A VAMPIRE, DO THEY?
LISTEN— MIKAGE, WAS IT? IT'S NOT THAT SIMPLE—
YOU CAN DRINK MY BLOOD.
...
AREN'T YOU AFRAID ...?
WHY?
YOU'RE KIND. I CAN TELL.

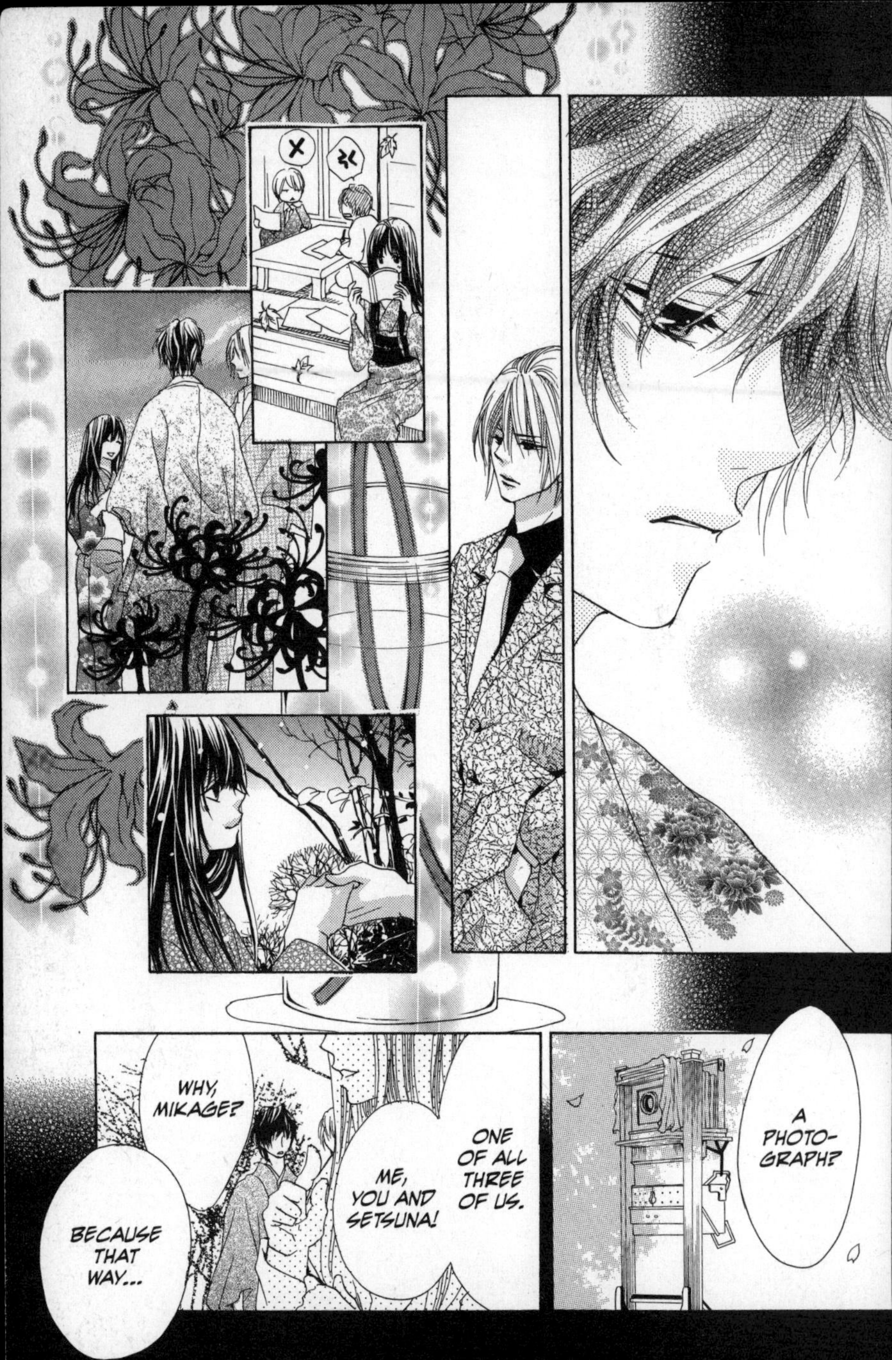
A PHOTO-GRAPH?
ONE OF ALL THREE OF US.
ME, YOU AND SETSUNA!
WHY, MIKAGE?
BECAUSE THAT WAY...

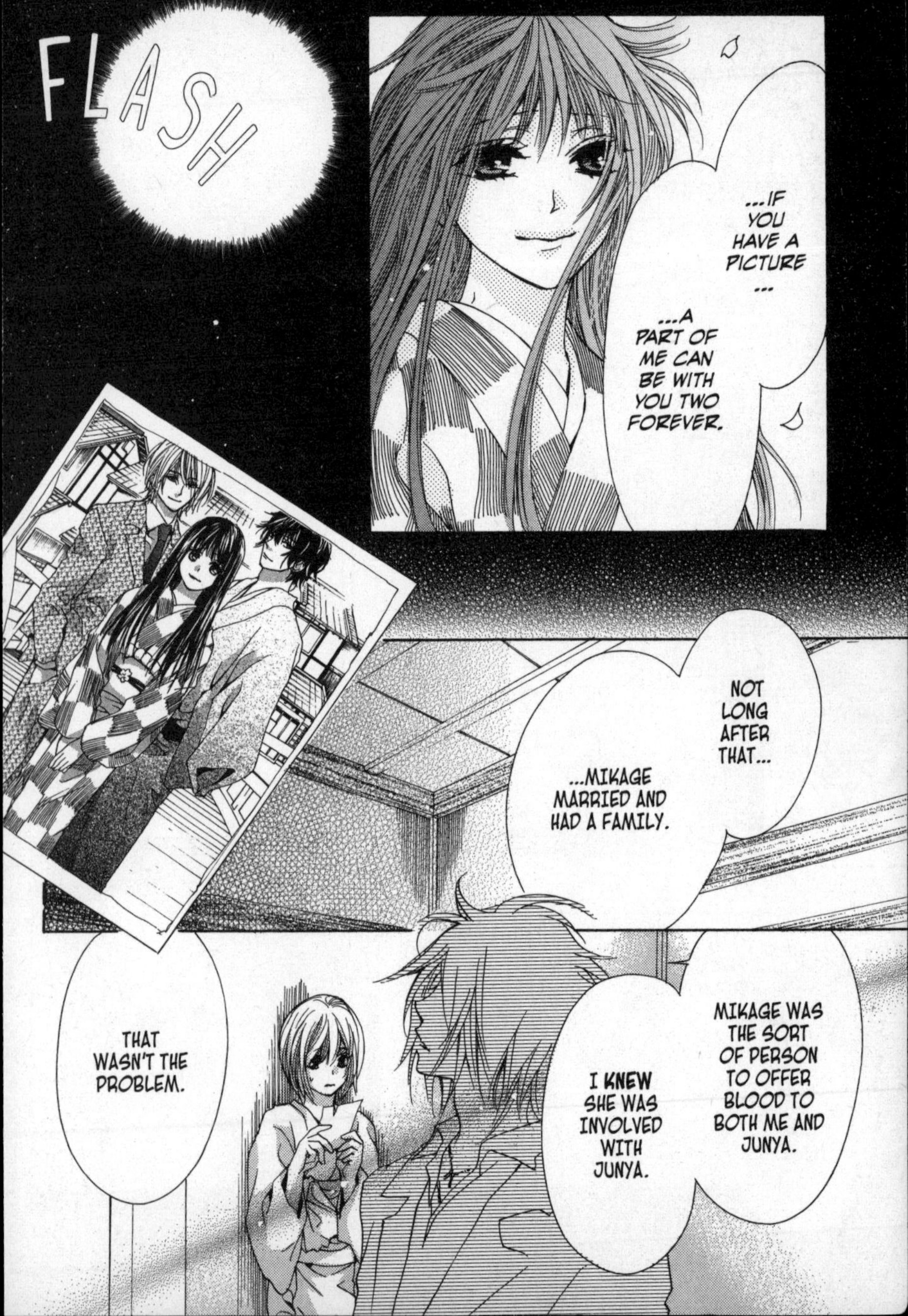
...IF YOU HAVE A PICTURE ...
...A PART OF ME CAN BE WITH YOU TWO FOREVER.
FLASH
NOT LONG AFTER THAT...
...MIKAGE MARRIED AND HAD A FAMILY.
MIKAGE WAS THE SORT OF PERSON TO OFFER BLOOD TO BOTH ME AND JUNYA.
I KNEW SHE WAS INVOLVED WITH JUNYA.
THAT WASN'T THE PROBLEM.

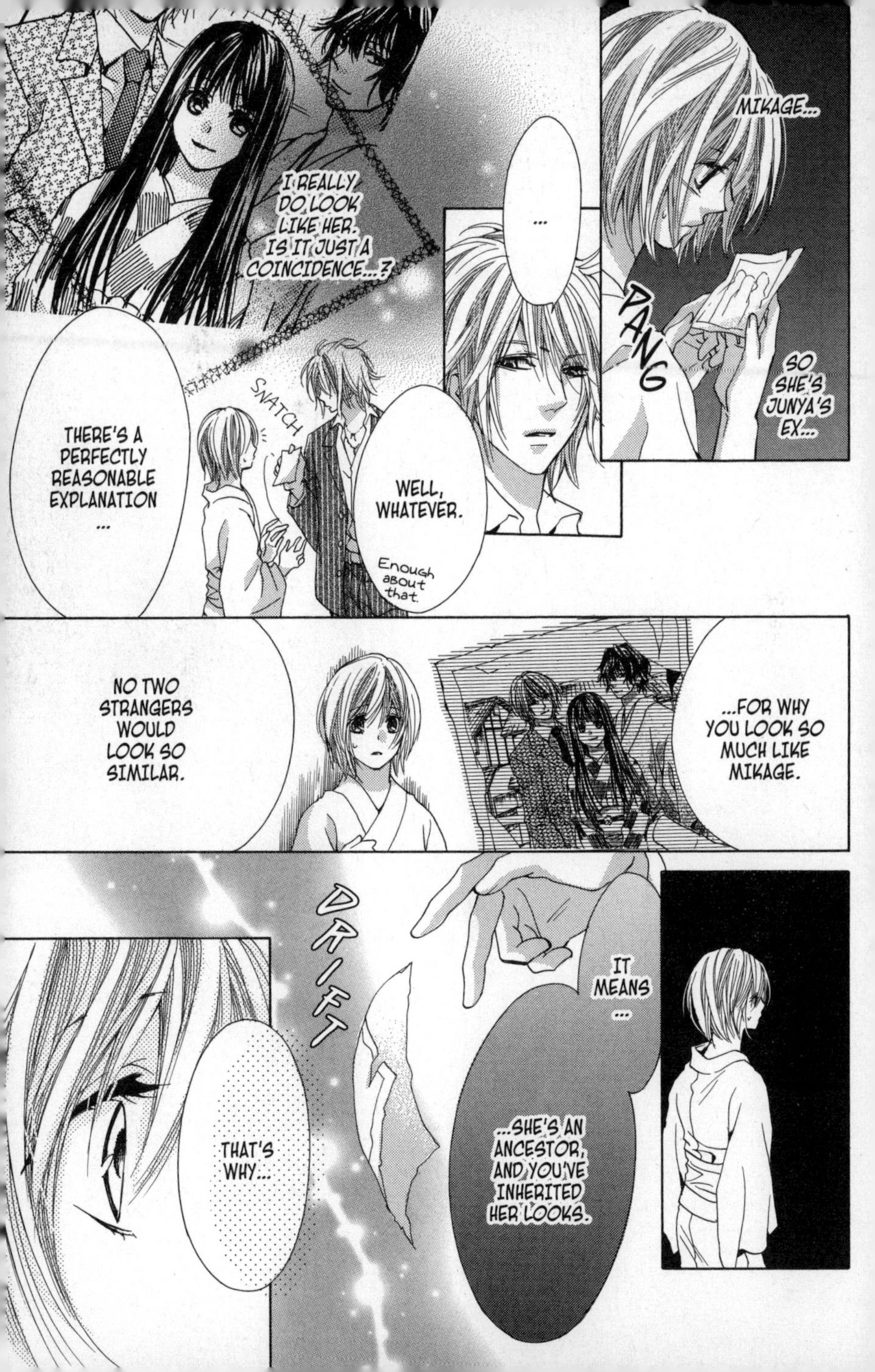
MIKAGE...
PANG
SO SHE'S JUNYA'S EX...
I REALLY DO LOOK LIKE HER. IS IT JUST A COINCIDENCE...?
...
WELL, WHATEVER.
Enough about that.
SNATCH
THERE'S A PERFECTLY REASONABLE EXPLANATION...
...FOR WHY YOU LOOK SO MUCH LIKE MIKAGE.
NO TWO STRANGERS WOULD LOOK SO SIMILAR.
IT MEANS...
...SHE'S AN ANCESTOR, AND YOU'VE INHERITED HER LOOKS.
DRIFT
THAT'S WHY...

...JUNYA APPROACHED YOU.
YOU REMIND HIM OF HER.
"THERE'S SOMEONE IRREPLACEABLE IN MY HEART."
"I WONDER WHY JUNYA CHOSE ME..."
JUNYA'S NOT IN LOVE WITH YOU AT ALL.

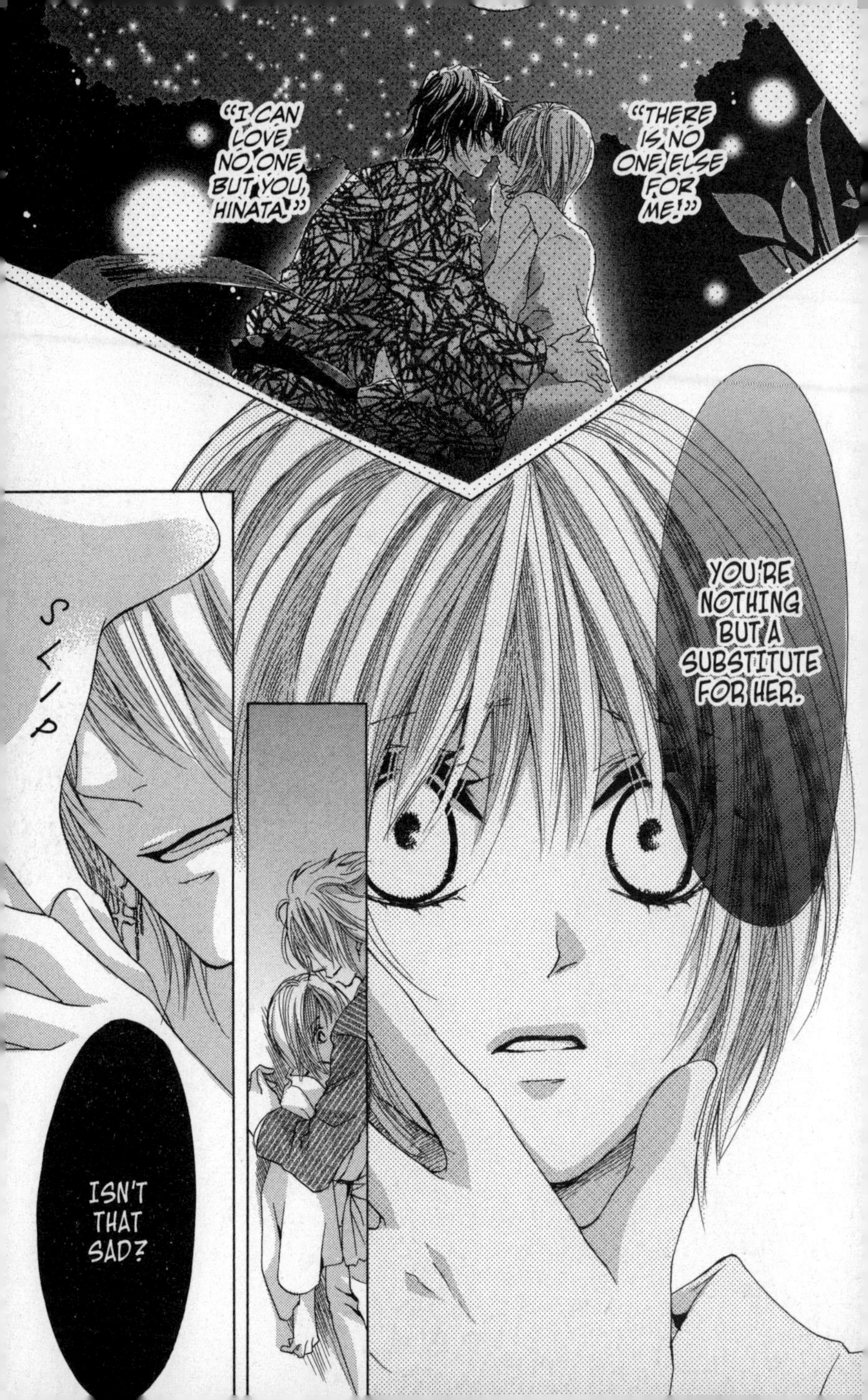
"THERE IS NO ONE ELSE FOR ME!"
"I CAN LOVE NO ONE BUT YOU, HINATA."
YOU'RE NOTHING BUT A SUBSTITUTE FOR HER.
SLIP
ISN'T THAT SAD?

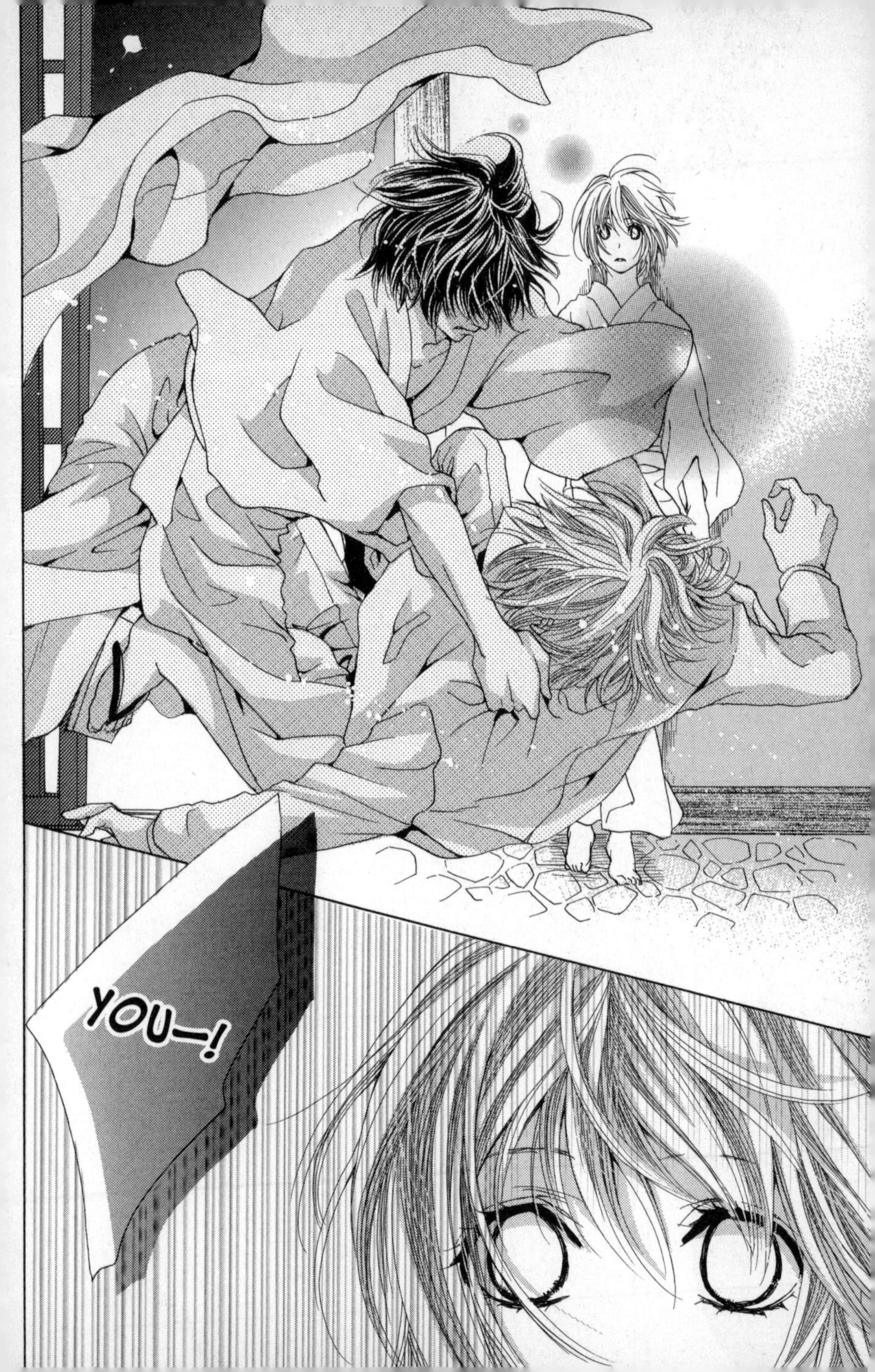
YOU—!

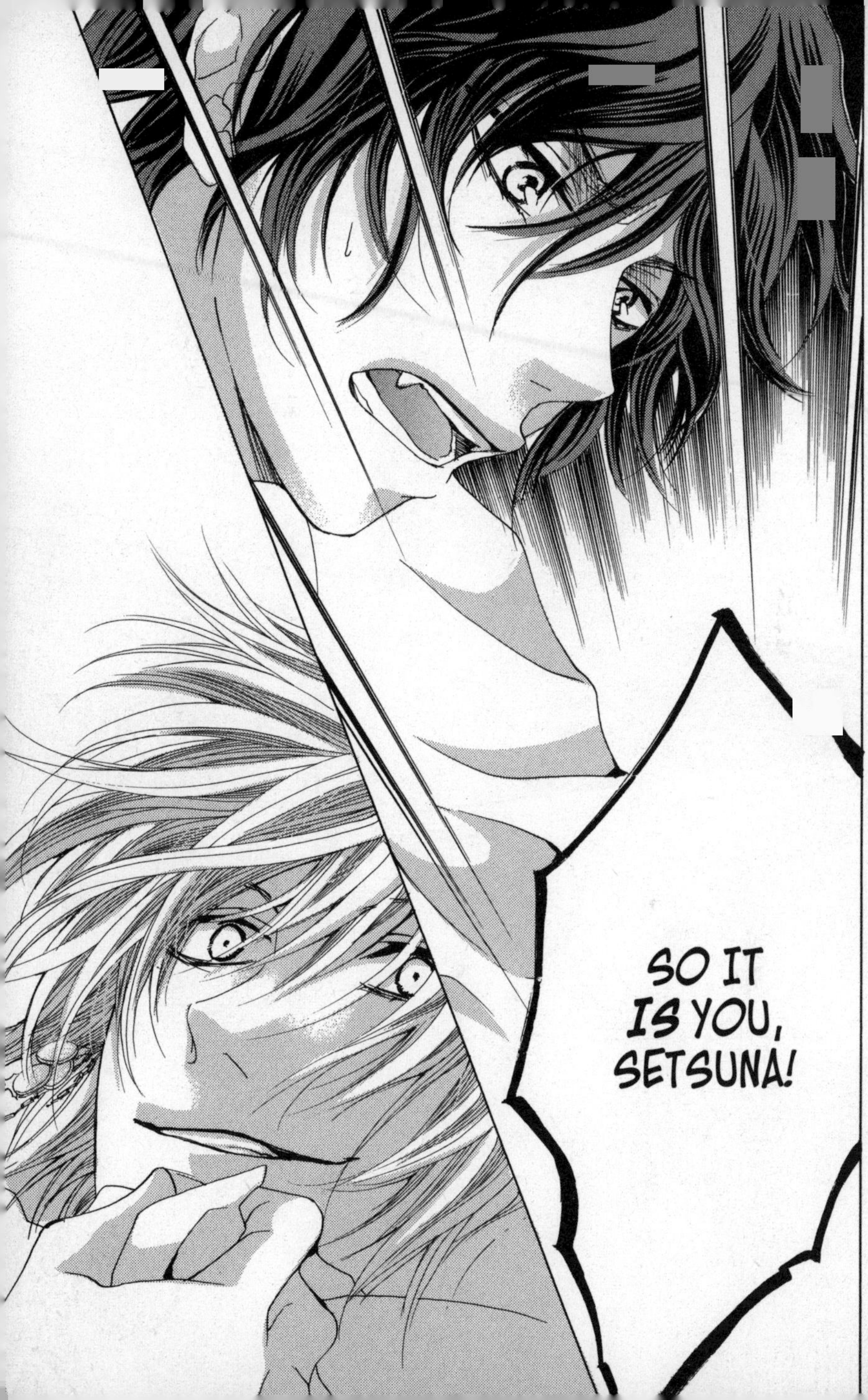
SO IT IS YOU, SETSUNA!

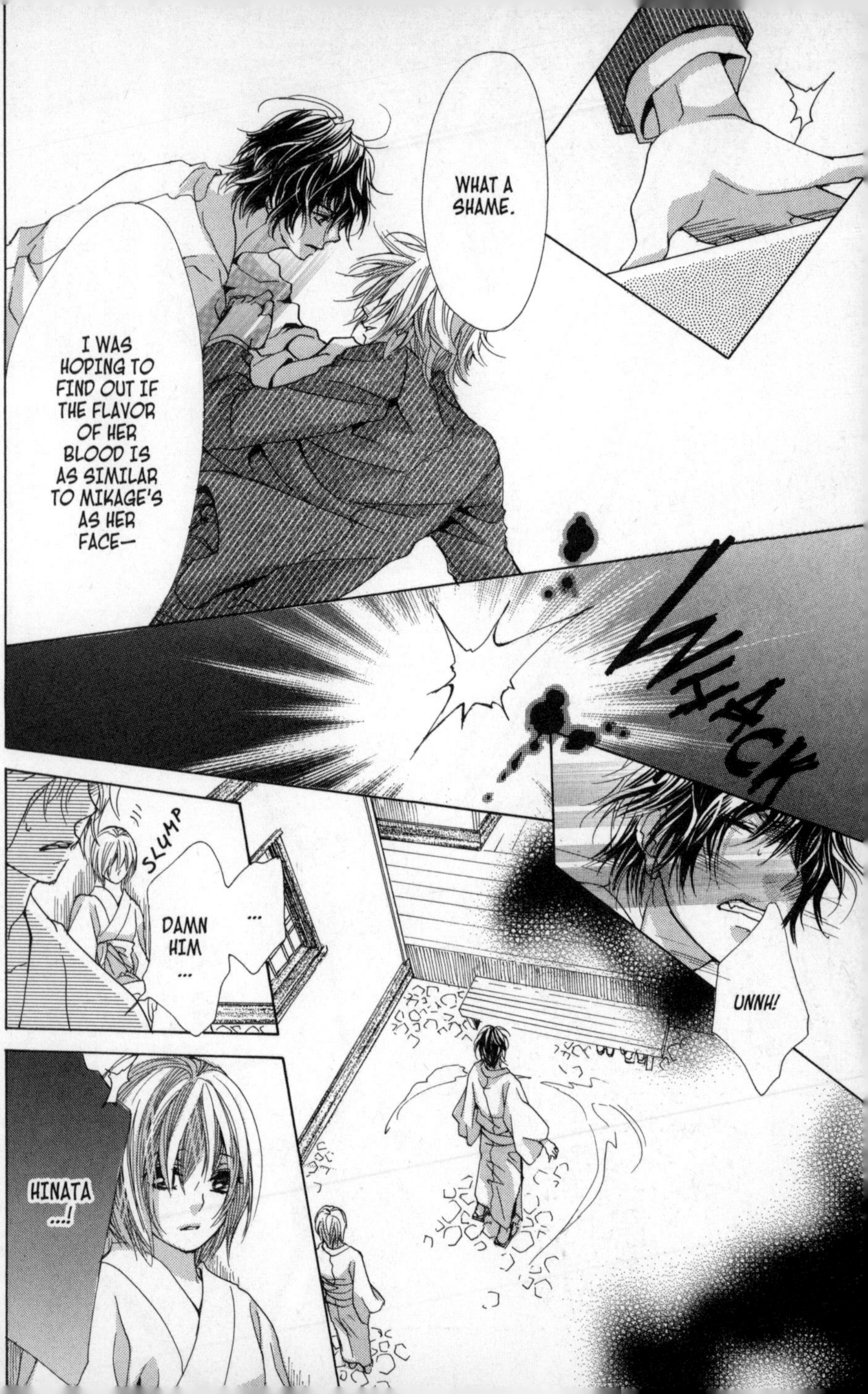
WHAT A SHAME.
I WAS HOPING TO FIND OUT IF THE FLAVOR OF HER BLOOD IS AS SIMILAR TO MIKAGE'S AS HER FACE—
WHACK
UNNH!
SLUMP
DAMN HIM ... ...
HINATA ...!

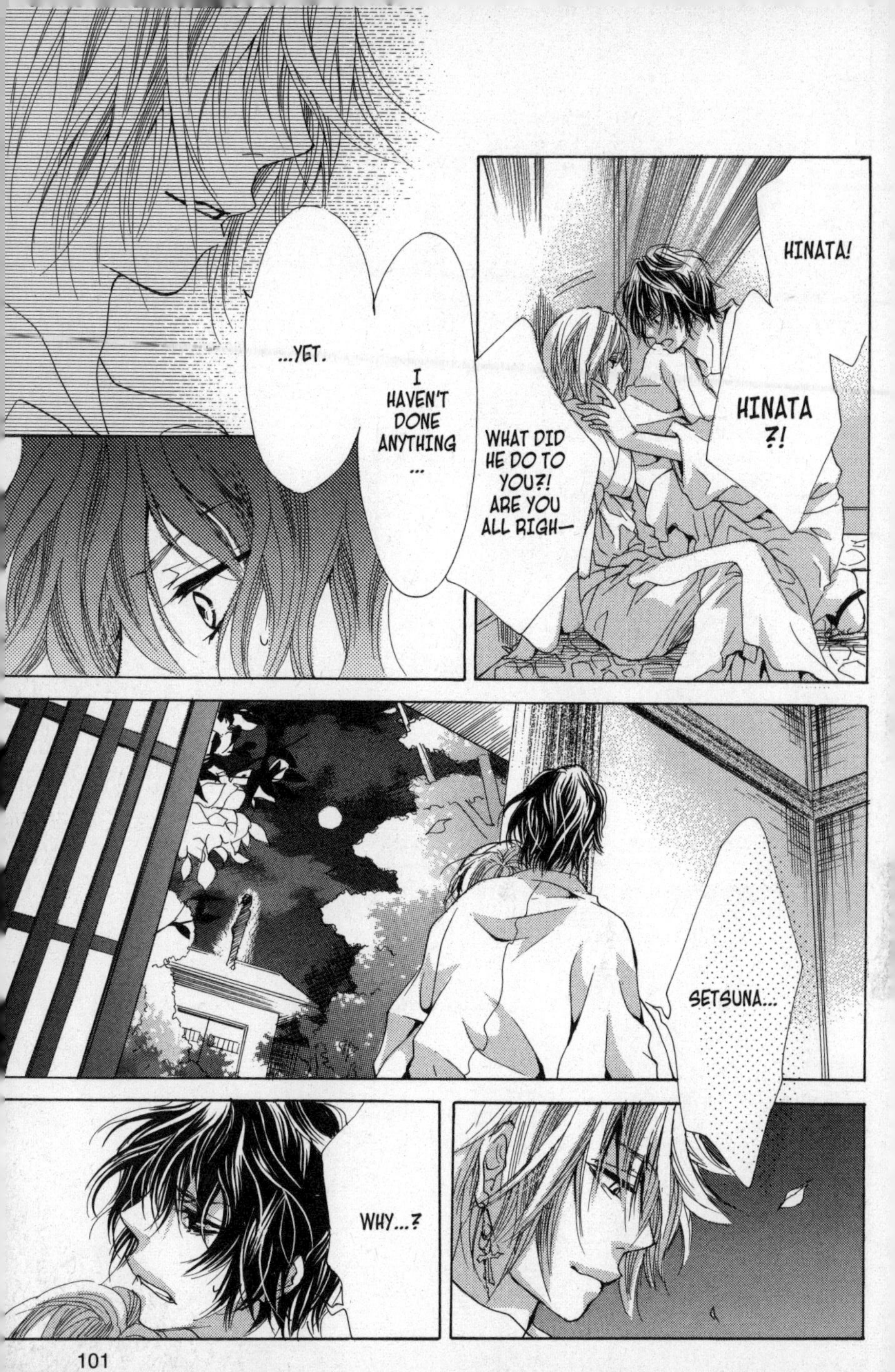
HINATA!
HINATA ?!
WHAT DID HE DO TO YOU?! ARE YOU ALL RIGH—
I HAVEN'T DONE ANYTHING ...
...YET.
SETSUNA...
WHY...?

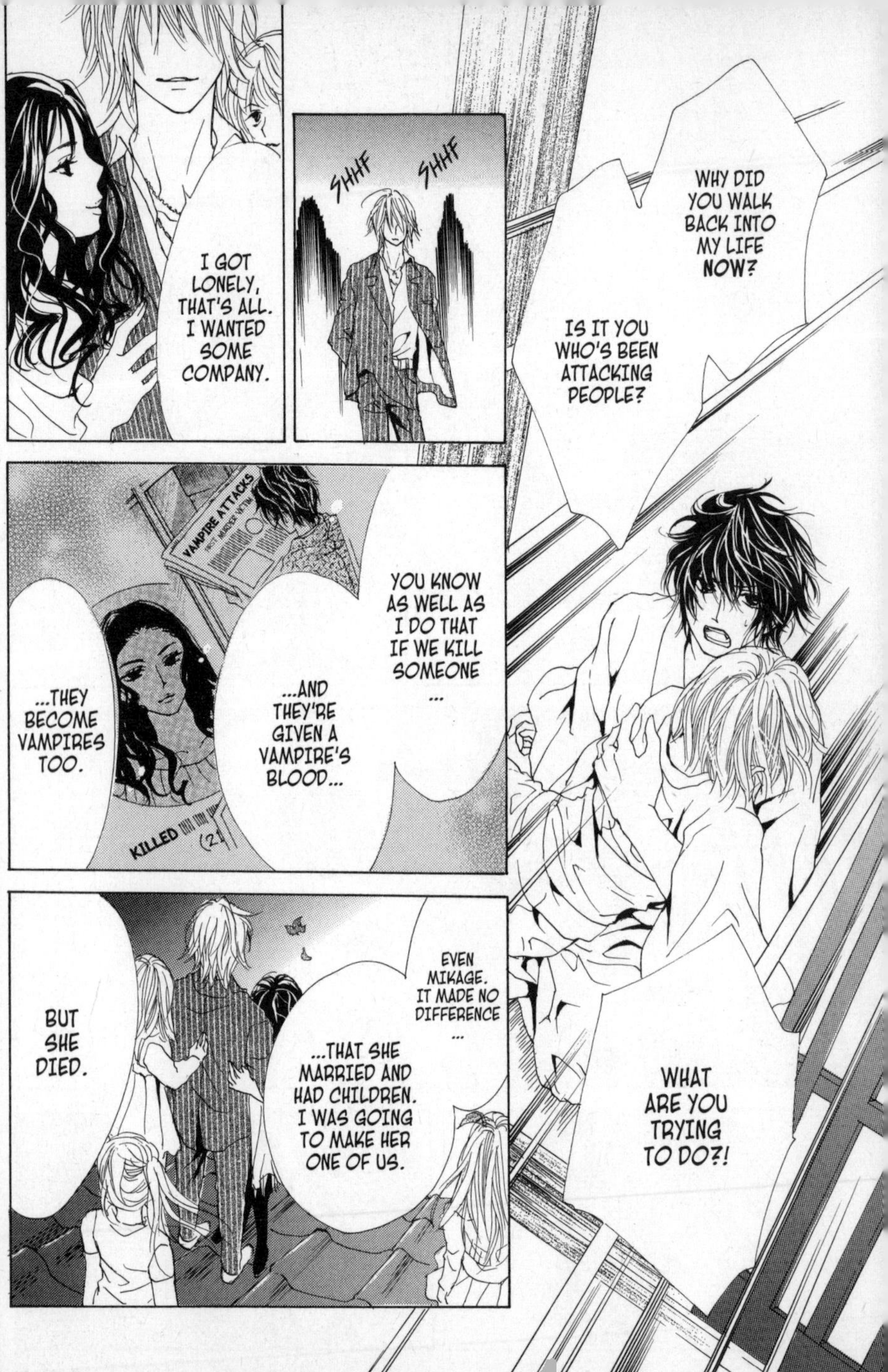
WHY DID YOU WALK BACK INTO MY LIFE NOW?
IS IT YOU WHO'S BEEN ATTACKING PEOPLE?
WHAT ARE YOU TRYING TO DO?!
SHHF
SHHF
I GOT LONELY, THAT'S ALL. I WANTED SOME COMPANY.
VAMPIRE ATTACKS
YOU KNOW AS WELL AS I DO THAT IF WE KILL SOMEONE ...
...AND THEY'RE GIVEN A VAMPIRE'S BLOOD...
...THEY BECOME VAMPIRES TOO.
KILLED
EVEN MIKAGE. IT MADE NO DIFFERENCE ...
...THAT SHE MARRIED AND HAD CHILDREN. I WAS GOING TO MAKE HER ONE OF US.
BUT SHE DIED.

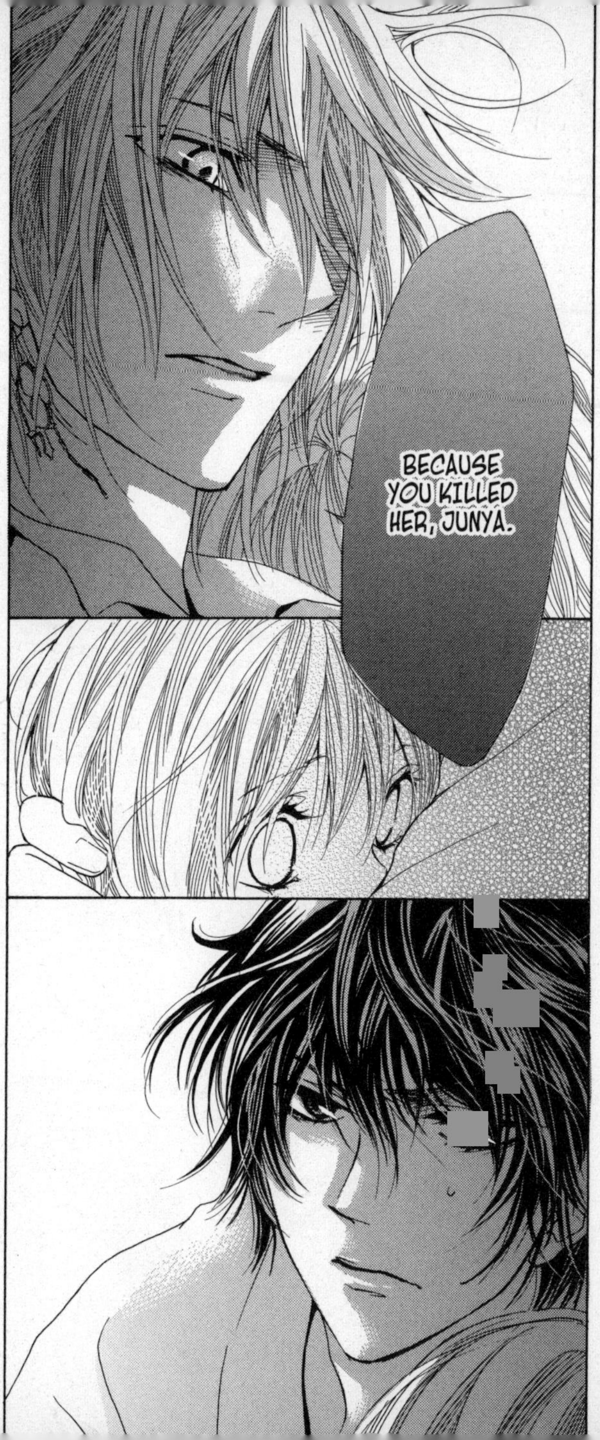
BECAUSE YOU KILLED HER, JUNYA.

Small Talk

3

Things I've Received Recently

RILAKKUMA MERCHANDISE!

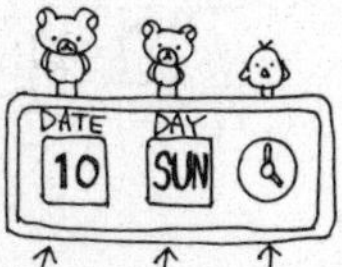
DATE
DAY
10
SUN

The date, day of the week and time are displayed on this calendar clock.

If you push the Rilakkuma figure on top, it adjusts the date or day of the week. It's pink and unbelievably adorable, and it's one of my favorite things. ♥

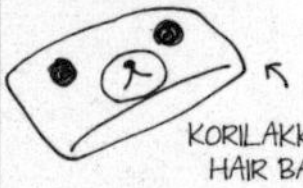

KORILAKKUMA HAIR BAND

If I wear this to pull my bangs back, I'm just like Korilakkuma!

I can't really do that when my assistants are around. But it's soooo cute! My love for Korilakkuma is getting ridiculous.

I've gotten a lot of other stuff too.

193-chan, thank you! ♥ ♥

Oops... This may not be an appropriate sidebar with such serious stuff happening right here in the manga!

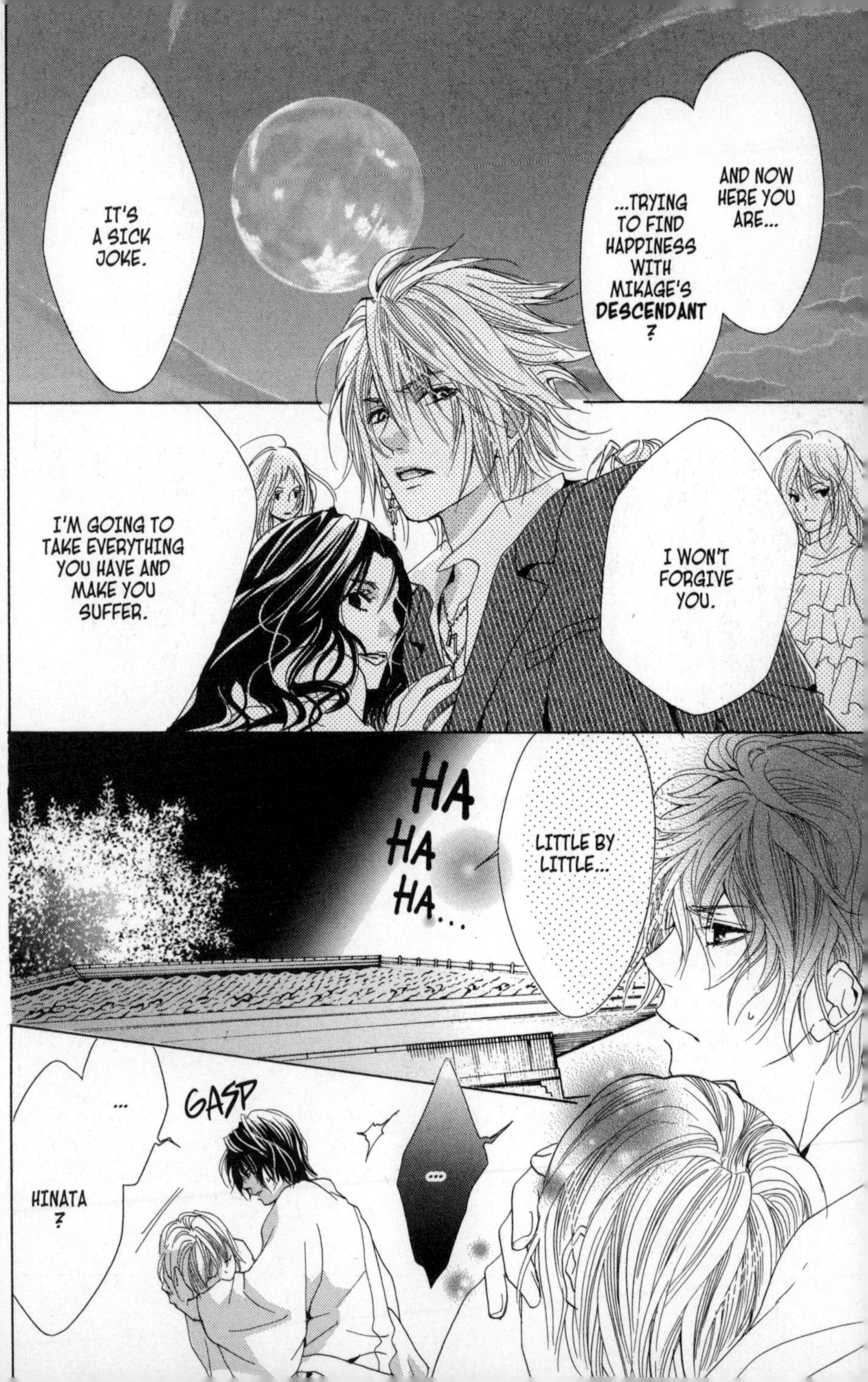
AND NOW HERE YOU ARE...
...TRYING TO FIND HAPPINESS WITH MIKAGE'S DESCENDANT?
IT'S A SICK JOKE.
I WON'T FORGIVE YOU.
I'M GOING TO TAKE EVERYTHING YOU HAVE AND MAKE YOU SUFFER.
LITTLE BY LITTLE...
HA HA HA...
...
GASP
...
HINATA?

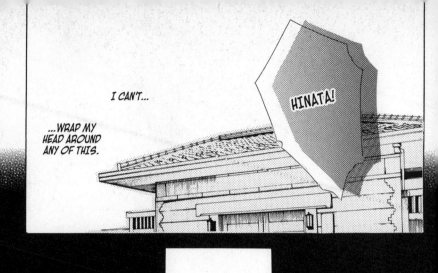

I CAN'T...

...WRAP MY HEAD AROUND ANY OF THIS.

HINATA!

"JUNYA'S NOT IN LOVE WITH *YOU* AT ALL."

PHEW...

HINATA...

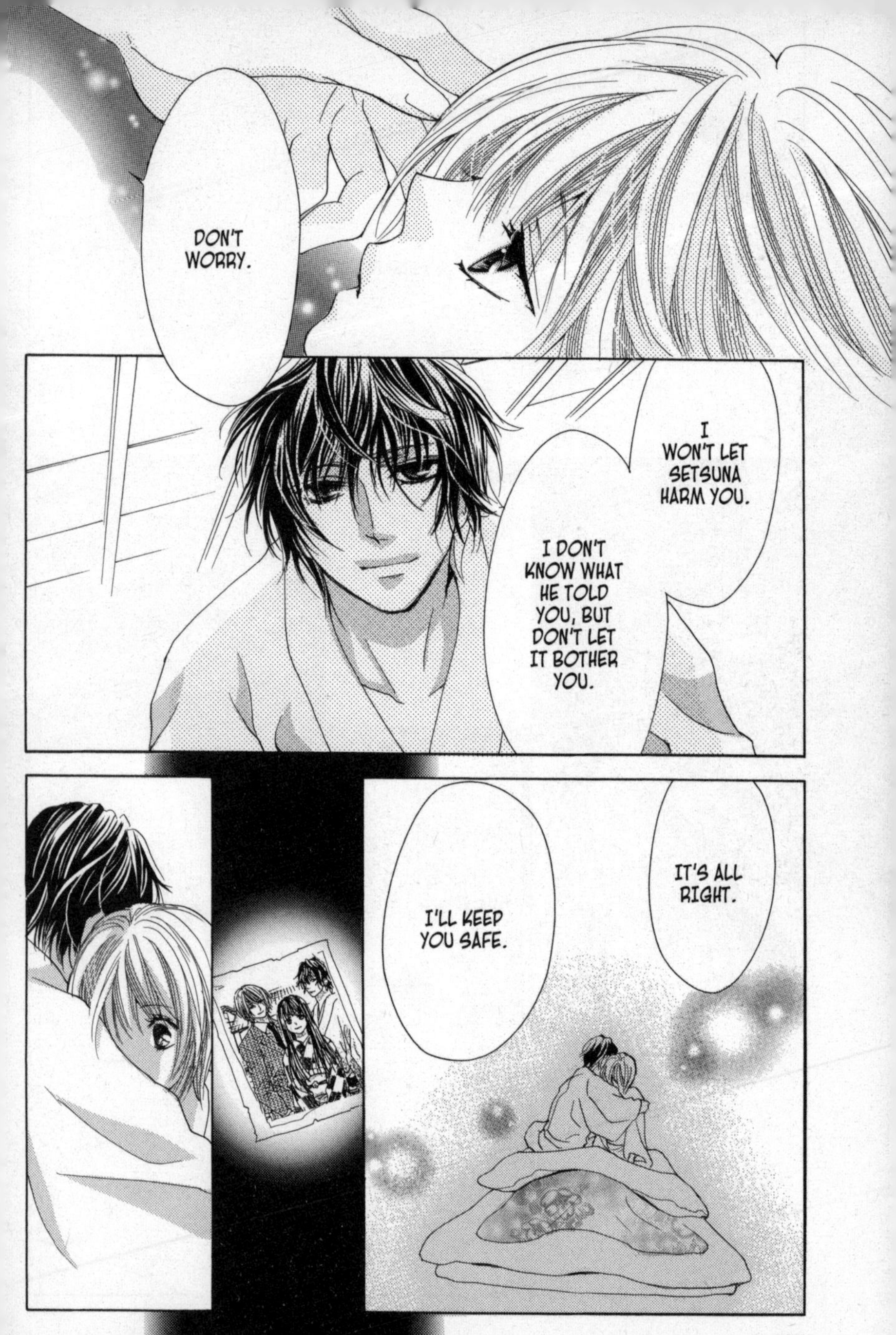
DON'T WORRY.
I WON'T LET SETSUNA HARM YOU.
I DON'T KNOW WHAT HE TOLD YOU, BUT DON'T LET IT BOTHER YOU.
IT'S ALL RIGHT.
I'LL KEEP YOU SAFE.

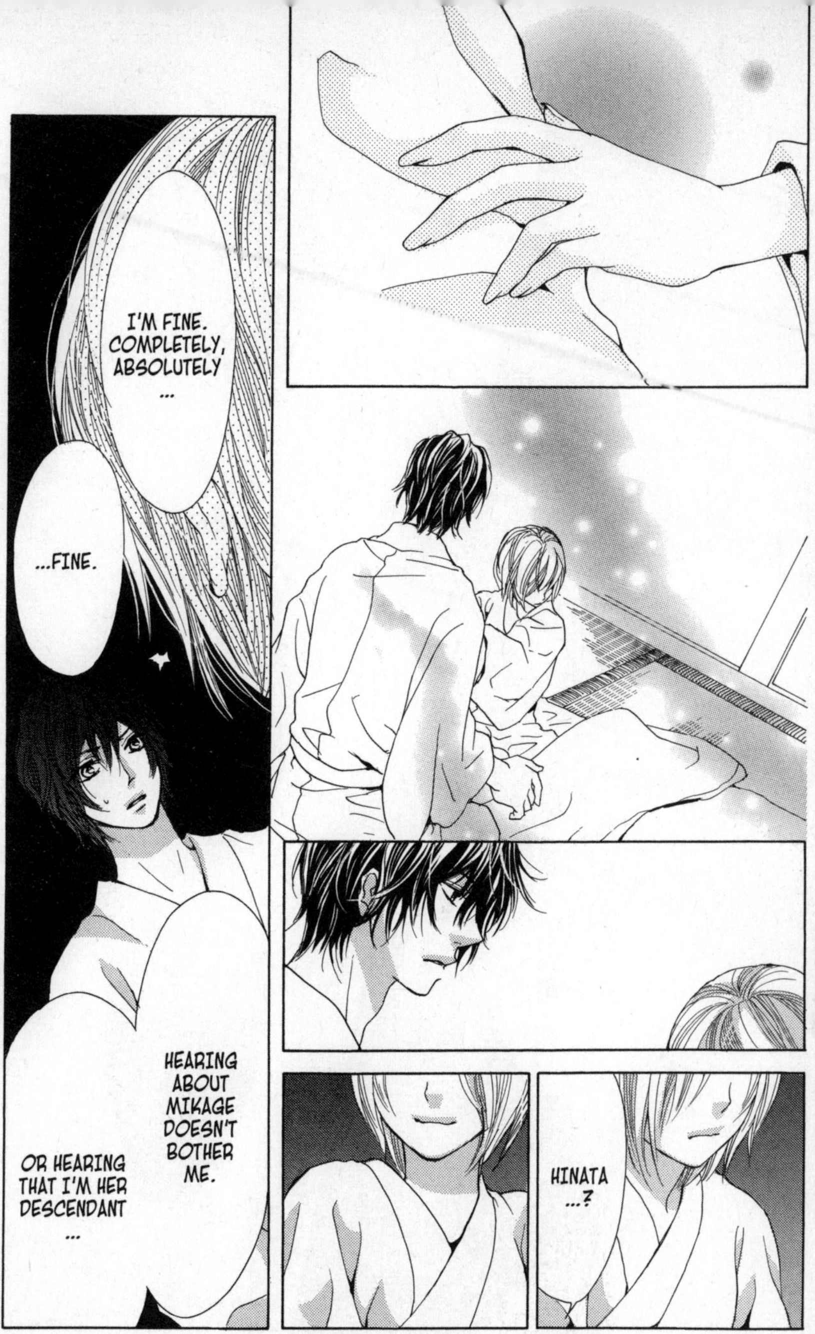
HINATA ...?
I'M FINE. COMPLETELY, ABSOLUTELY ...
...FINE.
HEARING ABOUT MIKAGE DOESN'T BOTHER ME.
OR HEARING THAT I'M HER DESCENDANT ...

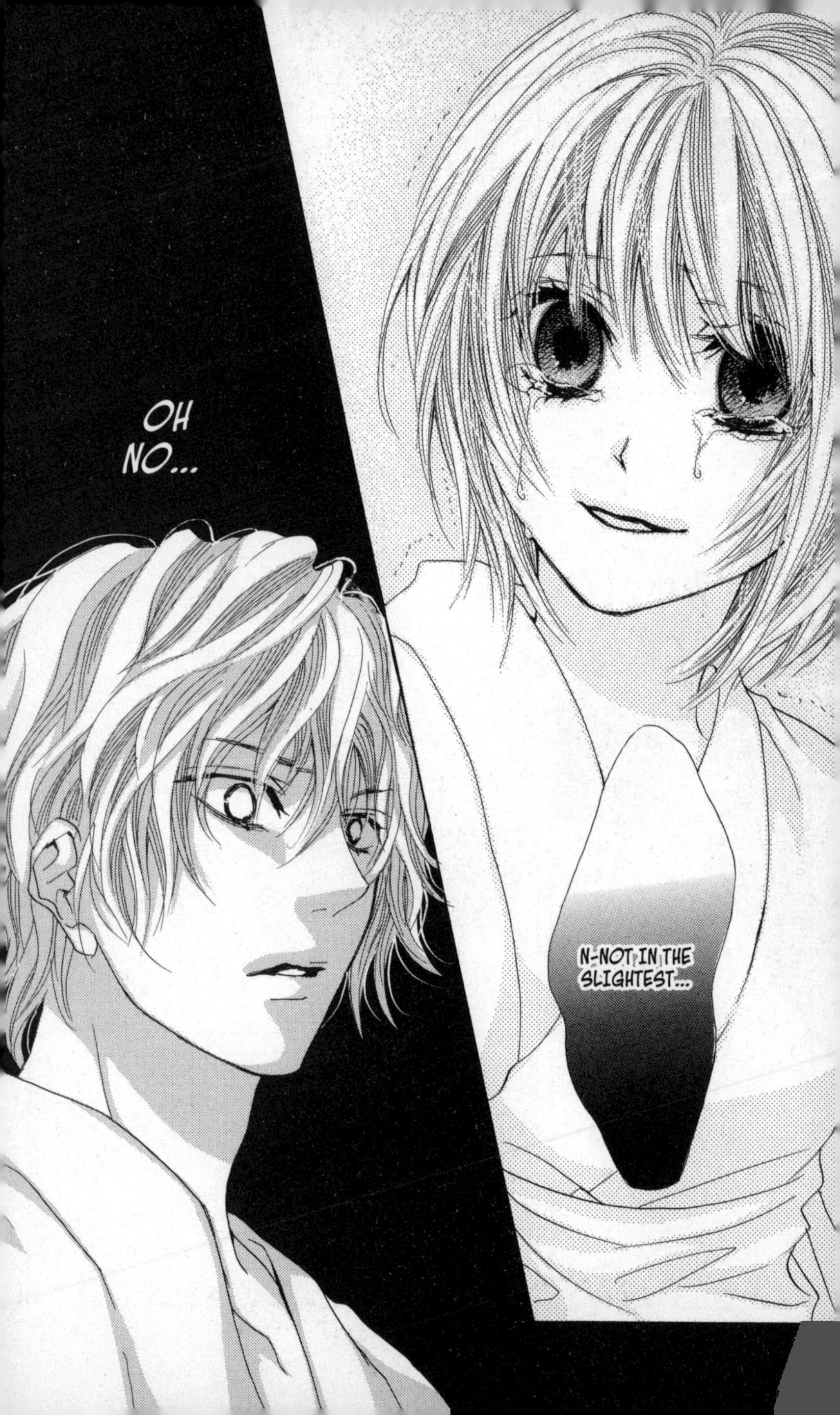
N-NOT IN THE SLIGHTEST...
OH NO...

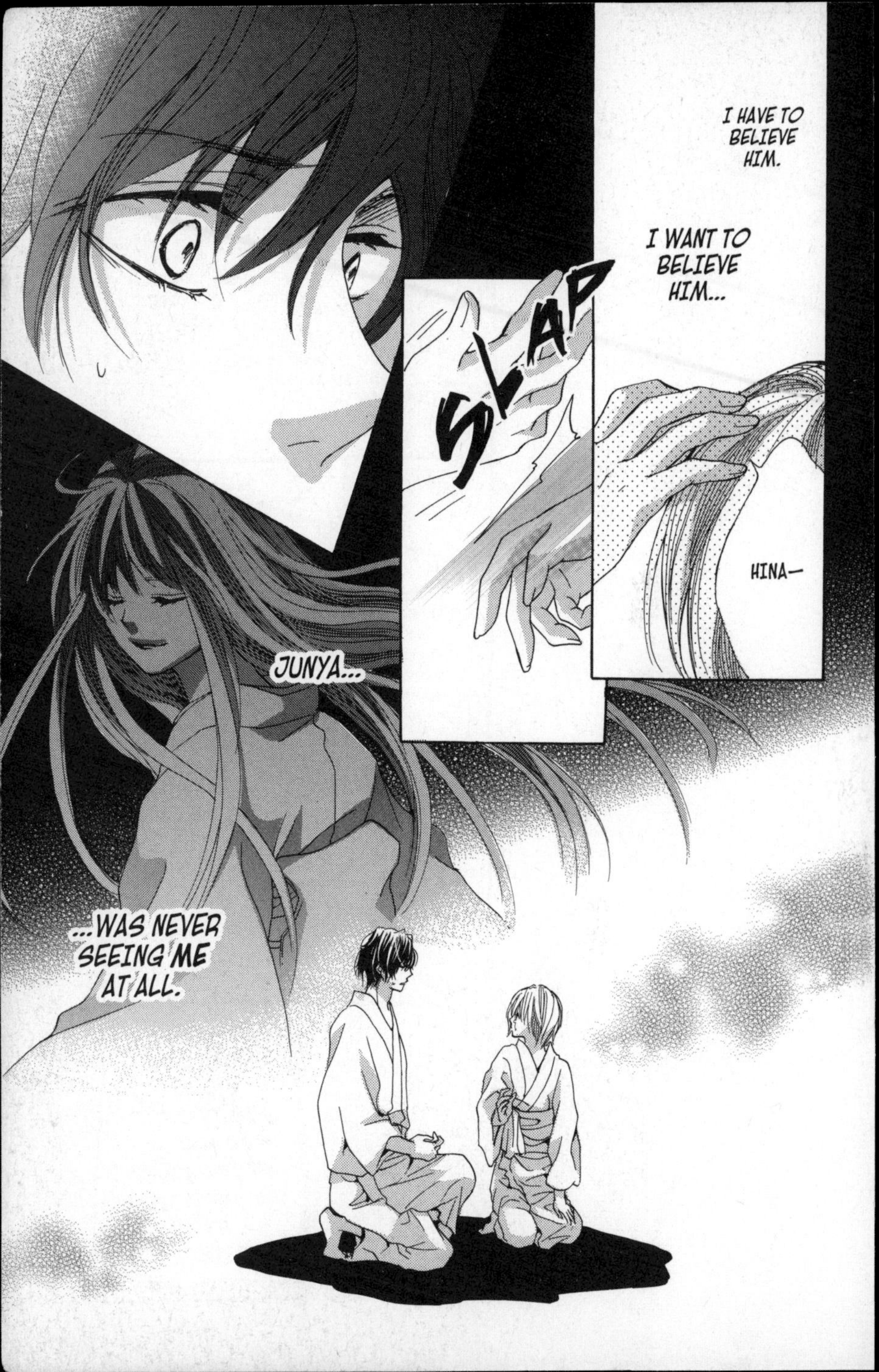

I HAVE TO BELIEVE HIM.
I WANT TO BELIEVE HIM...
HINA—
SLAP
JUNYA...
...WAS NEVER SEEING ME AT ALL.

I Moved

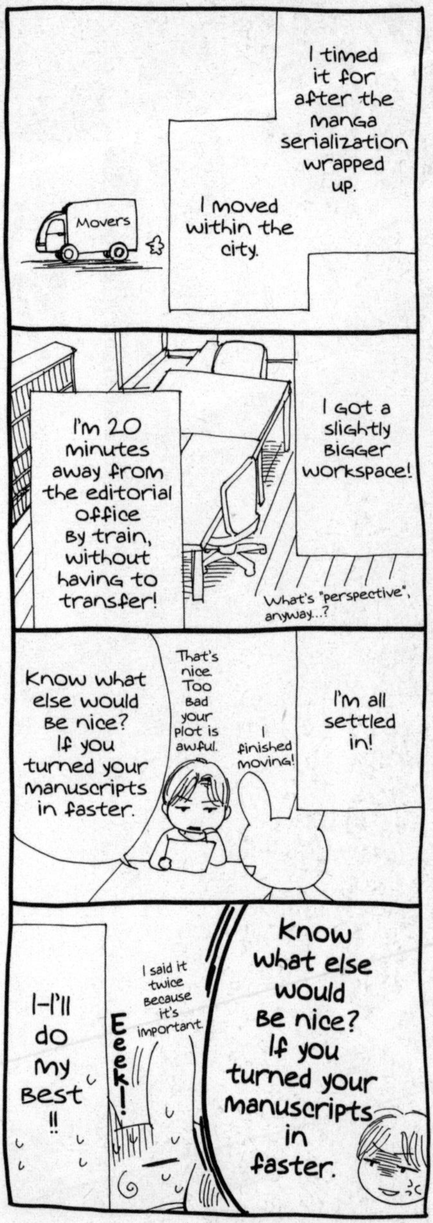
I timed it for after the manga serialization wrapped up.
I moved within the city.
Movers
I got a slightly bigger workspace!
I'm 20 minutes away from the editorial office by train, without having to transfer!
What's "perspective", anyway...?
I'm all settled in!
I finished moving!
That's nice. Too bad your plot is awful.
Know what else would be nice? If you turned your manuscripts in faster.
Know what else would be nice? If you turned your manuscripts in faster.
I said it twice because it's important.
Eeek!
I-I'll do my best!!

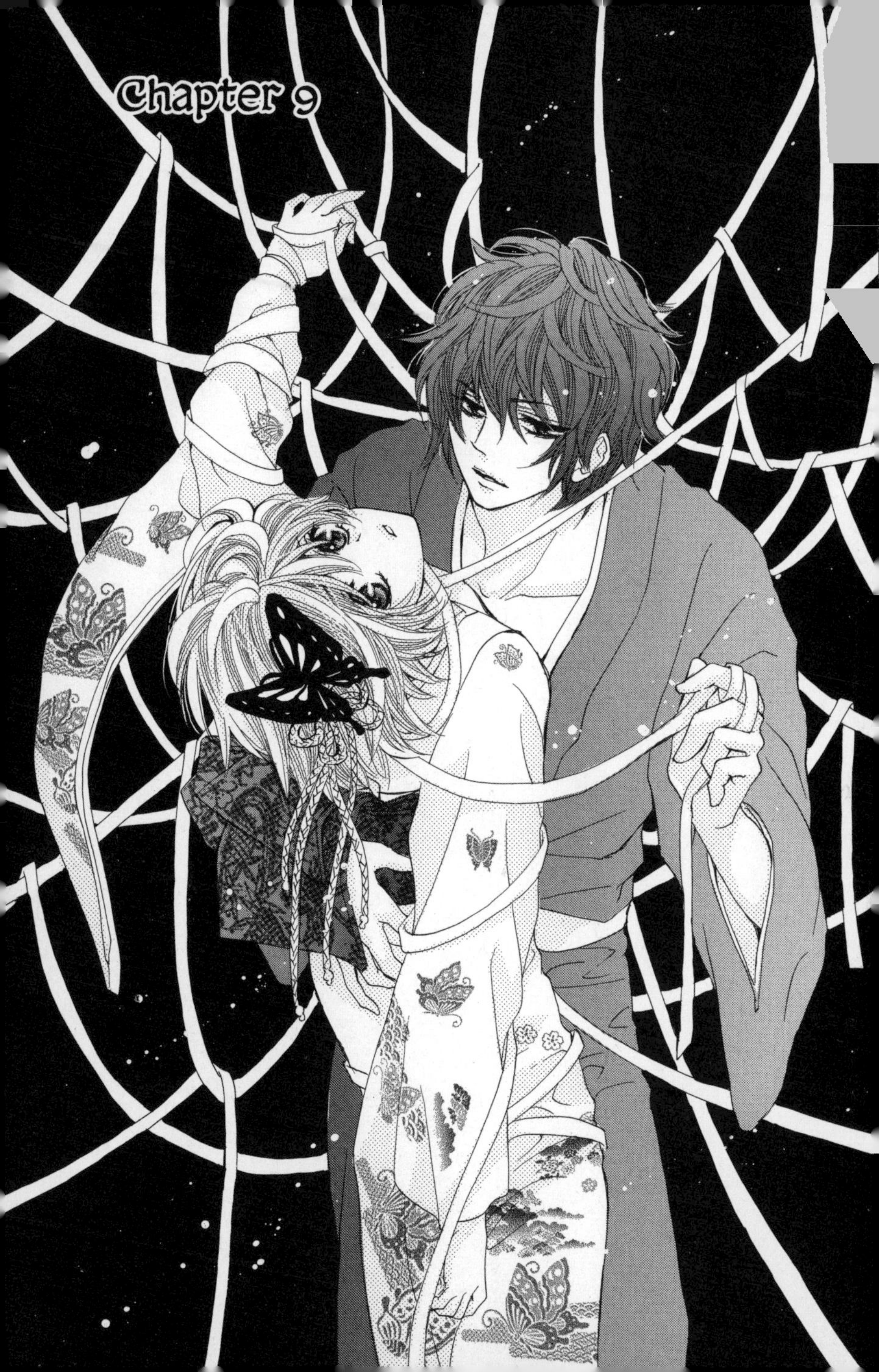
Chapter 9

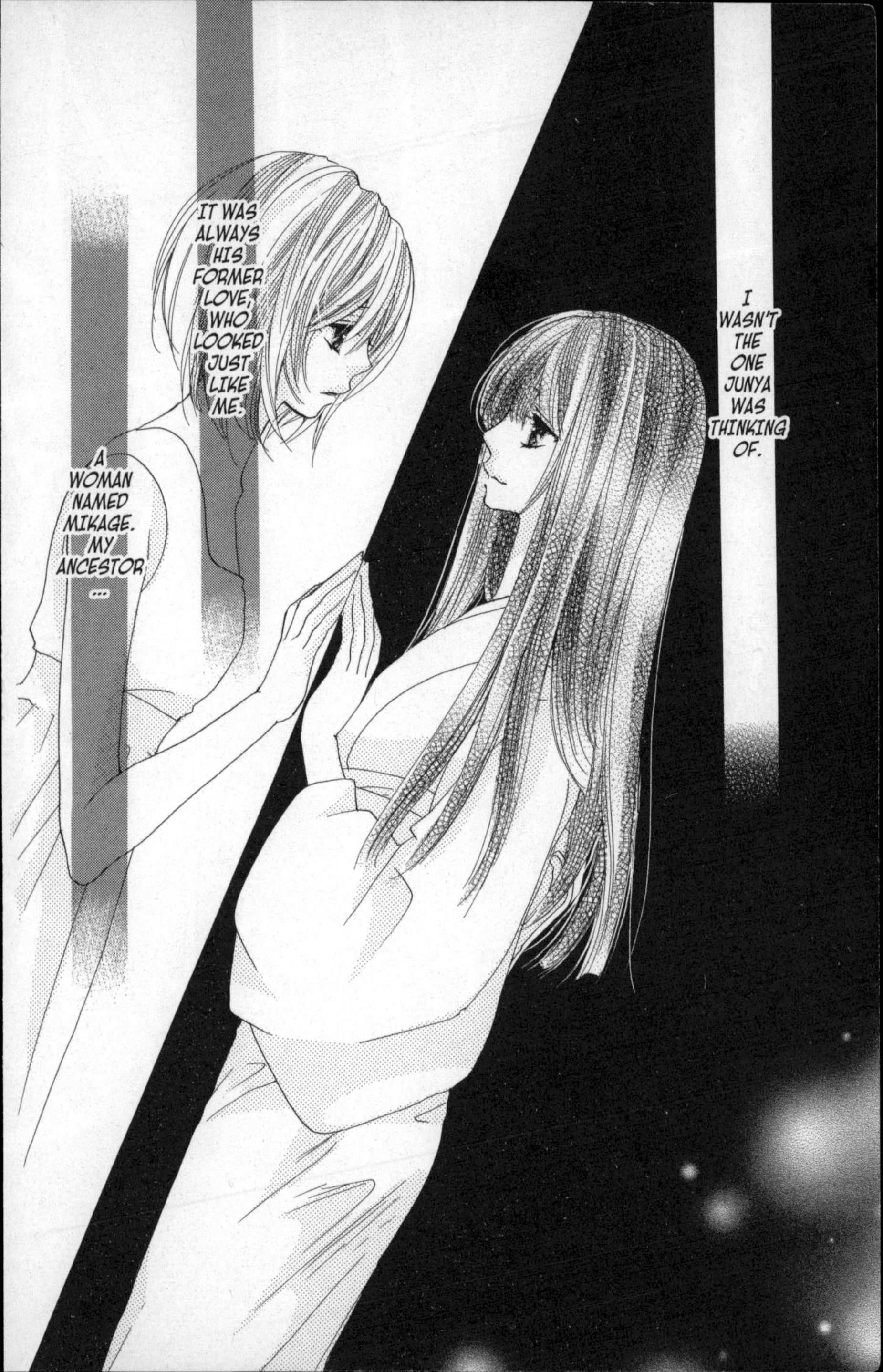
I WASN'T THE ONE JUNYA WAS THINKING OF.
IT WAS ALWAYS HIS FORMER LOVE, WHO LOOKED JUST LIKE ME.
A WOMAN NAMED MIKAGE. MY ANCESTOR...

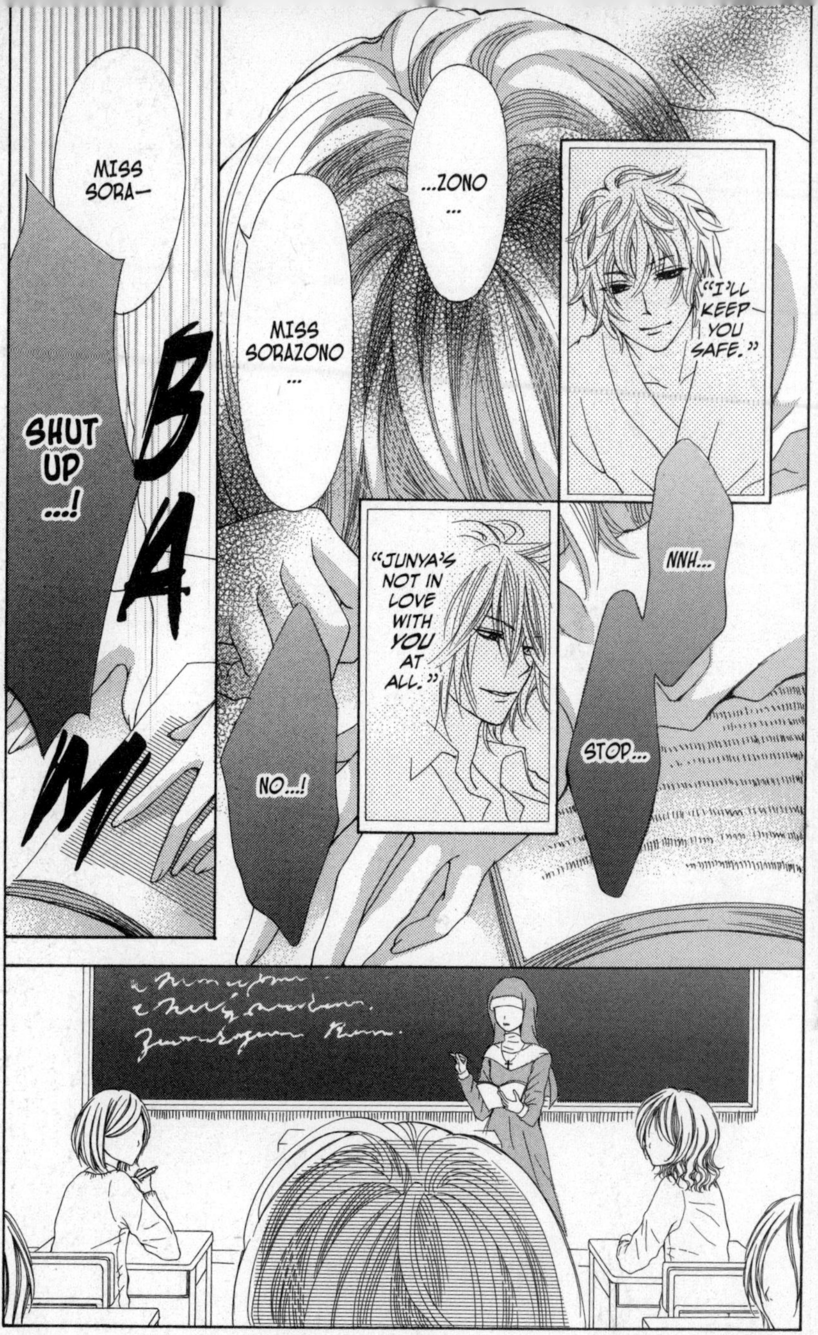
"I'LL KEEP YOU SAFE."
NNH...
STOP...
"JUNYA'S NOT IN LOVE WITH YOU AT ALL."
NO...!
...ZONO ...
MISS SORAZONO ...
MISS SORA—
SHUT UP ...!
BAM

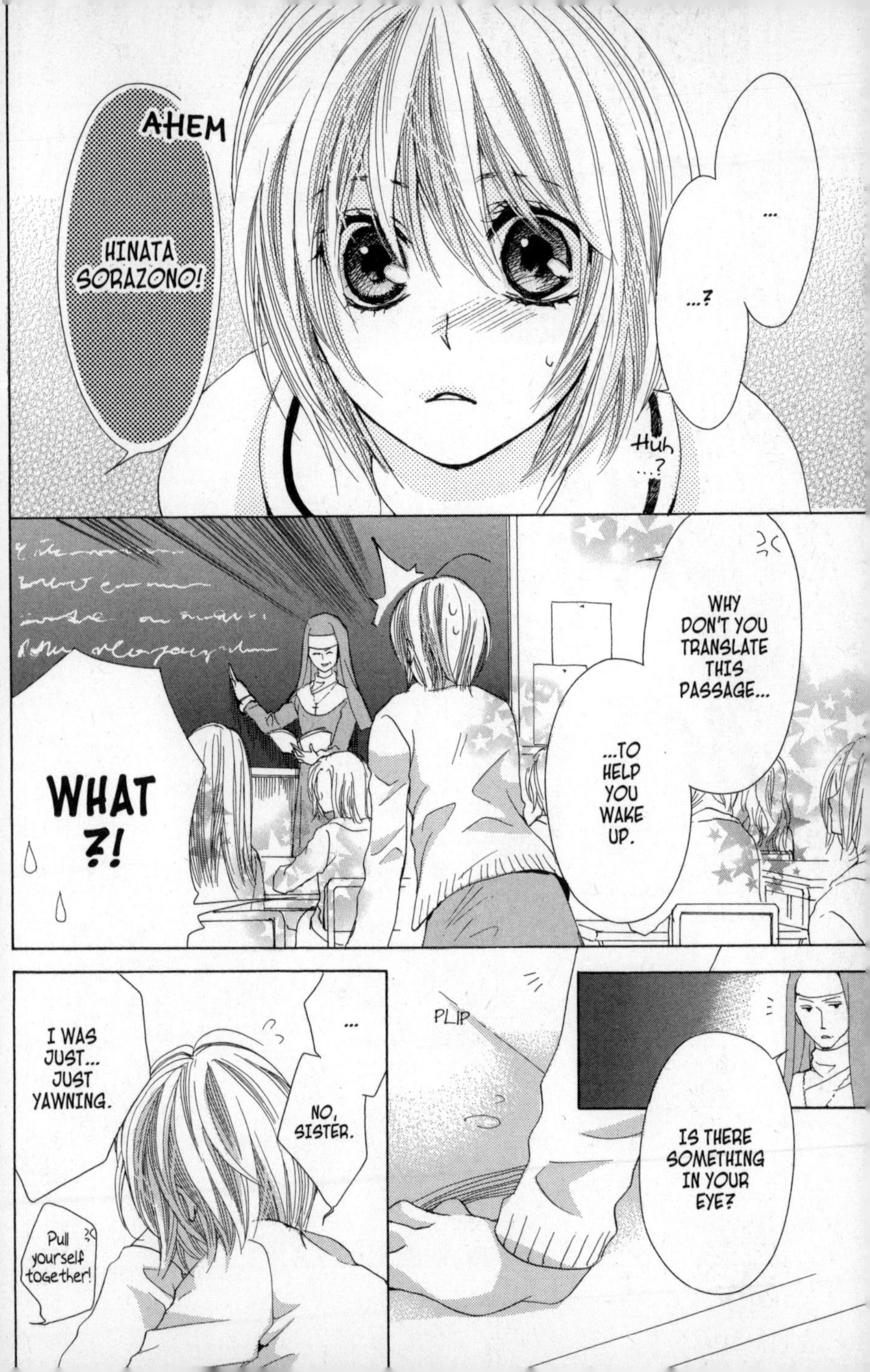
...
...?
Huh ...?
AHEM
HINATA SORAZONO!
WHY DON'T YOU TRANSLATE THIS PASSAGE...
...TO HELP YOU WAKE UP.
WHAT ?!
IS THERE SOMETHING IN YOUR EYE?
PLIP
...
NO, SISTER.
I WAS JUST... JUST YAWNING.
Pull yourself together!

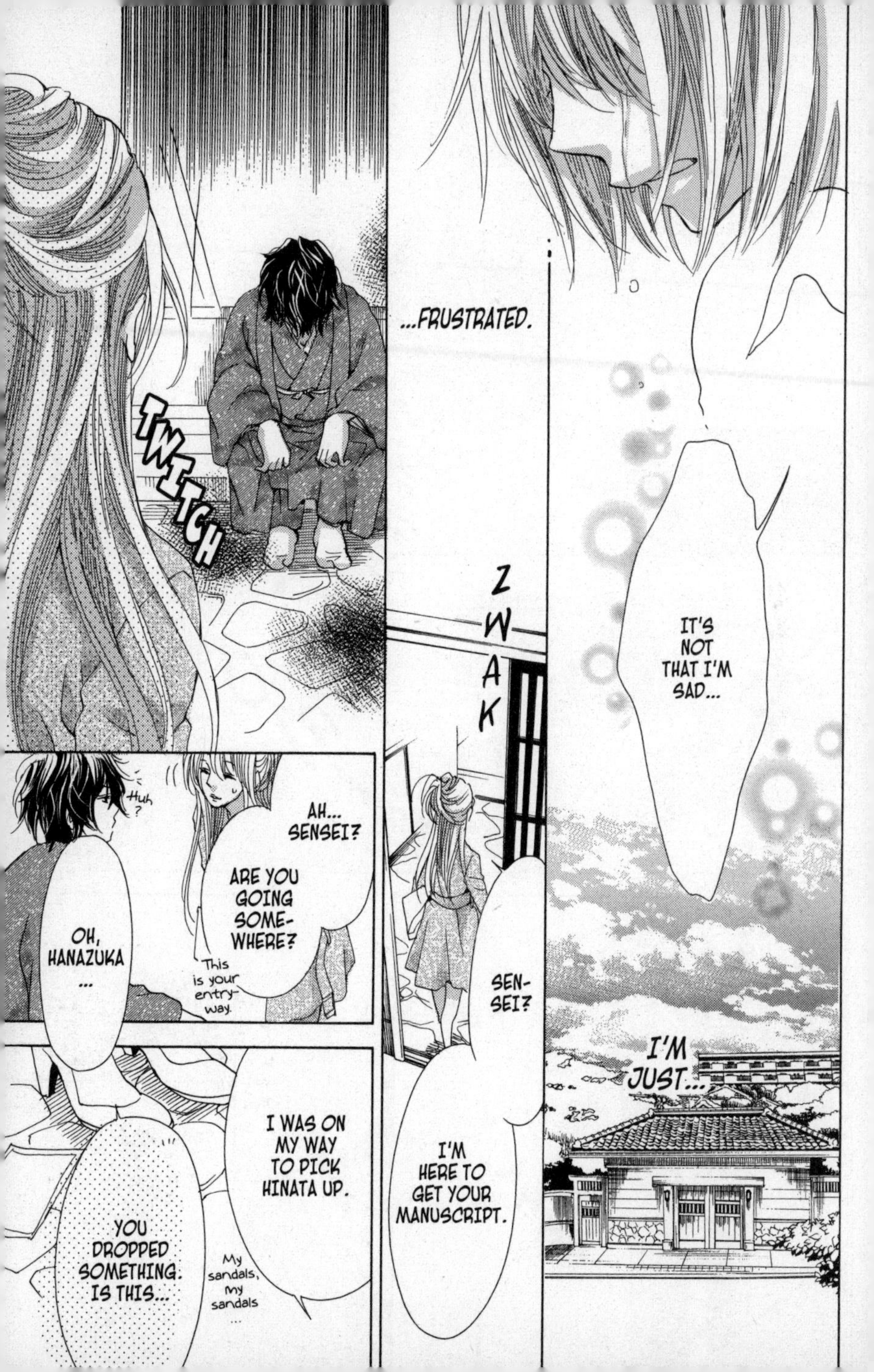
IT'S NOT THAT I'M SAD...
I'M JUST...
...FRUSTRATED.
ZWAK
SEN-SEI?
I'M HERE TO GET YOUR MANUSCRIPT.
TWITCH
AH... SENSEI?
ARE YOU GOING SOME-WHERE?
This is your entry-way.
Huh?
OH, HANAZUKA...
I WAS ON MY WAY TO PICK HINATA UP.
My sandals, my sandals...
YOU DROPPED SOMETHING. IS THIS...

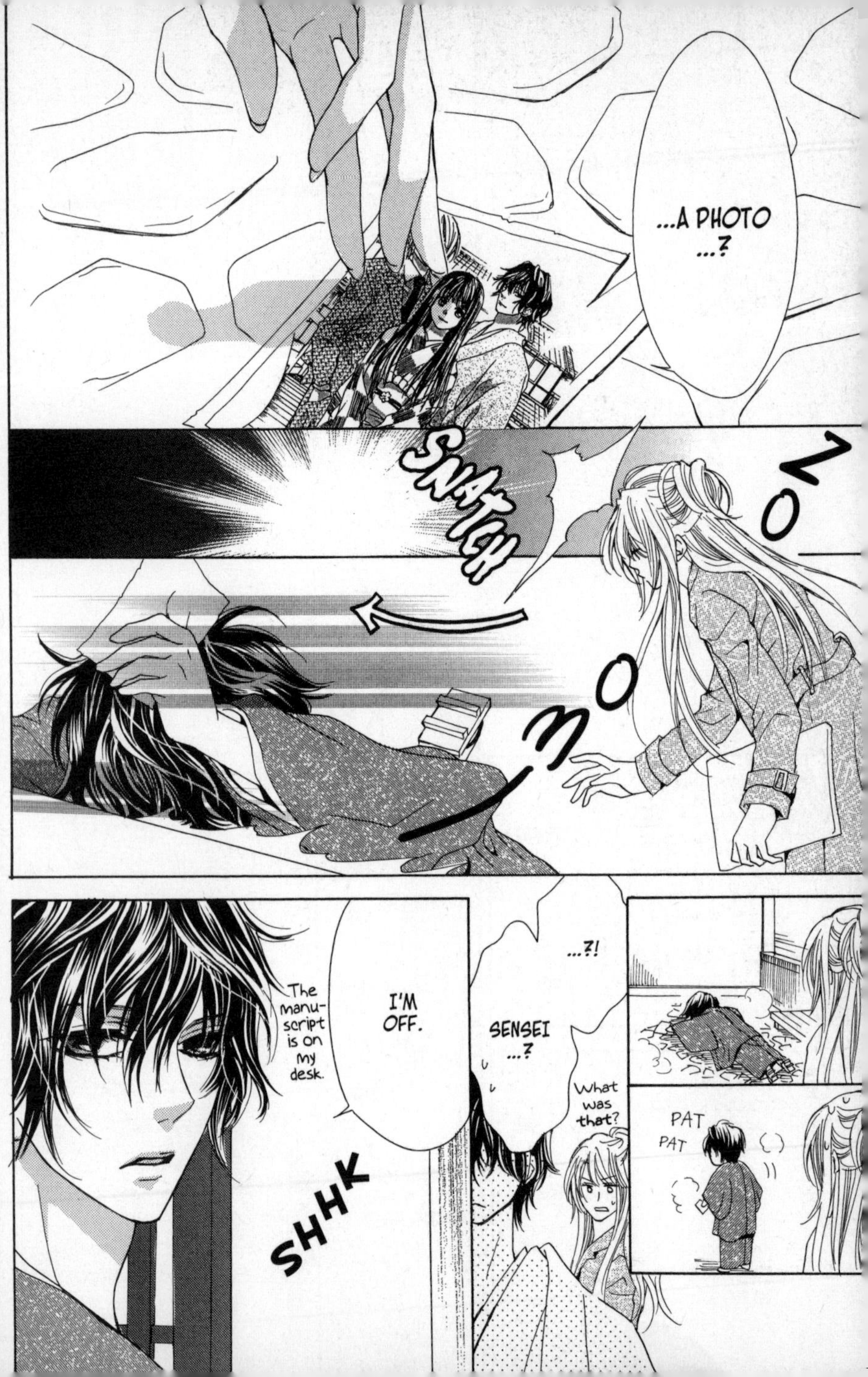
...A PHOTO ...?
SNATCH
ZOOM
PAT PAT
...?!
SENSEI ...?
What was that?
I'M OFF.
The manu-script is on my desk.
SHHK

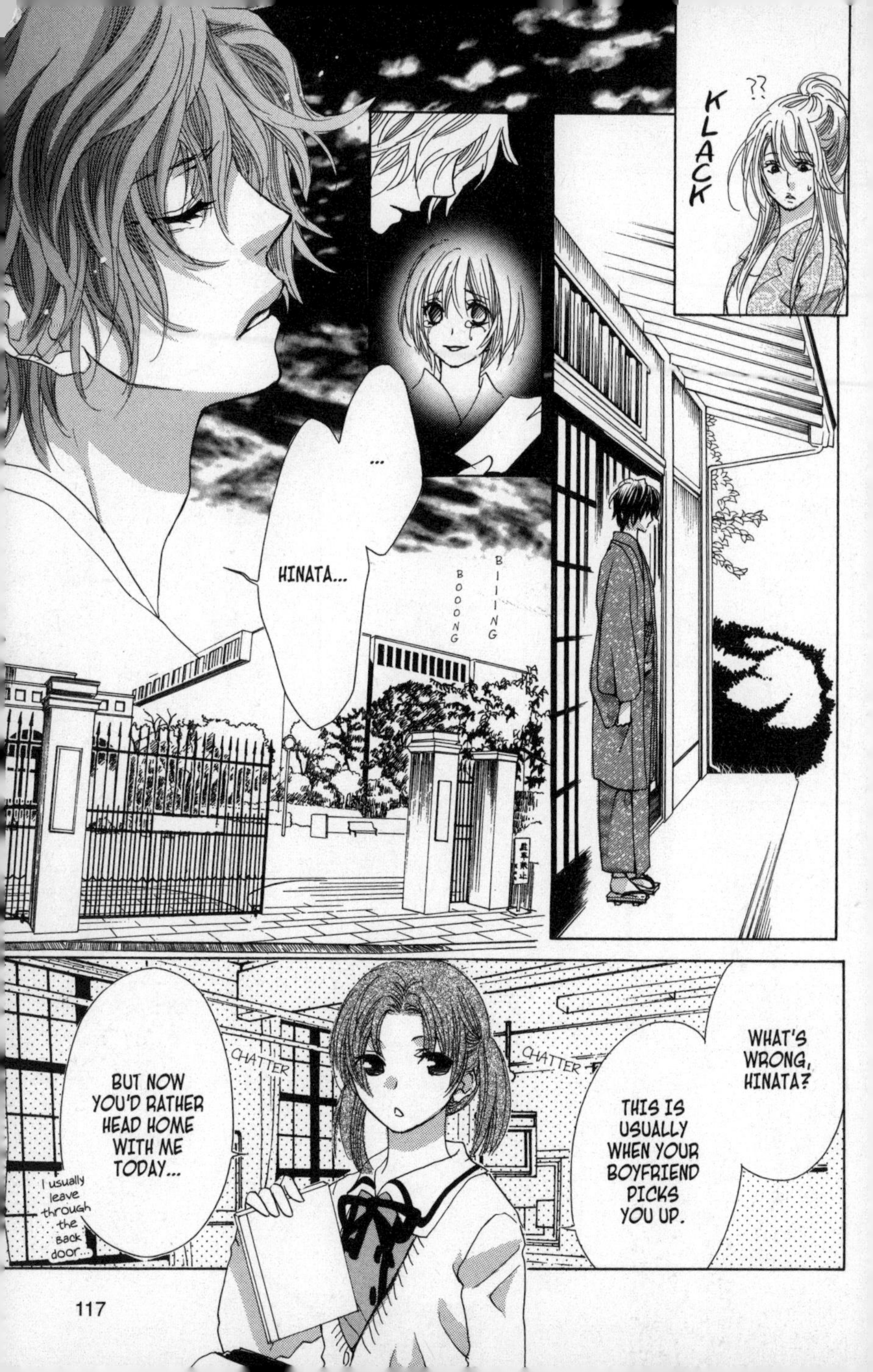
KLACK
??
...
HINATA...
BIIING
BOOONG
WHAT'S WRONG, HINATA?
THIS IS USUALLY WHEN YOUR BOYFRIEND PICKS YOU UP.
CHATTER
CHATTER
BUT NOW YOU'D RATHER HEAD HOME WITH ME TODAY...
I usually leave through the back door...

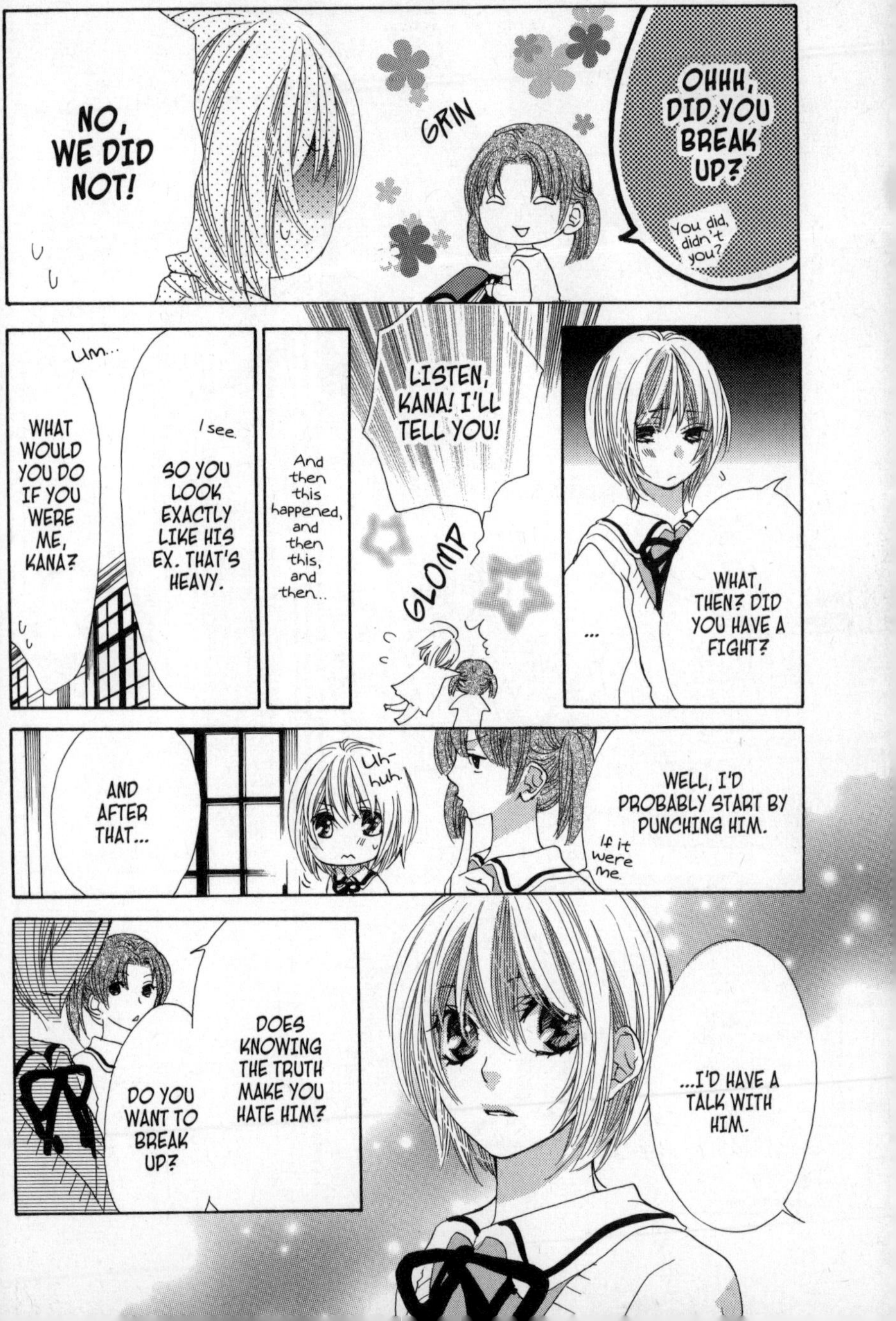
OHHH, DID YOU BREAK UP?
You did, didn't you?
GRIN
NO, WE DID NOT!
WHAT, THEN? DID YOU HAVE A FIGHT?
...
LISTEN, KANA! I'LL TELL YOU!
GLOMP
And then this happened, and then this, and then..
I see.
SO YOU LOOK EXACTLY LIKE HIS EX. THAT'S HEAVY.
Um...
WHAT WOULD YOU DO IF YOU WERE ME, KANA?
WELL, I'D PROBABLY START BY PUNCHING HIM.
If it were me.
Uh-huh.
AND AFTER THAT...
...I'D HAVE A TALK WITH HIM.
DOES KNOWING THE TRUTH MAKE YOU HATE HIM?
DO YOU WANT TO BREAK UP?

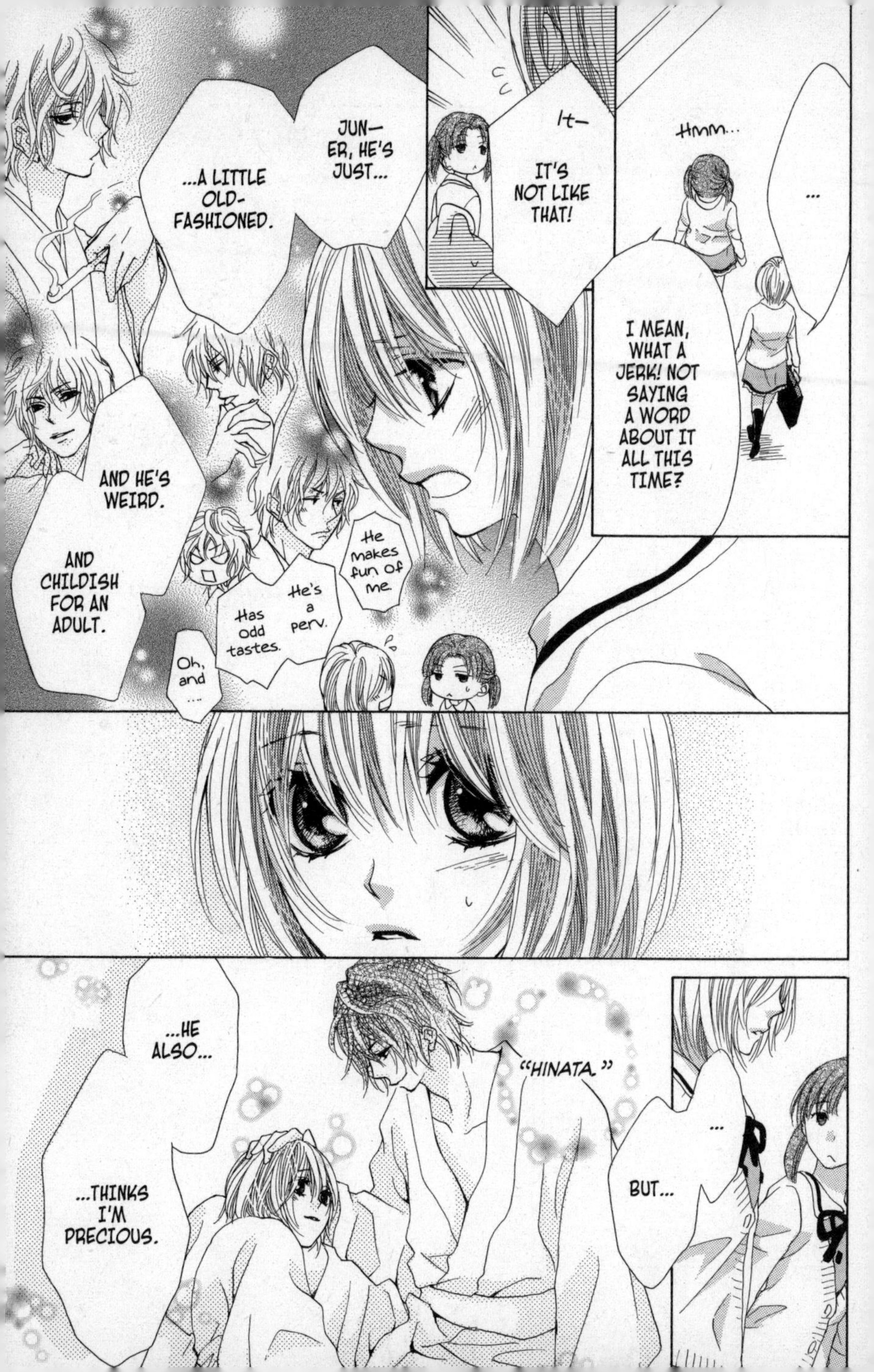
Hmm...
...
I MEAN, WHAT A JERK! NOT SAYING A WORD ABOUT IT ALL THIS TIME?
It—
IT'S NOT LIKE THAT!
JUN—ER, HE'S JUST...
...A LITTLE OLD-FASHIONED.
AND HE'S WEIRD.
AND CHILDISH FOR AN ADULT.
He makes fun of me.
He's a perv.
Has odd tastes.
Oh, and ...
...
BUT...
"HINATA."
...HE ALSO...
...THINKS I'M PRECIOUS.

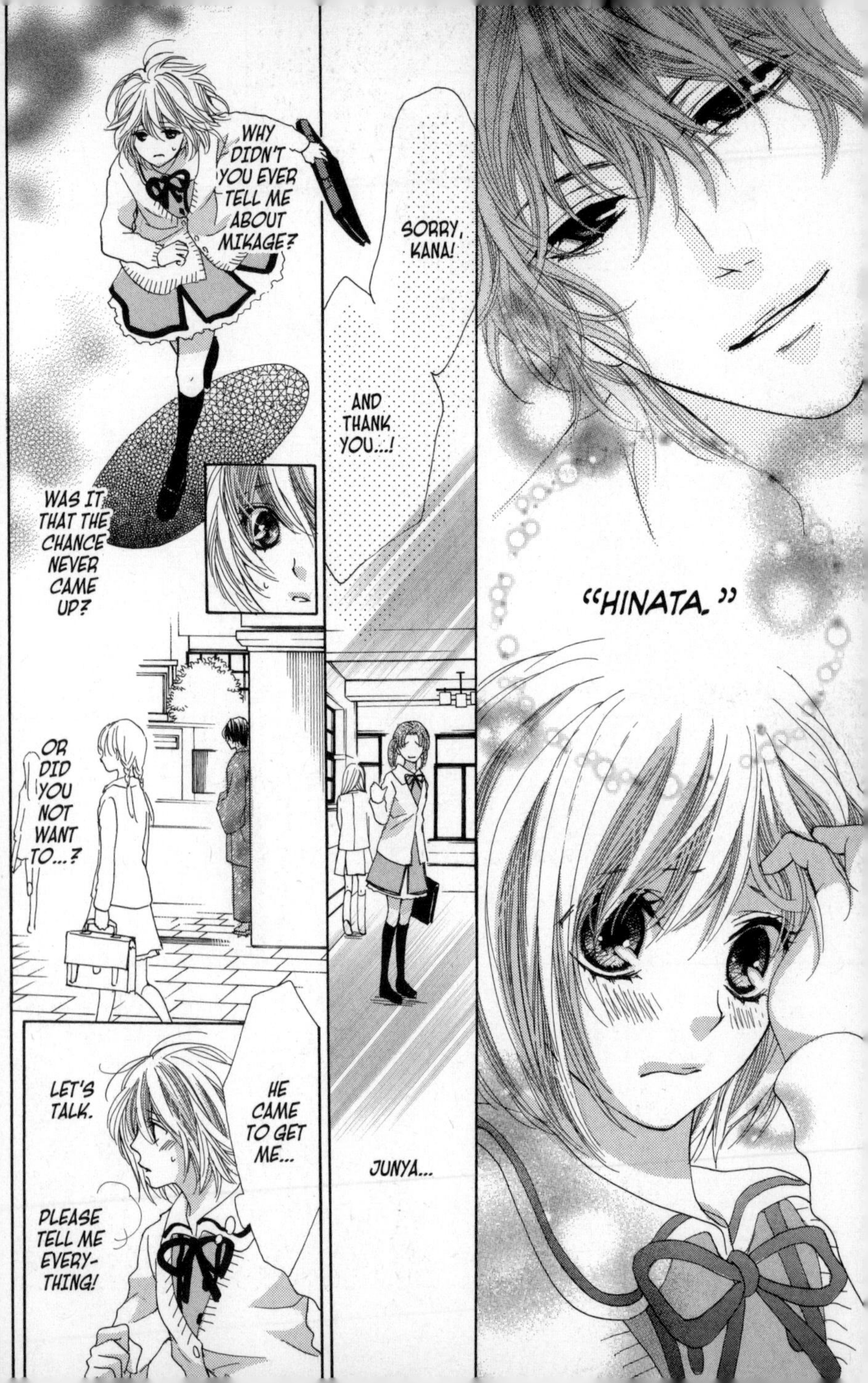
"HINATA."
SORRY, KANA!
AND THANK YOU...!
WHY DIDN'T YOU EVER TELL ME ABOUT MIKAGE?
WAS IT THAT THE CHANCE NEVER CAME UP?
OR DID YOU NOT WANT TO...?
JUNYA...
HE CAME TO GET ME...
LET'S TALK.
PLEASE TELL ME EVERY-THING!

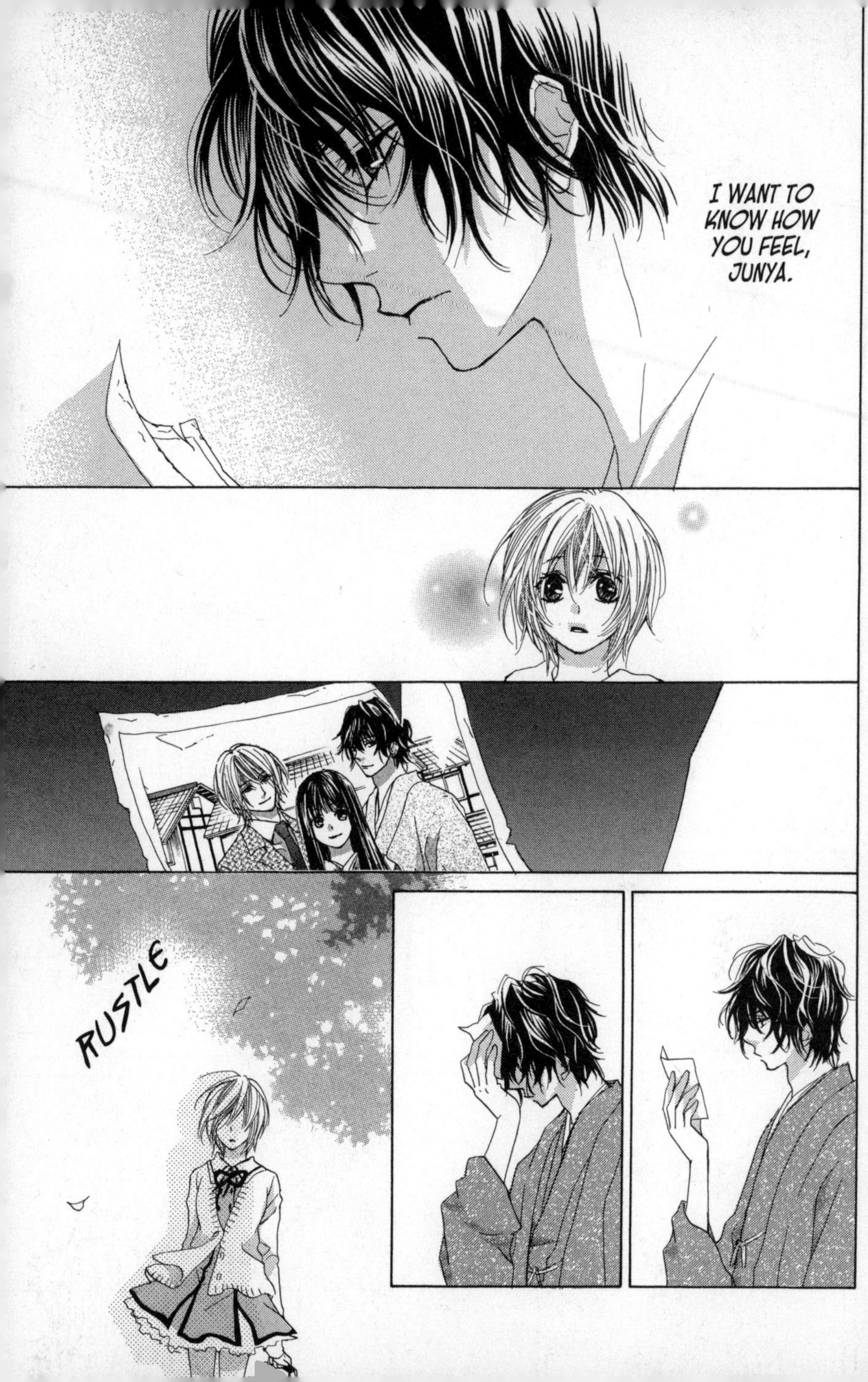
I WANT TO KNOW HOW YOU FEEL, JUNYA.
RUSTLE

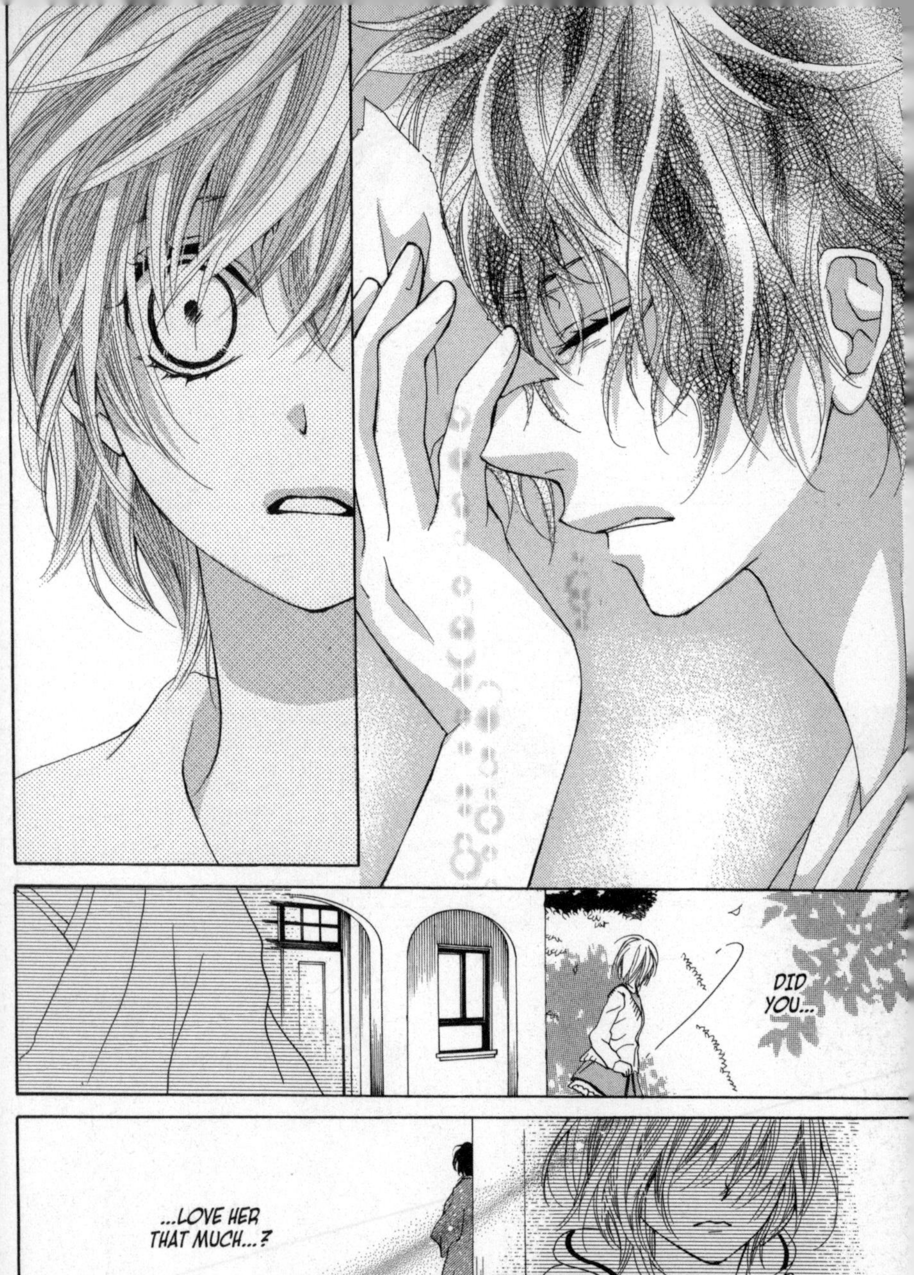
DID YOU...
...LOVE HER THAT MUCH...?

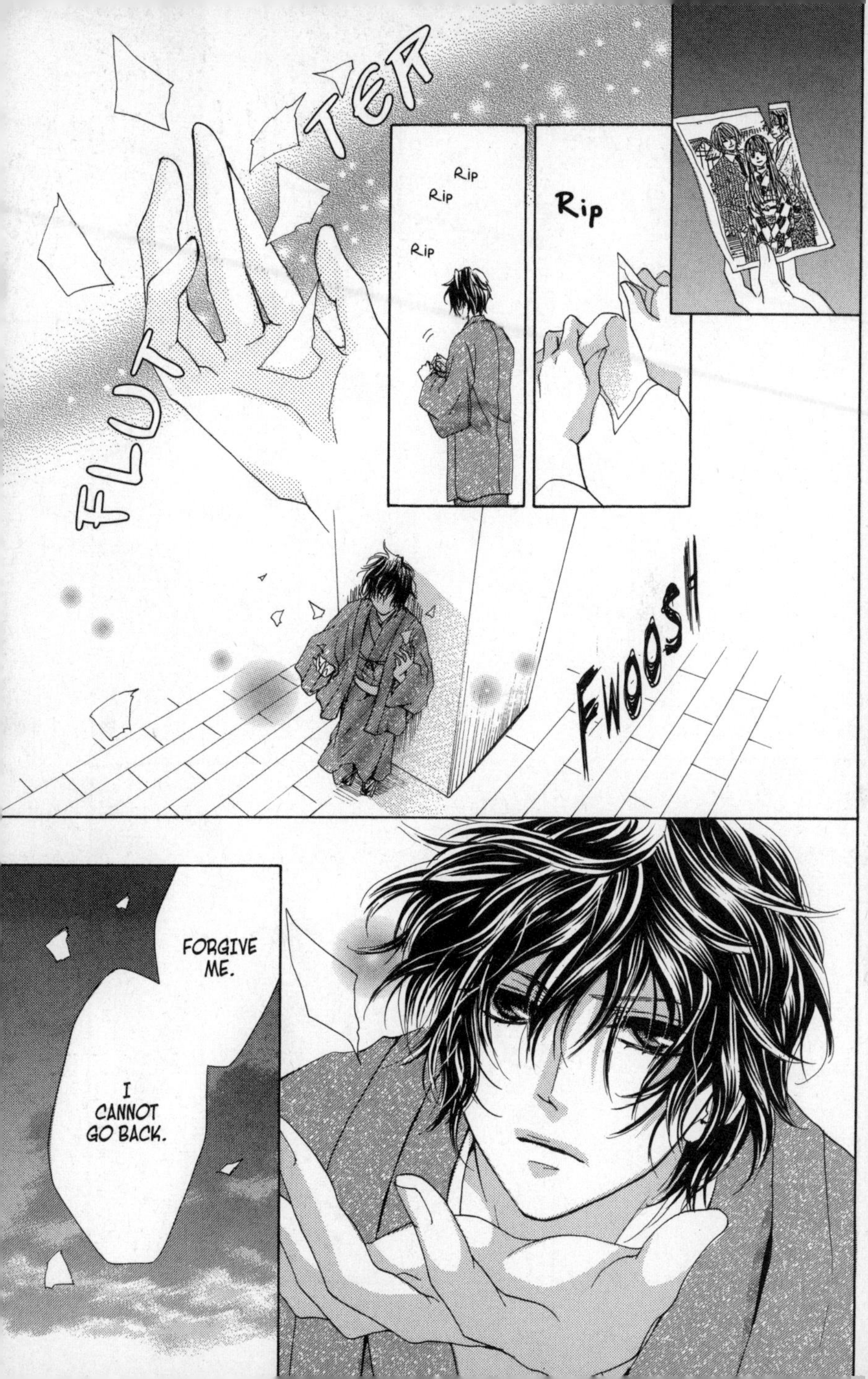
Rip
Rip
Rip
Rip
FLUTTER
FWOOSH
FORGIVE ME.
I CANNOT GO BACK.

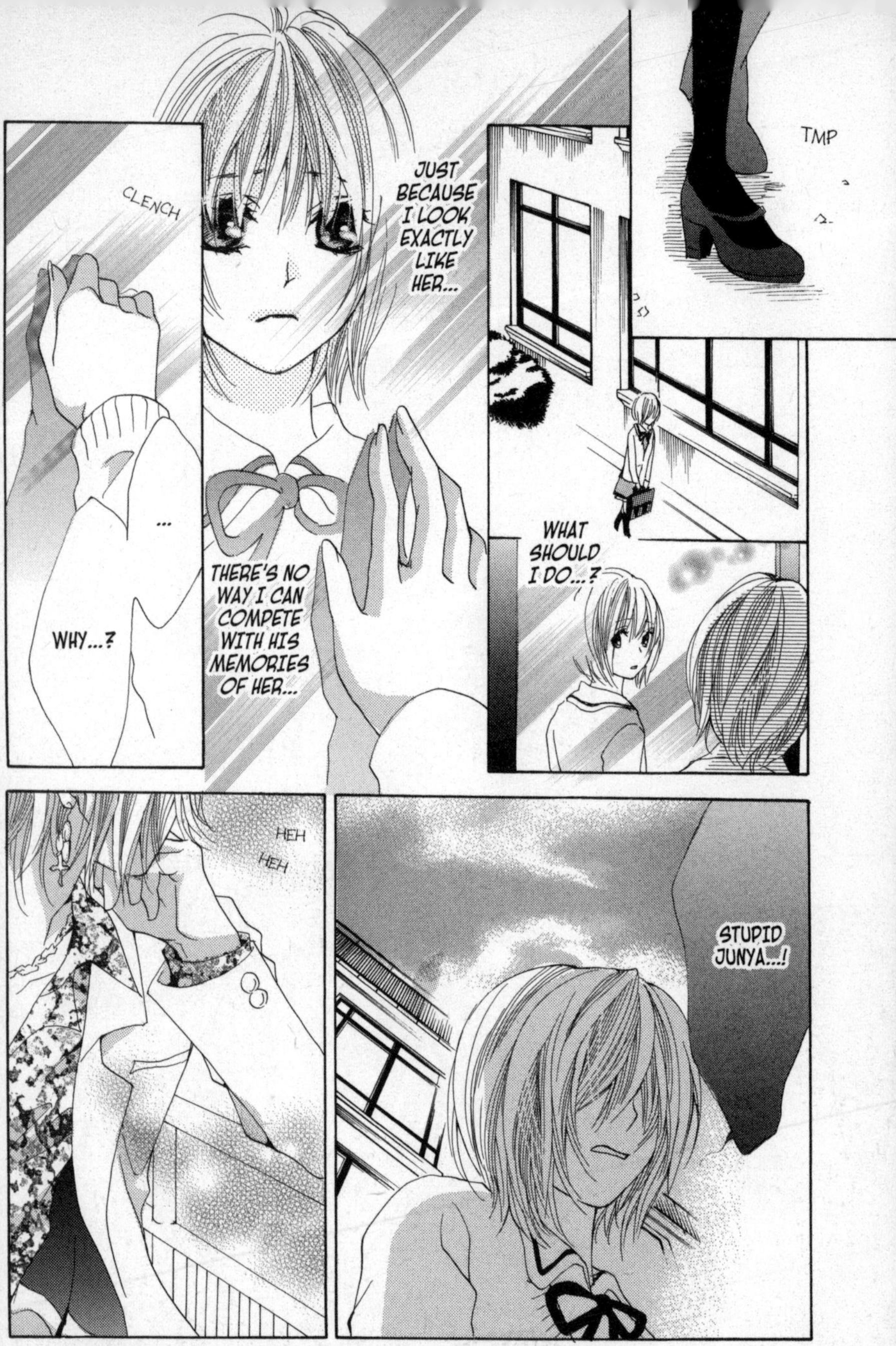
TMP
WHAT SHOULD I DO...?
JUST BECAUSE I LOOK EXACTLY LIKE HER...
THERE'S NO WAY I CAN COMPETE WITH HIS MEMORIES OF HER...
CLENCH
...
WHY...?
STUPID JUNYA...!
HEH
HEH

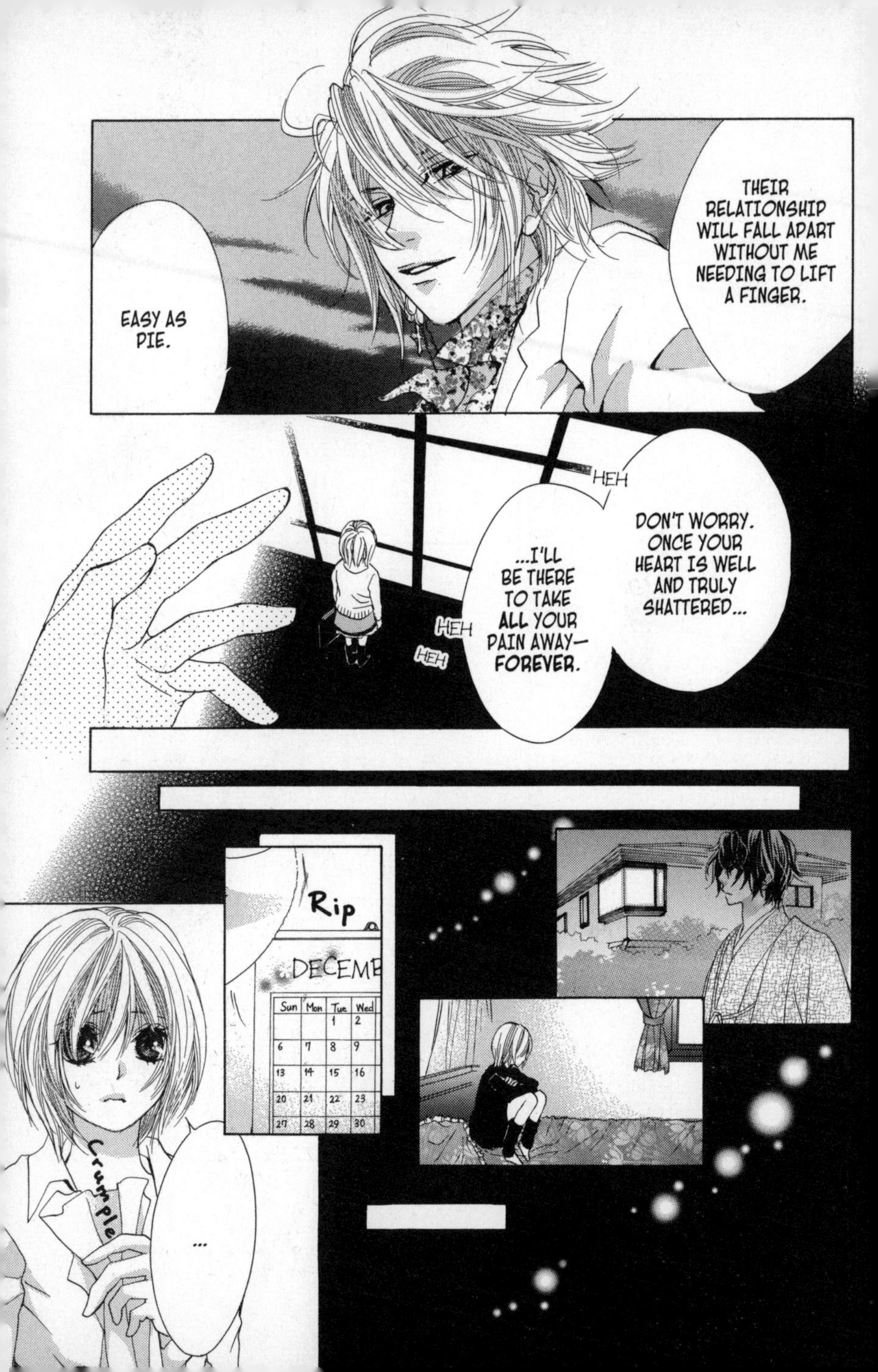
THEIR RELATIONSHIP WILL FALL APART WITHOUT ME NEEDING TO LIFT A FINGER.
EASY AS PIE.
HEH
DON'T WORRY. ONCE YOUR HEART IS WELL AND TRULY SHATTERED...
...I'LL BE THERE TO TAKE ALL YOUR PAIN AWAY—FOREVER.
HEH
HEH
Rip
DECEMB
Sun Mon Tue Wed
1 2
6 7 8 9
13 14 15 16
20 21 22 23
27 28 29 30
Crumple
...

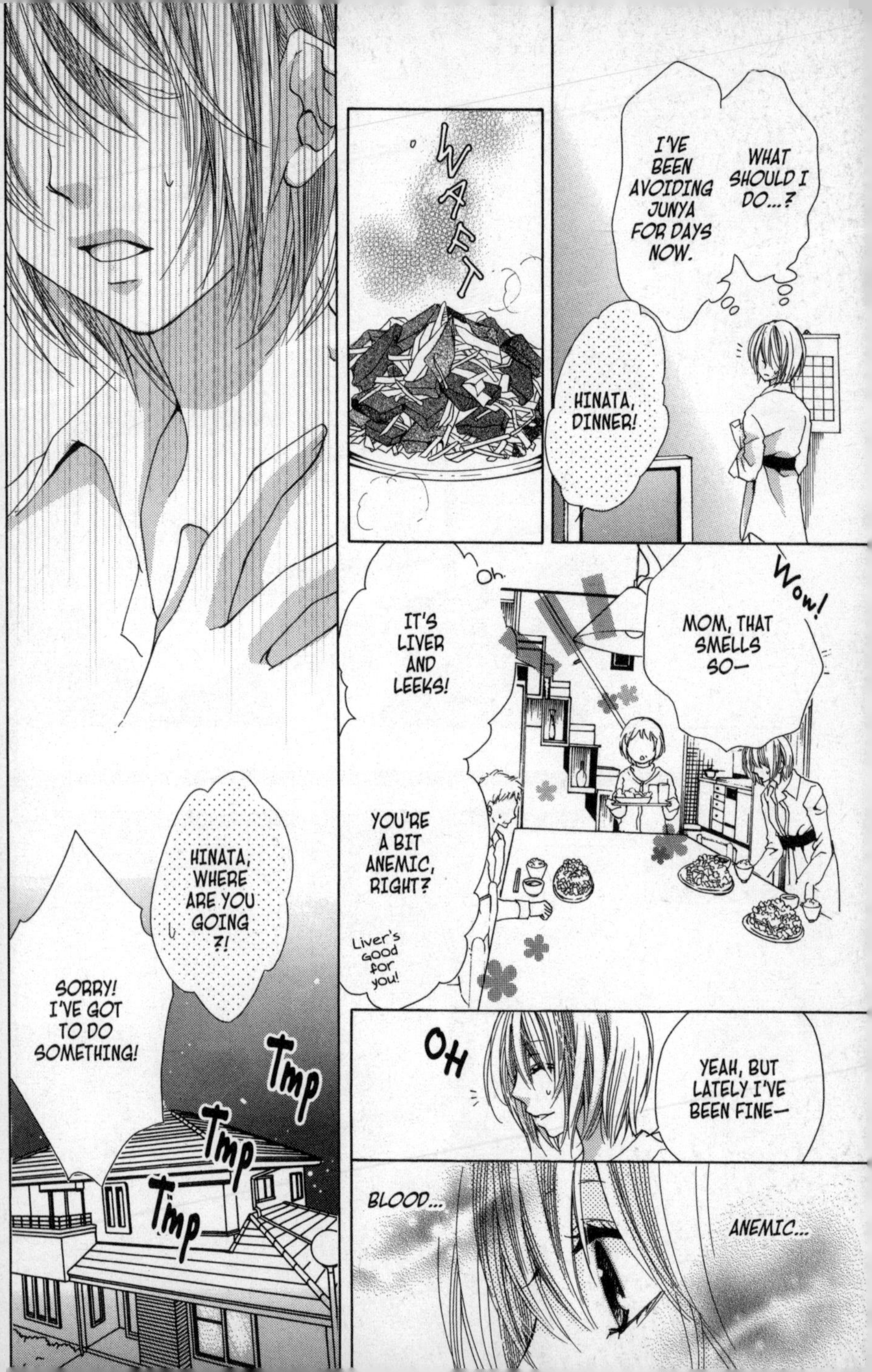
WHAT SHOULD I DO...?
I'VE BEEN AVOIDING JUNYA FOR DAYS NOW.
HINATA, DINNER!
WAFT
WOW!
MOM, THAT SMELLS SO—
Oh.
IT'S LIVER AND LEEKS!
YOU'RE A BIT ANEMIC, RIGHT?
Liver's good for you!
OH
YEAH, BUT LATELY I'VE BEEN FINE—
ANEMIC...
BLOOD...
HINATA, WHERE ARE YOU GOING?!
SORRY! I'VE GOT TO DO SOMETHING!
Tmp
Tmp
Tmp

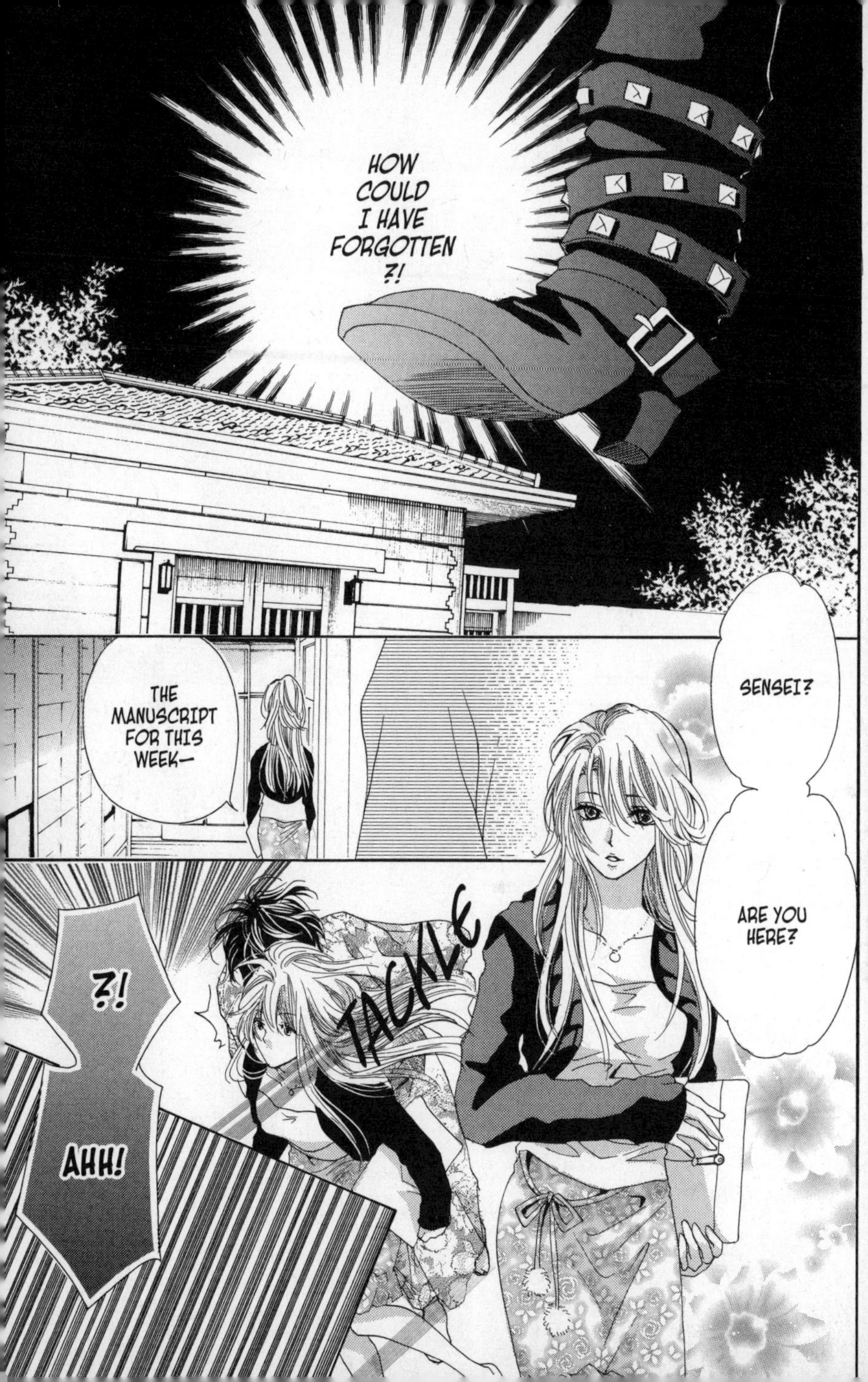
HOW COULD I HAVE FORGOTTEN ?!
SENSEI?
ARE YOU HERE?
THE MANUSCRIPT FOR THIS WEEK—
TACKLE
?!
AHH!

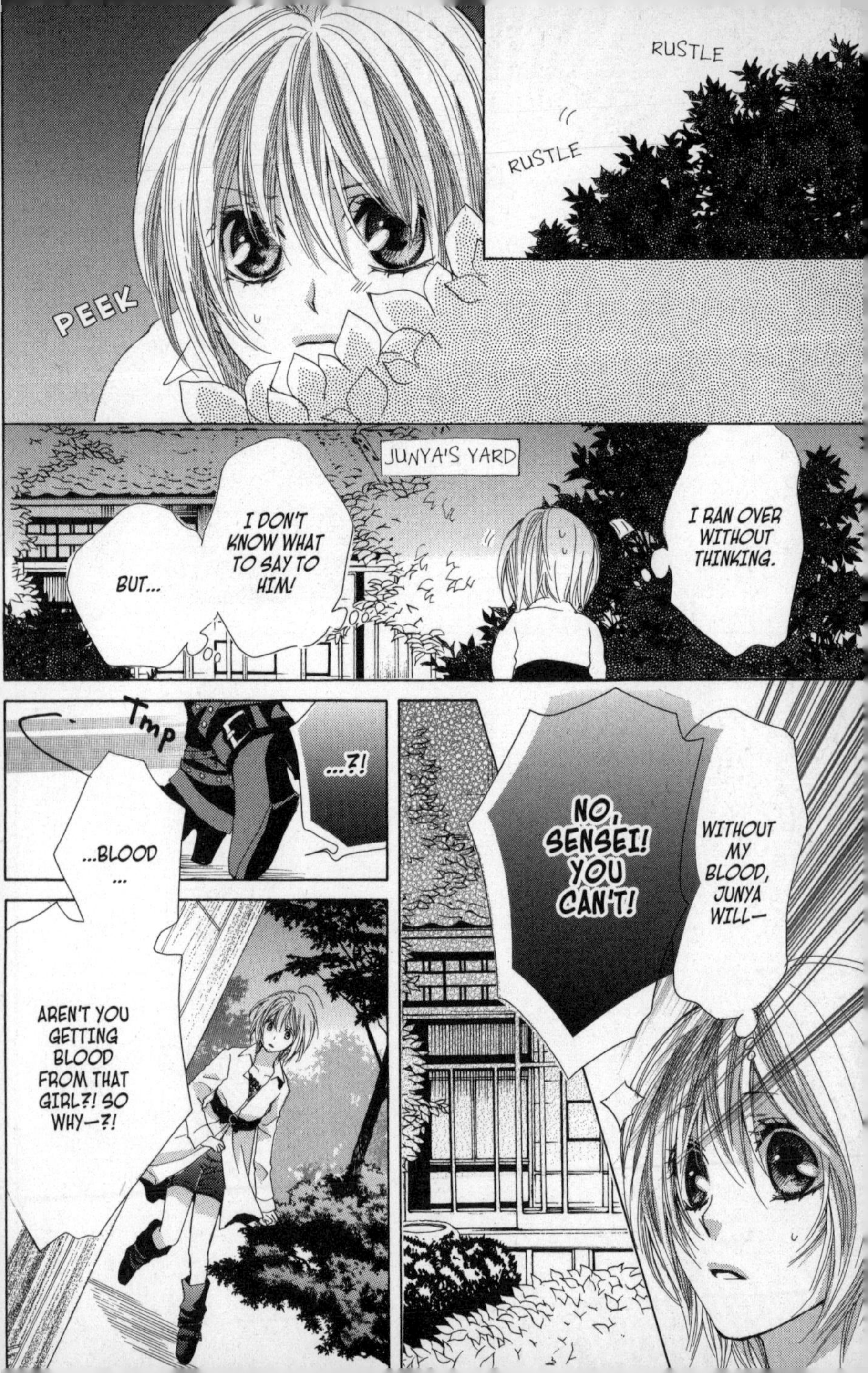
RUSTLE
RUSTLE
PEEK
I RAN OVER WITHOUT THINKING.
JUNYA'S YARD
I DON'T KNOW WHAT TO SAY TO HIM!
BUT...
WITHOUT MY BLOOD, JUNYA WILL—
NO, SENSEI! YOU CAN'T!
Tmp
...?!
...BLOOD ...
AREN'T YOU GETTING BLOOD FROM THAT GIRL?! SO WHY—?!

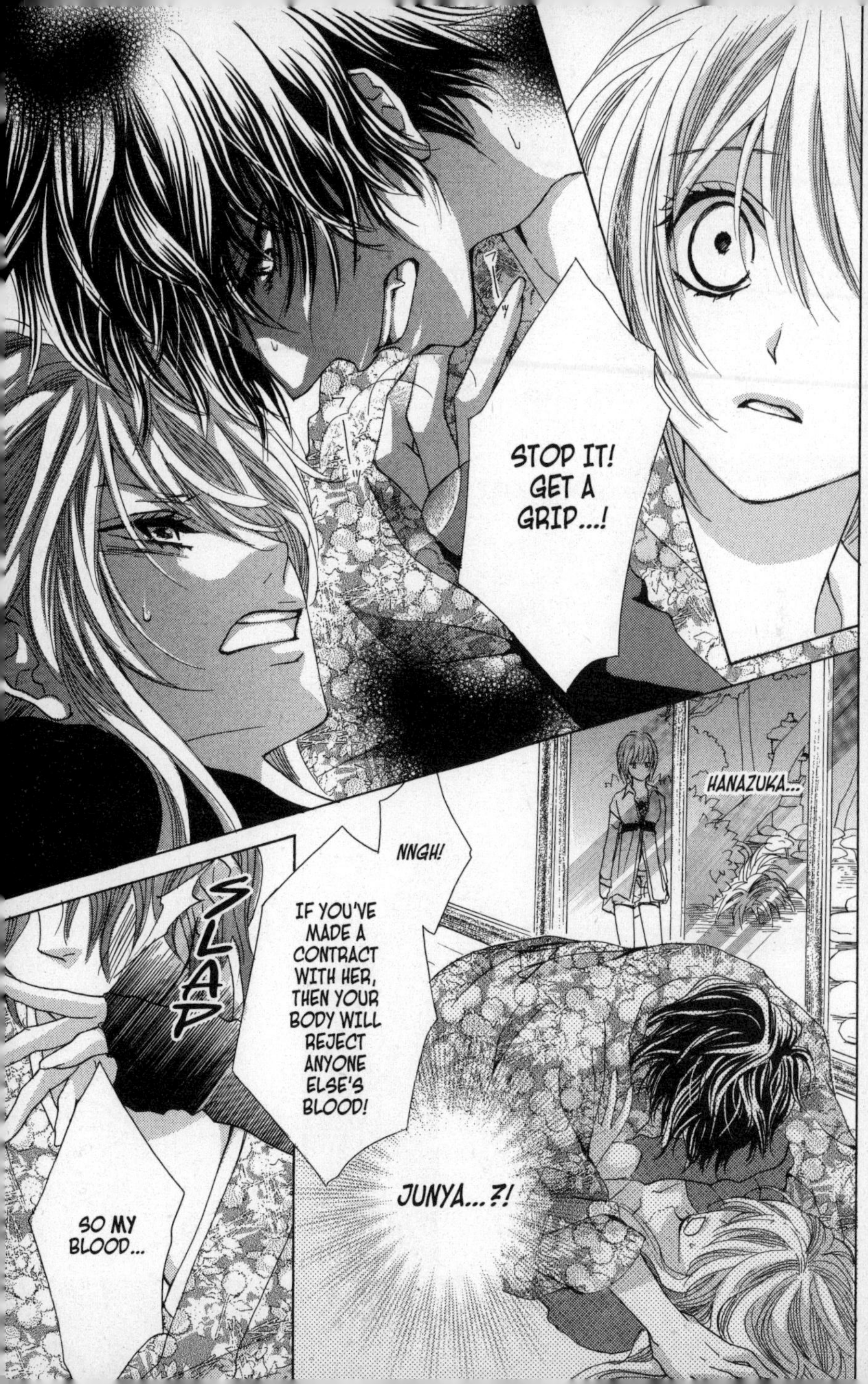
STOP IT! GET A GRIP...!
HANAZUKA...
NNGH!
IF YOU'VE MADE A CONTRACT WITH HER, THEN YOUR BODY WILL REJECT ANYONE ELSE'S BLOOD!
JUNYA...?!
SLAP
SO MY BLOOD...

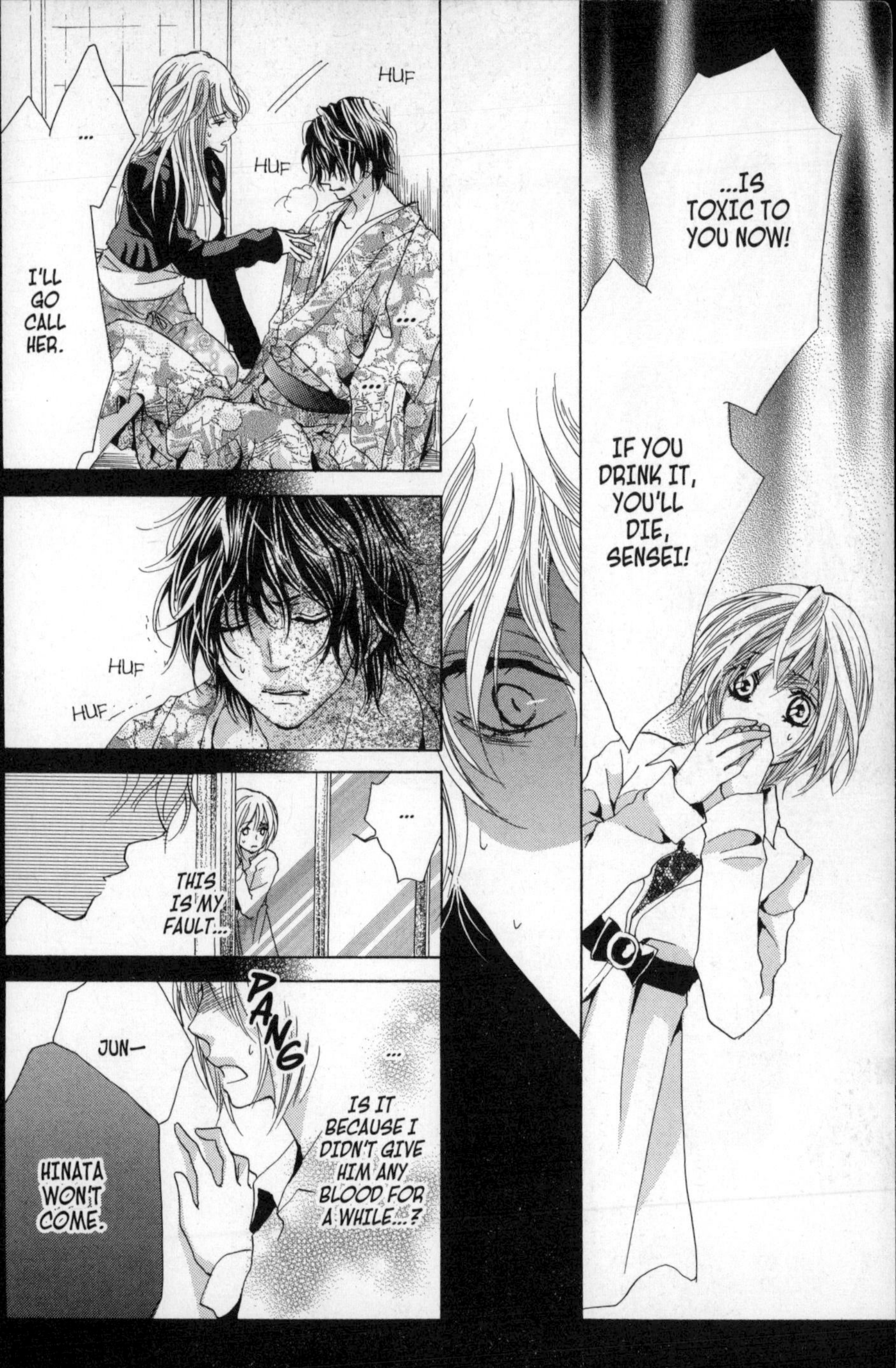

...IS TOXIC TO YOU NOW!
IF YOU DRINK IT, YOU'LL DIE, SENSEI!
HUF
...
HUF
...
...
I'LL GO CALL HER.
HUF
HUF
...
THIS IS MY FAULT...
PANG
...
JUN—
IS IT BECAUSE I DIDN'T GIVE HIM ANY BLOOD FOR A WHILE...?
HINATA WON'T COME.

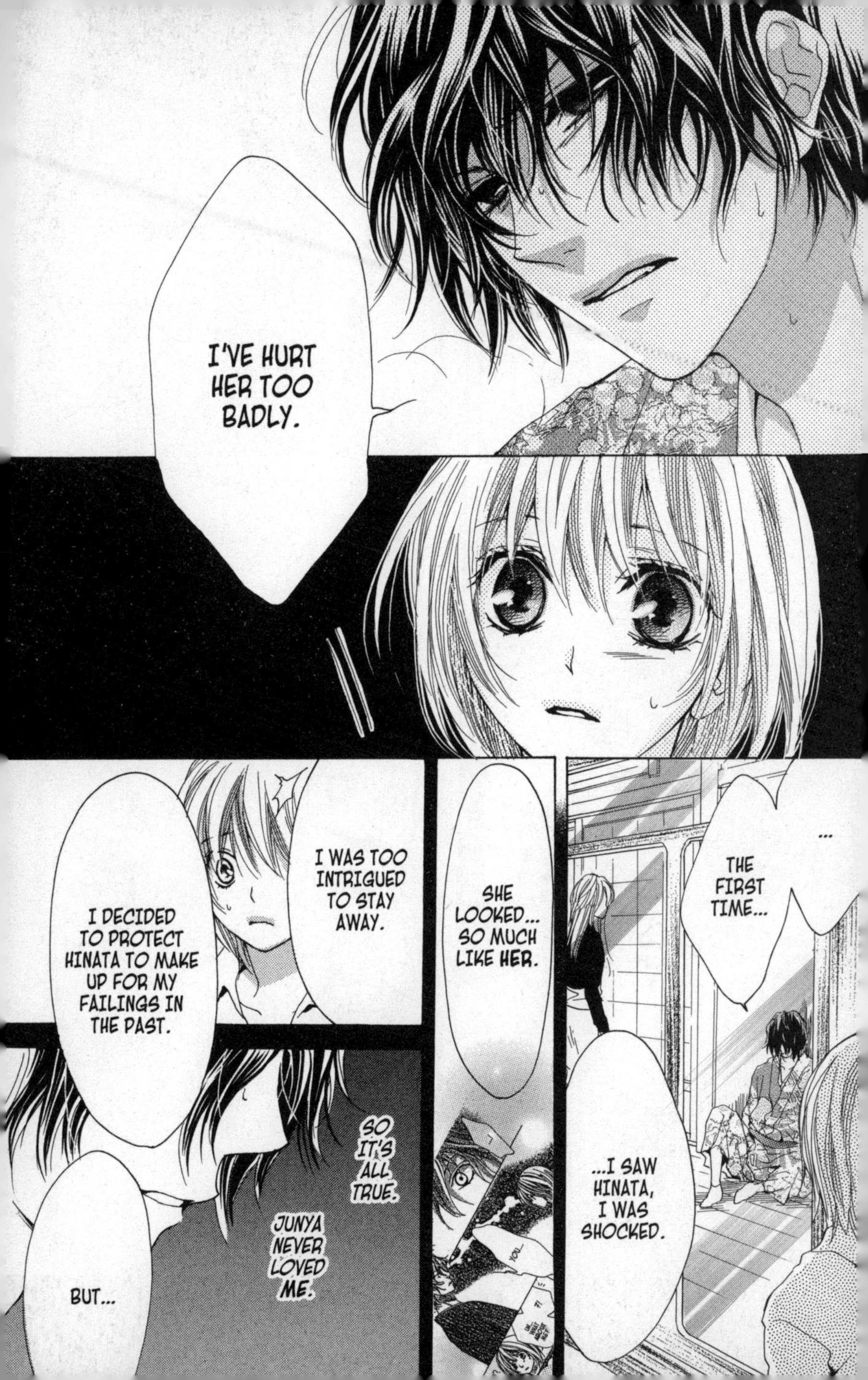
I'VE HURT HER TOO BADLY.
...
THE FIRST TIME...
...I SAW HINATA, I WAS SHOCKED.
SHE LOOKED... SO MUCH LIKE HER.
YOU...
I WAS TOO INTRIGUED TO STAY AWAY.
I DECIDED TO PROTECT HINATA TO MAKE UP FOR MY FAILINGS IN THE PAST.
SO IT'S ALL TRUE.
JUNYA NEVER LOVED ME.
BUT...

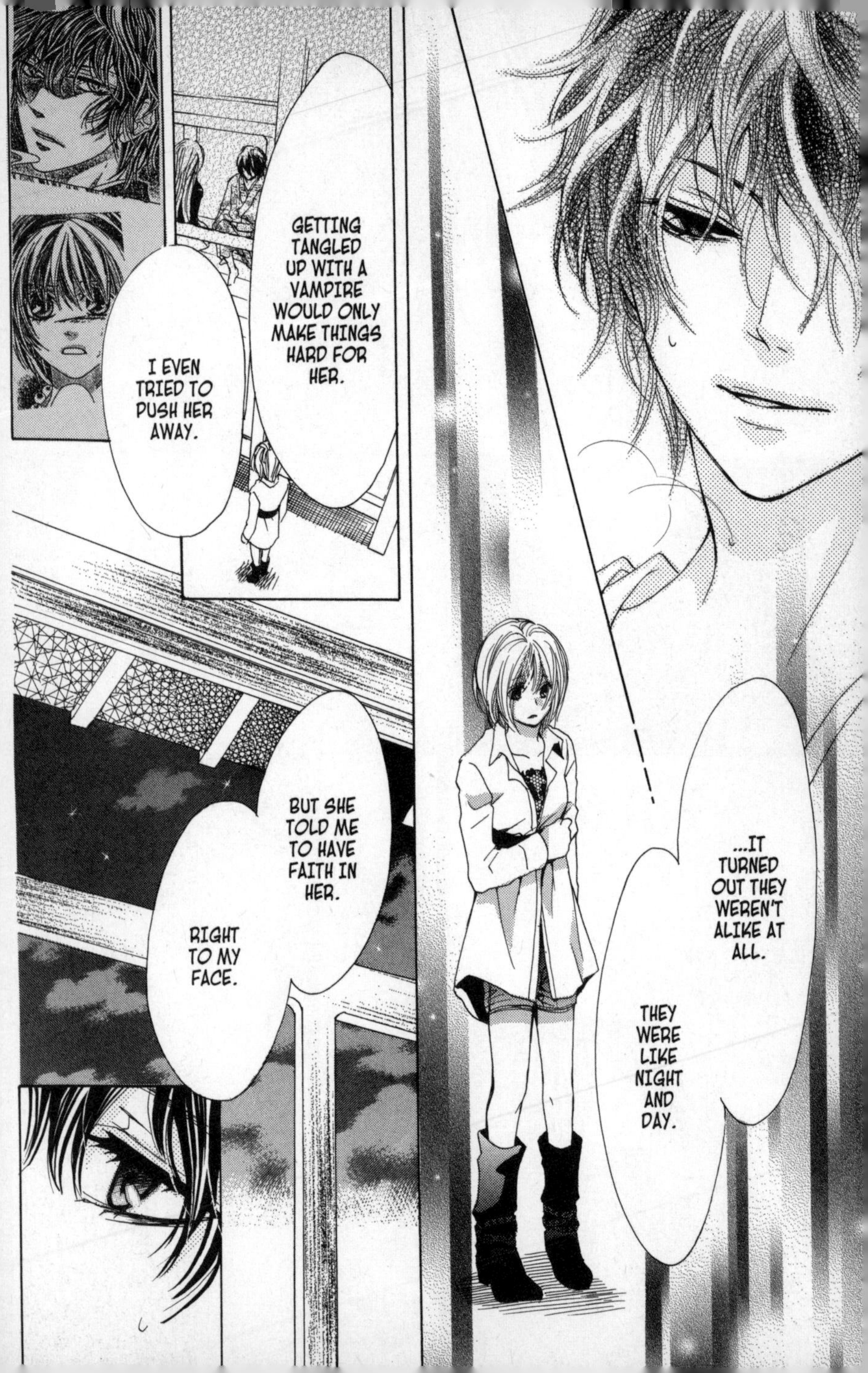
...IT TURNED OUT THEY WEREN'T ALIKE AT ALL.
THEY WERE LIKE NIGHT AND DAY.
GETTING TANGLED UP WITH A VAMPIRE WOULD ONLY MAKE THINGS HARD FOR HER.
I EVEN TRIED TO PUSH HER AWAY.
BUT SHE TOLD ME TO HAVE FAITH IN HER.
RIGHT TO MY FACE.

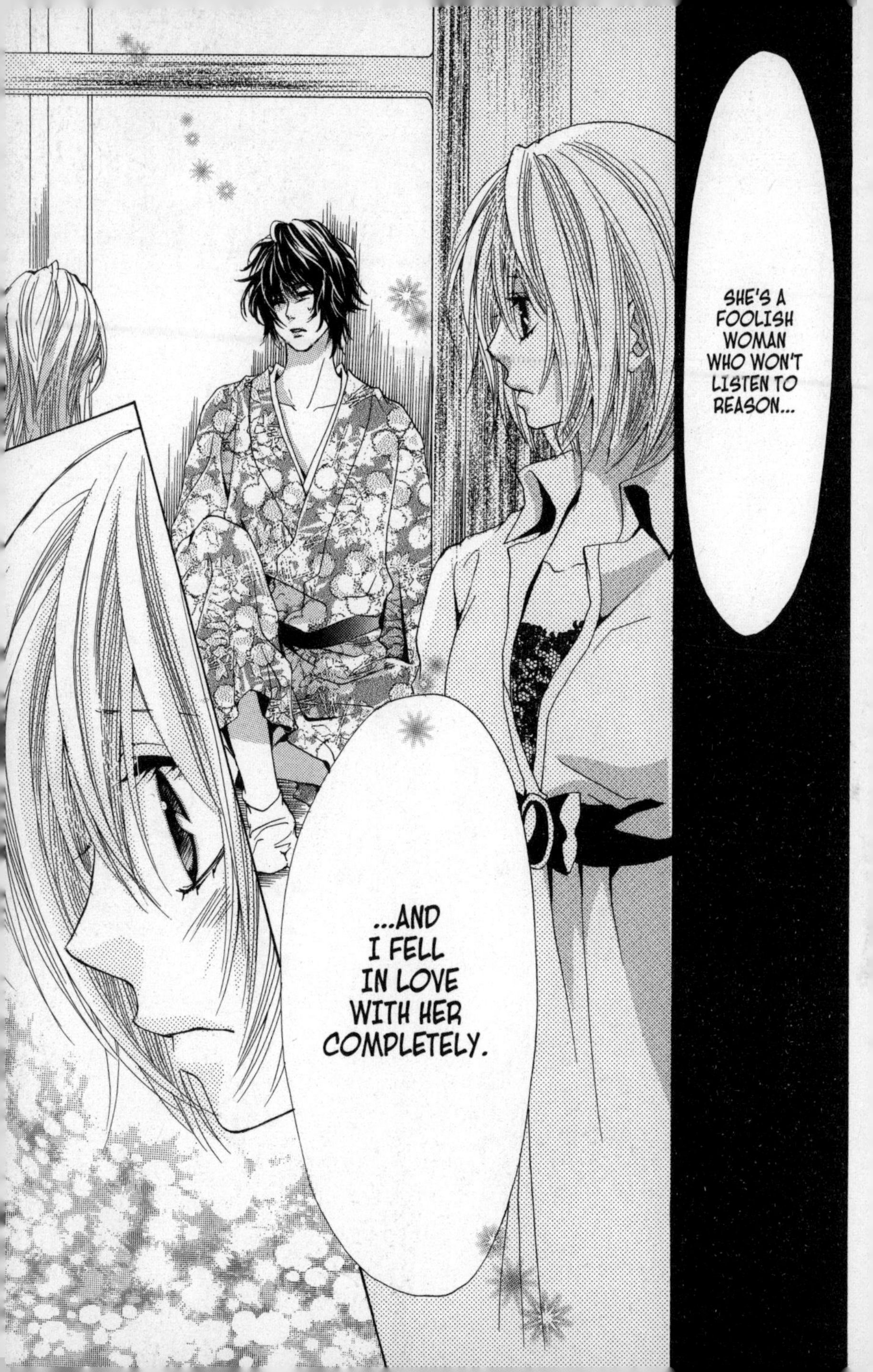
SHE'S A FOOLISH WOMAN WHO WON'T LISTEN TO REASON...
...AND I FELL IN LOVE WITH HER COMPLETELY.

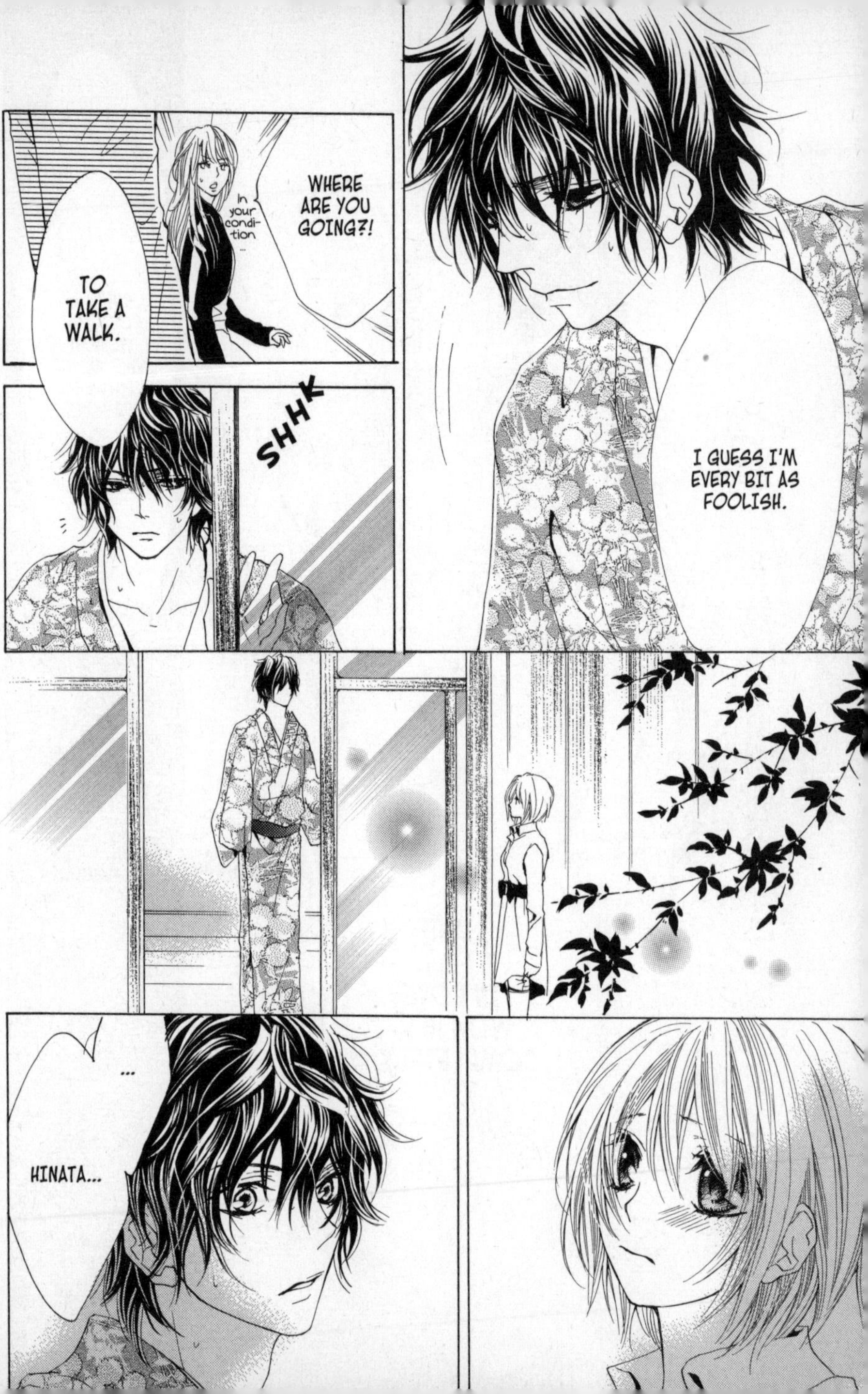
I GUESS I'M EVERY BIT AS FOOLISH.
WHERE ARE YOU GOING?!
In your condition...
TO TAKE A WALK.
SHHK
...
HINATA...

Small Talk

4

Somewhere I've Been Recently

KAGOSHIMA

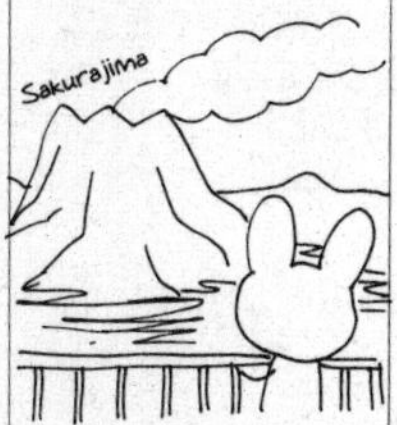
Sakurajima

Uhh, yes. It's my hometown. Sorry...

After the serialization ended, I had the chance to take a long break and go home.

I went to a party at a newlywed friend's place for some hot pot—**tomato-based** hot pot. I was a little overenthusiastic and it got all over my clothes.

Sorry I was such a slob, Sachiko.

I got my friends to read my manuscript and help me with character development.

Spending time with my friends makes me so happy!

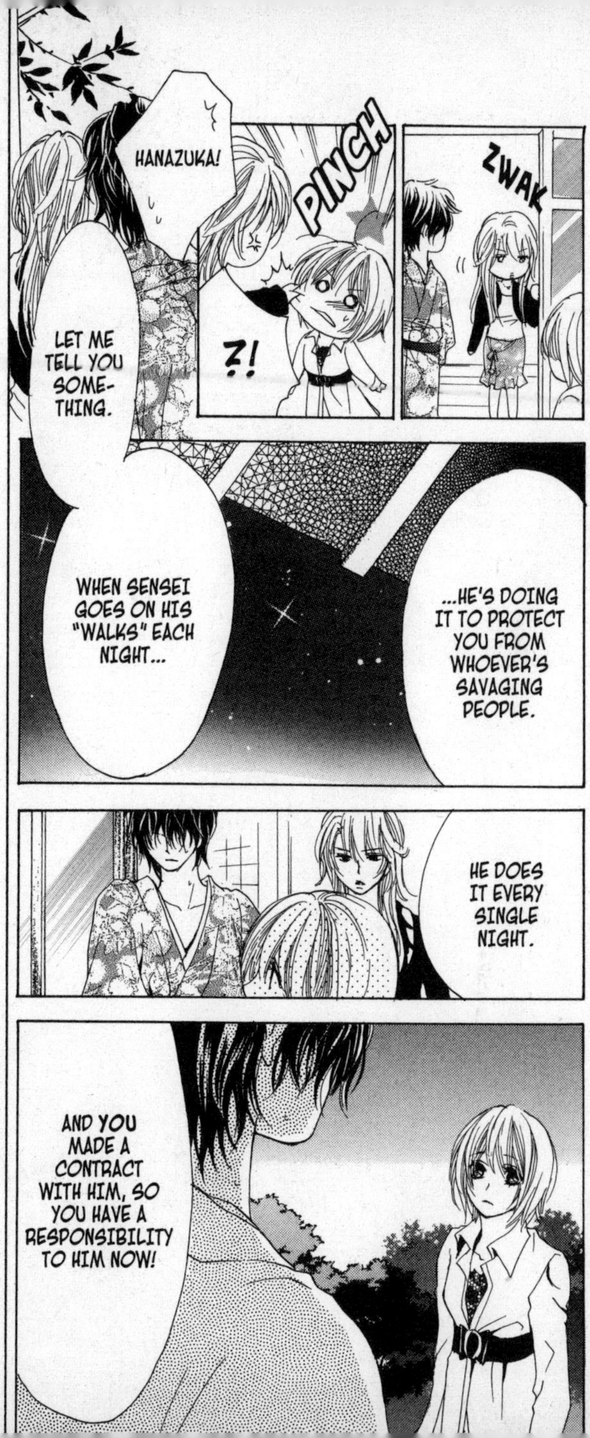
ZWAK
PINCH
?!
HANAZUKA!
LET ME TELL YOU SOMETHING.
WHEN SENSEI GOES ON HIS "WALKS" EACH NIGHT...
...HE'S DOING IT TO PROTECT YOU FROM WHOEVER'S SAVAGING PEOPLE.
HE DOES IT EVERY SINGLE NIGHT.
AND YOU MADE A CONTRACT WITH HIM, SO YOU HAVE A RESPONSIBILITY TO HIM NOW!

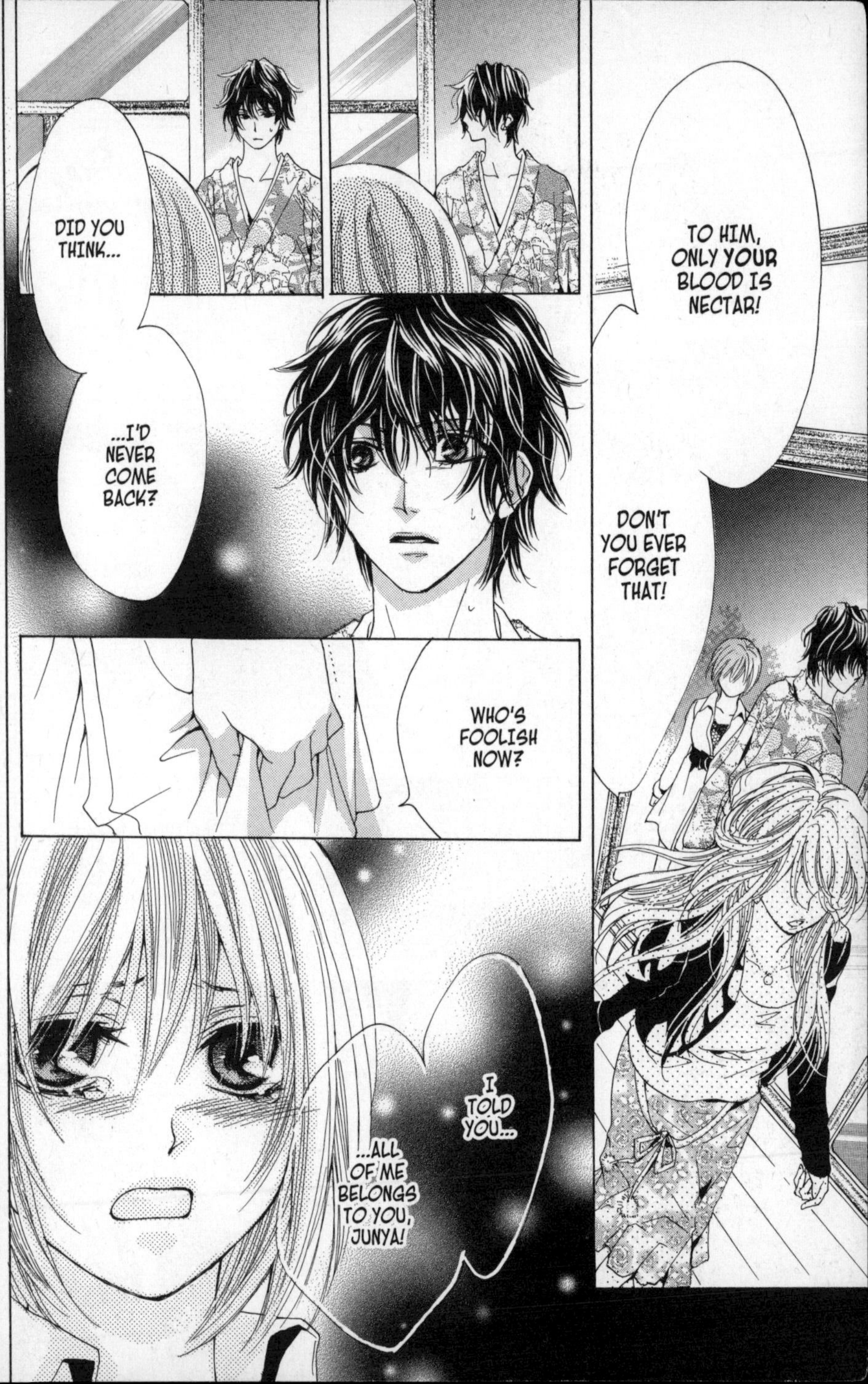
TO HIM, ONLY YOUR BLOOD IS NECTAR!
DON'T YOU EVER FORGET THAT!
DID YOU THINK...
...I'D NEVER COME BACK?
WHO'S FOOLISH NOW?
I TOLD YOU...
...ALL OF ME BELONGS TO YOU, JUNYA!

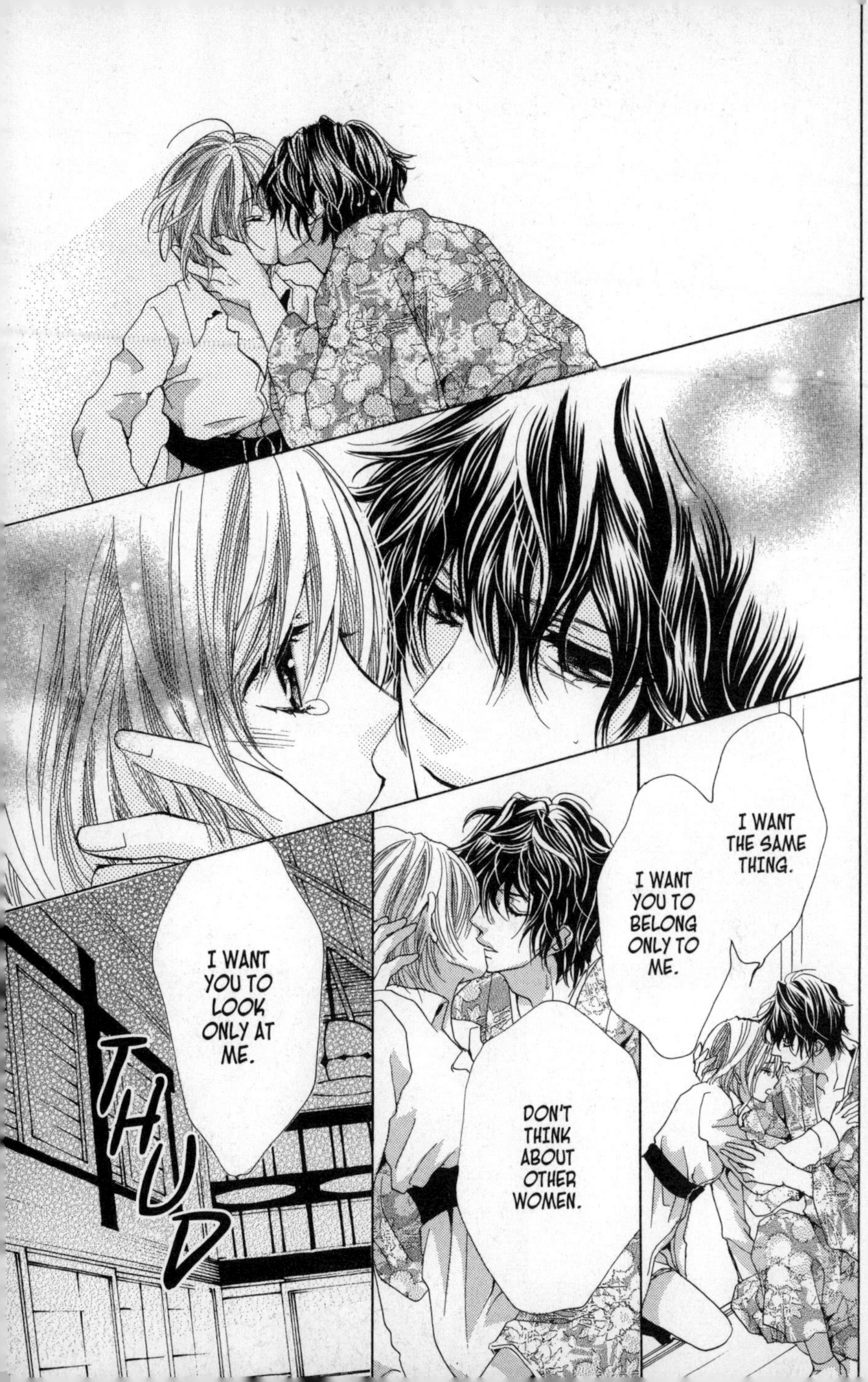
I WANT THE SAME THING.
I WANT YOU TO BELONG ONLY TO ME.
DON'T THINK ABOUT OTHER WOMEN.
I WANT YOU TO LOOK ONLY AT ME.
THUD

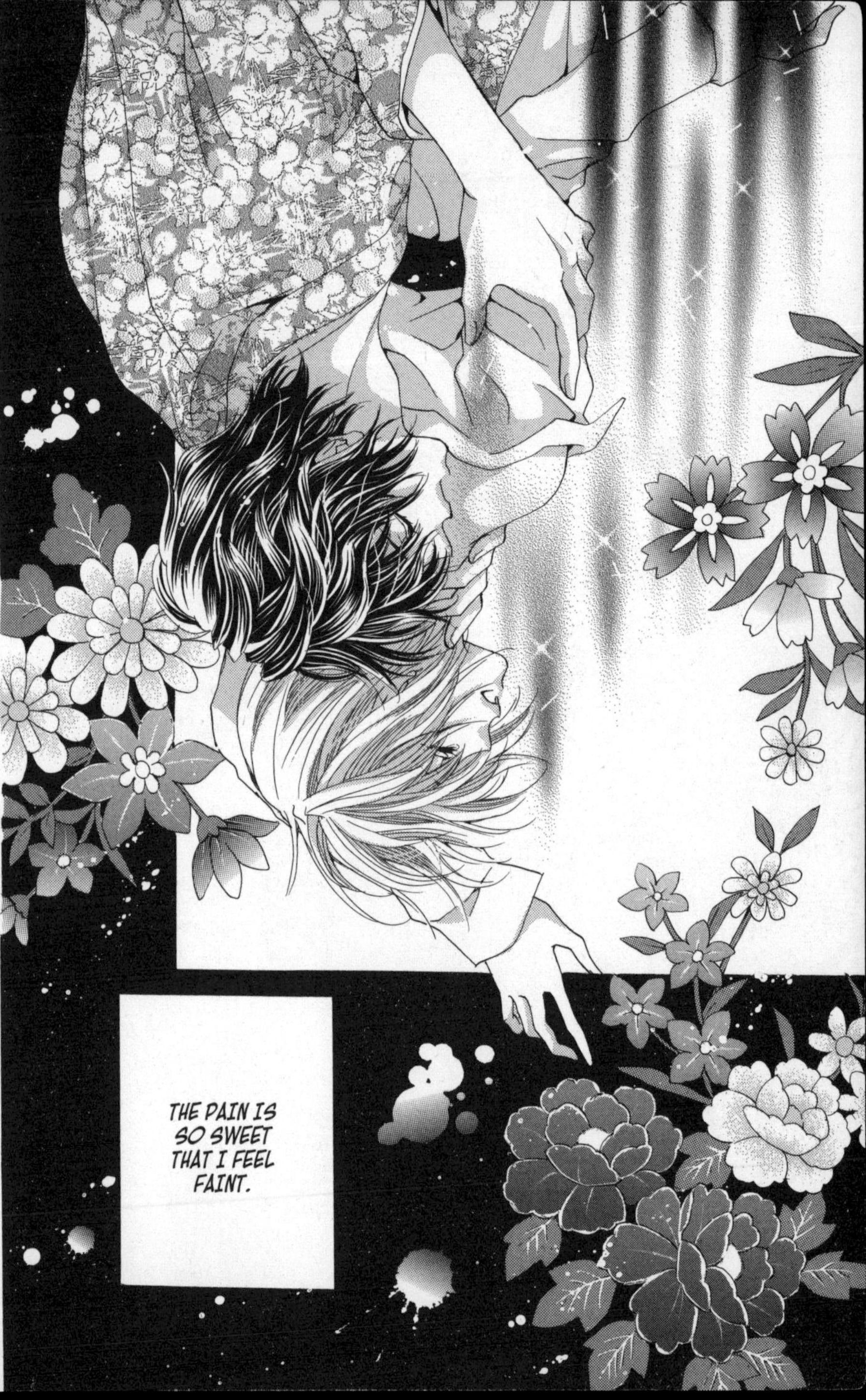
THE PAIN IS SO SWEET THAT I FEEL FAINT.

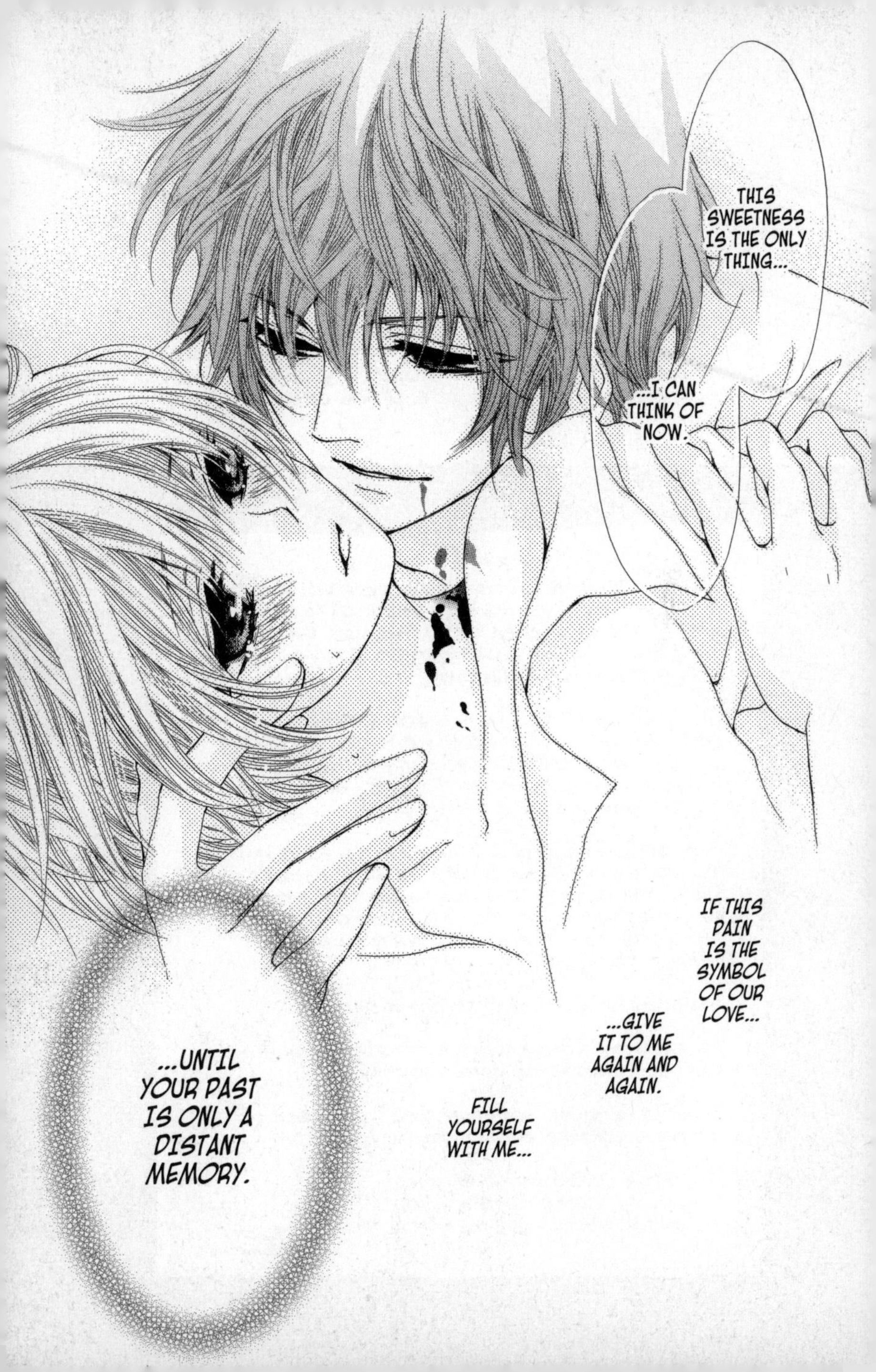
THIS SWEETNESS IS THE ONLY THING...
...I CAN THINK OF NOW.
IF THIS PAIN IS THE SYMBOL OF OUR LOVE...
...GIVE IT TO ME AGAIN AND AGAIN.
FILL YOURSELF WITH ME...
...UNTIL YOUR PAST IS ONLY A DISTANT MEMORY.

About *Honey Blood*

This second volume marks the conclusion to *Honey Blood*. But we're not at the end of the book yet, so this could be a little bit of a spoiler. If you haven't finished reading, I'd appreciate it if you came back to this page once you're done.

After the serialization ended I received lots of letters. "I want you to keep writing." "Is this the end?" "What happened to...?" This was the first time I got that kind of reaction, so I was thrilled. I read each and every letter.

To be honest, I was hoping for a longer serialization, but I couldn't pull it off. I'm sorry I couldn't wrap things up properly. In my head, I have a continuation of the story as well as the final ending.

But of course, this is a business, so what I want to write isn't as important as what readers want to read. So I'll have to keep that more personal, full-blown (Ha ha) version of *Honey Blood* in the back of my mind and let it rest for a while.

Maybe if I'm ever given another chance...

Maybe if my manga work ever dries up... (Ugh, no! I don't want to think about that!)

Even if it never gets published, I still want to draw out the ending I imagined.

To those readers who enjoyed this story, I want to thank you from the bottom of my heart. ♥

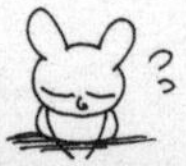

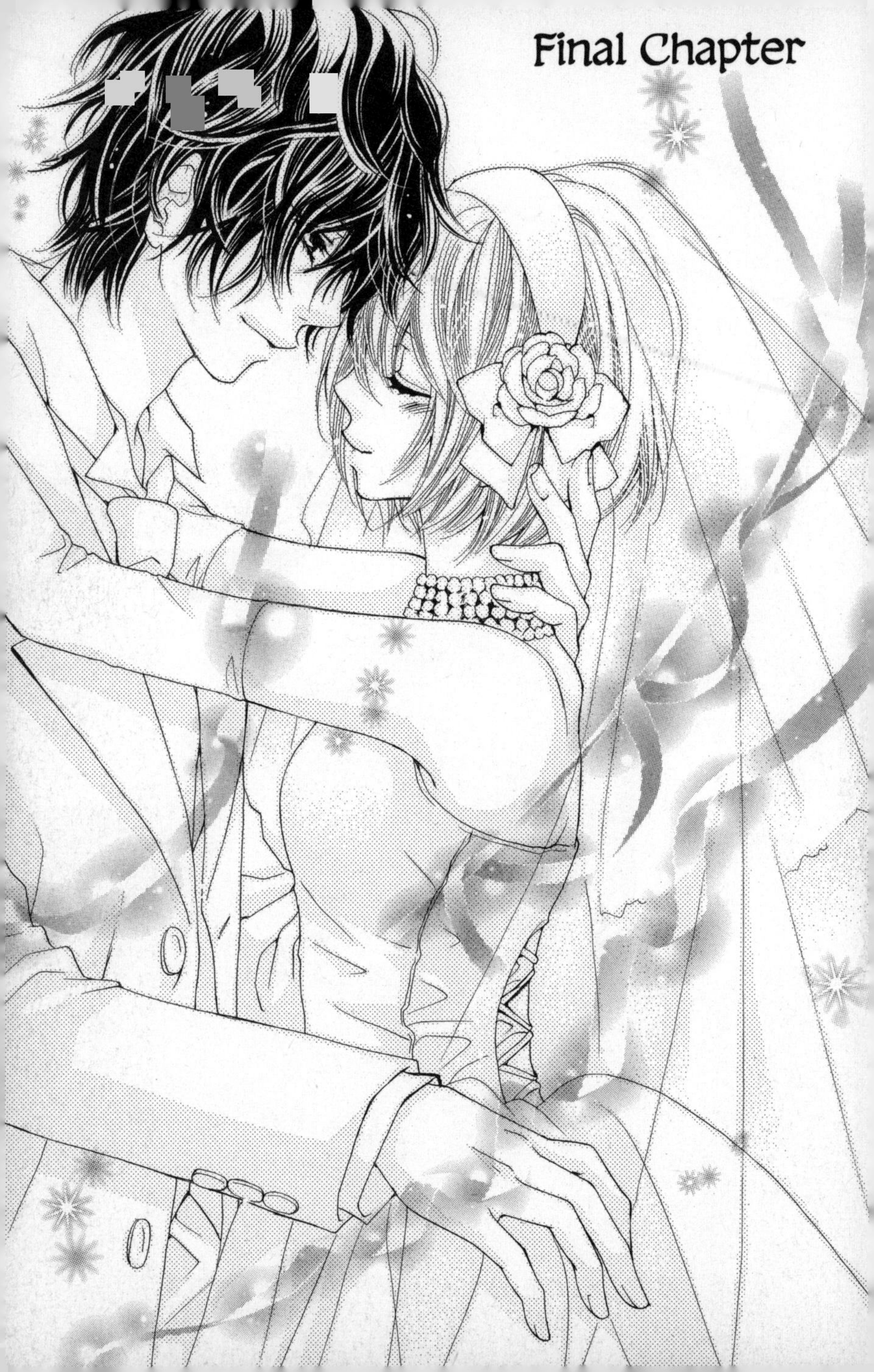
Final Chapter

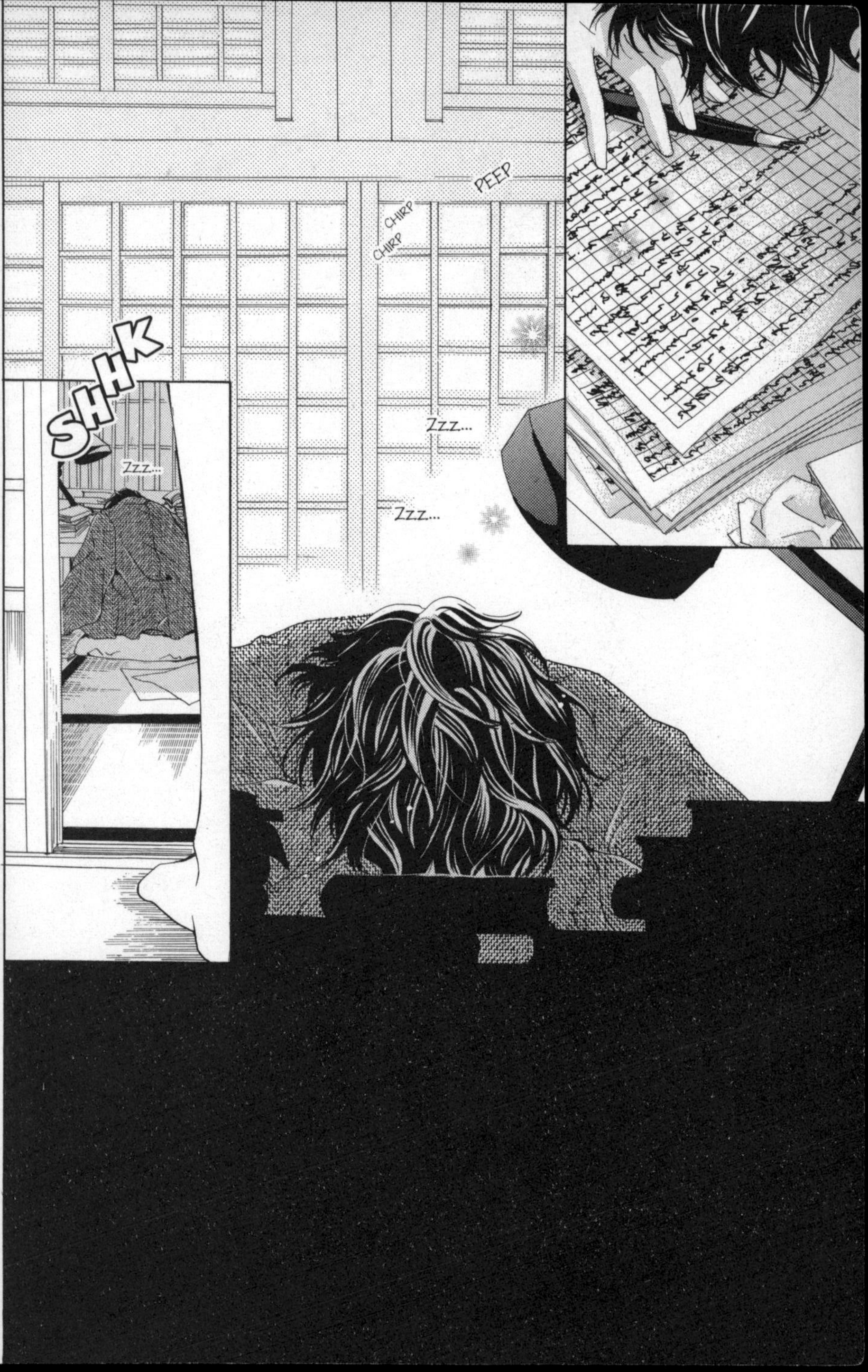
PEEP
CHIRP
CHIRP
Zzz...
Zzz...
SHHK
Zzz...

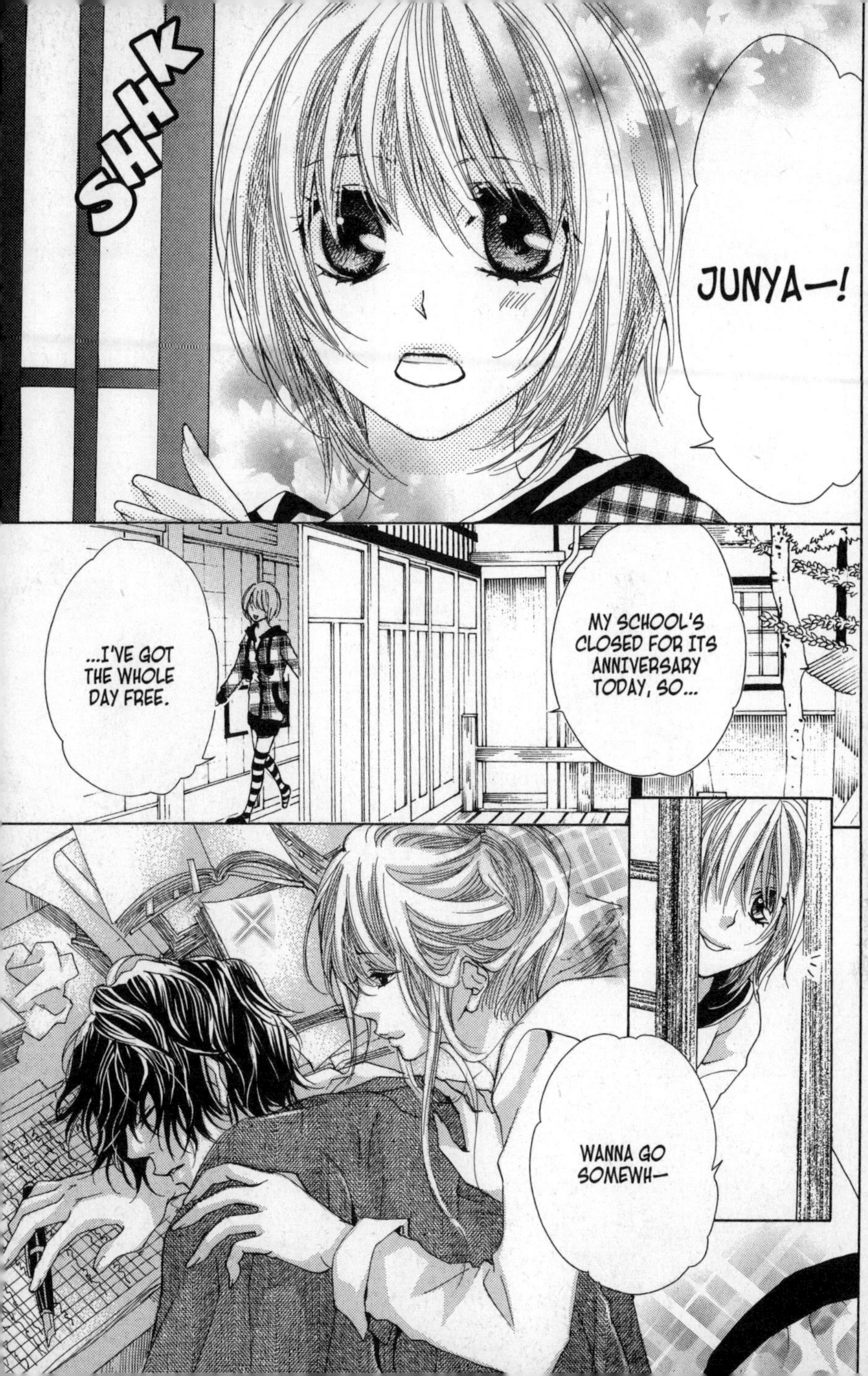
SHHK
JUNYA—!
MY SCHOOL'S CLOSED FOR ITS ANNIVERSARY TODAY, SO...
...I'VE GOT THE WHOLE DAY FREE.
WANNA GO SOMEWH—

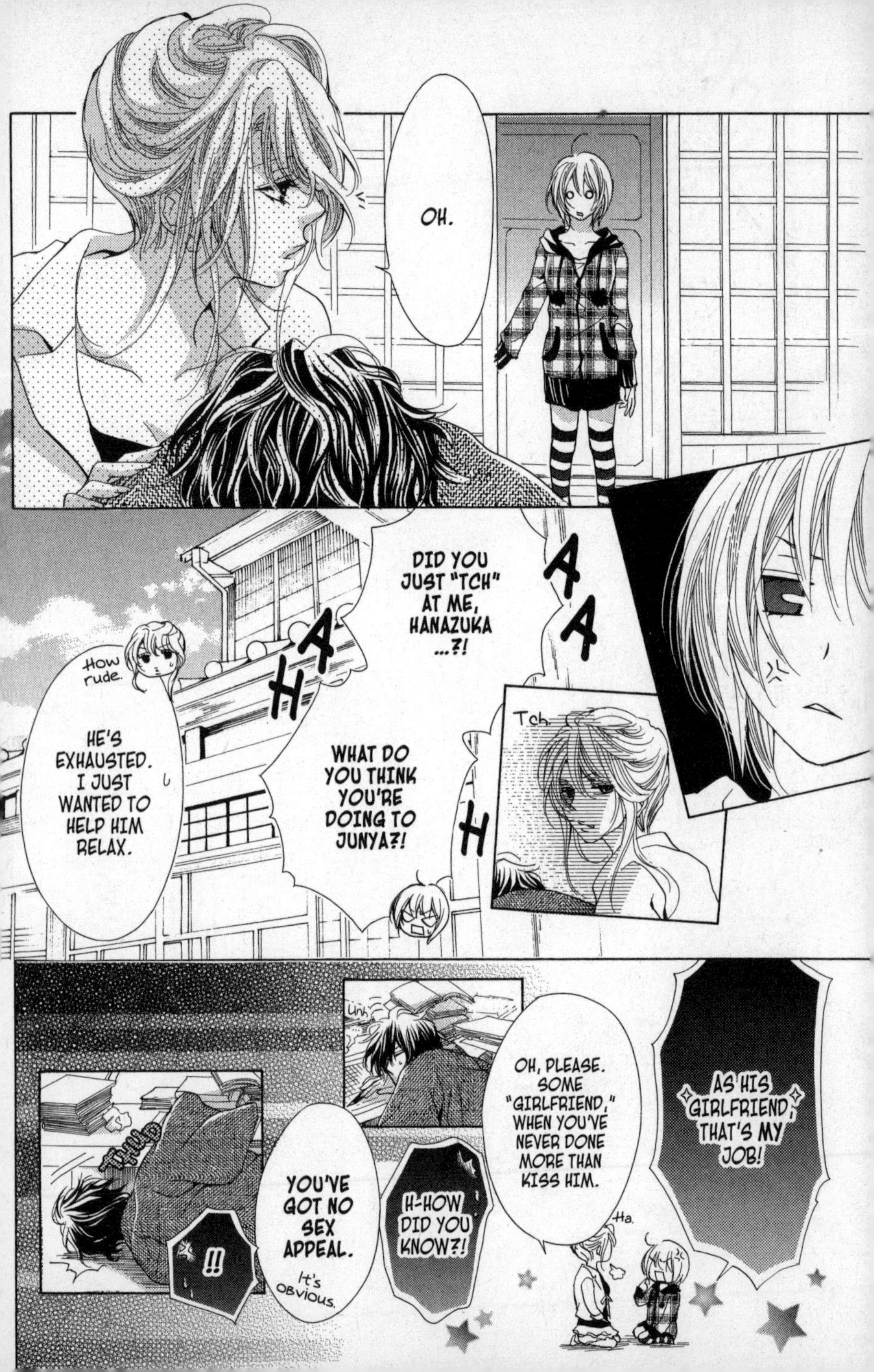
OH.
Tch.
DID YOU JUST "TCH" AT ME, HANAZUKA ...?!
WHAT DO YOU THINK YOU'RE DOING TO JUNYA?!
HE'S EXHAUSTED. I JUST WANTED TO HELP HIM RELAX.
How rude.
AS HIS GIRLFRIEND, THAT'S MY JOB!
OH, PLEASE. SOME "GIRLFRIEND," WHEN YOU'VE NEVER DONE MORE THAN KISS HIM.
Ha.
Unh
H-HOW DID YOU KNOW?!
YOU'VE GOT NO SEX APPEAL.
It's obvious.
!!

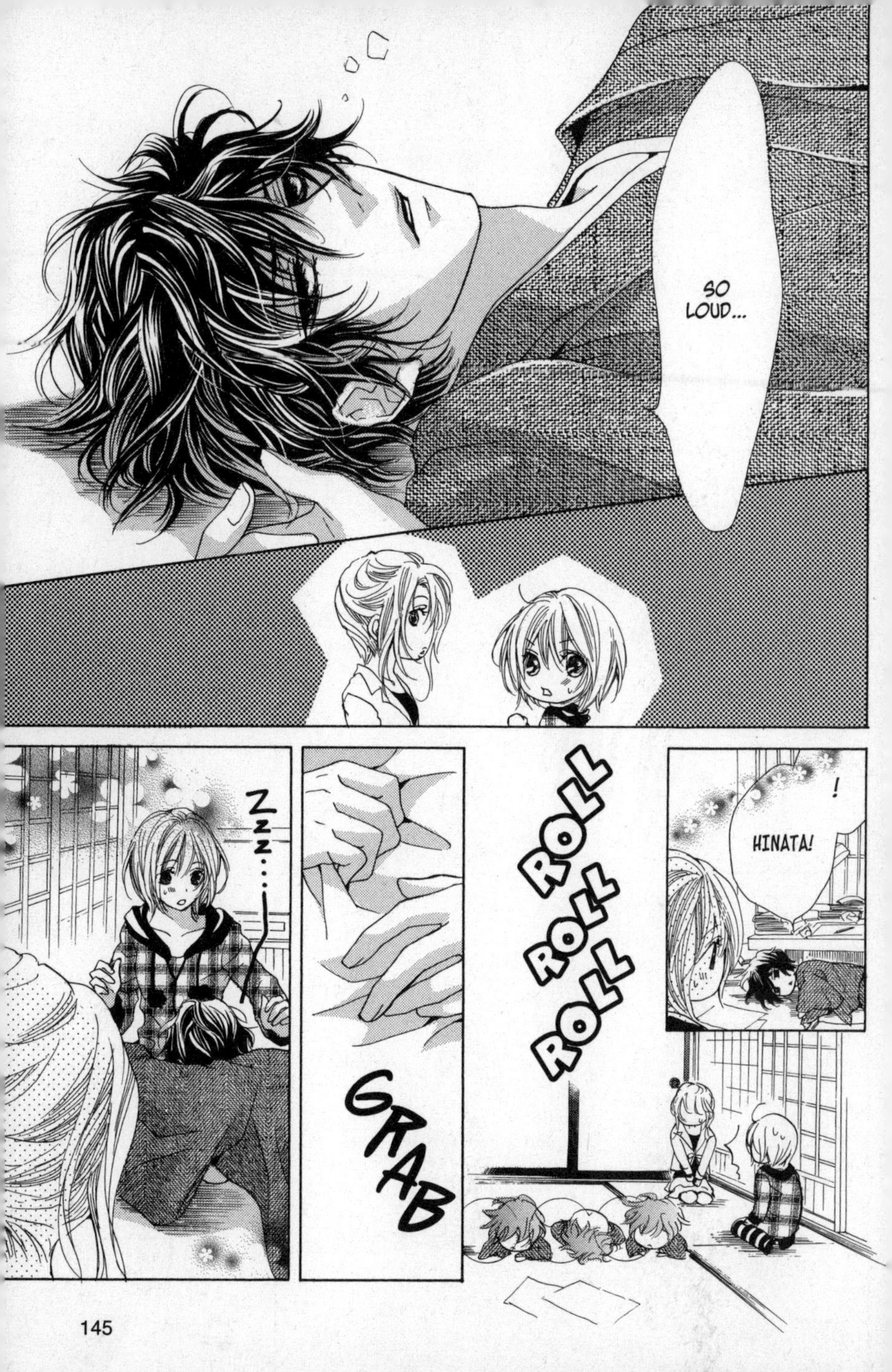
SO LOUD...
!
HINATA!
ROLL ROLL ROLL
GRAB
Zzz...

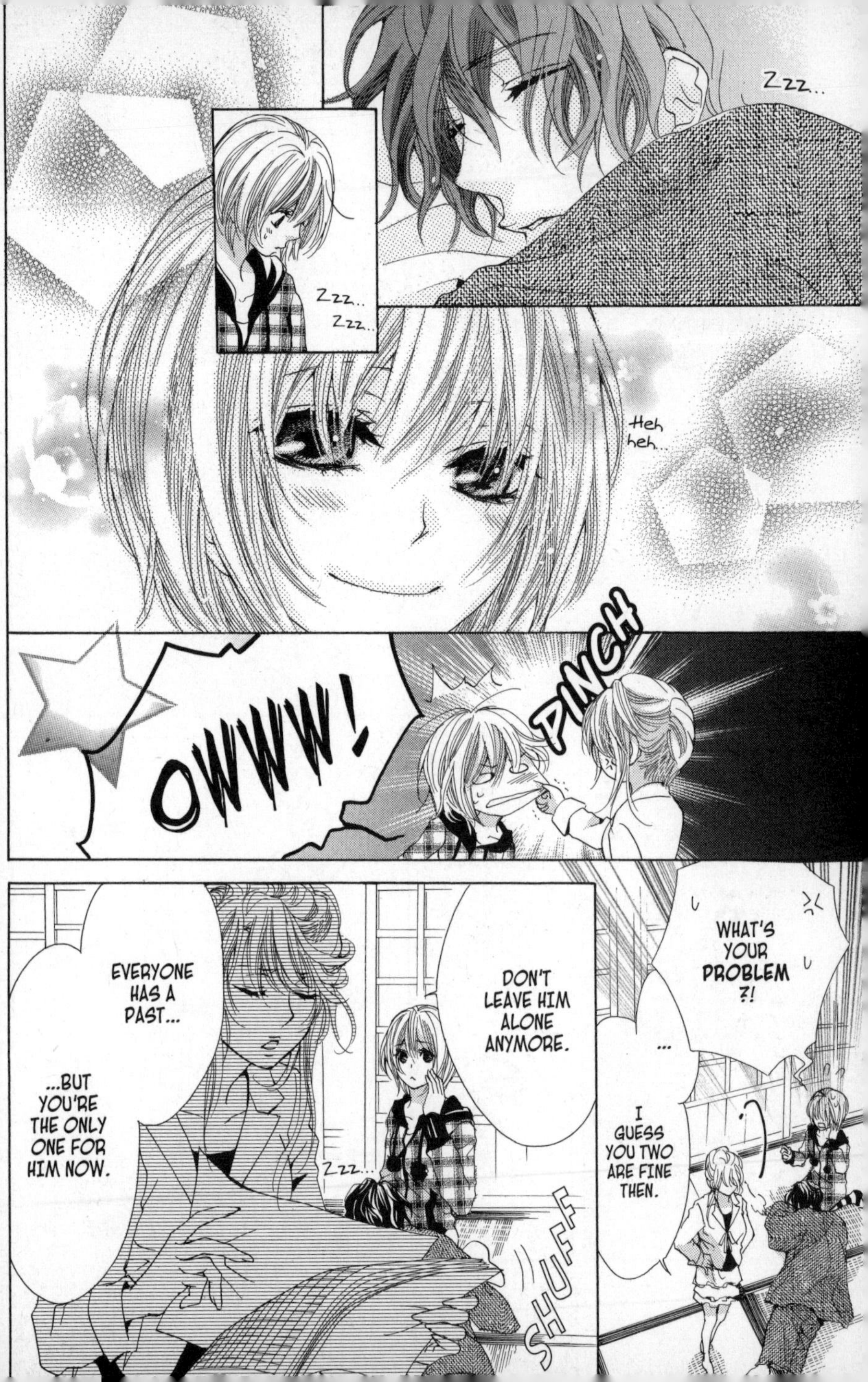
Zzz...
Zzz..
Zzz...
Heh heh...
PINCH
OWWW!
WHAT'S YOUR PROBLEM?!
...
I GUESS YOU TWO ARE FINE THEN.
DON'T LEAVE HIM ALONE ANYMORE.
EVERYONE HAS A PAST...
Zzz...
...BUT YOU'RE THE ONLY ONE FOR HIM NOW.
SHUFF

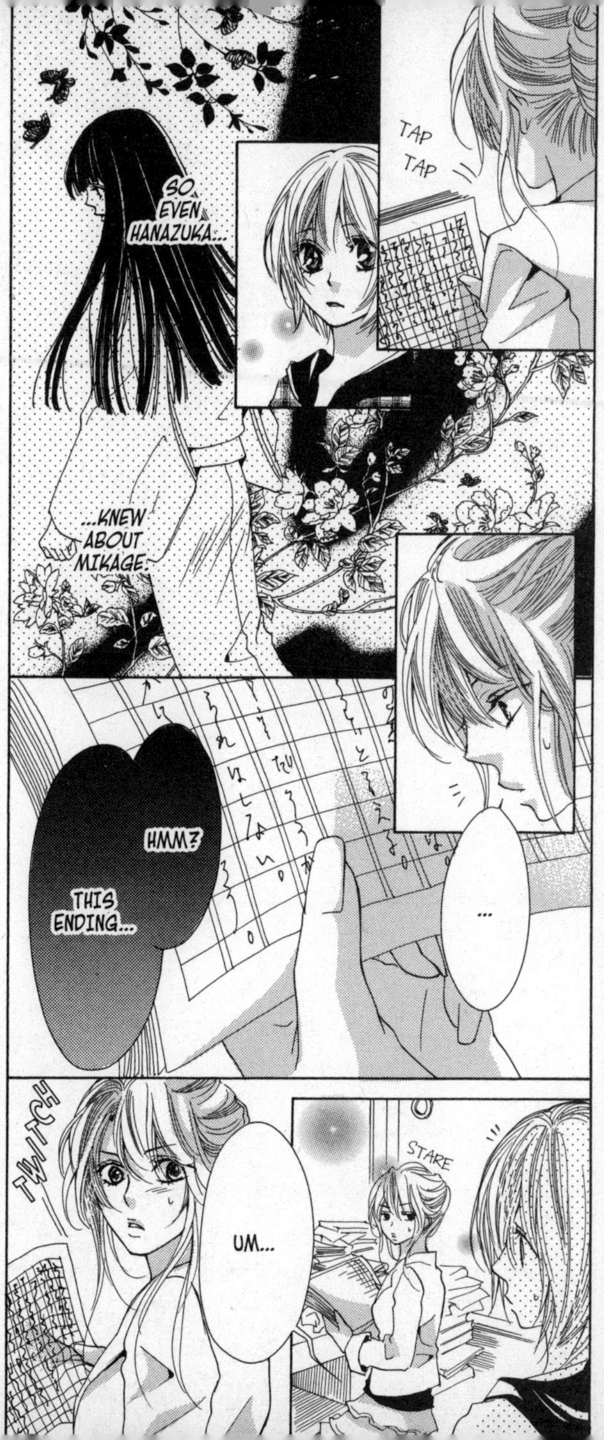
TAP
TAP
SO EVEN HANAZUKA...
...KNEW ABOUT MIKAGE.
...
HMM?
THIS ENDING...
STARE
TWITCH
UM...

Small Talk

⑤

People I've Met Recently

MANGA ARTISTS

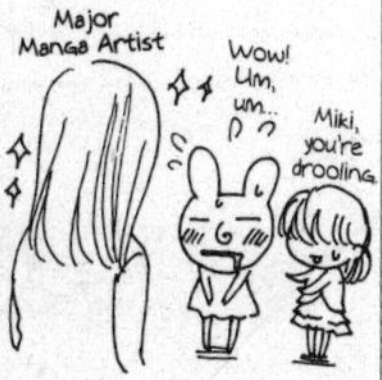
Major Manga Artist
Wow! Um, um...
Miki, you're drooling.

Oh, this isn't recent anymore. It happened at the end of last year.

My publisher, Shogakukan, threw a thank-you party. I'd just pulled an all-nighter, but I still attended.

Momiji Sensei and I were introduced to a lot of manga artists. I don't mingle with people on a regular basis, so I was very nervous, and I acted strange.

However, it's such a rare opportunity to meet other artists that I savored every precious moment!

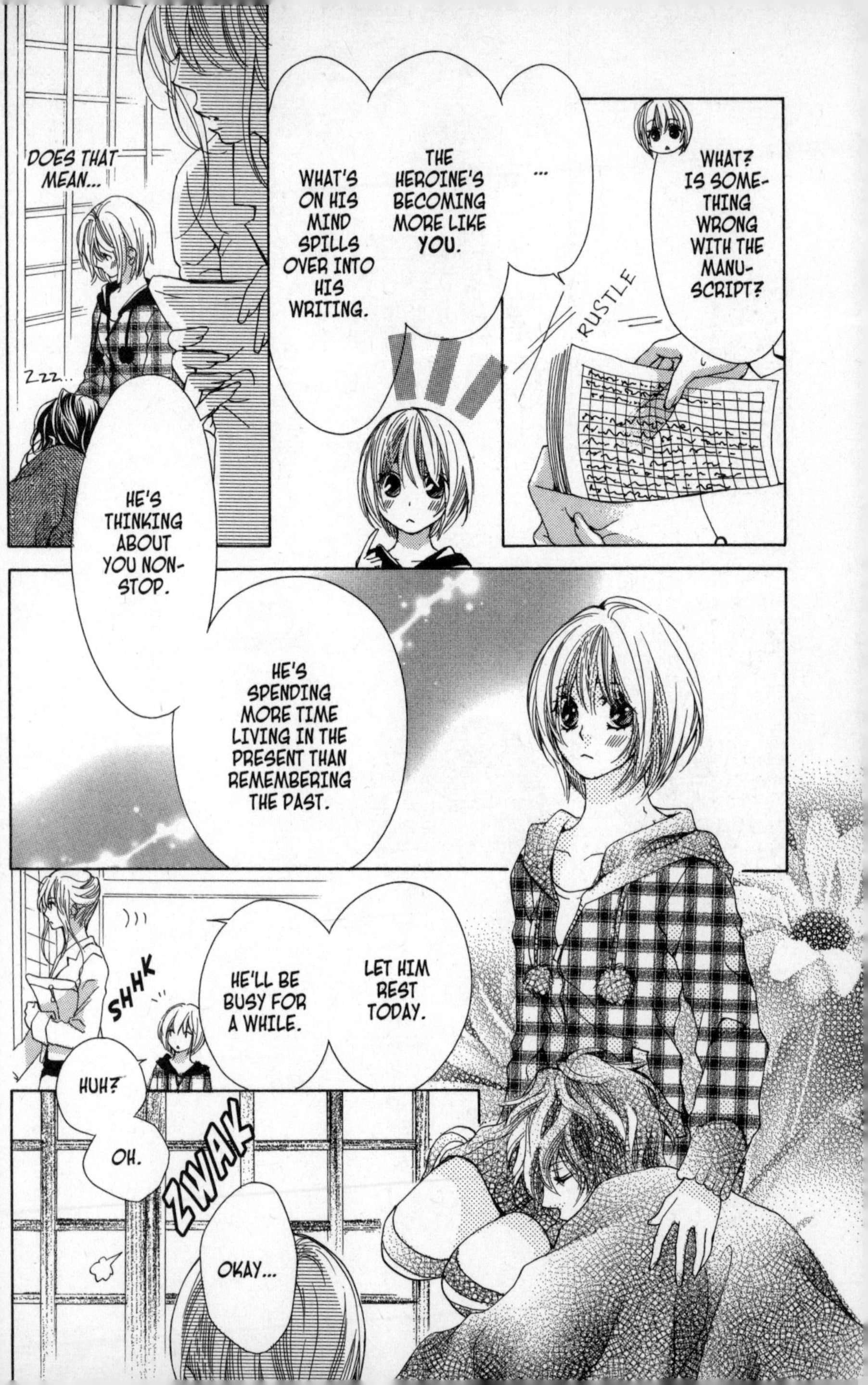
WHAT? IS SOME-THING WRONG WITH THE MANU-SCRIPT?
RUSTLE
...
THE HEROINE'S BECOMING MORE LIKE YOU.
WHAT'S ON HIS MIND SPILLS OVER INTO HIS WRITING.
DOES THAT MEAN...
Zzz...
HE'S THINKING ABOUT YOU NON-STOP.
HE'S SPENDING MORE TIME LIVING IN THE PRESENT THAN REMEMBERING THE PAST.
LET HIM REST TODAY.
HE'LL BE BUSY FOR A WHILE.
SHHK
HUH?
OH.
ZWAK
OKAY...

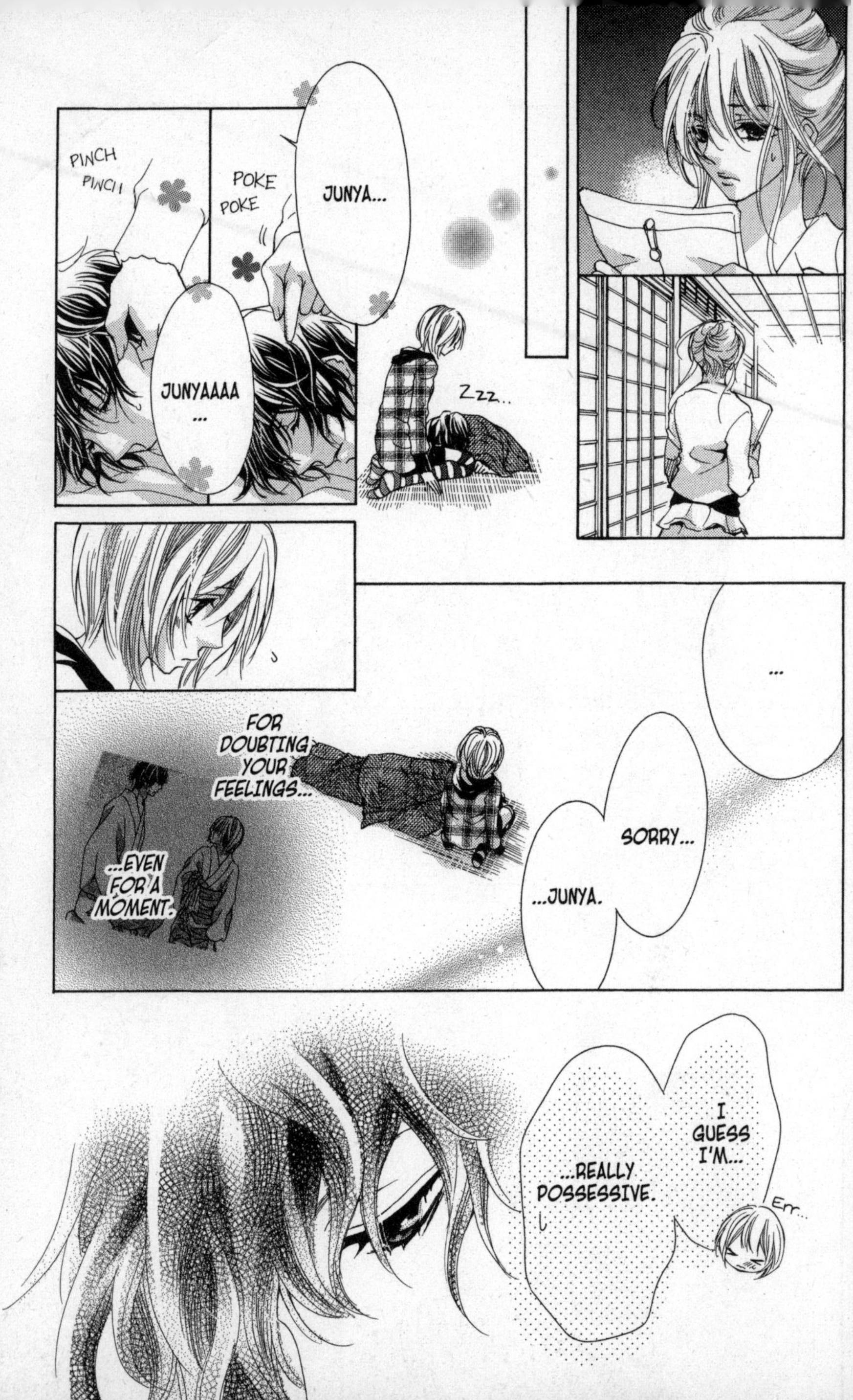
Zzz..
POKE POKE
JUNYA...
PINCH PINCH
JUNYAAAA...
...
SORRY...
...JUNYA.
FOR DOUBTING YOUR FEELINGS...
...EVEN FOR A MOMENT.
I GUESS I'M...
...REALLY POSSESSIVE.
Err...

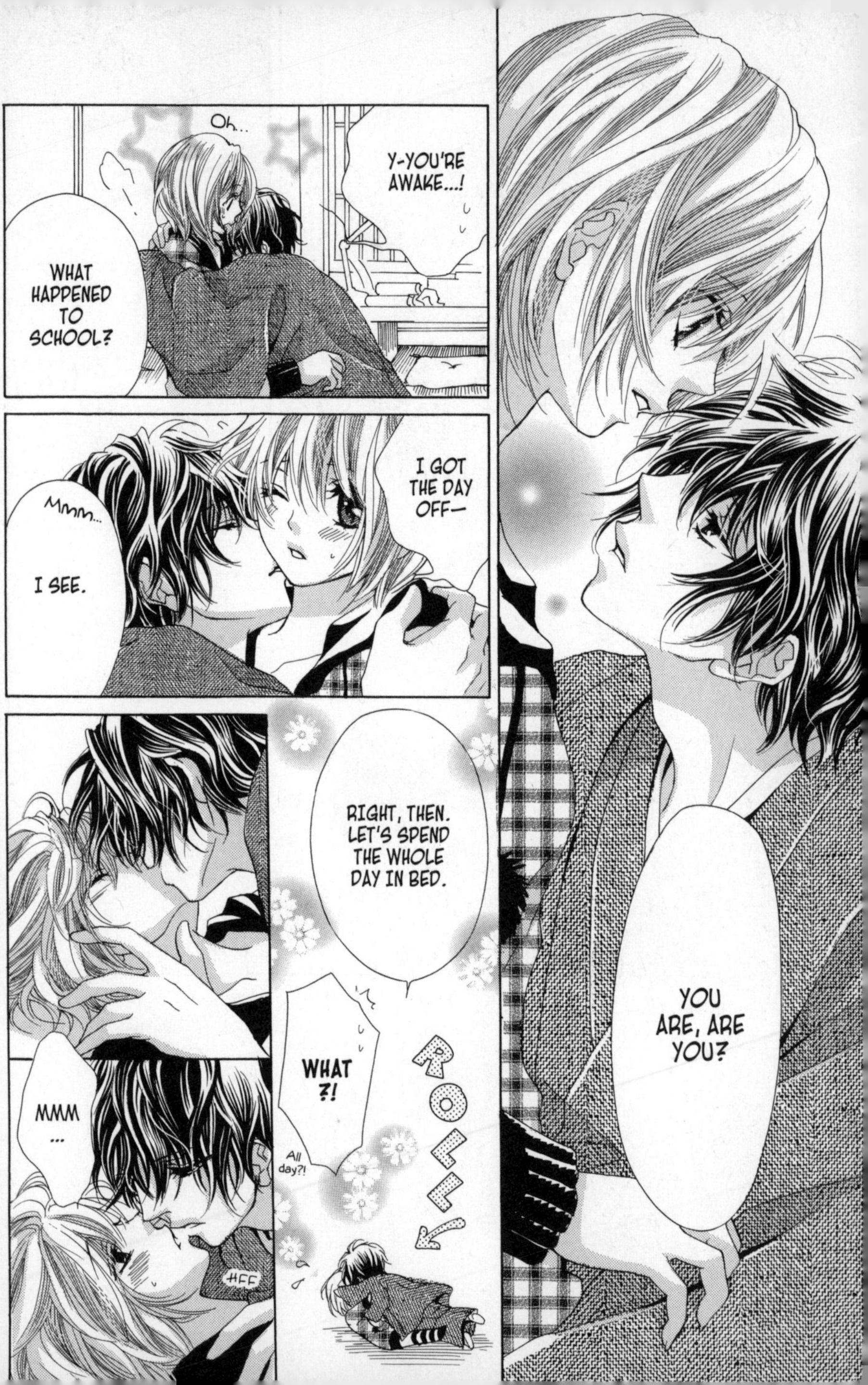
YOU ARE, ARE YOU?
Y-YOU'RE AWAKE...!
Oh...
WHAT HAPPENED TO SCHOOL?
I GOT THE DAY OFF—
Mmm...
I SEE.
RIGHT, THEN. LET'S SPEND THE WHOLE DAY IN BED.
WHAT?!
All day?!
ROLL
MMM ...
HFF

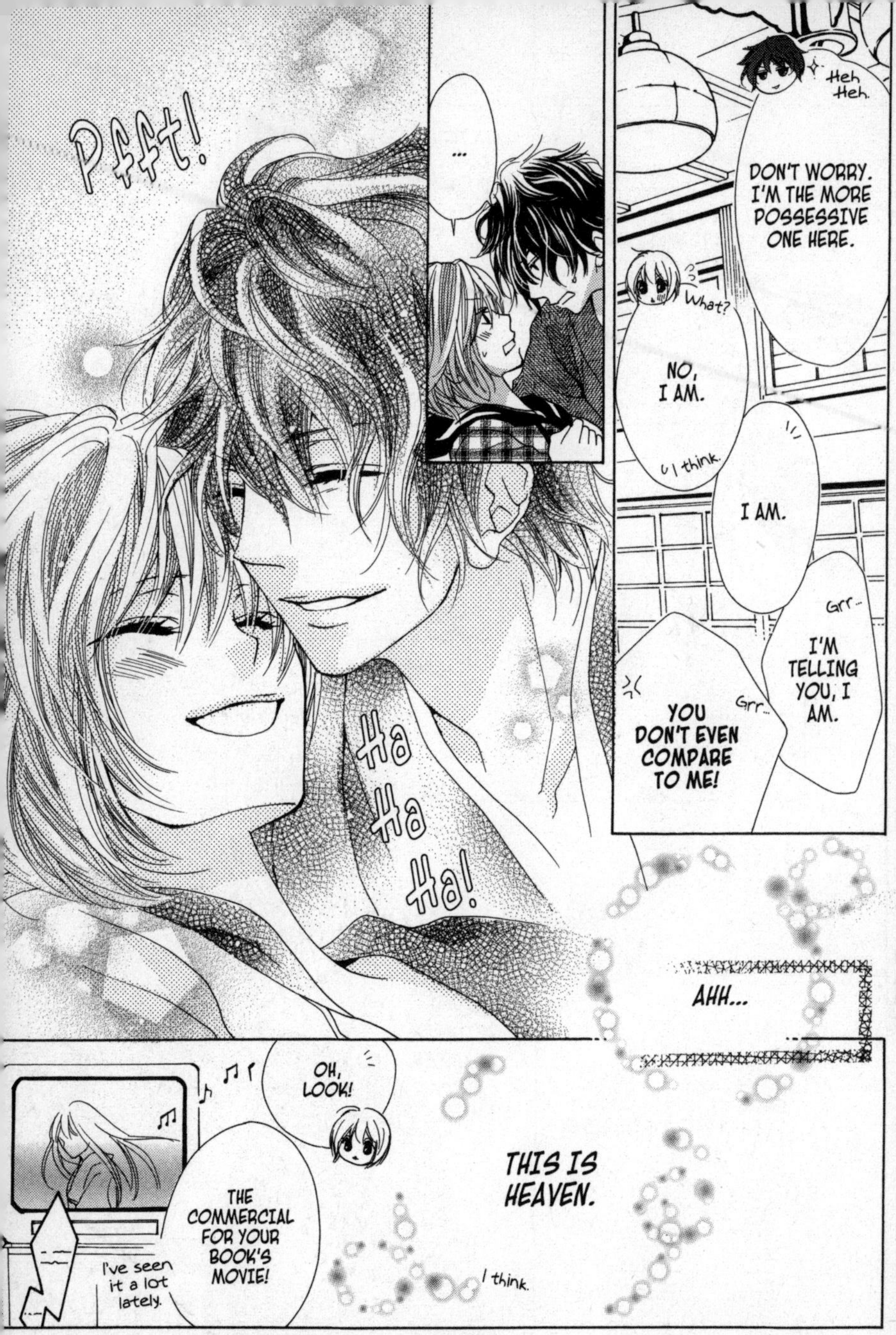

Heh Heh.
DON'T WORRY. I'M THE MORE POSSESSIVE ONE HERE.
What?
NO, I AM.
I think.
I AM.
Grr...
I'M TELLING YOU, I AM.
Grr...
YOU DON'T EVEN COMPARE TO ME!
...
Pfft!
Ha Ha Ha!
AHH...
THIS IS HEAVEN.
I think.
OH, LOOK!
THE COMMERCIAL FOR YOUR BOOK'S MOVIE!
I've seen it a lot lately.

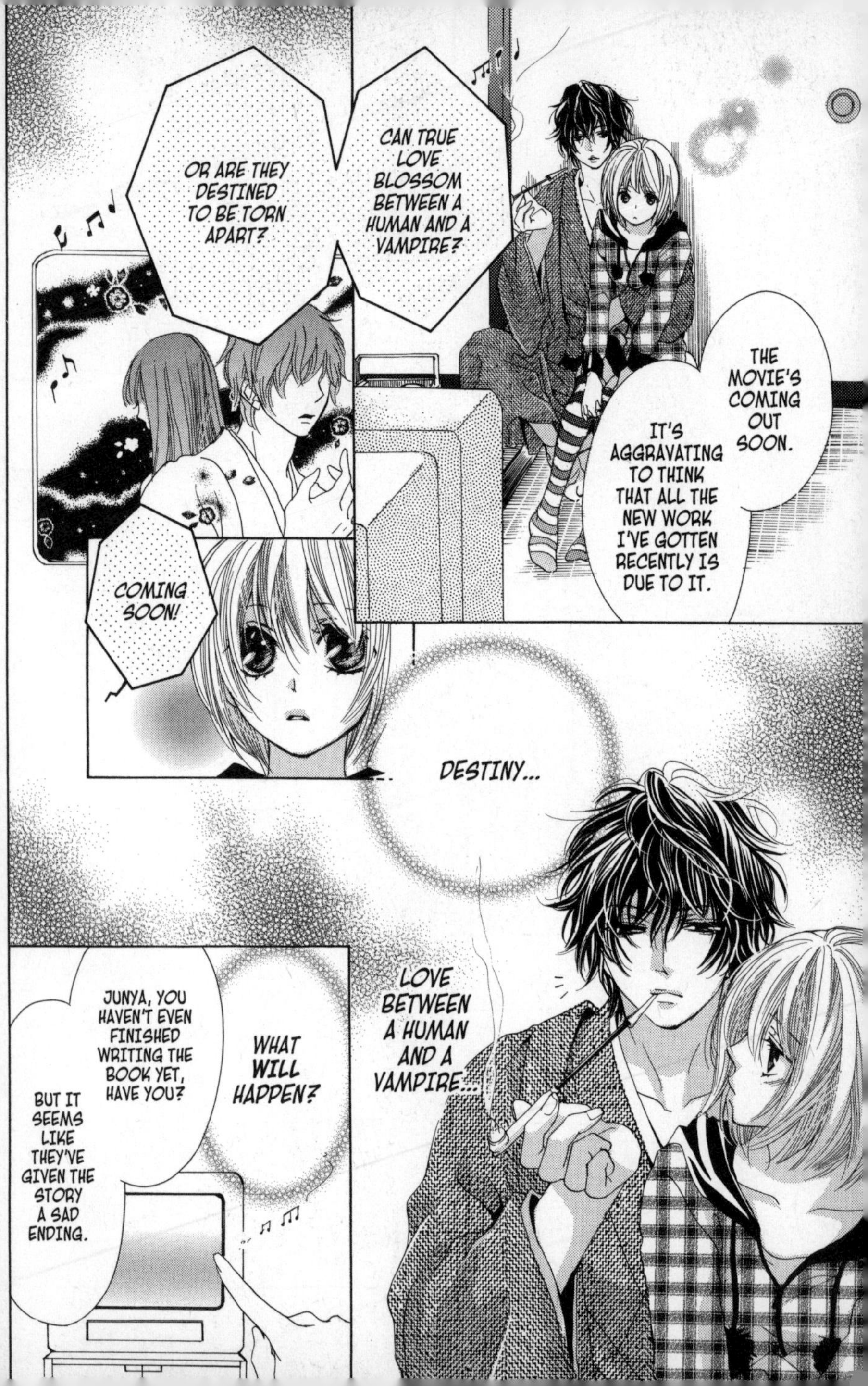
CAN TRUE LOVE BLOSSOM BETWEEN A HUMAN AND A VAMPIRE?
OR ARE THEY DESTINED TO BE TORN APART?
THE MOVIE'S COMING OUT SOON.
IT'S AGGRAVATING TO THINK THAT ALL THE NEW WORK I'VE GOTTEN RECENTLY IS DUE TO IT.
COMING SOON!
DESTINY...
LOVE BETWEEN A HUMAN AND A VAMPIRE...
WHAT **WILL** HAPPEN?
JUNYA, YOU HAVEN'T EVEN FINISHED WRITING THE BOOK YET, HAVE YOU?
BUT IT SEEMS LIKE THEY'VE GIVEN THE STORY A SAD ENDING.

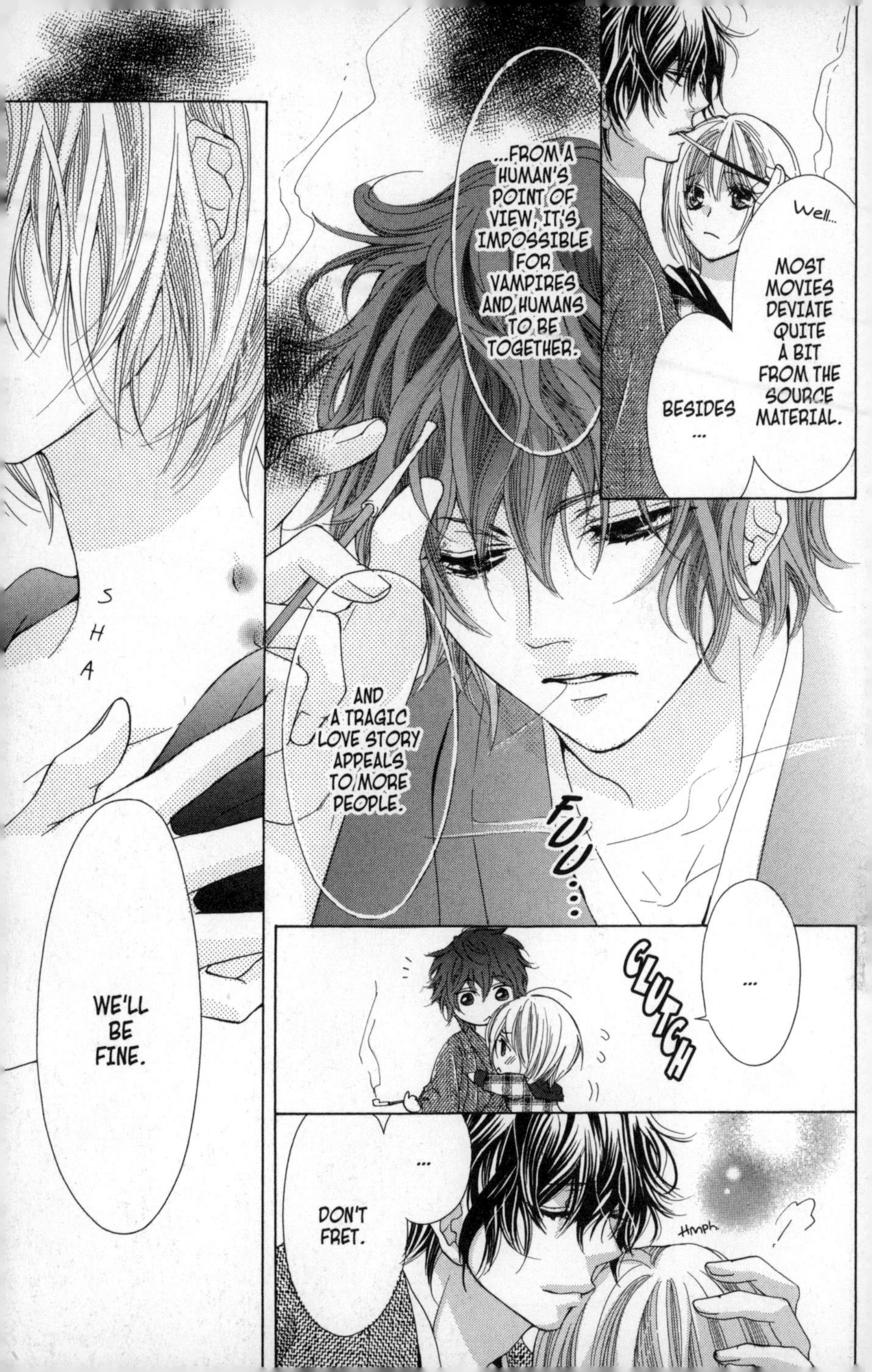

Well...
MOST MOVIES DEVIATE QUITE A BIT FROM THE SOURCE MATERIAL.
BESIDES...
...FROM A HUMAN'S POINT OF VIEW, IT'S IMPOSSIBLE FOR VAMPIRES AND HUMANS TO BE TOGETHER.
AND A TRAGIC LOVE STORY APPEALS TO MORE PEOPLE.
FUU...
...
CLUTCH
...
DON'T FRET.
Hmph.
SHA
WE'LL BE FINE.

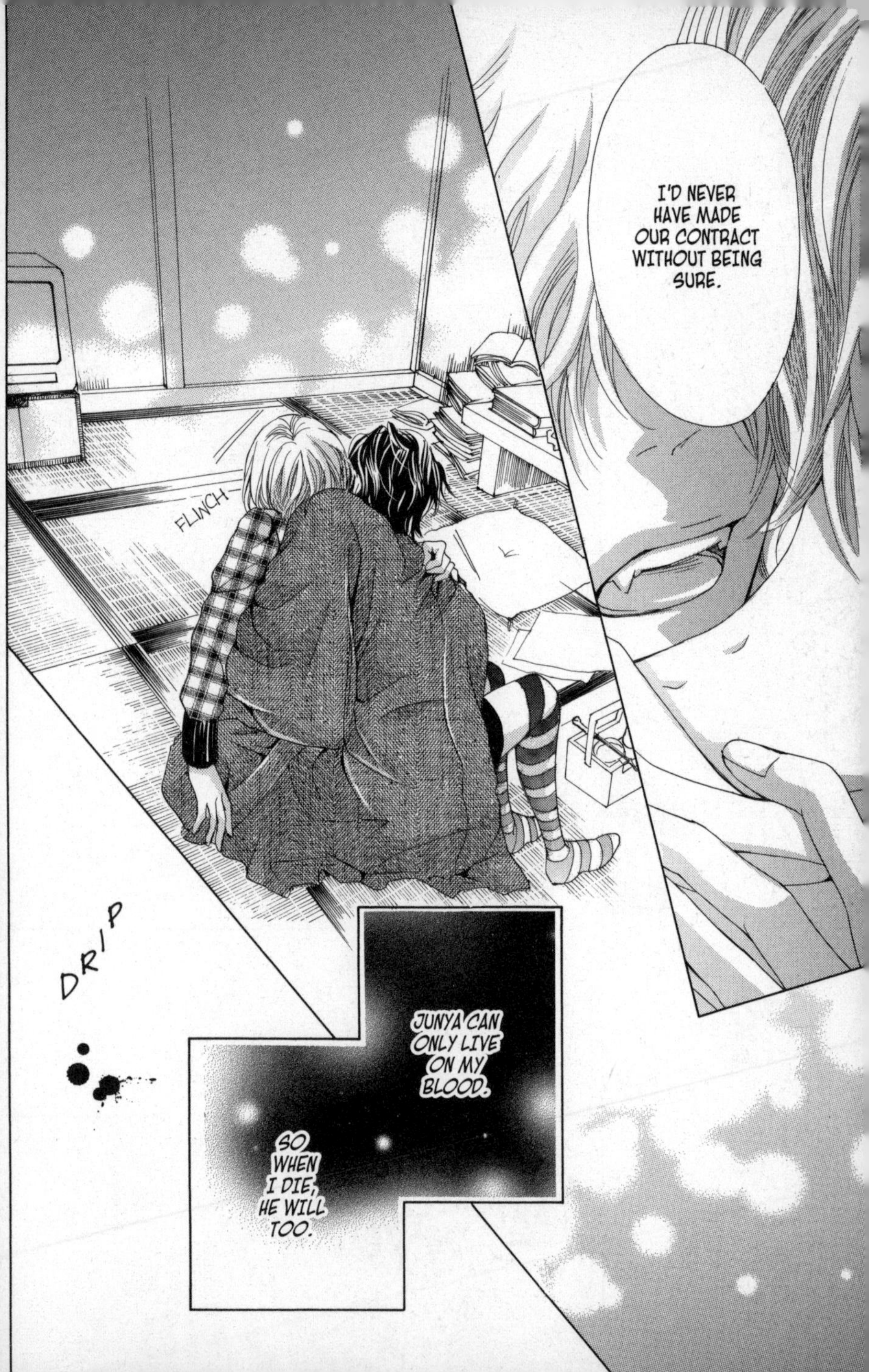
I'D NEVER HAVE MADE OUR CONTRACT WITHOUT BEING SURE.
FLINCH
DRIP
JUNYA CAN ONLY LIVE ON MY BLOOD.
SO WHEN I DIE, HE WILL TOO.

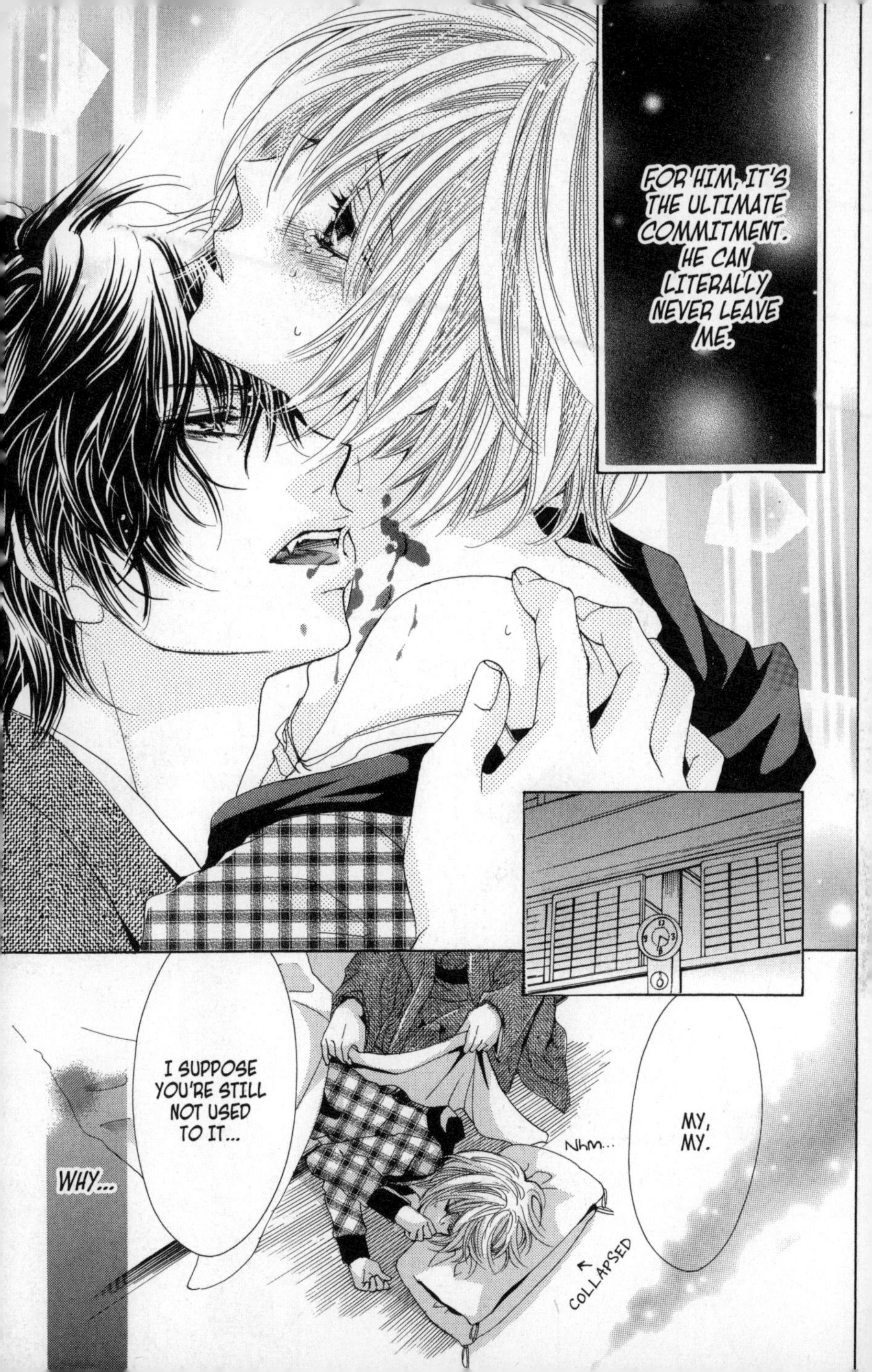
FOR HIM, IT'S THE ULTIMATE COMMITMENT. HE CAN LITERALLY NEVER LEAVE ME.
MY, MY.
Nhm...
COLLAPSED
I SUPPOSE YOU'RE STILL NOT USED TO IT...
WHY...

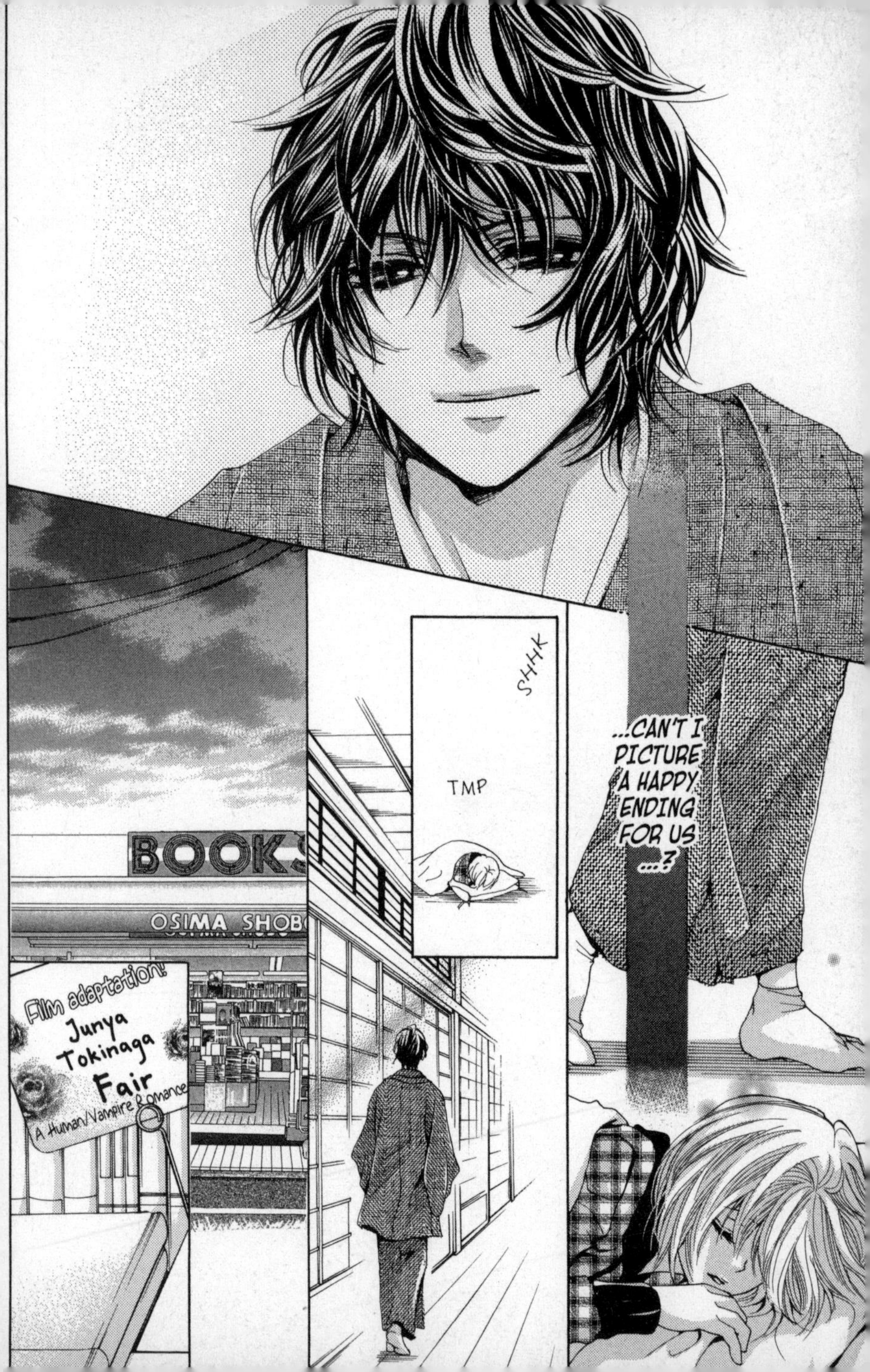
...CAN'T I PICTURE A HAPPY ENDING FOR US ...?
SHHK
TMP
BOOKS
OSIMA SHOBO
Film adaptation!
Junya Tokinaga Fair
A Human/Vampire Romance

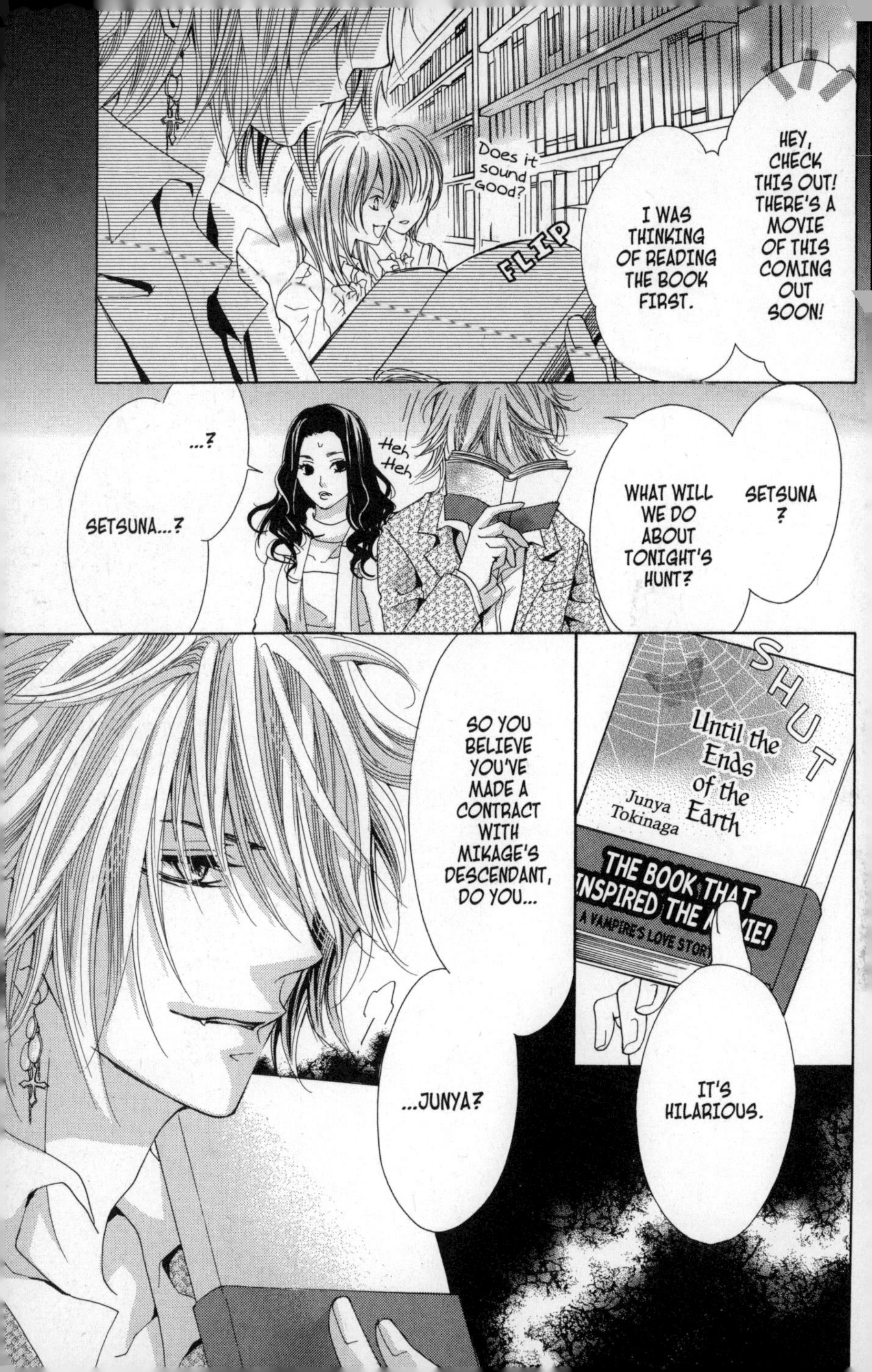
HEY, CHECK THIS OUT! THERE'S A MOVIE OF THIS COMING OUT SOON!
I WAS THINKING OF READING THE BOOK FIRST.
FLIP
Does it sound good?
SETSUNA?
WHAT WILL WE DO ABOUT TONIGHT'S HUNT?
Heh, Heh
...?
SETSUNA...?
SHUT
Until the Ends of the Earth
Junya Tokinaga
THE BOOK THAT
IT'S HILARIOUS.
SO YOU BELIEVE YOU'VE MADE A CONTRACT WITH MIKAGE'S DESCENDANT, DO YOU...
...JUNYA?

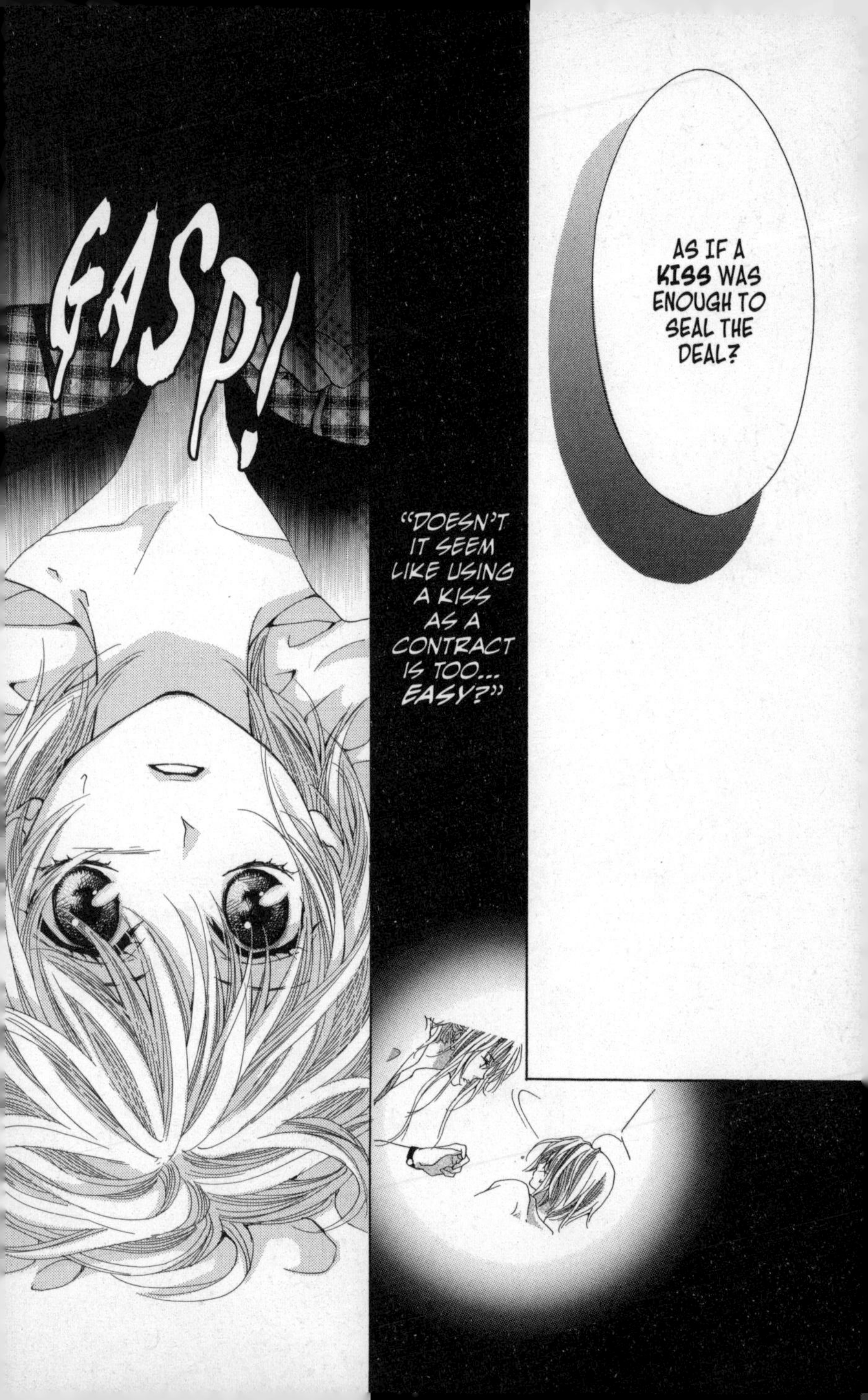
AS IF A KISS WAS ENOUGH TO SEAL THE DEAL?
"DOESN'T IT SEEM LIKE USING A KISS AS A CONTRACT IS TOO... EASY?"
GASP!

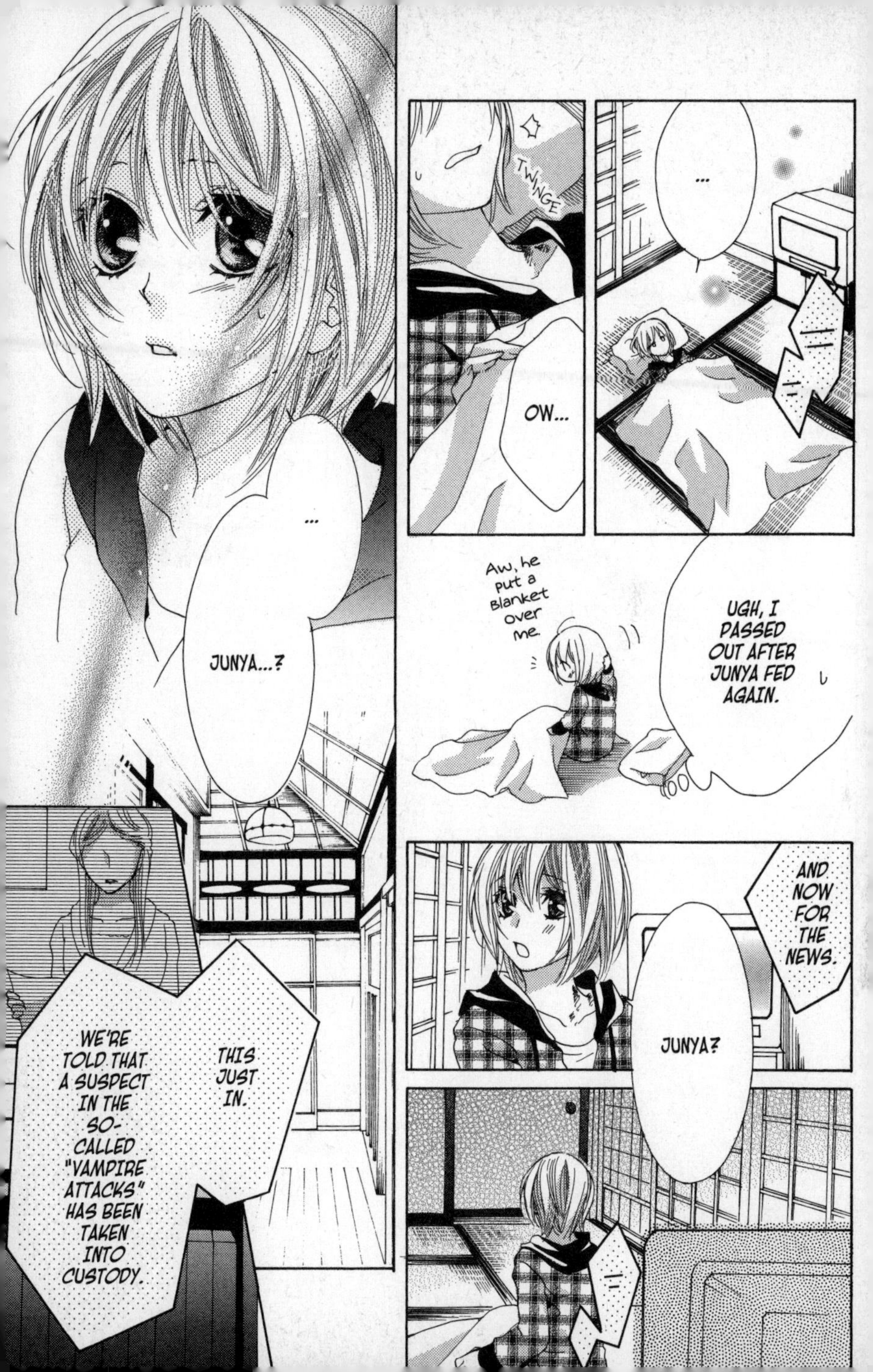
...
TWINGE
OW...
UGH, I PASSED OUT AFTER JUNYA FED AGAIN.
Aw, he put a Blanket over me.
AND NOW FOR THE NEWS.
JUNYA?
...
JUNYA...?
THIS JUST IN.
WE'RE TOLD THAT A SUSPECT IN THE SO-CALLED "VAMPIRE ATTACKS" HAS BEEN TAKEN INTO CUSTODY.

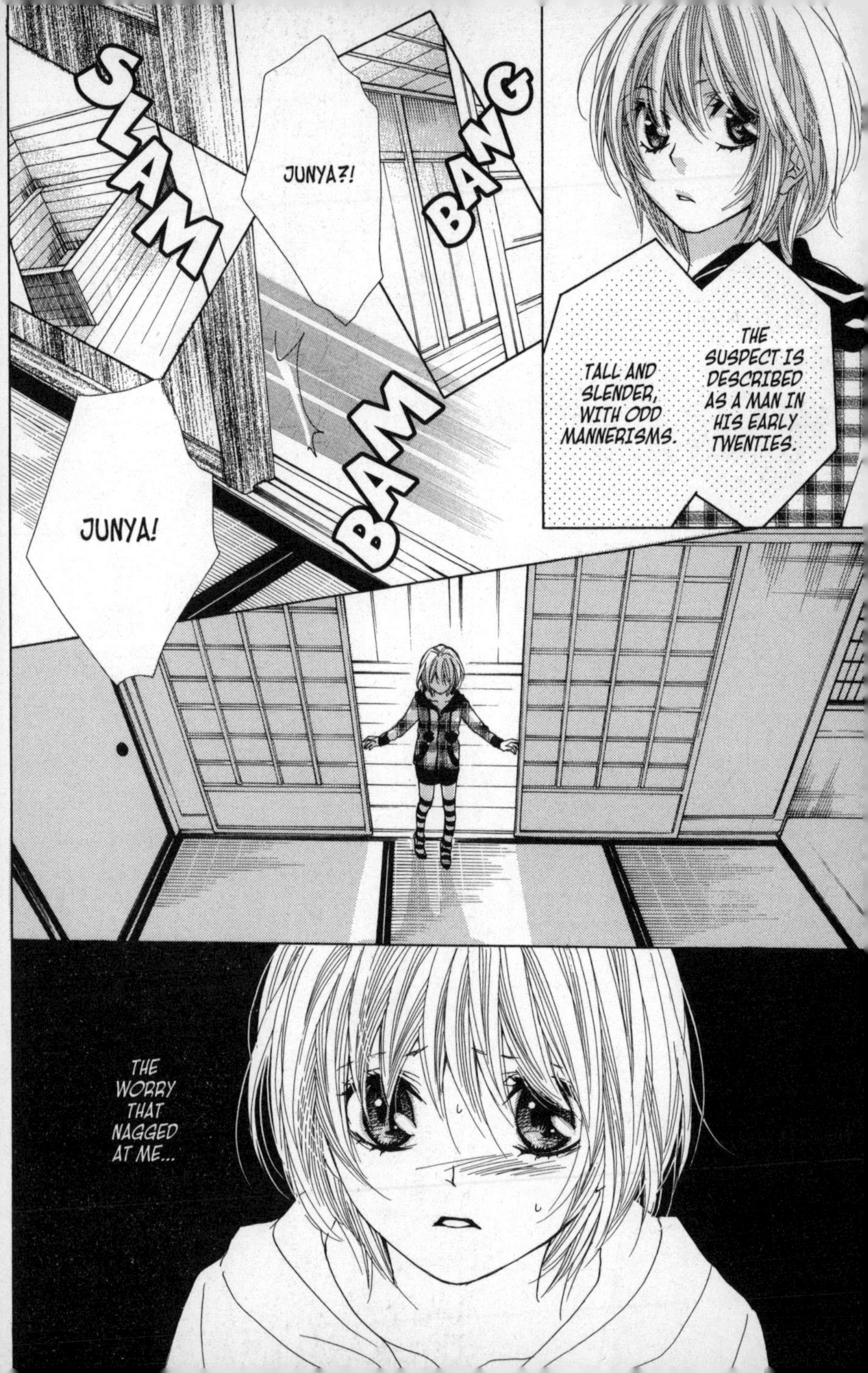
THE SUSPECT IS DESCRIBED AS A MAN IN HIS EARLY TWENTIES.
TALL AND SLENDER, WITH ODD MANNERISMS.
BANG
JUNYA?!
SLAM
BAM
JUNYA!
THE WORRY THAT NAGGED AT ME...

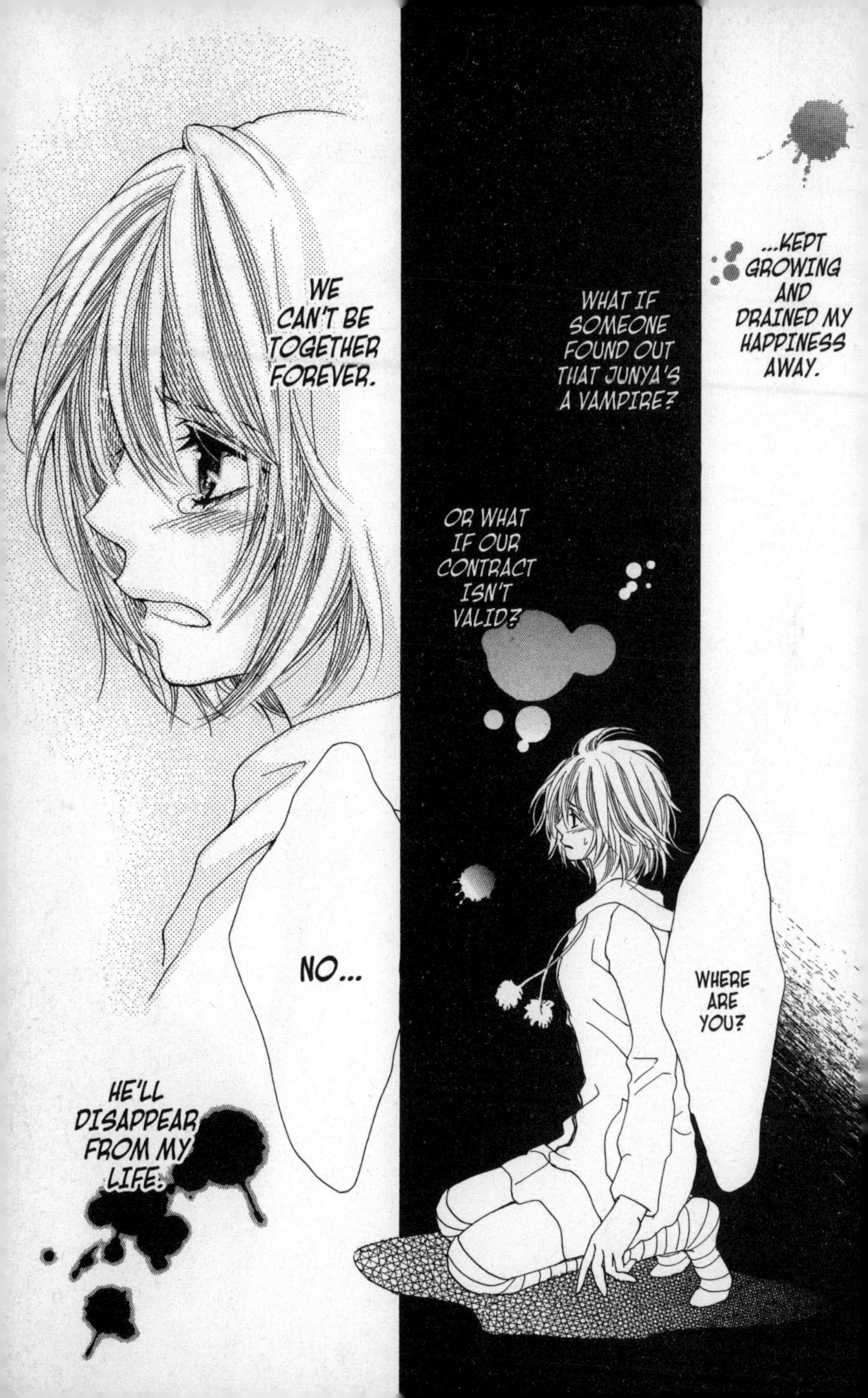
...KEPT GROWING AND DRAINED MY HAPPINESS AWAY.
WHAT IF SOMEONE FOUND OUT THAT JUNYA'S A VAMPIRE?
OR WHAT IF OUR CONTRACT ISN'T VALID?
WHERE ARE YOU?
WE CAN'T BE TOGETHER FOREVER.
NO...
HE'LL DISAPPEAR FROM MY LIFE.

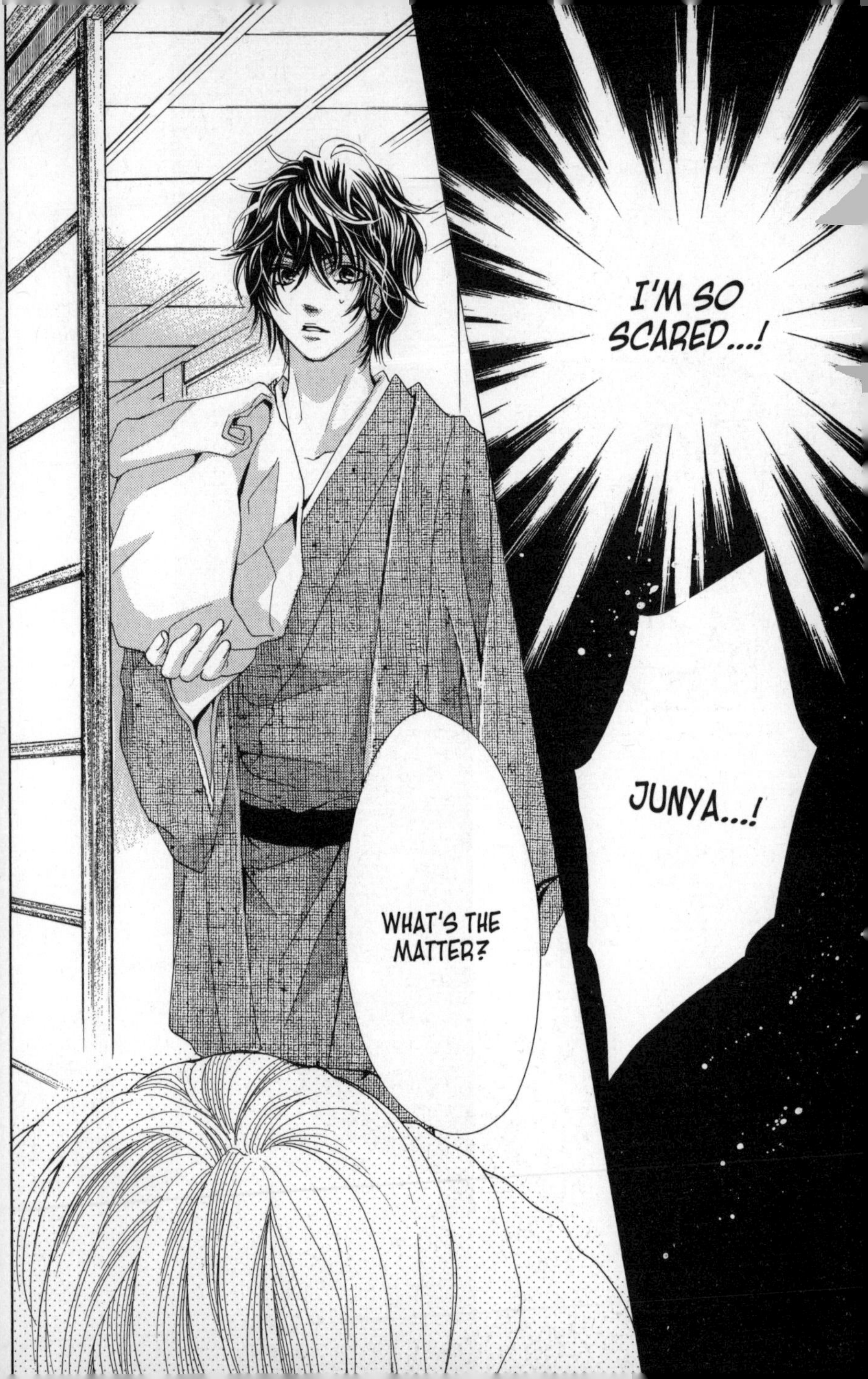
I'M SO SCARED...!
JUNYA...!
WHAT'S THE MATTER?

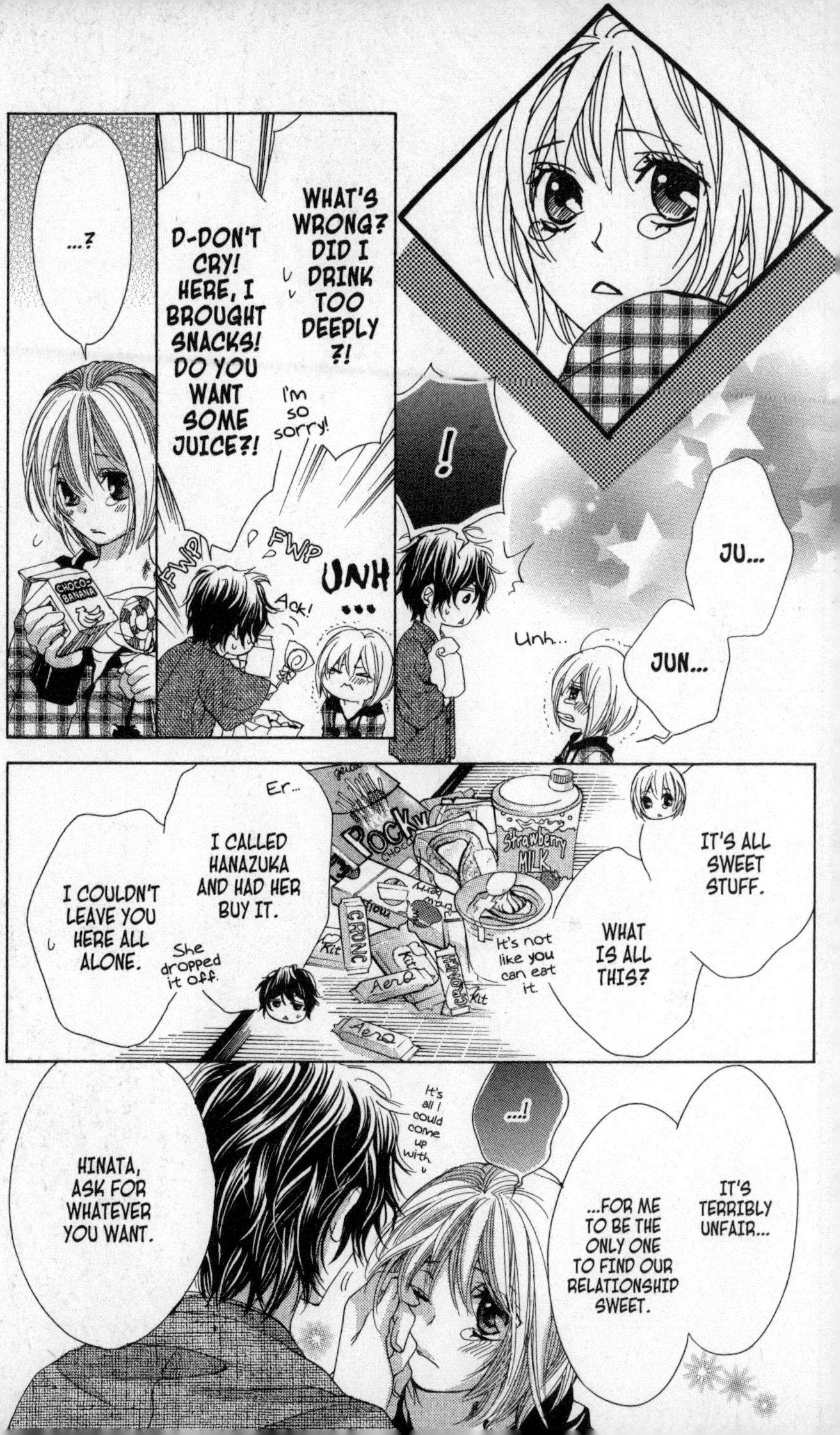
JU...
JUN...
!
Unh...
WHAT'S WRONG? DID I DRINK TOO DEEPLY?!
D-DON'T CRY! HERE, I BROUGHT SNACKS! DO YOU WANT SOME JUICE?!
I'm so sorry!
FWP
FWP
UNH
Ack!
...?
CHOCO-BANANA
IT'S ALL SWEET STUFF.
WHAT IS ALL THIS?
It's not like you can eat it.
Er...
I CALLED HANAZUKA AND HAD HER BUY IT.
She dropped it off.
I COULDN'T LEAVE YOU HERE ALL ALONE.
Strawberry MILK
CRUNCH
Aero
IT'S TERRIBLY UNFAIR...
...FOR ME TO BE THE ONLY ONE TO FIND OUR RELATIONSHIP SWEET.
...!
It's all I could come up with.
HINATA, ASK FOR WHATEVER YOU WANT.

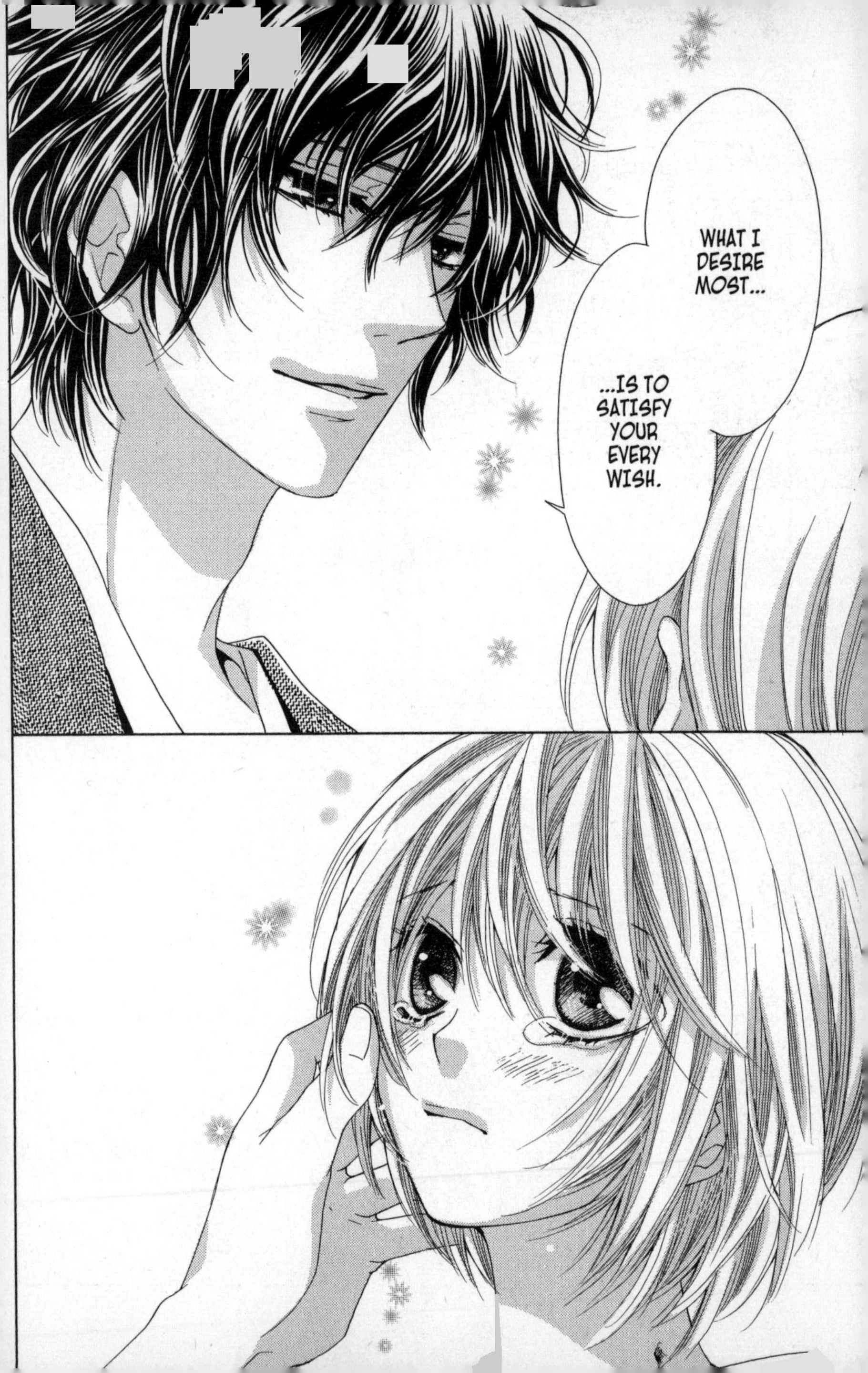
WHAT I DESIRE MOST...
...IS TO SATISFY YOUR EVERY WISH.

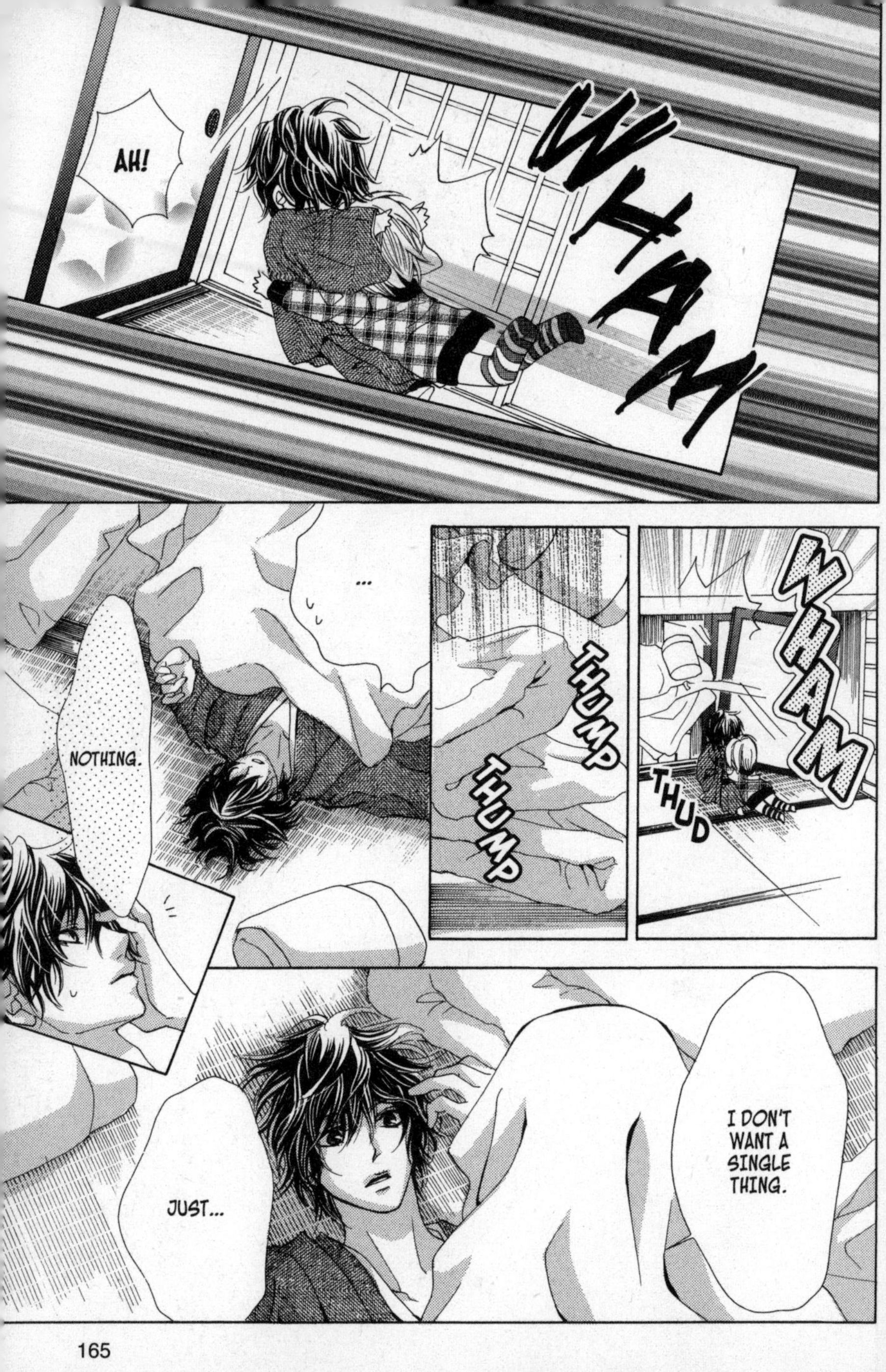
WHAM
AH!
WHAM
THUD
THUMP
THUMP
...
NOTHING.
I DON'T WANT A SINGLE THING.
JUST...

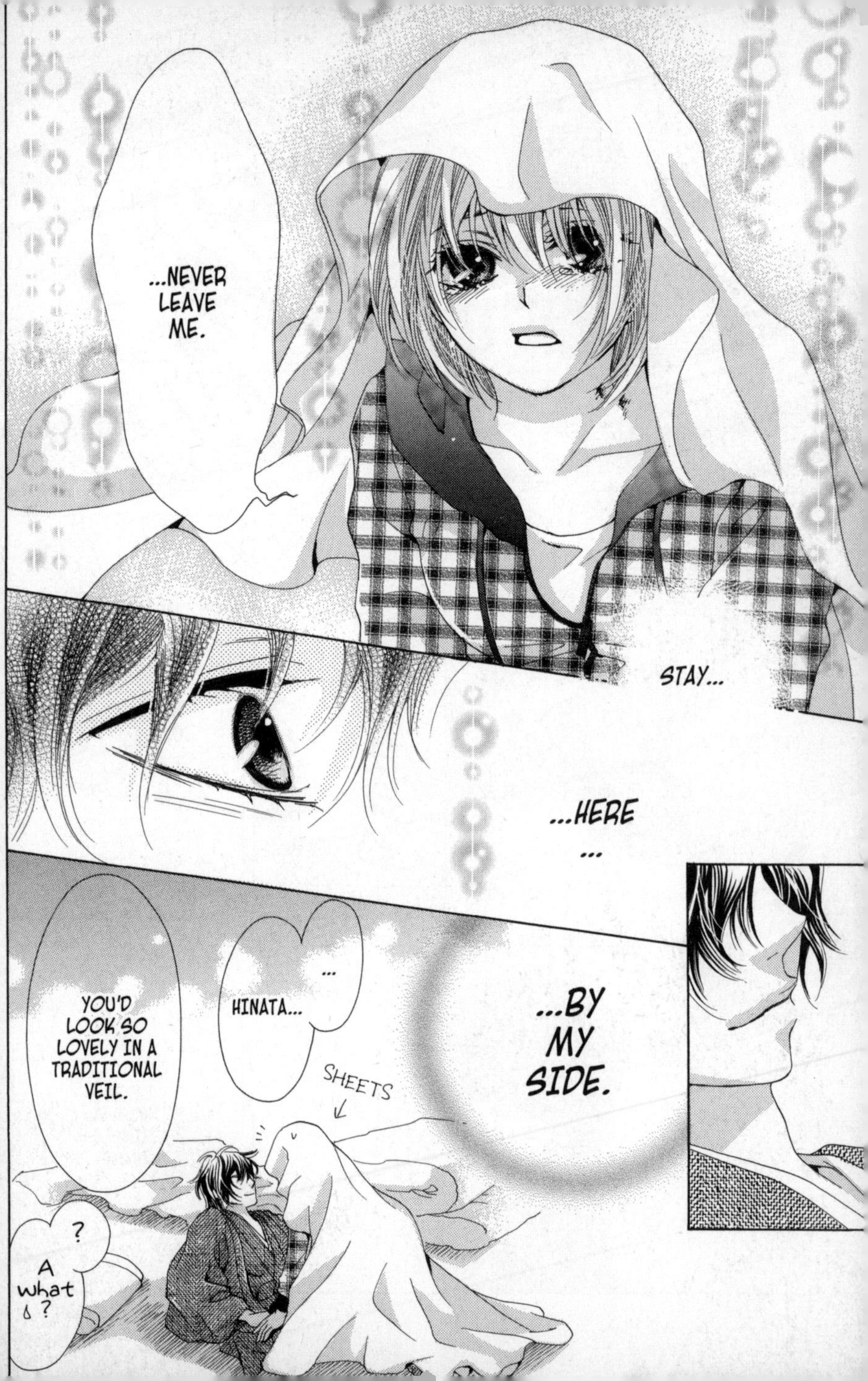
...NEVER LEAVE ME.
STAY...
...HERE ...
...BY MY SIDE.
... HINATA...
YOU'D LOOK SO LOVELY IN A TRADITIONAL VEIL.
SHEETS
? A what?

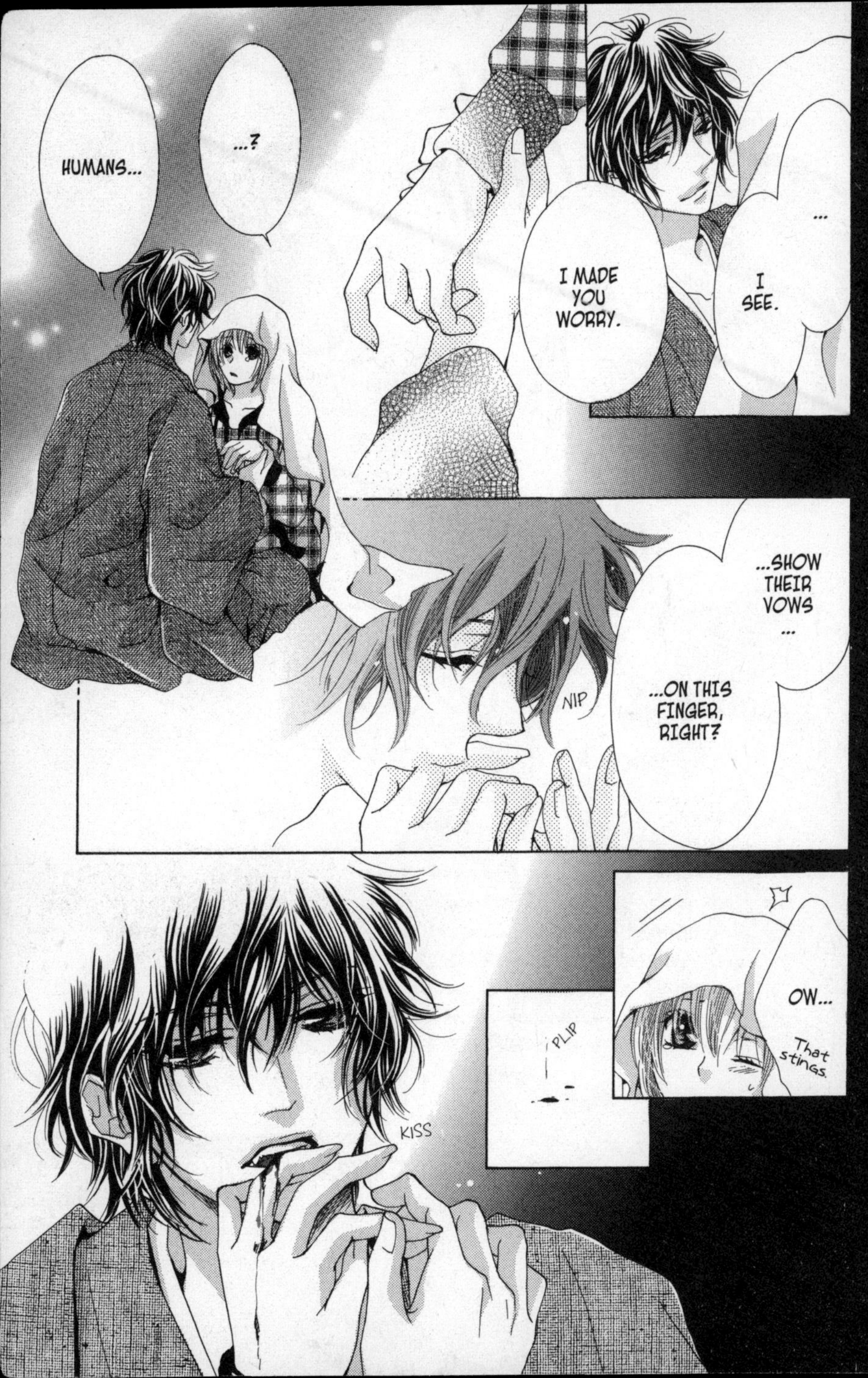

...
I SEE.
I MADE YOU WORRY.
...?
HUMANS...
...SHOW THEIR VOWS ...
...ON THIS FINGER, RIGHT?
NIP
OW...
That stings.
PLIP
KISS

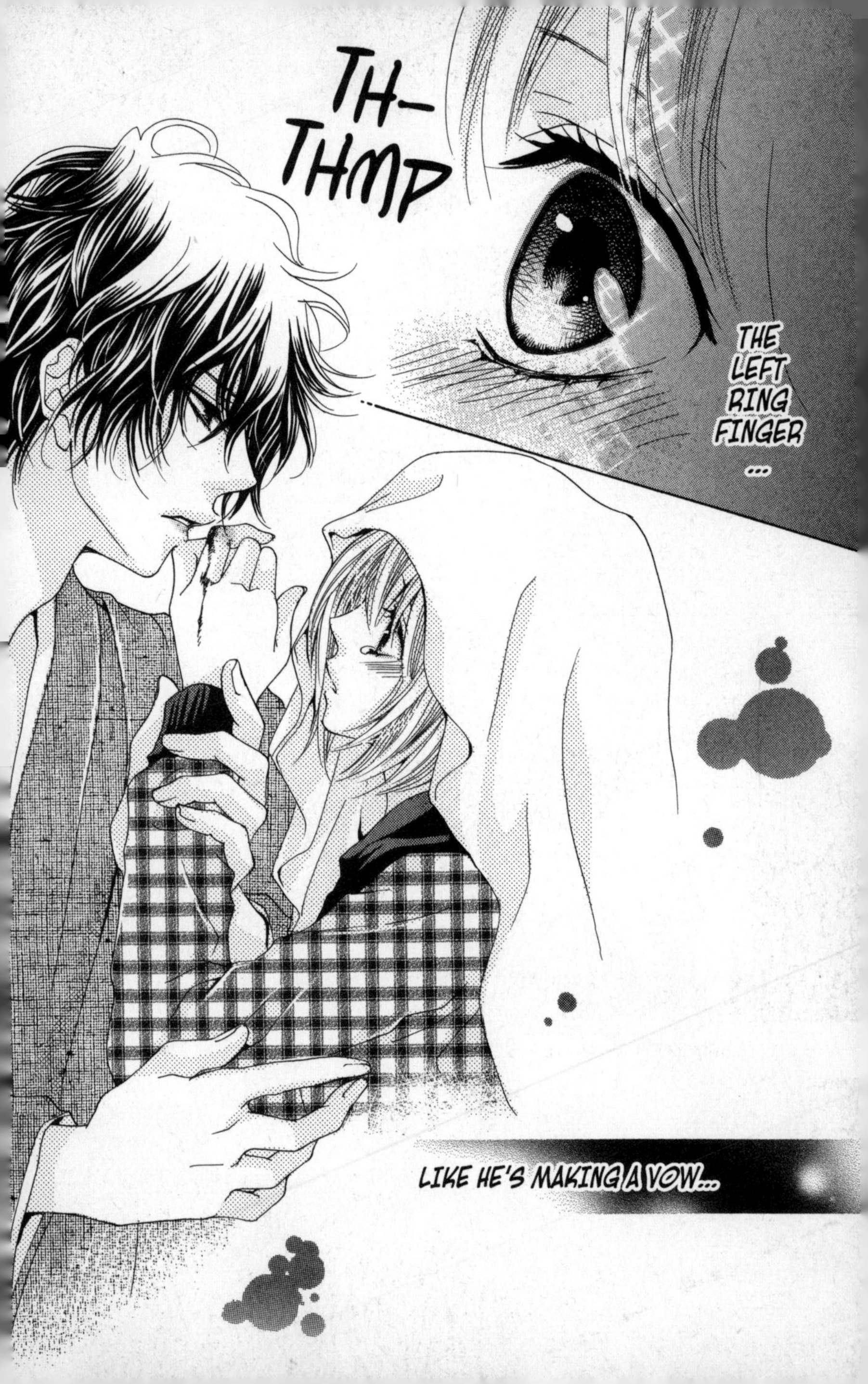
TH-THMP
THE LEFT RING FINGER...
LIKE HE'S MAKING A VOW...

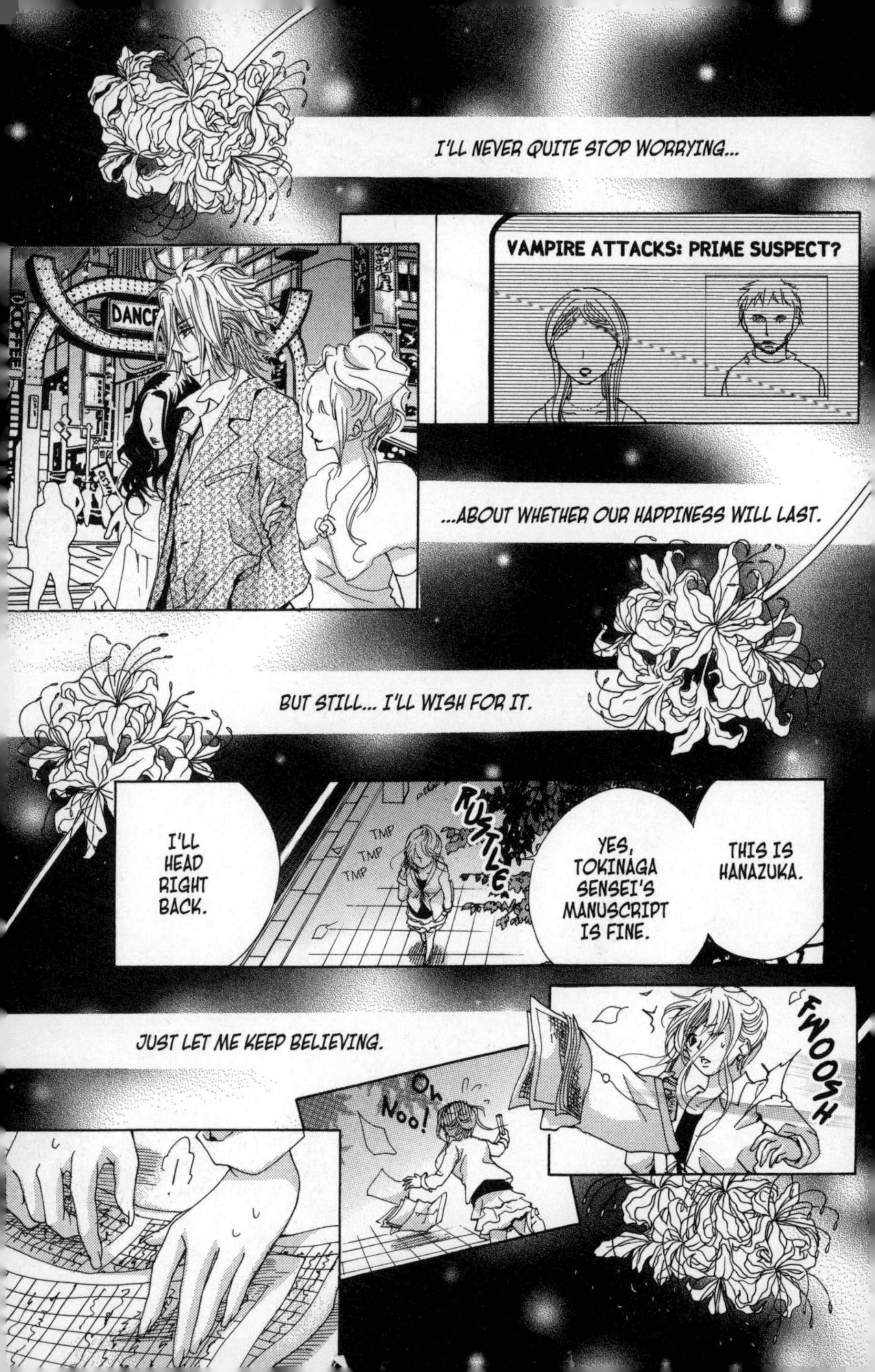
I'LL NEVER QUITE STOP WORRYING...
VAMPIRE ATTACKS: PRIME SUSPECT?
DANCE
COFFEE
...ABOUT WHETHER OUR HAPPINESS WILL LAST.
BUT STILL... I'LL WISH FOR IT.
THIS IS HANAZUKA.
YES, TOKINAGA SENSEI'S MANUSCRIPT IS FINE.
RUSTLE
TMP TMP TMP
I'LL HEAD RIGHT BACK.
JUST LET ME KEEP BELIEVING.
FWOOSH
Oh Noo!

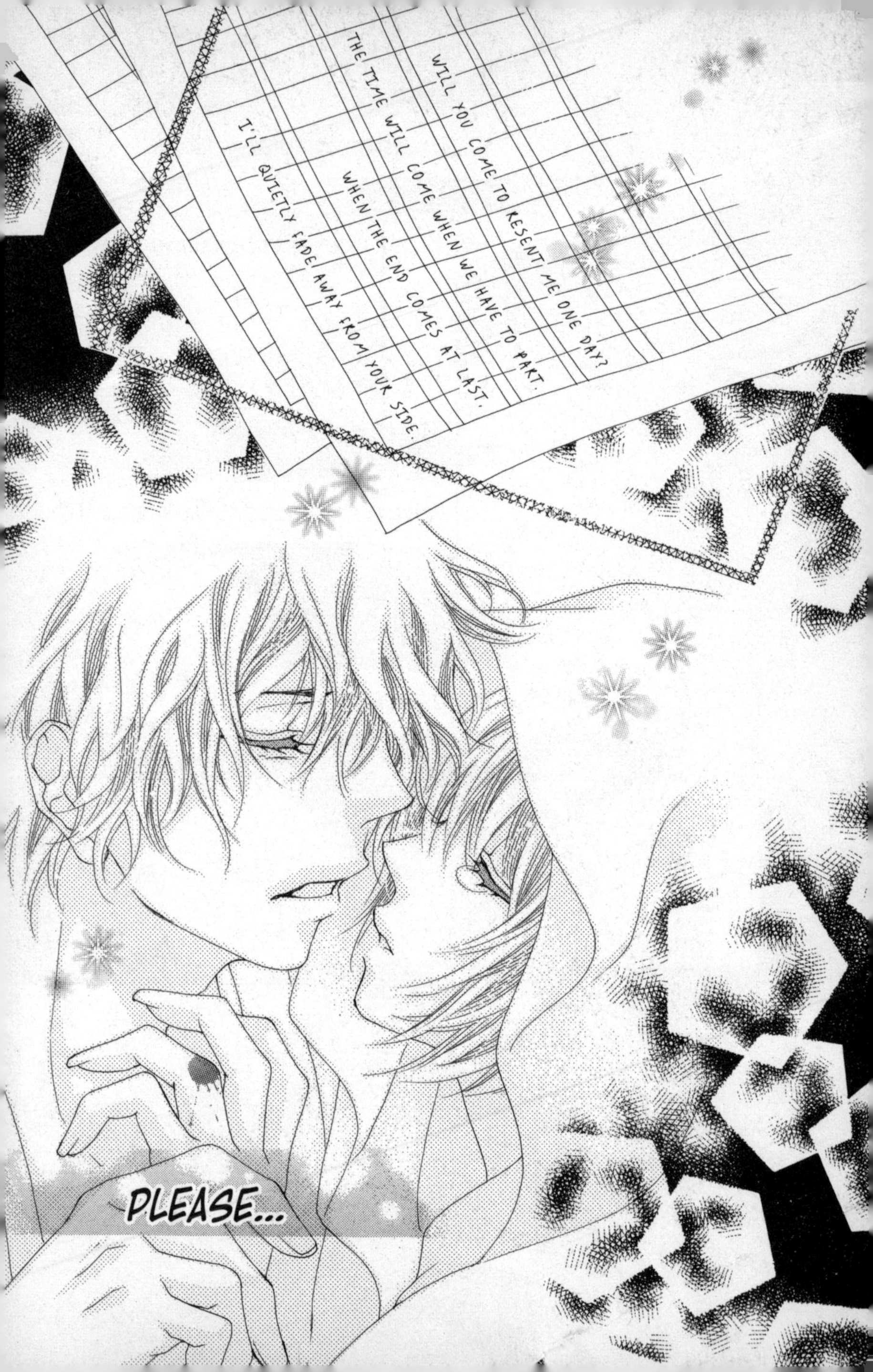
WILL YOU COME TO RESENT ME ONE DAY?
THE TIME WILL COME WHEN WE HAVE TO PART.
WHEN THE END COMES AT LAST.
I'LL QUIETLY FADE AWAY FROM YOUR SIDE.
PLEASE...

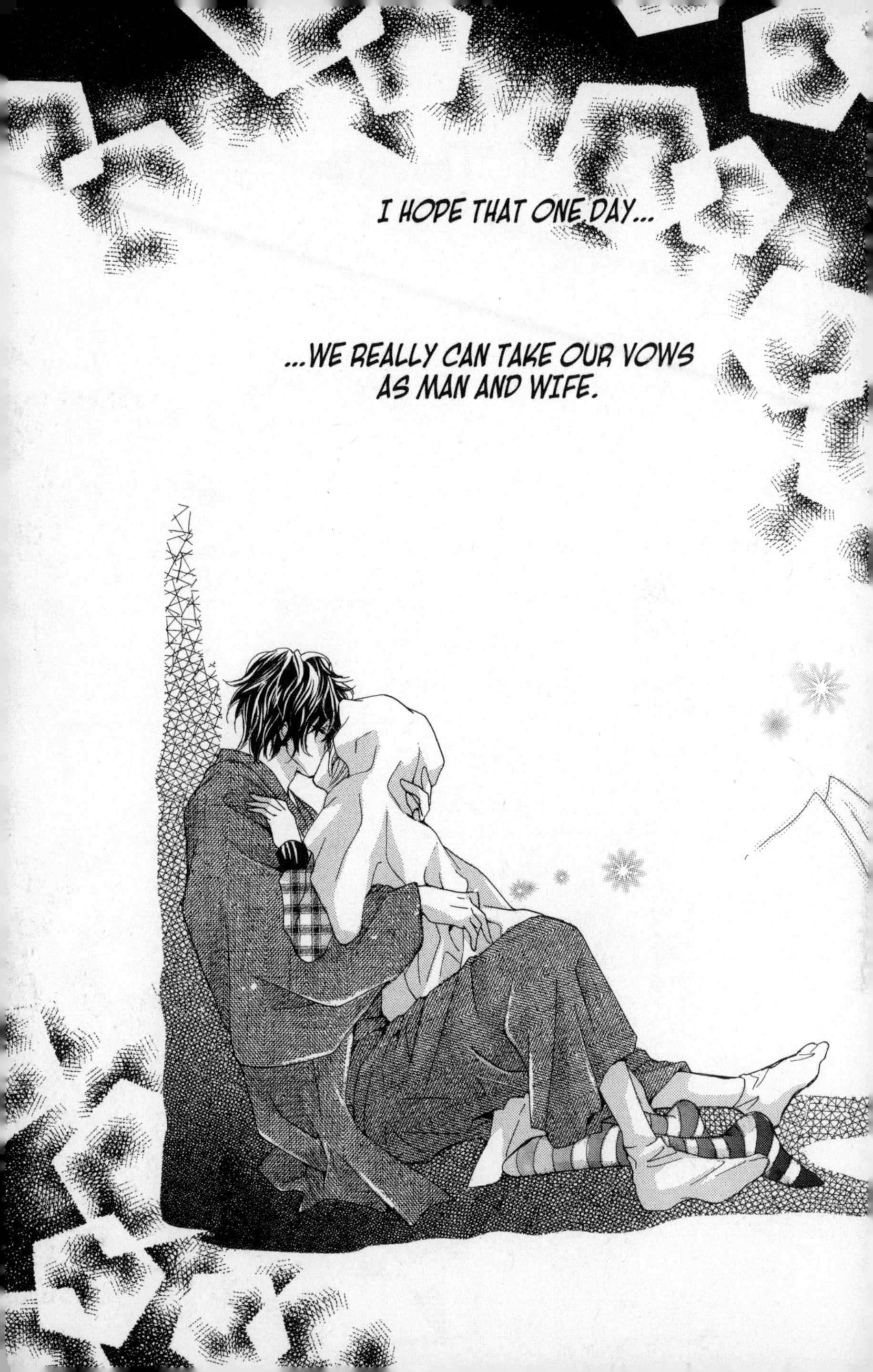
I HOPE THAT ONE DAY...
...WE REALLY CAN TAKE OUR VOWS AS MAN AND WIFE.

♥ Special Thanks ♥

EDITOR:

Nakamura

ASSISTANTS:

Alice · Kuon
Hana · Mizuki
Aki · Momizi

• The editorial staff at *Sho-Comi* magazine •

• My family and friends •

• Everyone who was involved with the making of this manga •

✿ The readers! ✿

Thank you from the bottom of my heart!

Miko Mitsuki
c/o Honey Blood Editor
Viz Media
P.O. Box 77010
San Francisco, CA 94107

I'd love to hear from you!

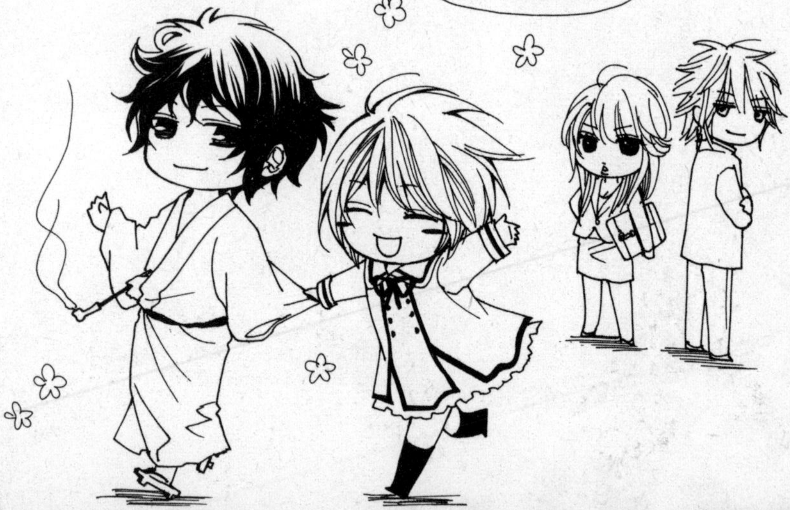

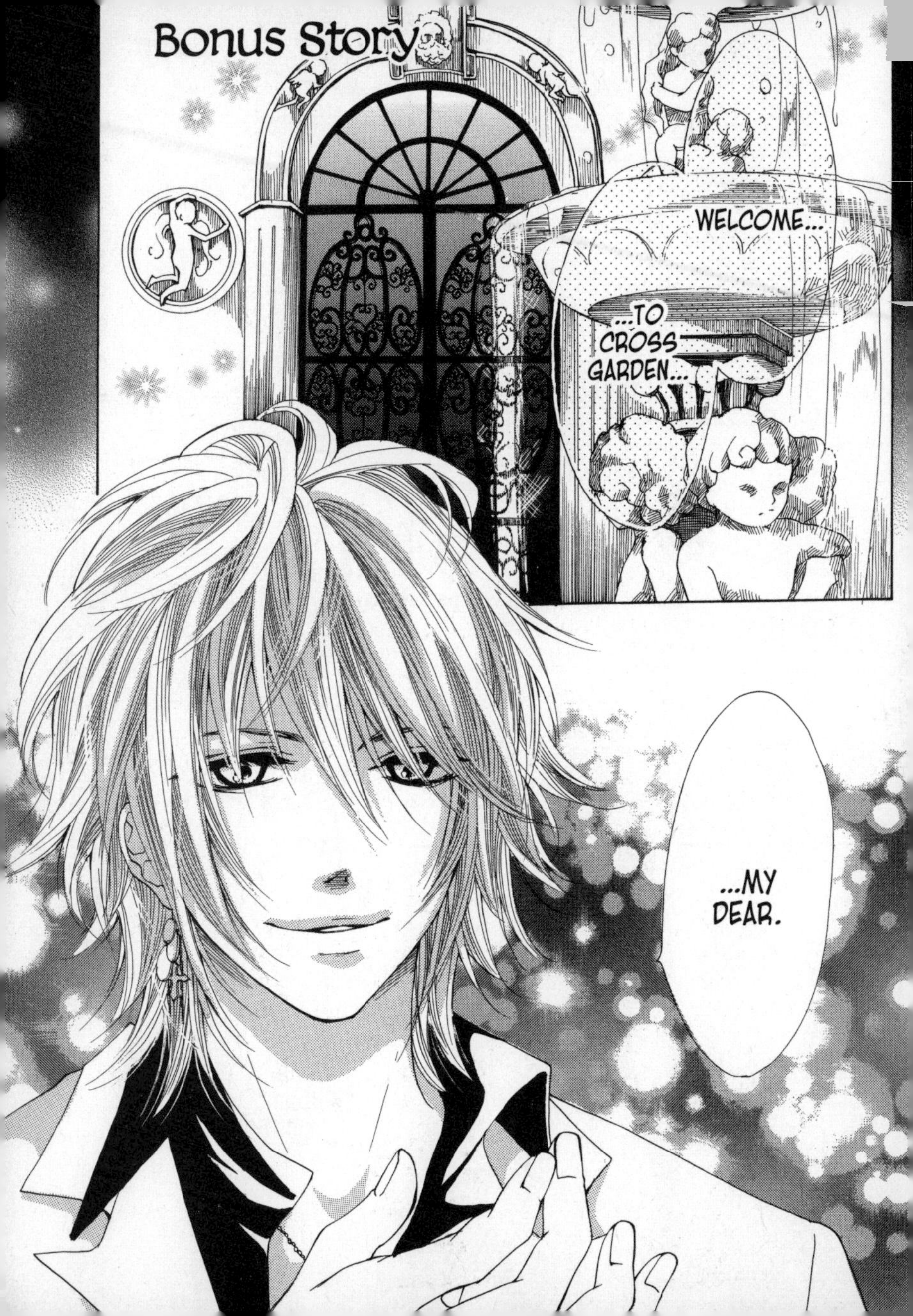
Bonus Story
WELCOME...
...TO CROSS GARDEN...
...MY DEAR.

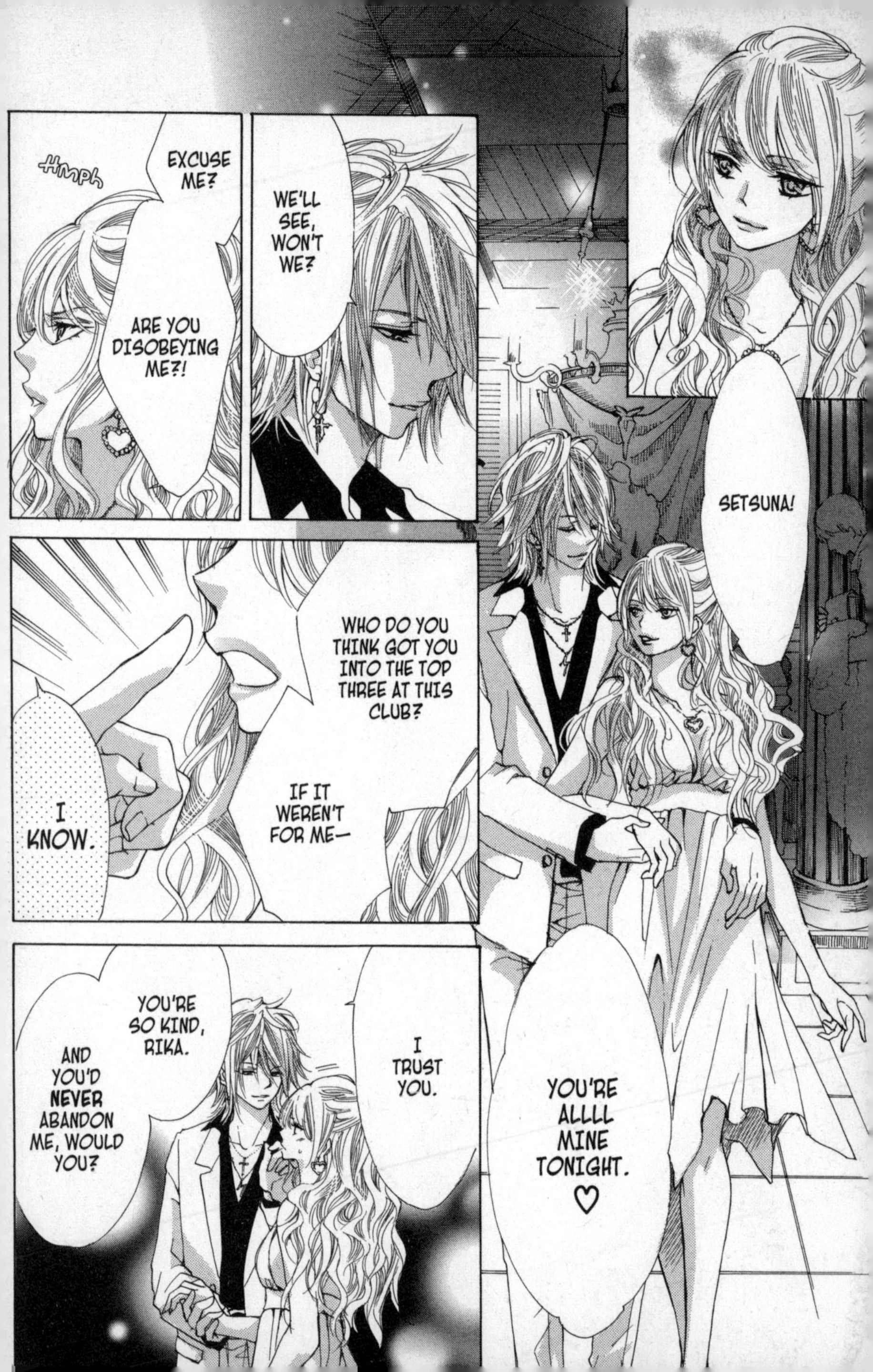
SETSUNA!
YOU'RE ALLLL MINE TONIGHT. ♡
WE'LL SEE, WON'T WE?
EXCUSE ME?
ARE YOU DISOBEYING ME?!
Hmph
WHO DO YOU THINK GOT YOU INTO THE TOP THREE AT THIS CLUB?
IF IT WEREN'T FOR ME—
I KNOW.
I TRUST YOU.
YOU'RE SO KIND, RIKA.
AND YOU'D NEVER ABANDON ME, WOULD YOU?

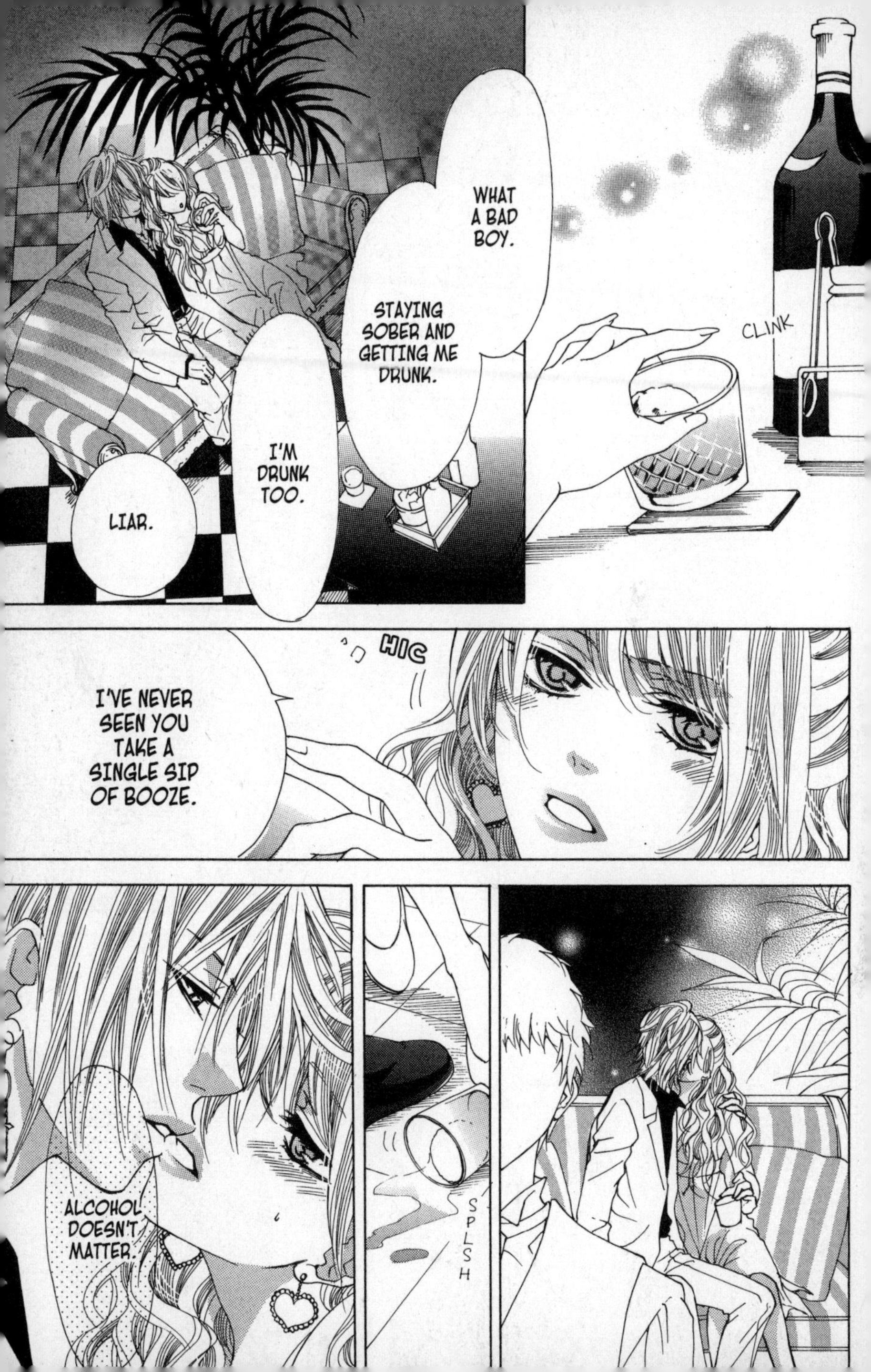
CLINK
WHAT A BAD BOY.
STAYING SOBER AND GETTING ME DRUNK.
I'M DRUNK TOO.
LIAR.
HIC
I'VE NEVER SEEN YOU TAKE A SINGLE SIP OF BOOZE.
SPLSH
ALCOHOL DOESN'T MATTER.

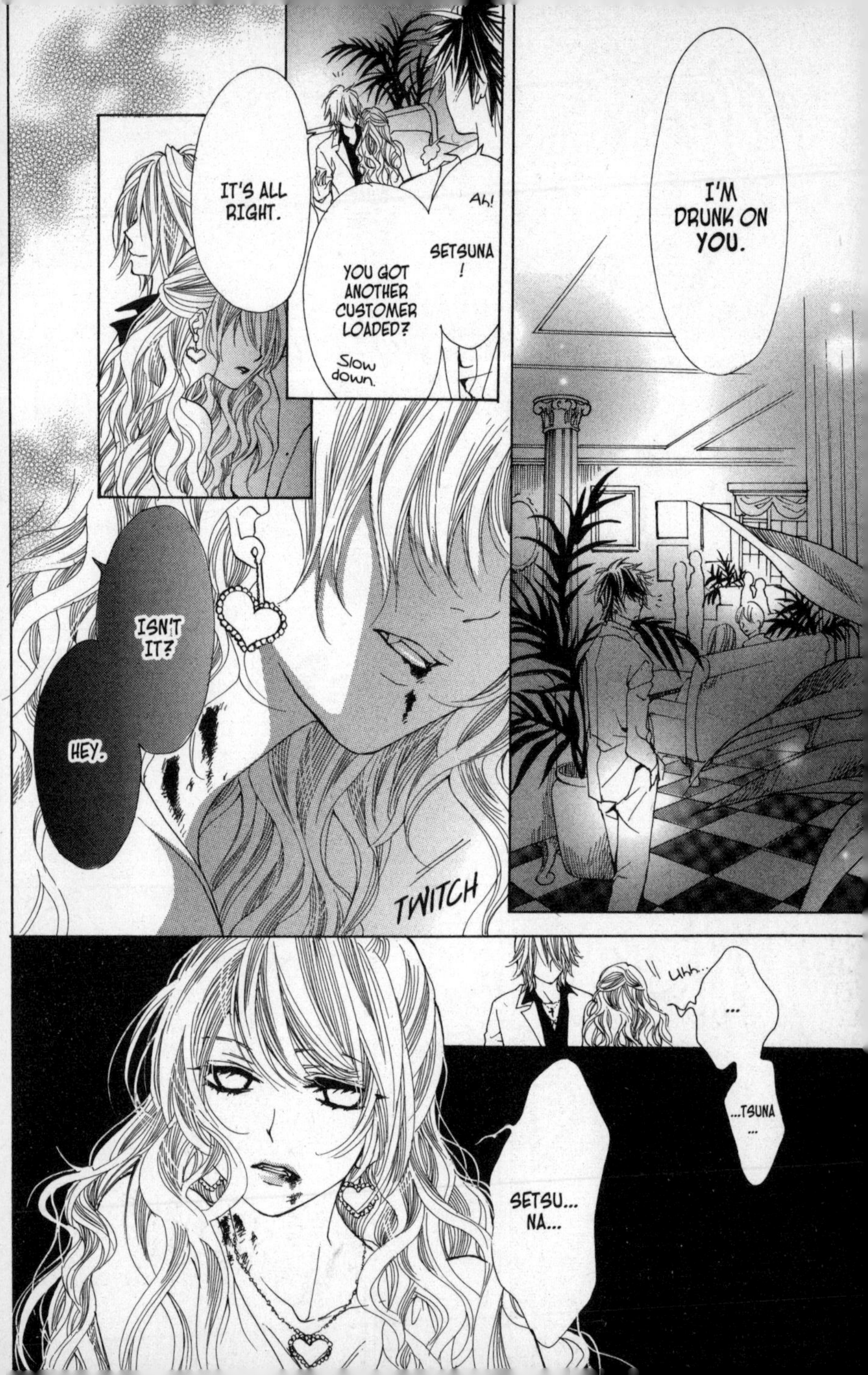
I'M DRUNK ON YOU.
Ah!
SETSUNA!
YOU GOT ANOTHER CUSTOMER LOADED?
Slow down.
IT'S ALL RIGHT.
ISN'T IT?
HEY.
TWITCH
Uhh...
...
...TSUNA...
SETSU... NA...

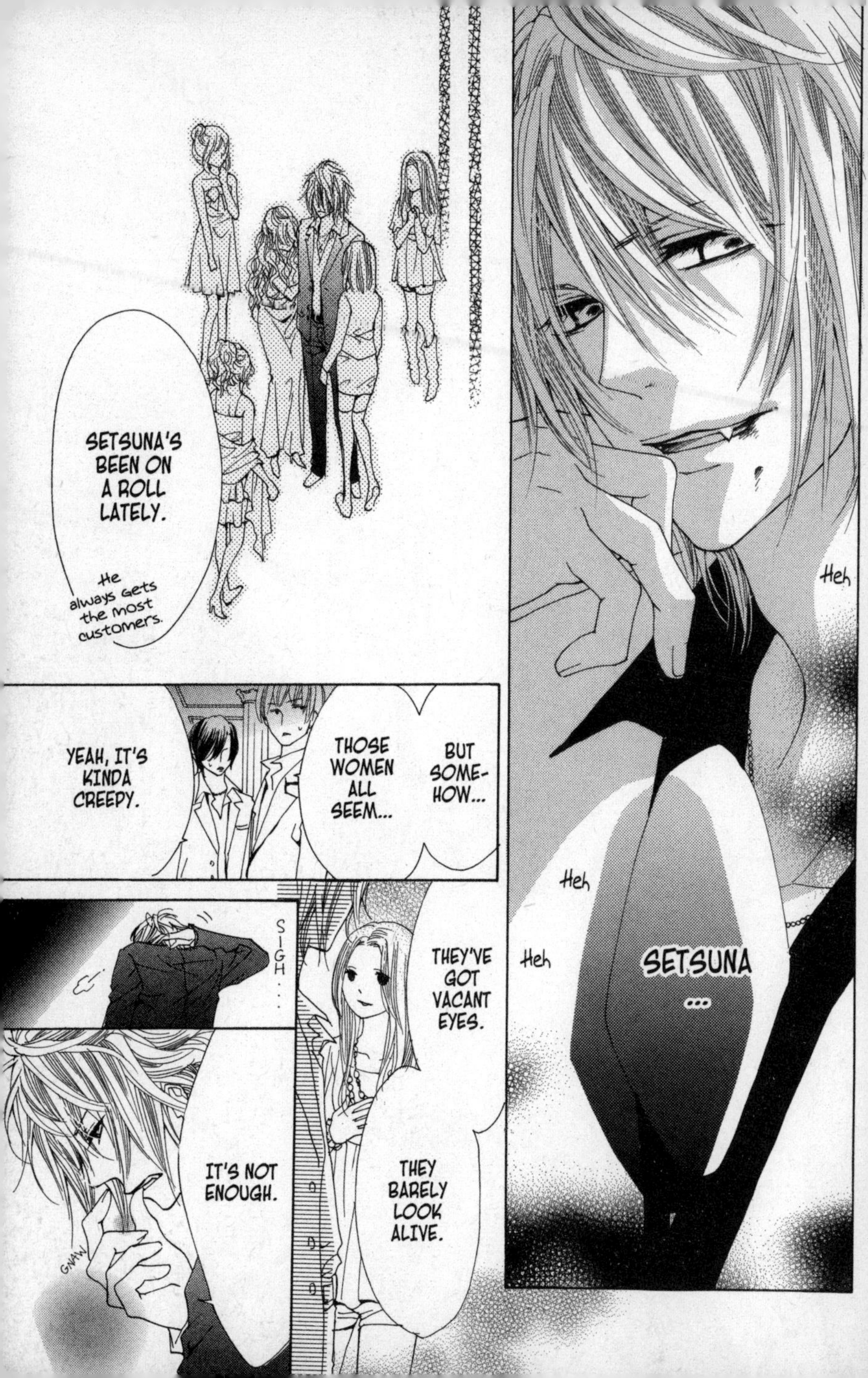
Heh
Heh
Heh
SETSUNA ...
SETSUNA'S BEEN ON A ROLL LATELY.
He always gets the most customers.
BUT SOME-HOW...
THOSE WOMEN ALL SEEM...
YEAH, IT'S KINDA CREEPY.
THEY'VE GOT VACANT EYES.
THEY BARELY LOOK ALIVE.
SIGH...
IT'S NOT ENOUGH.
GNAW

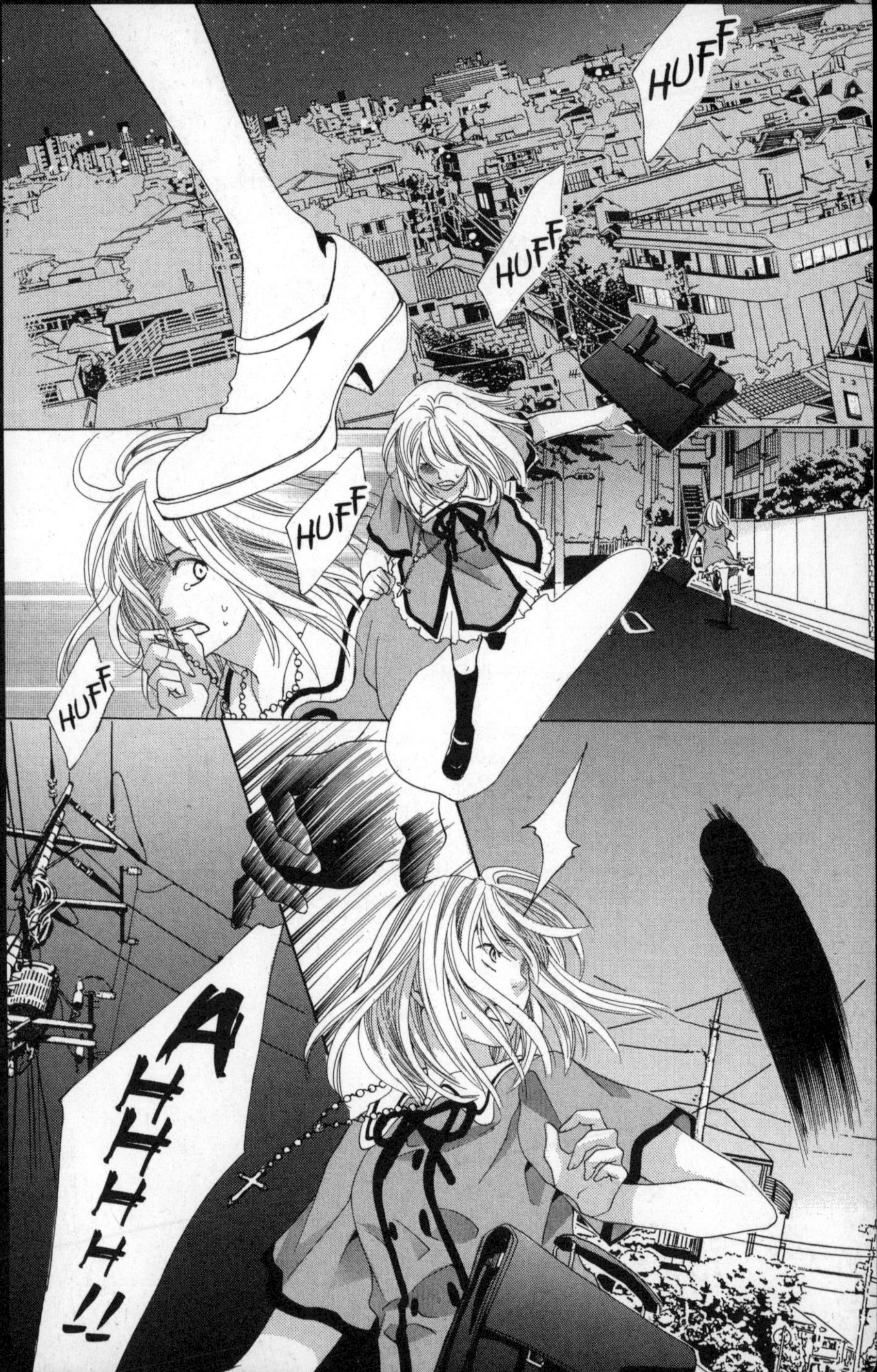
HUFF
HUFF
HUFF
HUFF
AHHHHH!!

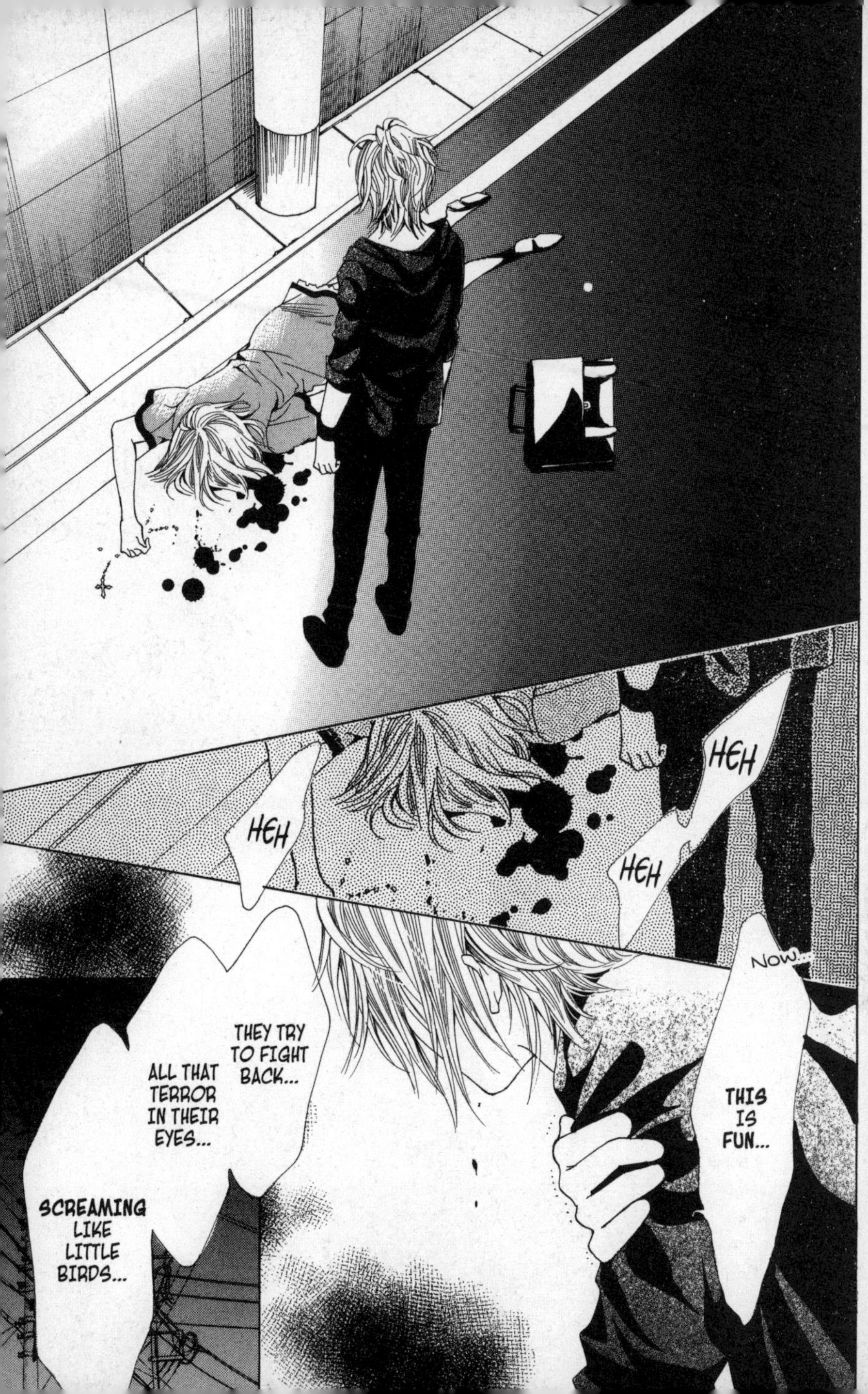
HEH
HEH
HEH
NOW...
THIS IS FUN...
THEY TRY TO FIGHT BACK...
ALL THAT TERROR IN THEIR EYES...
SCREAMING LIKE LITTLE BIRDS...

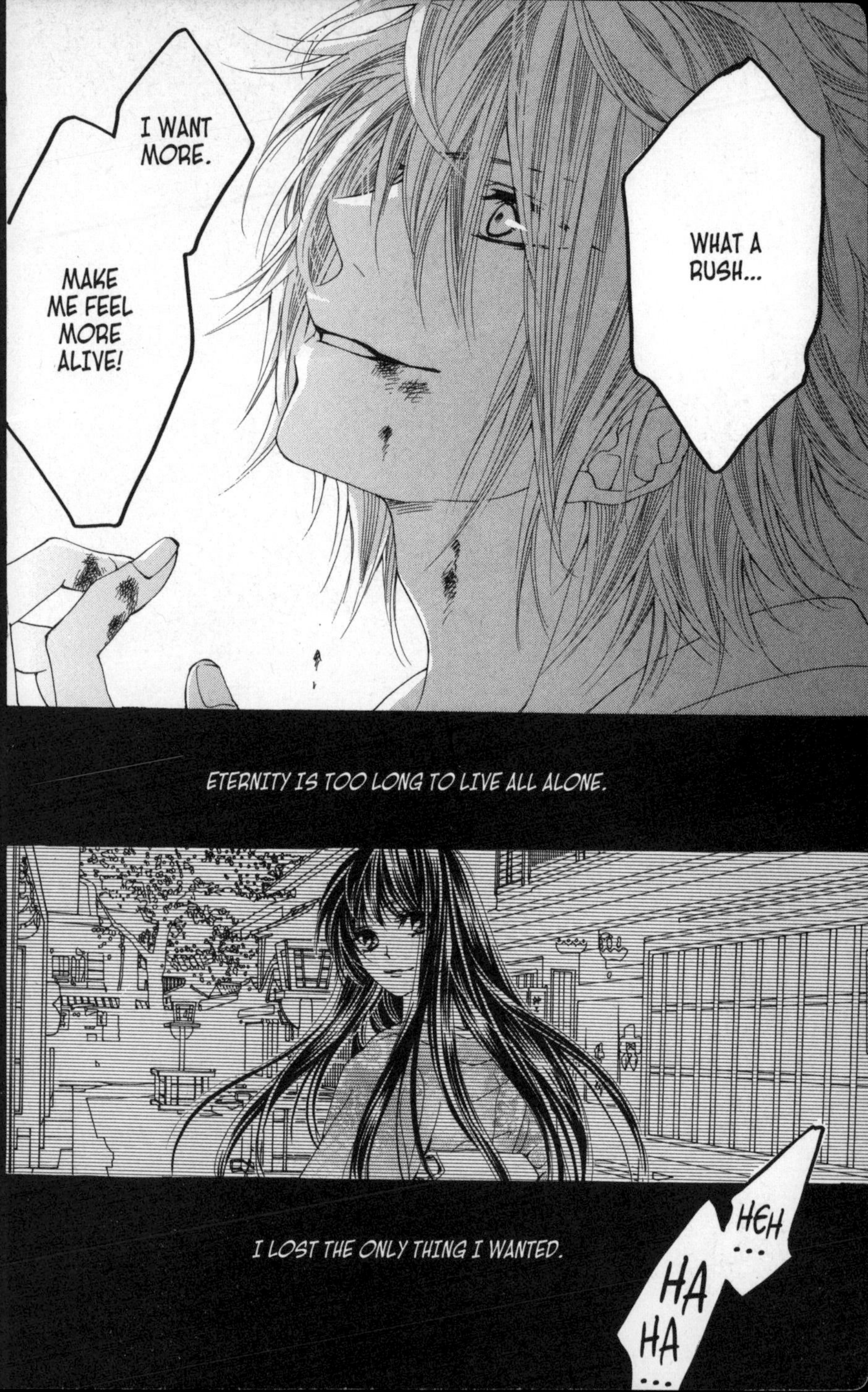
WHAT A RUSH...
I WANT MORE.
MAKE ME FEEL MORE ALIVE!
ETERNITY IS TOO LONG TO LIVE ALL ALONE.
HEH... HA HA...
I LOST THE ONLY THING I WANTED.

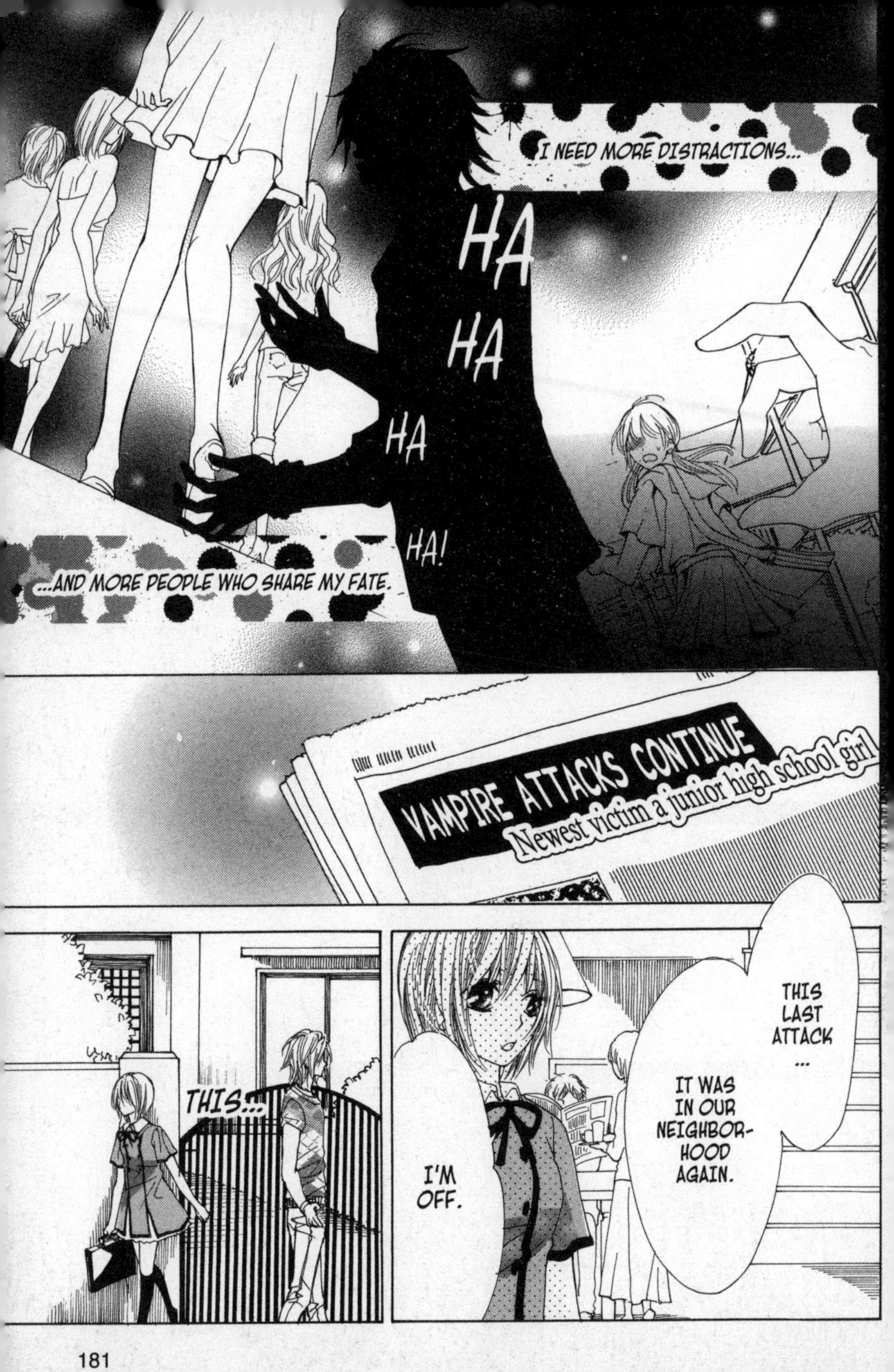
I NEED MORE DISTRACTIONS...
HA HA HA HA!
...AND MORE PEOPLE WHO SHARE MY FATE.
VAMPIRE ATTACKS CONTINUE
Newest victim a junior high school girl
THIS LAST ATTACK...
IT WAS IN OUR NEIGHBOR-HOOD AGAIN.
I'M OFF.
THIS...

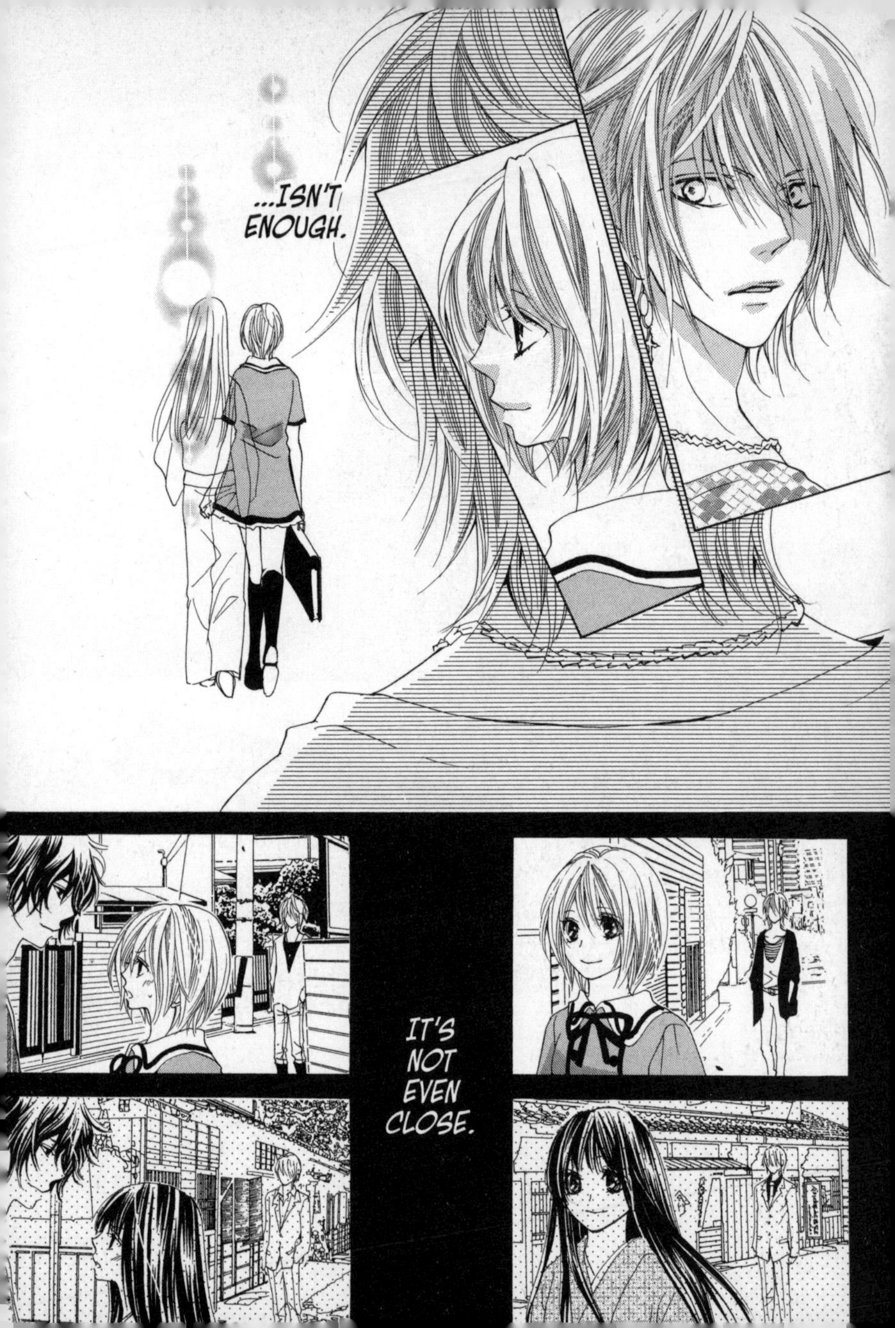
...ISN'T ENOUGH.
IT'S NOT EVEN CLOSE.

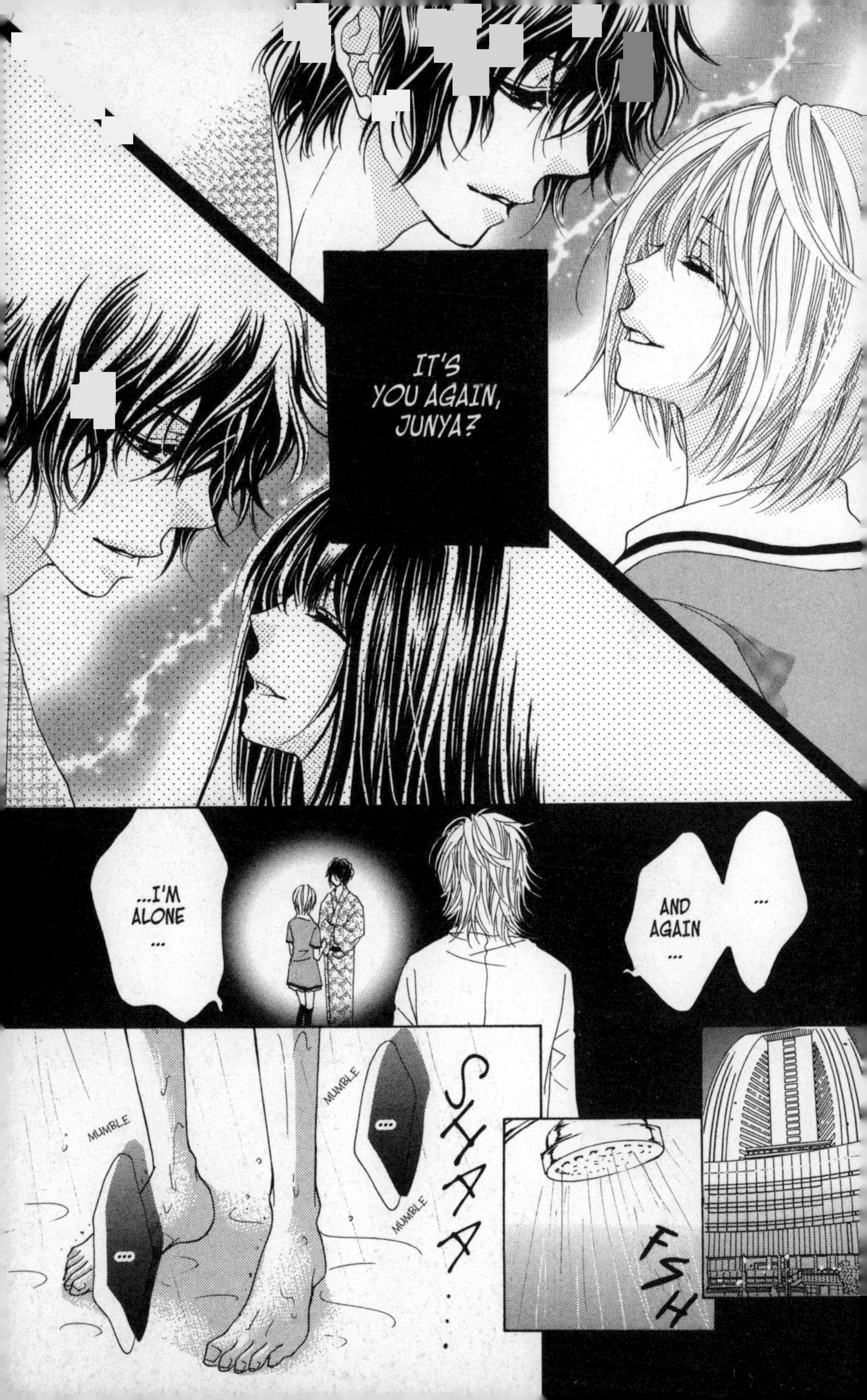
IT'S YOU AGAIN, JUNYA?
...
AND AGAIN ...
...I'M ALONE ...
FSH
SHAA...
MUMBLE
...
MUMBLE
MUMBLE
...

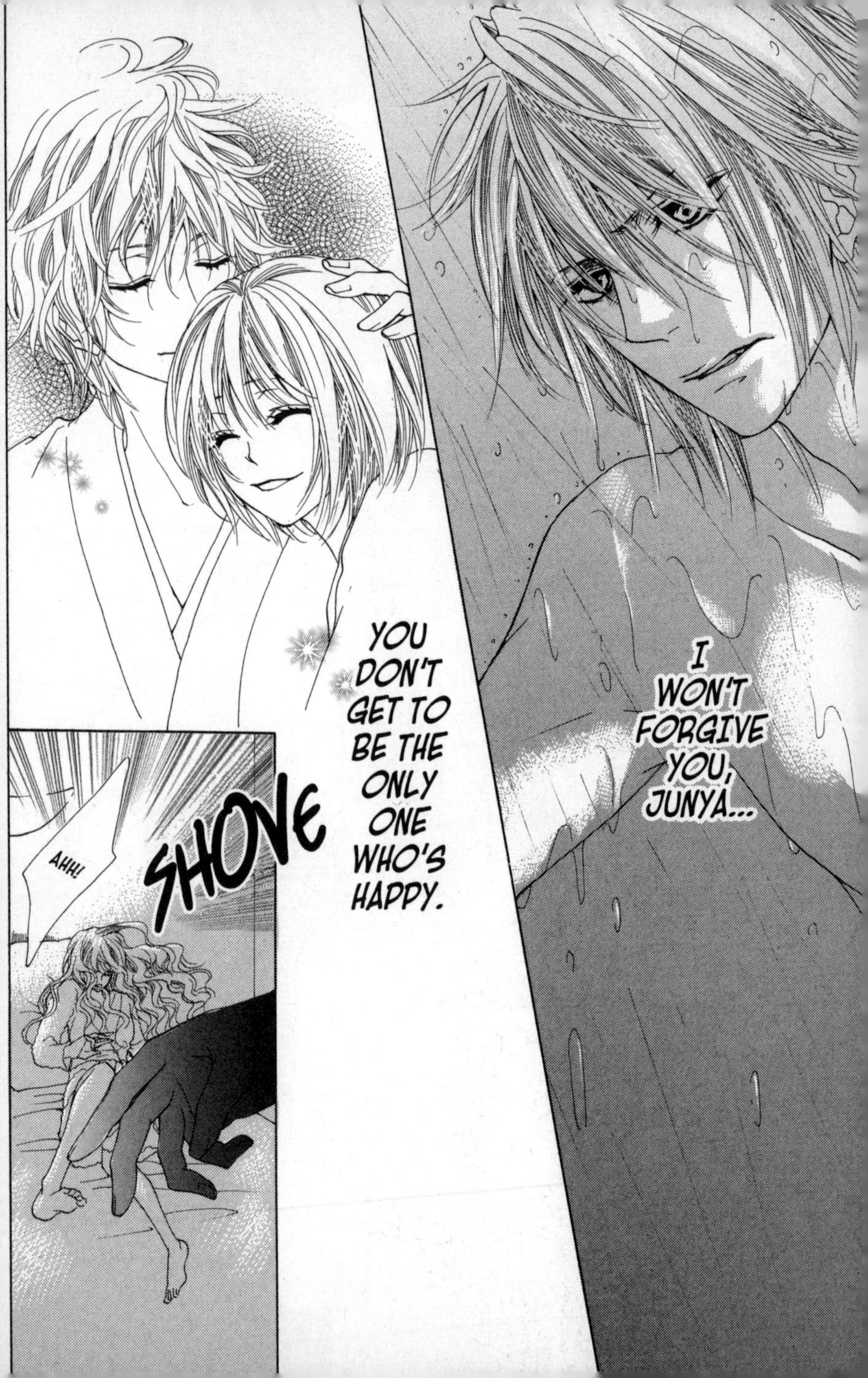
I WON'T FORGIVE YOU, JUNYA...
YOU DON'T GET TO BE THE ONLY ONE WHO'S HAPPY.
SHOVE
AHH!

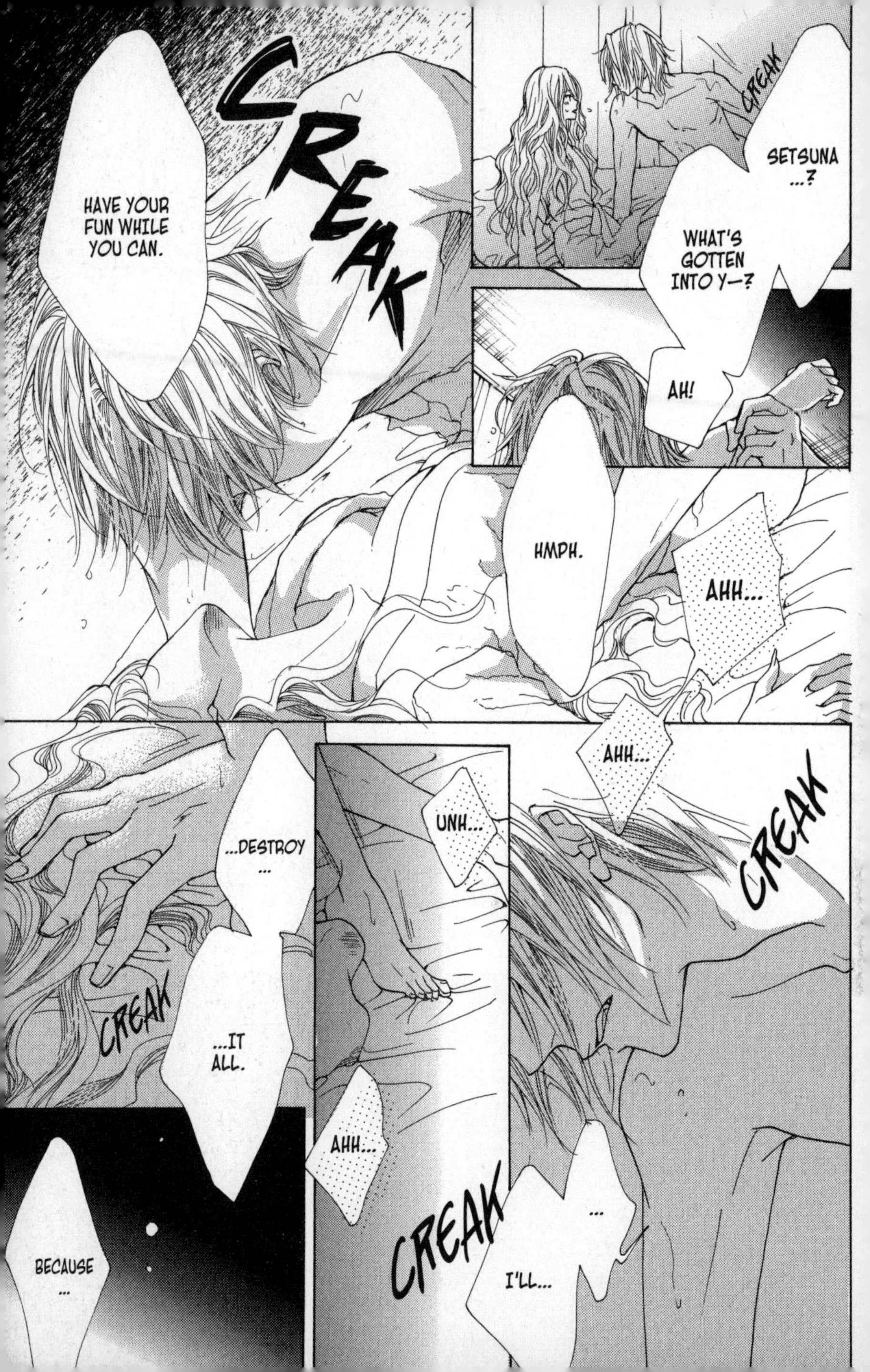
CREAK
SETSUNA ...?
WHAT'S GOTTEN INTO Y—?
AH!
CREAK
HAVE YOUR FUN WHILE YOU CAN.
HMPH.
AHH...
AHH...
CREAK
...
I'LL...
CREAK
UNH...
AHH...
...DESTROY ...
CREAK
...IT ALL.
BECAUSE ...

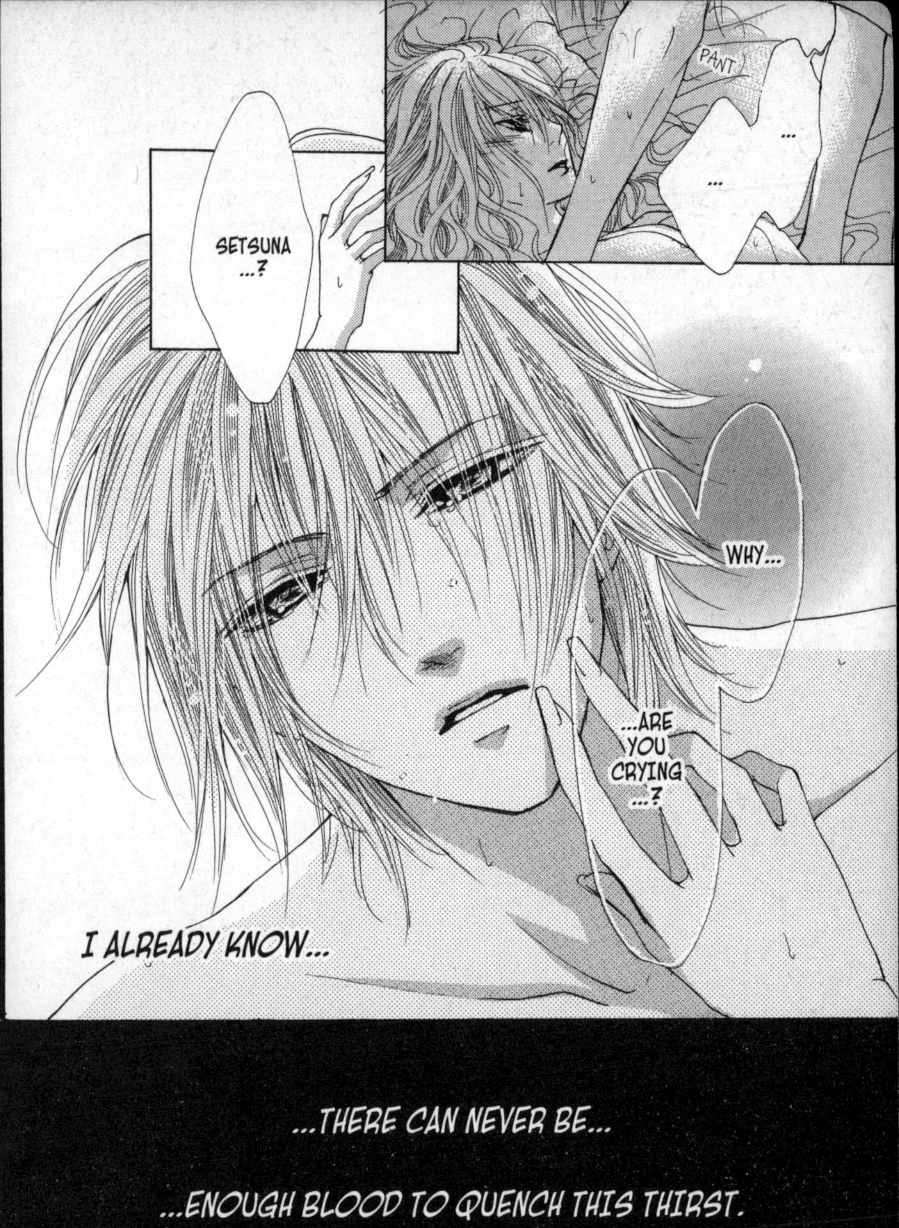
PANT
...
...
SETSUNA ...?
WHY...
...ARE YOU CRYING ...?
I ALREADY KNOW...
...THERE CAN NEVER BE...
...ENOUGH BLOOD TO QUENCH THIS THIRST.

Author Bio

Born on October 10, Miko
Mitsuki debuted with *Utakata*
in 2003. She is currently
working on projects for *Sho-
Comi* magazine. Mitsuki is
from Kagoshima Prefecture in
Japan, and her blood type is
O. She loves cats the most but
loves dogs as well.

Honey Blood

VOLUME 2
Shojo Beat Edition

STORY AND ART BY
MIKO MITSUKI

MITSUAJI BLOOD Vol. 2
by Miko MITSUKI
© 2009 Miko MITSUKI
All rights reserved.
Original Japanese edition published by SHOGAKUKAN.
English translation rights in the United States of America,
Canada, the United Kingdom,
and Ireland arranged with SHOGAKUKAN.

English Adaptation/Ysabet Reinhardt MacFarlane
Translation/pinkie-chan
Touch-up Art & Lettering/Joanna Estep
Design/Izumi Evers
Editor/Amy Yu

Printed in the U.S.A.

Published by VIZ Media, LLC
P.O. Box 77010
San Francisco, CA 94107

10 9 8 7 6 5 4 3 2 1
First printing, December 2014

www.viz.com   www.shojobeat.com

We Were There

By Yuki Obata

Also known as the award-winning series *Bokura ga Ita*

Get to the Bottom of a Broken Heart

It's love at first sight when Nanami Takahashi falls for Motoharu Yano, the most popular boy in her new class. But he's still grieving his girlfriend who died the year before. Can Nanami break through the wall that surrounds Motoharu's heart?

Find out in *We Were There*— manga series on sale now!

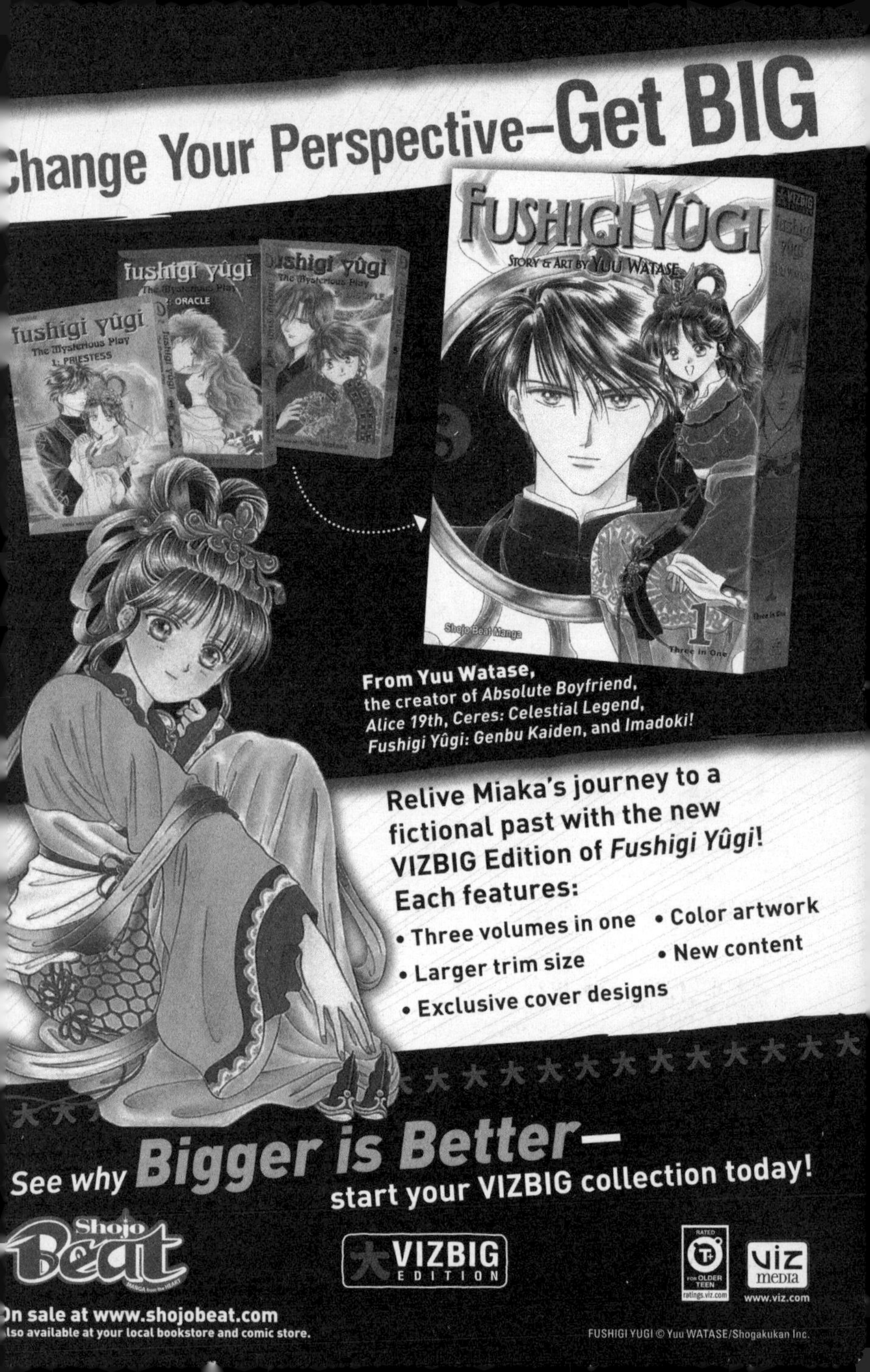
Change Your Perspective—Get BIG
fushigi yûgi
The Mysterious Play
1: PRIESTESS
2: ORACLE
FUSHIGI YÛGI
STORY & ART BY YUU WATASE
Shojo Beat Manga
1
Three in One
From Yuu Watase,
the creator of Absolute Boyfriend,
Alice 19th, Ceres: Celestial Legend,
Fushigi Yûgi: Genbu Kaiden, and Imadoki!
Relive Miaka's journey to a fictional past with the new VIZBIG Edition of Fushigi Yûgi!
Each features:
• Three volumes in one
• Larger trim size
• Exclusive cover designs
• Color artwork
• New content
See why Bigger is Better—
start your VIZBIG collection today!
Shojo Beat
MANGA from the HEART
VIZBIG EDITION
RATED T+ FOR OLDER TEEN
ratings.viz.com
viz media
www.viz.com
On sale at www.shojobeat.com
Also available at your local bookstore and comic store.
FUSHIGI YUGI © Yuu WATASE/Shogakukan Inc.

This is the last page.

In keeping with the original Japanese comic format, this book reads from right to left— so action, sound effects, and word balloons are completely reversed. This preserves the orientation of the original artwork—plus, it's fun! Check out the diagram shown here to get the hang of things, and then turn to the other side of the book to get started!

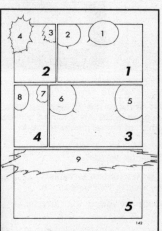